The Vicar of Bu

Anthony Trollope

Alpha Editions

This edition published in 2024

ISBN : 9789362926555

Design and Setting By
Alpha Editions
www.alphaedis.com
Email - info@alphaedis.com

As per information held with us this book is in Public Domain.
This book is a reproduction of an important historical work. Alpha Editions uses the best technology to reproduce historical work in the same manner it was first published to preserve its original nature. Any marks or number seen are left intentionally to preserve its true form.

Contents

PREFACE.	- 1 -
CHAPTER I.	- 3 -
CHAPTER II.	- 11 -
CHAPTER III.	- 17 -
CHAPTER IV.	- 24 -
CHAPTER V.	- 32 -
CHAPTER VI.	- 36 -
CHAPTER VII.	- 41 -
CHAPTER VIII.	- 46 -
CHAPTER IX.	- 56 -
CHAPTER X.	- 62 -
CHAPTER XI.	- 67 -
CHAPTER XII.	- 72 -
CHAPTER XIII.	- 78 -
CHAPTER XIV.	- 85 -
CHAPTER XV.	- 93 -
CHAPTER XVI.	- 101 -
CHAPTER XVII.	- 109 -
CHAPTER XVIII.	- 120 -
CHAPTER XIX.	- 125 -
CHAPTER XX.	- 131 -
CHAPTER XXI.	- 140 -
CHAPTER XXII.	- 146 -
CHAPTER XXIII.	- 151 -
CHAPTER XXIV.	- 156 -
CHAPTER XXV.	- 162 -

CHAPTER XXVI.	171
CHAPTER XXVII.	179
CHAPTER XXVIII.	186
CHAPTER XXIX.	191
CHAPTER XXX.	201
CHAPTER XXXI.	207
CHAPTER XXXII.	211
CHAPTER XXXIII.	216
CHAPTER XXXIV.	226
CHAPTER XXXV.	231
CHAPTER XXXVI.	239
CHAPTER XXXVII.	246
CHAPTER XXXVIII.	253
CHAPTER XXXIX.	261
CHAPTER XL.	266
CHAPTER XLI.	271
CHAPTER XLII.	277
CHAPTER XLIII.	290
CHAPTER XLIV.	294
CHAPTER XLV.	303
CHAPTER XLVI.	310
CHAPTER XLVII.	318
CHAPTER XLVIII.	326
CHAPTER XLIX.	333
CHAPTER L.	338
CHAPTER LI.	342
CHAPTER LII.	345
CHAPTER LIII.	352

CHAPTER LIV. ....- 363 -

CHAPTER LV. ....- 370 -

CHAPTER LVI. ....- 378 -

CHAPTER LVII. ....- 385 -

CHAPTER LVIII. ....- 390 -

CHAPTER LIX. ....- 396 -

CHAPTER LX. ....- 401 -

CHAPTER LXI. ....- 407 -

CHAPTER LXII. ....- 412 -

CHAPTER LXIII. ....- 417 -

CHAPTER LXIV. ....- 425 -

CHAPTER LXV. ....- 432 -

CHAPTER LXVI. ....- 440 -

CHAPTER LXVII. ....- 448 -

CHAPTER LXVIII. ....- 455 -

CHAPTER LXIX. ....- 462 -

CHAPTER LXX. ....- 471 -

CHAPTER LXXI. ....- 476 -

CHAPTER LXXII. ....- 483 -

CHAPTER LXXIII. ....- 489 -

PREFACE.

The writing of prefaces is, for the most part, work thrown away; and the writing of a preface to a novel is almost always a vain thing. Nevertheless, I am tempted to prefix a few words to this novel on its completion, not expecting that many people will read them, but desirous, in doing so, of defending myself against a charge which may possibly be made against me by the critics,—as to which I shall be unwilling to revert after it shall have been preferred.

I have introduced in the Vicar of Bullhampton the character of a girl whom I will call,—for want of a truer word that shall not in its truth be offensive,— a castaway. I have endeavoured to endow her with qualities that may create sympathy, and I have brought her back at last from degradation at least to decency. I have not married her to a wealthy lover, and I have endeavoured to explain that though there was possible to her a way out of perdition, still things could not be with her as they would have been had she not fallen.

There arises, of course, the question whether a novelist, who professes to write for the amusement of the young of both sexes, should allow himself to bring upon his stage such a character as that of Carry Brattle? It is not long since,—it is well within the memory of the author,—that the very existence of such a condition of life, as was hers, was supposed to be unknown to our sisters and daughters, and was, in truth, unknown to many of them. Whether that ignorance was good may be questioned; but that it exists no longer is beyond question. Then arises that further question,—how far the condition of such unfortunates should be made a matter of concern to the sweet young hearts of those whose delicacy and cleanliness of thought is a matter of pride to so many of us. Cannot women, who are good, pity the sufferings of the vicious, and do something perhaps to mitigate and shorten them, without contamination from the vice? It will be admitted probably by most men who have thought upon the subject that no fault among us is punished so heavily as that fault, often so light in itself but so terrible in its consequences to the less faulty of the two offenders, by which a woman falls. All her own sex is against her,—and all those of the other sex in whose veins runs the blood which she is thought to have contaminated, and who, of nature, would befriend her were her trouble any other than it is.

She is what she is, and remains in her abject, pitiless, unutterable misery, because this sentence of the world has placed her beyond the helping hand of Love and Friendship. It may be said, no doubt, that the severity of this judgment acts as a protection to female virtue,—deterring, as all known punishments do deter, from vice. But this punishment, which is horrible beyond the conception of those who have not regarded it closely, is not known beforehand. Instead of the punishment there is seen a false glitter of gaudy life,—a glitter which is damnably false,—and which, alas, has been more often portrayed in glowing colours, for the injury of young girls, than have those horrors, which ought to deter, with the dark shadowings which belong to them.

To write in fiction of one so fallen as the noblest of her sex, as one to be rewarded because of her weakness, as one whose life is happy, bright, and glorious, is certainly to allure to vice and misery. But it may perhaps be possible that if the matter be handled with truth to life, some girl, who would have been thoughtless, may be made thoughtful, or some parent's heart may be softened. It may also at last be felt that this misery is worthy of alleviation, as is every misery to which humanity is subject.

A. T.

CHAPTER I.

BULLHAMPTON.

I am disposed to believe that no novel reader in England has seen the little town of Bullhampton, in Wiltshire, except such novel readers as live there, and those others, very few in number, who visit it perhaps four times a year for the purposes of trade, and who are known as commercial gentlemen. Bullhampton is seventeen miles from Salisbury, eleven from Marlborough, nine from Westbury, seven from Haylesbury, and five from the nearest railroad station, which is called Bullhampton Road, and lies on the line from Salisbury to Yeovil. It is not quite on Salisbury Plain, but probably was so once, when Salisbury Plain was wider than it is now. Whether it should be called a small town or a large village I cannot say. It has no mayor, and no market, but it has a fair. There rages a feud in Bullhampton touching this want of a market, as there are certain Bullhamptonites who aver that the charter giving all rights of a market to Bullhampton does exist; and that at one period in its history the market existed also,—for a year or two; but the three bakers and two butchers are opposed to change; and the patriots of the place, though they declaim on the matter over their evening pipes and gin-and-water, have not enough of matutinal zeal to carry out their purpose. Bullhampton is situated on a little river, which meanders through the chalky ground, and has a quiet, slow, dreamy prettiness of its own. A mile above the town,—for we will call it a town,—the stream divides itself into many streamlets, and there is a district called the Water Meads, in which bridges are more frequent than trustworthy, in which there are hundreds of little sluice-gates for regulating the irrigation, and a growth of grass which is a source of much anxiety and considerable trouble to the farmers. There is a water-mill here, too, very low, with ever a floury, mealy look, with a pasty look often, as the flour becomes damp with the spray of the water as it is thrown by the mill-wheel. It seems to be a tattered, shattered, ramshackle concern, but it has been in the same family for many years; and as the family has not hitherto been in distress, it may be supposed that the mill still affords a fair means of livelihood. The Brattles,—for Jacob Brattle is the miller's name,—have ever been known as men who paid their way, and were able to hold up their heads. But nevertheless Jacob Brattle is ever at war with his landlord in regard to repairs wanted for his mill, and Mr. Gilmore, the landlord in question, declares that he wishes that the Avon would some night run so high as to carry off the mill altogether. Bullhampton is very quiet. There is no special trade in the place. Its interests are altogether agricultural. It has no newspaper. Its tendencies are altogether conservative. It is a good deal given to religion; and the Primitive Methodists have a very strong holding there, although in all Wiltshire there is not a clergyman more popular in his own parish than the Rev. Frank Fenwick. He himself, in his inner heart, rather likes his rival, Mr. Puddleham, the dissenting minister; because Mr. Puddleham is an earnest man, who, in spite of the intensity of his ignorance, is efficacious among the poor. But Mr. Fenwick is bound to keep up the fight; and Mr. Puddleham considers it to be his duty to put down Mr. Fenwick and the Church Establishment altogether.

The men of Bullhampton, and the women also, are aware that the glory has departed from them, in that Bullhampton was once a borough, and returned two members to Parliament. No borough more close, or shall we say more rotten, ever existed. It was not that the Marquis of Trowbridge had, what has often delicately been called, an interest in it; but he held it absolutely in his breeches pocket, to do with it as he liked; and it had been the liking of the late Marquis to sell one of the seats at every election to the highest bidder on his side in politics. Nevertheless, the people of Bullhampton had gloried in being a borough, and the shame, or at least the regret of their downfall, had not yet altogether passed away when the tidings of a new Reform Bill came upon them. The people of Bullhampton are notoriously slow to learn, and slow to forget. It was told of a farmer of Bullhampton, in old days, that he asked what had become of Charles I., when told that Charles II. had been restored. Cromwell had come and gone, and had not disturbed him at Bullhampton.

At Bullhampton there is no public building, except the church, which indeed is a very handsome edifice with a magnificent tower, a thing to go to see, and almost as worthy of a visit as its neighbour the cathedral at Salisbury. The body of the church is somewhat low, but its yellow-gray colour is perfect, and there is, moreover, a Norman door, and there are Early English windows in the aisle, and a perfection of perpendicular architecture in the chancel, all of which should bring many visitors to Bullhampton; and there are brasses in the nave, very curious, and one or two tombs of the Gilmore family, very rare in their construction, and the churchyard is large and green, and bowery, with the Avon flowing close under it, and nooks in it which would make a man wish to die that he might be buried there. The church and churchyard of Bullhampton are indeed perfect, and yet but few people go to see it. It has not as yet had its own bard to sing its praises. Properly it is called Bullhampton Monachorum, the living having belonged to the friars of Chiltern. The great tithes now go to the Earl of Todmorden, who has no other interest in the place whatever, and who never saw it. The benefice belongs to St. John's, Oxford, and as the vicarage is not worth more than £400 a year, it happens that a clergyman generally accepts it before he has lived for twenty or thirty years in the common room of his college. Mr. Fenwick took it on his marriage, when he was about twenty-seven, and Bullhampton has been lucky.

The bulk of the parish belongs to the Marquis of Trowbridge, who, however, has no residence within ten miles of it. The squire of the parish is Squire Gilmore,—Harry Gilmore,—and he possesses every acre in it that is not owned by the Marquis. With the village, or town as it may be, Mr. Gilmore has no concern; but he owns a large tract of the water meads, and again has a farm or two up on the downs as you go towards Chiltern. But they lie out of the parish of Bullhampton. Altogether he is a man of about fifteen hundred a year, and as he is not as yet married, many a Wiltshire mother's eye is turned towards Hampton Privets, as Mr. Gilmore's house is, somewhat fantastically, named.

Mr. Gilmore's character must be made to develop itself in these pages,—if such developing may be accomplished. He is to be our hero,—or at least one of two. The author will not, in these early words, declare that the squire will be his favourite hero, as he will wish that his readers should form their own opinions on that matter. At this period he was a man somewhat over thirty,—perhaps thirty-three years of age, who had done fairly well at Harrow and at Oxford, but had never done enough to make his friends regard him as a swan. He still read a good deal; but he shot and fished more than he read, and had become, since his residence at the Privets, very fond of the outside of his books. Nevertheless, he went on buying books, and was rather proud of his library. He had travelled a good deal, and was a politician,—somewhat scandalising his own tenants and other Bullhamptonites by voting for the liberal candidates for his division of the county. The Marquis of Trowbridge did not know him, but regarded him as an objectionable person, who did not understand the nature of the duties which devolved upon him as a country gentleman; and the Marquis himself was always spoken of by Mr. Gilmore as—an idiot. On these various grounds the squire has hitherto regarded himself as being a little in advance of other squires, and has, perhaps, given himself more credit than he has deserved for intellectuality. But he is a man with a good heart, and a pure mind, generous, desirous of being just, somewhat sparing of that which is his own, never desirous of that which is another's. He is good-looking, though, perhaps, somewhat ordinary in appearance; tall, strong, with dark-brown hair, and dark-brown whiskers, with small, quick grey eyes, and teeth which are almost too white and too perfect for a man. Perhaps it is his greatest fault that he thinks that as a liberal politician and as an English country gentleman he has combined in his own position all that is most desirable upon earth. To have the acres without the acre-laden brains, is, he thinks, everything.

And now it may be as well told at once that Mr. Gilmore is over head and ears in love with a young lady to whom he has offered his hand and all that can be made to appertain to the future mistress of Hampton Privets. And the lady is one who has nothing to give in return but her hand, and her heart, and herself. The neighbours all round the country have been saying for the last five years that Harry Gilmore was looking out for an heiress; for it has always been told of Harry, especially among those who have opposed him in politics, that he had a keen eye for the main chance. But Mary Lowther has not, and never can have, a penny with which to make up for any deficiency in her own personal attributes. But Mary is a lady, and Harry Gilmore thinks her the sweetest woman on whom his eye ever rested. Whatever resolutions as to fortune-hunting he may have made,—though probably none were ever made,—they have all now gone to the winds. He is so absolutely in love that nothing in the world is, to him, at present worth thinking about except Mary Lowther. I do not doubt that he would vote for a conservative candidate if Mary Lowther so ordered him; or consent to go and live in New York if Mary Lowther would accept him on no other condition. All Bullhampton parish is nothing to him at the present moment, except as far as it is connected with Mary Lowther. Hampton Privets is dear to him only as far as it can be made to look attractive in the eyes of Mary Lowther. The mill is to be repaired, though he knows he will never get any interest on the outlay, because Mary Lowther has said that Bullhampton water-meads would be destroyed if the mill were to tumble down. He has drawn for himself mental pictures of Mary Lowther till he has invested her with every charm and grace and virtue that can adorn a woman. In very truth he believes her to be perfect. He is actually and absolutely in love. Mary Lowther has hitherto neither accepted nor rejected him. In a very few lines further on we will tell how the matter stands between them.

It has already been told that the Rev. Frank Fenwick is Vicar of Bullhampton. Perhaps he was somewhat guided in his taking of the living by the fact that Harry Gilmore, the squire of the parish, had been his very intimate friend at Oxford. Fenwick, at the period with which we are about to begin our story, had been six years at Bullhampton, and had been married about five and a half. Of him something has already been said, and perhaps it may be only necessary further to state that he is a tall, fair-haired man, already becoming somewhat bald on the top of his head, with bright eyes, and the slightest possible amount of whiskers, and a look about his nose and mouth which seems to imply that he could be severe if he were not so thoroughly good-humoured. He has more of breeding in his appearance than his friend,—a show of higher blood; though whence comes such show, and how one discerns that appearance, few of us can tell. He was a man who read more and thought more than Harry Gilmore, though given much to athletics and very fond of field sports. It shall only further be said of Frank Fenwick that he esteemed both his churchwardens and his bishop, and was afraid of neither.

His wife had been a Miss Balfour, from Loring, in Gloucestershire, and had had some considerable fortune. She was now the mother of four children, and, as Fenwick used to say, might have fourteen for anything he knew. But as he also had possessed some small means of his own, there was no poverty, or prospect of poverty at the vicarage, and the babies were made welcome as they came. Mrs. Fenwick is as good a specimen of an English country parson's wife as you shall meet in a county,—gay, good-looking, fond of the society around her, with a little dash of fun, knowing in blankets and corduroys and coals and tea; knowing also as to beer and gin and tobacco; acquainted with every man and woman in the parish; thinking her husband to be quite as good as the squire in regard to position, and to be infinitely superior to the squire, or any other man in the world, in regard to his personal self;—a handsome, pleasant, well-dressed lady, who has no nonsense about her. Such a one was, and is, Mrs. Fenwick.

Now the Balfours were considerable people at Loring, though their property was not county property; and it was always considered that Janet Balfour might have done better than she did, in a worldly point of view. Of that, however, little had been said at Loring, because it soon became known there that she and her husband stood rather well in the country round about Bullhampton; and when she asked Mary Lowther to come and stay with her for six months, Mary Lowther's aunt, Miss Marrable, had nothing to say against the arrangement, although she herself was a most particular old lady, and always remembered that Mary Lowther was third or fourth cousin to some earl in Scotland. Nothing more shall be said of Miss Marrable at present, as it is expedient, for the sake of the story, that the reader should fix his attention on Bullhampton till he find himself quite at home there. I would wish him to know his way among the water meads, to be quite alive to the fact that the lodge of Hampton Privets is a mile and a quarter to the north of Bullhampton church, and half a mile across the fields west from Brattle's mill; that Mr. Fenwick's parsonage adjoins the churchyard, being thus a little farther from Hampton Privets than the church; and that there commences Bullhampton street, with its inn,—the Trowbridge Arms, its four public-houses, its three bakers, and its two butchers. The bounds of the parsonage run down to the river, so that the Vicar can catch his trout from his own bank,—though he much prefers to catch them at distances which admit of the appurtenances of sport.

Now there must be one word of Mary Lowther, and then the story shall be commenced. She had come to the vicarage in May, intending to stay a month, and it was now August, and she had been already three months with her friend. Everybody said that she was staying because she intended to become the mistress of Hampton Privets. It was a month since Harry Gilmore had formally made his offer, and as she had not refused him, and as she still stayed on, the folk of Bullhampton were justified in their conclusions. She was a tall girl, with dark brown hair, which she wore fastened in a knot at the back of her head, after the simplest fashion. Her eyes were large and grey, and full of lustre; but they were not eyes which would make you say that Mary Lowther was especially a bright-eyed girl. They were eyes, however, which could make you think, when they looked at you, that if Mary Lowther would only like you, how happy your lot would be,—that if she would love you, the world would have nothing higher or better to offer. If you judged her face by any rules of beauty, you would say that it was too thin; but feeling its influence with sympathy, you could never wish it to be changed. Her nose and mouth were perfect. How many little noses there are on young women's faces which of themselves cannot be said to be things of beauty, or joys for ever, although they do very well in their places! There is the softness and colour of youth, and perhaps a dash of fun, and the eyes above are bright, and the lips below alluring. In the midst of such sweet charms, what does it matter that the nose be puggish,—or even a nose of putty, such as you think you might improve in the original material by a squeeze of your thumb and forefinger? But with Mary Lowther her nose itself was a feature of exquisite beauty, a feature that could be eloquent with pity, reverence, or scorn. The curves of the nostrils, with their almost transparent membranes, told of the working of the mind within, as every portion of human face should tell—in some degree. And the mouth was equally expressive, though the lips were thin. It was a mouth to watch, and listen to, and read with curious interest, rather than a mouth to kiss. Not but that the desire to kiss would come, when there might be a hope to kiss with favour;—but they were lips which no man would think to ravage in boisterous play. It might have been said that there was a want of capability for passion in her face, had it not been for the well-marked dimple in her little chin,—that soft couch in which one may be always sure, when one sees it, that some little imp of Love lies hidden.

It has already been said that Mary Lowther was tall,—taller than common. Her back was as lovely a form of womanhood as man's eye ever measured and appreciated. Her movements, which were never naturally quick, had a grace about them which touched men and women alike. It was the very poetry of motion; but its chief beauty consisted in this, that it was what it was by no effort of her own. We have all seen those efforts, and it may be that many of us have liked them when they have been made on our own behalf. But no man as yet could ever have felt himself to be so far flattered by Miss Lowther. Her dress was very plain; as it became her that it should be, for she was living on the kindness of an aunt who was herself not a rich woman. But it may be doubted whether dress could have added much to her charms.

She was now turned one-and-twenty, and though, doubtless, there were young men at Loring who had sighed for her smiles, no young man had sighed with any efficacy. It must be acknowledged, indeed, that she was not a girl for whom the most susceptible of young men would sigh. Young men given to sigh are generally attracted by some outward and visible sign of softness which may be taken as an indication that sighing will produce some result, however small. At Loring it was said that Mary Lowther was cold and repellent, and, on that account, one who might very probably descend to the shades as an old maid in spite of the beauty of which she was the acknowledged possessor. No enemy, no friend, had ever accused her of being a flirt.

Such as she was, Harry Gilmore's passion for her much astonished his friends. Those who knew him best had thought that, as regarded his fate matrimonial,—or non-matrimonial,—there were three chances before him: he might carry out their presumed intention of marrying money; or he might become the sudden spoil of the bow and spear of some red-cheeked lass; or he might walk on as an old bachelor, too cautious to be caught at all. But none believed that he would become the victim of a grand passion for a poor, reticent, high-bred, high-minded specimen of womanhood. Such, however, was now his condition.

He had an uncle, a clergyman, living at Salisbury, a prebendary there, who was a man of the world, and in whom Harry trusted more than in any other member of his own family. His mother had been the sister of the Rev. Henry Fitzackerly Chamberlaine; and as Mr. Chamberlaine had never married, much of his solicitude was bestowed upon his nephew.

"Don't, my dear fellow," had been the prebendary's advice when he was taken over to see Miss Lowther. "She is a lady, no doubt; but you would never be your own master, and you would be a poor man till you died. An easy temper and a little money are almost as common in our rank of life as destitution and obstinacy." On the day after this advice was given, Harry Gilmore made his formal offer.

CHAPTER II.

FLO'S RED BALL.

"You should give him an answer, dear, one way or the other." These wise words were spoken by Mrs. Fenwick to her friend as they sat together, with their work in their hands, on a garden seat under a cedar tree. It was an August evening after dinner, and the Vicar was out about his parish. The two elder children were playing in the garden, and the two young women were alone together.

"You should give him an answer, dear, one way or the other."

"Of course I shall give him an answer. What answer does he wish?"

"You know what answer he wishes. If any man was ever in earnest he is."

"Am I not doing the best I can for him then in waiting—to see whether I can say yes?"

"It cannot be well for him to be in suspense on such a matter; and, dear Mary, it cannot be well for you either. One always feels that when a girl bids a man to wait, she will take him after a while. It always comes to that. If you had been at home at Loring, the time would not have been much; but, being so near to him, and seeing him every day, must be bad. You must both be in a state of fever."

"Then I will go back to Loring."

"No; not now, till you have positively made up your mind, and given him an answer one way or the other. You could not go now and leave him in doubt. Take him at once, and have done with it. He is as good as gold."

In answer to this, Mary for a while said nothing, but went sedulously on with her work.

"Mamma," said a little girl, running up, followed by a nursery-maid, "the ball's in the water!"

The child was a beautiful fair-haired little darling about four-and-a-half years old, and a boy, a year younger, and a little shorter, and a little stouter, was toddling after her.

"The ball in the water, Flo! Can't Jim get it out?"

"Jim's gone, mamma."

Then Jane, the nursery-maid, proceeded to explain that the ball had rolled in and had been carried down the stream to some bushes, and that it was caught there just out of reach of all that she, Jane, could do with a long stick for its recovery. Jim, the gardener, was not to be found; and they were in despair lest the ball should become wet through and should perish.

Mary at once saw her opportunity of escape,—her opportunity for that five minutes of thought by herself which she needed. "I'll come, Flo, and see what can be done," said Mary.

"Do; 'cause you is so big," said the little girl.

"We'll see if my long arms won't do as well as Jim's," said Mary; "only Jim would go in, perhaps, which I certainly shall not do." Then she took Flo by the hand, and together they ran down to the margin of the river.

There lay the treasure, a huge red inflated ball, just stopped in its downward current by a short projecting stick. Jim could have got it certainly, because he could have suspended himself over the stream from a bough, and could have dislodged the ball, and have floated it on to the bank.

"Lean over, Mary,—a great deal, and we'll hold you," said Flo, to whom her ball was at this moment worth any effort. Mary did lean over, and poked at it, and at last thought that she would trust herself to the bough, as Jim would have done, and became more and more venturous, and at last touched the ball, and then, at last,—fell into the river! Immediately there was a scream and a roar, and a splashing about of skirts and petticoats, and by the time that Mrs. Fenwick was on the bank, Mary Lowther had extricated herself, and had triumphantly brought out Flo's treasure with her.

"Mary, are you hurt?" said her friend.

"What should hurt me? Oh dear, oh dear! I never fell into a river before. My darling Flo, don't be unhappy. It's such good fun. Only you mustn't fall in yourself, till you're as big as I am." Flo was in an agony of tears, not deigning to look at the rescued ball.

"You do not mean that your head has been under?" said Mrs. Fenwick.

"My face was, and I felt so odd. For about half a moment I had a sound of Ophelia in my ears. Then I was laughing at myself for being such a goose."

"You'd better come up and go to bed, dear; and I'll get you something warm."

"I won't go to bed, and I won't have anything warm; but I will change my clothes. What an adventure! What will Mr. Fenwick say?"

"What will Mr. Gilmore say?" To this Mary Lowther made no answer, but went straight up to the house, and into her room, and changed her clothes.

While she was there Fenwick and Gilmore both appeared at the open window of the drawing-room in which Mrs. Fenwick was sitting. She had known well enough that Harry Gilmore would not let the evening pass without coming to the vicarage, and at one time had hoped to persuade Mary Lowther to give her verdict on this very day. Both she and her husband were painfully anxious that Harry might succeed. Fenwick had loved the man dearly for many years, and Janet Fenwick had loved him since she had known him as her husband's friend. They both felt that he was showing more of manhood than they had expected from him in the persistency of his love, and that he deserved his reward. And they both believed also that for Mary herself it would be a prosperous and a happy marriage. And then, where is the married woman who does not wish that the maiden friend who comes to stay with her should find a husband in her house? The parson and his wife were altogether of one mind in this matter, and thought that Mary Lowther ought to be made to give herself to Harry Gilmore.

"What do you think has happened?" said Mrs. Fenwick, coming to the window, which opened down to the ground. "Mary Lowther has fallen into the river."

"Fallen where?" shouted Gilmore, putting up both his hands, and seeming to prepare himself to rush away among the river gods in search of his love.

"Don't be alarmed, Mr. Gilmore, she's upstairs, quite safe,—only she has had a ducking." Then the circumstances were explained, and the papa declared magisterially that Flo must not play any more with her ball near the river,—an order to which it was not probable that much close attention would ever be paid.

"I suppose Miss Lowther will have gone to bed?" said Gilmore.

"On the contrary, I expect her every moment. I suggested bed, and warm drinks, and cosseting; but she would have none of it. She scrambled out all by herself, and seemed to think it very good fun."

"Come in at any rate and have some tea," said the Vicar. "If you start before eleven, I'll walk half the way back with you."

In the mean time, in spite of her accident, Mary had gained the opportunity that she had required. The point for self-meditation was not so much whether she would or would not accept Mr. Gilmore now, as that other point;—was she or was she not wrong to keep him in suspense. She knew very well that she would not accept him now. It seemed to her that a girl should know a man very thoroughly before she would be justified in trusting herself altogether to his hands, and she thought that her knowledge of Mr. Gilmore was insufficient. It might however be the case that in such circumstances duty required her to give him at once an unhesitating answer. She did not find herself to be a bit nearer to knowing him and to loving him than she was a month since. Her friend Janet had complained again and again of the suspense to which she was subjecting the man;—but she knew on the other hand that her friend Janet did this in her intense anxiety to promote the match. Was it wrong to say to the man—"I will wait and try?" Her friend told her that to say that she would wait and try, was in truth to say that she would take him at some future time;—that any girl who said so had almost committed herself to such a decision;—that the very fact that she was waiting and trying to love a man ought to bind her to the man at last. Such certainly had not been her own idea. As far as she could at present look into her own future feelings, she did not think that she could ever bring herself to say that she would be this man's wife. There was a solemnity about the position which had never come fully home to her before she had been thus placed.

Everybody around her told her that the man's happiness was really bound up in her reply. If this were so,—and she in truth believed that it was so,—was she not bound to give him every chance in her power? And yet because she still doubted, she was told by her friend that she was behaving badly! She would believe her friend, would confess her fault, and would tell her lover in what most respectful words of denial she could mould, that she would not be his wife. For herself personally, there would be no sorrow in this, and no regret.

Her ducking had given her time for all this thought; and then, having so decided, she went downstairs. She was met, of course, with various inquiries about her bath. Mr. Gilmore was all pity, as though the accident were the most serious thing in the world. Mr. Fenwick was all mirth, as though there had never been a better joke. Mrs. Fenwick, who was perhaps unwise in her impatience, was specially anxious that her two guests might be left together. She did not believe that Mary Lowther would ever say the final No; and yet she thought also that, if it were so, the time had quite come in which Mary Lowther ought to say the final Yes.

"Let us go down and look at the spot," she said, after tea.

So they went down. It was a beautiful August night. There was no moon, and the twilight was over; but still it was not absolutely dark; and the air was as soft as a mother's kiss to her sleeping child. They walked down together, four abreast, across the lawn, and thence they reached a certain green orchard path that led down to the river. Mrs. Fenwick purposely went on with the lover, leaving Mary with her husband, in order that there might be no appearance of a scheme. She would return with her husband, and then there might be a ramble among the paths, and the question would be pressed, and the thing might be settled.

They saw through the gloom the spot where Mary had scrambled, and the water which had then been bright and smiling, was now black and awful.

"To think that you should have been in there!" said Harry Gilmore, shuddering.

"To think that she should ever have got out again!" said the parson.

"It looks frightful in the dark," said Mrs. Fenwick. "Come away, Frank. It makes me sick." And the charming schemer took her husband's arm, and continued the round of the garden. "I have been talking to her, and I think she would take him if he would ask her now."

The other pair of course followed them. Mary's mind was so fully made up, at this moment, that she almost wished that her companion might ask the question. She had been told that she was misusing him; and she would misuse him no longer. She had a firm No, as it were, within her grasp, and a resolution that she would not be driven from it. But he walked on beside her talking of the water, and of the danger, and of the chance of a cold, and got no nearer to the subject than to bid her think what suffering she would have caused had she failed to extricate herself from the pool. He also had made up his mind. Something had been said by himself of a certain day when last he had pleaded his cause; and that day would not come round till the morrow. He considered himself pledged to restrain himself till then; but on the morrow he would come to her.

There was a little gate which led from the parsonage garden through the churchyard to a field path, by which was the nearest way to Hampton Privets.

"I'll leave you here," he said, "because I don't want to make Fenwick come out again to-night. You won't mind going up through the garden alone?"

"Oh dear, no."

"And, Miss Lowther,—pray, pray take care of yourself. I hardly think you ought to have been out again to-night."

"It was nothing, Mr. Gilmore. You make infinitely too much of it."

"How can I make too much of anything that regards you? You will be at home to-morrow?"

"Yes, I fancy so."

"Do remain at home. I intend to come down after lunch. Do remain at home." He held her by the hand as he spoke to her, and she promised him that she would obey him. He clearly was entitled to her obedience on such a point. Then she slowly made her way round the garden, and entered the house at the front door, some quarter of an hour after the others.

Why should she refuse him? What was it that she wanted in the world? She liked him, his manners, his character, his ways, his mode of life, and after a fashion she liked his person. If there was more of love in the world than this, she did not think that it would ever come in her way. Up to this time of her life she had never felt any such feeling. If not for her own sake, why should she not do it for him? Why should he not be made happy? She had risked a plunge in the water to get Flo her ball, and she liked him better than she liked Flo. It seemed that her mind had been altogether changed by that stroll through the dark alleys.

"Well," said Janet, "how is it to be?"

"He is to come to-morrow, and I do not know how it will be," she said, turning away to her own room.

CHAPTER III.

SAM BRATTLE.

It was about eleven o'clock when Gilmore passed through the wicket leading from the vicarage garden to the churchyard. The path he was about to take crossed simply a corner of the church precincts, as it came at once upon a public footway leading from the fields through the churchyard to the town. There was, of course, no stopping the public path, but Fenwick had been often advised to keep a lock on his own gate, as otherwise it almost seemed that the vicarage gardens were open to all Bullhampton. But the lock had never been put on. The gate was the way by which he and his family went to the church, and the parson was accustomed to say that however many keys there might be provided, he knew that there would never be one in his pocket when he wanted it. And he was wont to add, when his wife would tease him on the subject, that they who desired to come in decently were welcome, and that they who were minded to make an entrance indecently would not be debarred by such rails and fences as hemmed in the vicarage grounds. Gilmore, as he passed through the corner of the churchyard, clearly saw a man standing near to the stile leading from the fields. Indeed, this man was quite close to him, although, from the want of light and the posture of the man, the face was invisible to him. But he knew the fellow to be a stranger to Bullhampton. The dress was strange, the manner was strange, and the mode of standing was strange. Gilmore had lived at Bullhampton all his life, and, without much thought on the subject, knew Bullhampton ways. The jacket which the man wore was a town-made jacket, a jacket that had come farther a-field even than Salisbury; and the man's gaiters had a savour which was decidedly not of Wiltshire. Dark as it was, he could see so much as this. "Good night, my friend," said Gilmore, in a sharp cheery voice. The man muttered something, and passed on as though to the village. There had, however, been something in his position which made Gilmore think that the stranger had intended to trespass on his friend's garden. He crossed the stile into the fields, however, without waiting,—without having waited for half a moment, and immediately saw the figure of a second man standing down, hidden as it were in the ditch; and though he could discover no more than the cap and shoulders of the man through the gloom, he was sure he knew who it was that owned the cap and shoulders. He did not speak again, but passed on quickly, thinking what he might best do. The man whom he had seen and recognised had latterly been talked of as a discredit to his family, and anything but an honour to the usually respectable inhabitants of Bullhampton.

On the further side of the church from the town was a farmyard, in the occupation of one of Lord Trowbridge's tenants,—a man who had ever been very keen at preventing the inroads of trespassers, to which he had, perhaps, been driven by the fact that his land was traversed by various public pathways. Now a public pathway through pasture is a nuisance, as it is impossible to induce those who use it to keep themselves to one beaten track; but a pathway through cornfields is worse, for, let what pains may be taken, wheat, beans, and barley will be torn down and trampled under foot. And yet in apportioning his rents, no landlord takes all this into consideration. Farmer Trumbull considered it a good deal, and was often a wrathful man. There was at any rate no right of way across his farmyard, and here he might keep as big a dog as he chose, chained or unchained. Harry Gilmore knew the dog well, and stood for a moment leaning on the gate.

"Who be there?" said the voice of the farmer.

"Is that you, Mr. Trumbull? It is I,—Mr. Gilmore. I want to get round to the front of the parson's house."

"Zurely, zurely," said the farmer, coming forward and opening the gate. "Be there anything wrong about, Squire?"

"I don't know. I think there is. Speak softly. I fancy there are men lying in the churchyard."

"I be a-thinking so, too, Squire. Bone'm was a growling just now like the old 'un." Bone'm was the name of the bull-dog as to which Gilmore had been solicitous as he looked over the gate. "What is't t'ey're up to? Not bugglary?"

"Our friend's apricots, perhaps. But I'll just move round to the front. Do you and Bone'm keep a look-out here."

"Never fear, Squire; never fear. Me and Bone'm together is a'most too much for 'em, bugglars and all." Then he led Mr. Gilmore through the farmyard, and out on to the road, Bone'm growling a low growl as he passed away.

The Squire hurried along the high road, past the church, and in at the Vicarage front gate. Knowing the place well, he could have made his way round into the garden; but he thought it better to go to the front door. There was no light to be seen from the windows; but almost all the rooms of the house looked out into the garden at the back. He knocked sharply, and in a minute or two the door was opened by the parson in person.

"Frank," said the Squire.

"Halloo! is that you? What's up now?"

"Men who ought to be in bed. I came across two men hanging about your gate in the churchyard, and I'm not sure there wasn't a third."

"They're up to nothing. They often sit and smoke there."

"These fellows were up to something. The man I saw plainest was a stranger, and just the sort of man who won't do your parishioners any good to be among them. The other was Sam Brattle."

"Whew—w—w," said the parson.

"He has gone utterly to the dogs," said the Squire.

"He's on the road, Harry; but nobody has gone while he's still going. I had some words with him in his father's presence last week, and he followed me afterwards, and told me he'd see it out with me. I wouldn't tell you, because I didn't want to set you more against them."

"I wish they were out of the place,—the whole lot of them."

"I don't know that they'd do better elsewhere than here. I suppose Mr. Sam is going to keep his word with me."

"Only for the look of that other fellow, I shouldn't think they meant anything serious," said Gilmore.

"I don't suppose they do, but I'll be on the look-out."

"Shall I stay with you, Frank?"

"Oh, no; I've a life-preserver, and I'll take a round of the gardens. You come with me, and you can pass home that way. The chances are they'll mizzle away to bed, as they've seen you, and heard Bone'm,—and probably heard too every word you said to Trumbull."

He then got his hat and the short, thick stick of which he had spoken, and turning the key of the door, put it in his pocket. Then the two friends went round by the kitchen garden, and so through to the orchard, and down to the churchyard gate. Hitherto they had seen nothing, and heard nothing, and Fenwick was sure that the men had made their way through the churchyard to the village.

"But they may come back," said Gilmore.

"I'll be about if they do," said the parson.

"What is one against three? You had better let me stay."

Fenwick laughed at this, saying that it would be quite as rational to propose that they should keep watch every night.

"But, hark!" said the Squire, with a mind evidently perturbed.

"Don't you be alarmed about us," said the parson.

"If anything should happen to Mary Lowther!"

"That, no doubt, is matter of anxiety, to which may, perhaps, be added some trifle of additional feeling on the score of Janet and the children. But I'll do my best. If the women knew that you and I were patrolling the place, they'd be frightened out of their wits."

Then Gilmore, who never liked that there should be a laugh against himself, took his leave and walked home across the fields. Fenwick passed up through the garden, and, when he was near the terrace which ran along the garden front of the house, he thought that he heard a voice. He stood under the shade of a wall dark with ivy, and distinctly heard whispering on the other side of it. As far as he could tell there were the voices of more than two men. He wished now that he had kept Gilmore with him,—not that he was personally afraid of the trespassers, for his courage was of that steady settled kind which enables the possessor to remember that men who are doing deeds of darkness are ever afraid of those whom they are injuring; but had there been an ally with him his prospect of catching one or more of the ruffians would have been greatly increased. Standing where he was he would probably be able to interrupt them, should they attempt to enter the house; but in the mean time they might be stripping his fruit from the wall. They were certainly, at present, in the kitchen garden, and he was not minded to leave them there at such work as they might have in hand. Having paused to think of this, he crept along under the wall, close to the house, towards the passage by which he could reach them. But they had not heard him, nor had they waited among the fruit. When he was near the corner of the wall, one leading man came round within a foot or two of the spot on which he stood; and, before he could decide on what he would do, the second had appeared. He rushed forward with the loaded stick in his hand, but, knowing its weight, and remembering the possibility of the comparative innocence of the intruders, he hesitated to strike. A blow on the head would have brained a man, and a knock on the arm with such an instrument would break the bone. In a moment he found his left hand on the leading man's throat, and the man's foot behind his heel. He fell, but as he fell he did strike heavily, cutting upwards with his weapon, and bringing the heavy weight of lead at the end of it on to the man's shoulder. He stumbled rather than fell, but when he regained his footing, the man was gone. That man was gone, and two others were following him down towards the gate at the bottom of the orchard. Of these two, in a few strides, he was able to catch the hindermost, and then he found himself wrestling with Sam Brattle.

"Sam," said he, speaking as well as he could with his short breath, "if you don't stand, I'll strike you with the life-preserver."

Sam made another struggle, trying to seize the weapon, and the parson hit him with it on the right arm.

"You've smashed that anyway, Mr. Fenwick," said the man.

"I hope not; but do you come along with me quietly, or I'll smash something else. I'll hit you on the head if you attempt to move away. What were you doing here?"

Brattle made no answer, but walked along towards the house at the parson's left hand, the parson holding him the while by the neck of his jacket, and swinging the life-preserver in his right hand. In this way he took him round to the front of the house, and then began to think what he would do with him.

"That, after all, you should be at this work, Sam!"

"What work is it, then?"

"Prowling about my place, after midnight, with a couple of strange blackguards."

"There ain't so much harm in that, as I knows of."

"Who were the men, Sam?"

"Who was the men?"

"Yes;—who were they?"

"Just friends of mine, Mr. Fenwick. I shan't say no more about 'em. You've got me, and you've smashed my arm, and now what is it you're a-going to do with me? I ain't done no harm,—only just walked about, like."

To tell the truth, our friend the parson did not quite know what he meant to do with the Tartar he had caught. There were reasons which made him very unwilling to hand over Sam Brattle to the village constable. Sam had a mother and sister who were among the Vicar's first favourites in the parish; and though old Jacob Brattle, the father, was not so great a favourite, and was a man whom the Squire, his landlord, held in great disfavour, Mr. Fenwick would desire, if possible, to spare the family. And of Sam, himself, he had had high hopes, though those hopes, for the last eighteen months had been becoming fainter and fainter. Upon the whole, he was much averse to knocking up the groom, the only man who lived on the parsonage except himself, and dragging Sam into the village. "I wish I knew," he said, "what you and your friends were going to do. I hardly think it has come to that with you, that you'd try to break into the house and cut our throats."

"We warn't after no breaking in, nor no cutting of throats, Mr. Fenwick. We warn't indeed!"

"What shall you do with yourself, to-night, if I let you off?"

"Just go home to father's, sir; not a foot else, s'help me."

"One of your friends, as you call them, will have to go to the doctor, if I am not very much mistaken; for the rap I gave you was nothing to what he got. You're all right?"

"It hurt, sir, I can tell ye;—but that won't matter."

"Well, Sam,—there; you may go. I shall be after you to-morrow, and the last word I say to you, to-night, is this;—as far as I can see, you're on the road to the gallows. It isn't pleasant to be hung, and I would advise you to change your road." So saying, he let go his hold, and stood waiting till Sam should have taken his departure.

"Don't be a-coming after me, to-morrow, parson, please," said the man.

"I shall see your mother, certainly."

"Dont'ee tell her of my being here, Mr. Fenwick, and nobody shan't ever come anigh this place again,—not in the way of prigging anything."

"You fool, you!" said the parson. "Do you think that it is to save anything that I might lose, that I let you go now? Don't you know that the thing I want to save is you,—you,—you; you helpless, idle, good-for-nothing reprobate? Go home, and be sure that I shall do the best I can according to my lights. I fear that my lights are bad lights, in that they have allowed me to let you go."

When he had seen Sam take his departure through the front gate, he returned to the house, and found that his wife, who had gone to bed, had come downstairs in search of him.

"Frank, you have frightened me so terribly! Where have you been?"

"Thief-catching. And I'm afraid I've about split one fellow's back. I caught another, but I let him go."

"What on earth do you mean, Frank?"

Then he told her the whole story,—how Gilmore had seen the men, and had come up to him; how he had gone out and had a tussle with one man, whom he had, as he thought, hurt; and how he had then caught another, while the third escaped.

"We ain't safe in our beds, then," said the wife.

"You ain't safe in yours, my dear, because you chose to leave it; but I hope you're safe out of it. I doubt whether the melons and peaches are safe. The truth is, there ought to be a gardener's cottage on the place, and I must build one. I wonder whether I hurt that fellow much. I seemed to hear the bone crunch."

"Oh, Frank!"

"But what could I do? I got that thing because I thought it safer than a pistol, but I really think it's worse. I might have murdered them all, if I'd lost my temper,—and just for half-a-dozen apricots!"

"And what became of the man you took?"

"I let him go."

"Without doing anything to him?"

"Well; he got a tap too."

"Did you know him?"

"Yes, I knew him,—well."

"Who was he, Frank?"

The parson was silent for a moment, and then he answered her. "It was Sam Brattle."

"Sam Brattle, coming to rob?"

"He's been at it, I fear, for months, in some shape."

"And what shall you do?"

"I hardly know as yet. It would about kill her and Fanny, if they were told all that I suspect. They are stiff-necked, obstinate, ill-conditioned people—that is, the men. But I think Gilmore has been a little hard on them. The father and brother are honest men. Come;—we'll go to bed."

CHAPTER IV.

THERE IS NO ONE ELSE.

On the following morning there was of course a considerable amount of conversation at the Vicarage as to the affairs of the previous evening. There was first of all an examination of the fruit; but as this was made without taking Jem the gardener into confidence, no certain conclusion could be reached. It was clear, however, that no robbery for the purpose of sale had been made. An apricot or two might have been taken, and perhaps an assault made on an unripe peach. Mr. Fenwick was himself nearly sure that garden spoliation was not the purpose of the assailants, though it suited him to let his wife entertain that idea. The men would hardly have come from the kitchen garden up to the house and round the corner at which he had met them, if they were seeking fruit. Presuming it to have been their intention to attempt the drawing-room windows, he would have expected to meet them as he did meet them. From the garden the Vicar and the two ladies went down to the gate, and from thence over the stile to Farmer Trumbull's farmyard. The farmer had not again seen the men, after the Squire had left him, nor had he heard them. To him the parson said nothing of his encounter, and nothing of that blow on the man's back. From thence Mr. Fenwick went on to the town, and the ladies returned to the Vicarage.

The only person whom the parson at once consulted was the surgeon,—Dr. Cuttenden, as he was called. No man with an injured shoulder-blade had come to him last night or that morning. A man, he said, might receive a very violent blow on his back, in the manner in which the fellow had been struck, and might be disabled for days from any great personal exertion, without having a bone broken. If the blade of his shoulder were broken, the man—so thought the doctor—could not travel far on foot, would hardly be able to get away to any of the neighbouring towns unless he were carried. Of Sam Brattle the parson said nothing to the doctor; but when he had finished his morning's work about the town, he walked on to the mill.

In the mean time the two ladies remained at home at the Parsonage. The excitement occasioned by the events of the previous night was probably a little damaged by the knowledge that Mr. Gilmore was coming. The coming of Mr. Gilmore on this occasion was so important that even the terrible idea of burglars, and the sensation arising from the use of that deadly weapon which had been produced at the breakfast table during the morning, were robbed of some of their interest. They did not keep possession of the minds of the two ladies as they would have done had there been no violent interrupting cause. But here was the violent interrupting cause, and by the time that lunch was on the table, Sam Brattle and his comrades were forgotten.

Very little was said between the two women on that morning respecting Mr. Gilmore. Mrs. Fenwick, who had allowed herself to be convinced that Mary would act with great impropriety if she did not accept the man, thought that further speech might only render her friend obstinate. Mary, who knew the inside of her friend's mind very clearly, and who loved and respected her friend, could hardly fix her own mind. During the past night it had been fixed, or nearly fixed, two different ways. She had first determined that she would refuse her lover,—as to which resolve, for some hours or so, she had been very firm; then that she would accept him,—as to which she had ever, when most that way inclined, entertained some doubt as to the possibility of her uttering that word "Yes."

"If it be that other women don't love better than I love him, I wonder that they ever get married at all," she said to herself.

She was told that she was wrong to keep the man in suspense, and she believed it. Had she not been so told, she would have thought that some further waiting would have been of the three alternatives the best.

"I shall be upstairs with the bairns," said Mrs. Fenwick, as she left the dining-room after lunch, "so that if you prefer the garden to the drawing-room, it will be free."

"Oh dear, how solemn and ceremonious you make it."

"It is solemn, Mary; I don't know how anything can be more solemn, short of going to heaven or the other place. But I really don't see why there should be any doubt or difficulty."

There was something in the tone in which these words were said which almost made Mary Lowther again decide against the man. The man had a home and an income, and was Squire of the parish; and therefore there need be no difficulty! When she compared Mr. Fenwick and Mr. Gilmore together, she found that she liked Mr. Fenwick the best. She thought him to be the more clever, the higher spirited, the most of a man of the two. She certainly was not the least in love with her friend's husband; but then she was just as little in love with Mr. Gilmore.

At about half-past two Mr. Gilmore made his appearance, standing at the open window.

"May I come in?" he said.

"Of course you may come in."

"Mrs. Fenwick is not here?"

"She is in the house, I think, if you want her."

"Oh no. I hope you were not frightened last night. I have not seen Frank this morning; but I hear from Mr. Trumbull that there was something of a row."

"There was a row, certainly. Mr. Fenwick struck some of the men, and he is afraid that he hurt one of them."

"I wish he had broken their heads. I take it there was a son of one of my tenants there, who is about as bad as he can be. Frank will believe me now. I hope you were not frightened here."

"I heard nothing of it till this morning."

After that there was a pause. He had told himself as he came along that the task before him could not be easy and pleasant. To declare a passion to the girl he loves may be very pleasant work to the man who feels almost sure that his answer will not be against him. It may be an easy task enough even when there is a doubt. The very possession of the passion,—or even its pretence,—gives the man a liberty which he has a pleasure and a pride in using. But this is the case when the man dashes boldly at his purpose without preconcerted arrangements. Such pleasure, if it ever was a pleasure to him,— such excitement at least, was come and gone with Harry Gilmore. He had told his tale, and had been desired to wait. Now he had come again at a fixed hour to be informed—like a servant waiting for a place—whether it was thought that he would suit. The servant out of place, however, would have had this advantage, that he would receive his answer without the necessity of further eloquence on his own part. With the lover it was different. It was evident that Mary Lowther would not say to him, "I have considered the matter, and I think that, upon the whole, you will do." It was necessary that he should ask the question again, and ask it as a suppliant.

"Mary," he said, beginning with words that he had fixed for himself as he came up the garden, "it is six weeks, I think, since I asked you to be my wife; and now I have come to ask you again."

She made him no immediate answer, but sat as though waiting for some further effort of his eloquence.

"I do not think you doubt my truth, or the warmth of my affection. If you trust in them—"

"I do; I do."

"Then I don't know that I can say anything further. Nothing that I can say now will make you love me. I have not that sort of power which would compel a girl to come into my arms."

"I don't understand that kind of power,—how any man can have it with any girl."

"They say that it is so; but I do not flatter myself that it is so with me; and I do not think that it would be so with any man over you. Perhaps I may assure you that, as far as I know myself at present, all my future happiness must depend on your answer. It will not kill me—to be refused; at least, I suppose not. But it will make me wish that it would." Having so spoken he waited for her reply.

She believed every word that he said. And she liked him so well that, for his own sake, she desired that he might be gratified. As far as she knew herself, she had no desire to be Harry Gilmore's wife. The position was not even one in which she could allow herself to look for consolation on one side, for disappointments on the other. She had read about love, and talked about love; and she desired to be in love. Certainly she was not in love with this man. She had begun to doubt whether it would ever be given to her to love,—to love as her friend Janet loved Frank Fenwick. Janet loved her husband's very footsteps, and seemed to eat with his palate, hear with his ears, and see with his eyes. She was, as it were, absolutely a bone from her husband's rib. Mary thought that she was sure that she could never have that same feeling towards Henry Gilmore. And yet it might come; or something might come which would do almost as well. It was likely that Janet's nature was softer and sweeter than her own,—more prone to adapt itself, like ivy to a strong tree. For herself, it might be, that she could never become as the ivy; but that, nevertheless, she might be the true wife of a true husband. But if ever she was to be the true wife of Harry Gilmore, she could not to-day say that it should be so.

"I suppose I must answer you," she said, very gently.

"If you tell me that you are not ready to do so I will wait, and come again. I shall never change my mind. You may be sure of that."

"But that is just what I may not do, Mr. Gilmore."

"Who says so?"

"My own feelings tell me so. I have no right to keep you in suspense, and I will not do it. I respect and esteem you most honestly. I have so much liking for you that I do not mind owning that I wish that it were more. Mr. Gilmore, I like you so much that I would make a great sacrifice for you; but I cannot sacrifice my own honesty or your happiness by making believe that I love you."

For a few moments he sat silent, and then there came over his face a look of inexpressible anguish,—a look as though the pain were almost more than he could bear. She could not keep her eyes from his face; and, in her woman's pity, she almost wished that her words had been different.

"And must that be all?" he asked.

"What else can I say, Mr. Gilmore?"

"If that must be all, it will be to me a doom that I shall not know how to bear. I cannot live here without you. I have thought about you till you have become mixed with every tree and every cottage about the place. I did not know of myself that I could become such a slave to a passion. Mary, say that you will wait again. Try it once more. I would not ask for this, but that you have told me that there was no one else."

"Certainly, there is no one else."

"Then let me wait again. It can do you no harm. If there should come any man more fortunate than I am, you can tell me, and I shall know that it is over. I ask no sacrifice from you, and no pledge; but I give you mine. I shall not change."

"There must be no such promise, Mr. Gilmore."

"But there is the promise. I certainly shall not change. When three months are over I will come to you again."

She tried to think whether she was bound to tell him that her answer must be taken as final, or whether she might allow the matter to stand as he proposed, with some chance of a result that might be good for him. On one point she was quite sure,—that if she left him now, with an understanding that he should again renew his offer after a period of three months, she must go away from Bullhampton. If there was any possibility that she should learn to love him, such feeling would arise within her more quickly in his absence than in his presence. She would go home to Loring, and try to bring herself to accept him.

"I think," she said, "that what we now say had better be the last of it."

"It shall not be the last of it. I will try again. What is there that I can do, so that I may make myself worthy of you?"

"It is no question of worthiness, Mr. Gilmore. Who can say how his heart is moved,—and why? I shall go home to Loring; and you may be sure of this, that if there be anything that you should hear of me, I will let you know."

Then he took her hand in his own, held it for a while, pressed it to his lips, and left her. She was by no means contented with herself, and, to tell the truth, was ashamed to let her friend know what she had done. And yet how could she have answered him in other words? It might be that she could teach herself to be contented with the amount of regard which she entertained for him. It might be that she could persuade herself to be his wife; and if so, why should he not have the chance,—the chance which he professed that he was so anxious to retain? He had paid her the greatest compliment which a man can pay a woman, and she owed him everything,—except herself. She was hardly sure even now that if the proposition had come to her by letter the answer might not have been of a different nature.

As soon as he was gone she went upstairs to the nursery, and thence to Mrs. Fenwick's bedroom. Flo was there, but Flo was soon dismissed. Mary began her story instantly, before a question could be asked.

"Janet," she said, "I am going home—at once."

"Why so?"

"Because it is best. Nothing more is settled than was settled before. When he asks me whether he may come again, how can I say that he may not? What can I say, except that as far I can see now, I cannot be his wife?"

"You have not accepted him, then?"

"No."

"I believe that you would, if he had asked you last night."

"Most certainly I should not. I may doubt when I am talking behind his back; but when I meet him face to face I cannot do it."

"I think you have been wrong,—very wrong and very foolish."

"In not taking a man I do not love?" said Mary.

"You do love him; but you are longing for you do not know what; some romance,—some grand passion,—something that will never come."

"Shall I tell you what I want?"

"If you please."

"A feeling such as you have for Frank. You are my model; I want nothing beyond that."

"That comes after marriage. Frank was very little to me till we were man and wife. He'll tell you the same. I don't know whether I didn't almost dislike him when I married him."

"Oh, Janet!"

"Certainly the sort of love you are thinking of comes afterwards;—when the interests of two people are the same. Frank was very well as a lover."

"Don't I remember it?"

"You were a child."

"I was fifteen; and don't I remember how all the world used to change for you when he was coming? There wasn't a ribbon you wore but you wore it for him; you dressed yourself in his eyes; you lived by his thoughts."

"That was all after I was engaged. If you would accept Harry Gilmore, you would do just the same."

"I must be sure that it would be so. I am now almost sure that it would not."

"And why do you want to go home?"

"That he may not be pestered by having me near him. I think it will be better for him that I should go."

"And he is to ask you again?"

"He says that he will—in three months. But you should tell him that it will be better that he should not. I would advise him to travel,—if I were his friend, like you."

"And leave all his duties, and his pleasures, and his house, and his property, because of your face and figure, my dear! I don't think any woman is worth so much to a man."

Mary bit her lips in sorrow for what she had said. "I was thinking of his own speech about himself, Janet, not of my worth. It does not astonish you more than it does me that such a man as Mr. Gilmore should be perplexed in spirit for such a cause. But he says that he is perplexed."

"Of course he is perplexed, and of course I was in joke. Only it does seem so hard upon him! I should like to shake you till you fell into his arms. I know it would be best for you. You will go on examining your own feelings and doubting about your heart, and waiting for something that will never come till you will have lost your time. That is the way old maids are made. If you married Harry, by the time your first child was born you would think that he was Jupiter,—just as I think that Frank is."

Mrs. Fenwick owned, however, that as matters stood at present, it would be best that Mary should return home; and letters were written that afternoon to say that she would be at Loring by the middle of next week.

The Vicar was not seen till dinner-time, and then he came home in considerable perplexity of spirit. It was agreed between the two women that the fate of Harry Gilmore, as far as it had been decided, should be told to Mr. Fenwick by his wife; and she, though she was vexed, and almost angry with Mary, promised to make the best of it.

"She'll lose him at last; that'll be the end of it," said the parson, as he scoured his face with a towel after washing it.

"I never saw a man so much in love in my life," said Mrs. Fenwick.

"But iron won't remain long at red heat," said he. "What she says herself would be the best for him. He'll break up and go away for a time, and then, when he comes back, there'll be somebody else. She'll live to repent it."

"When she's away from him there may be a change."

"Fiddlestick!" said the parson.

Mary, when she met him before dinner, could see that he was angry with her, but she bore it with the utmost meekness. She believed of herself that she was much to blame in that she could not fall in love with Harry Gilmore. Mrs. Fenwick had also asked a question or two about Sam Brattle during the dressing of her husband; but he had declined to say anything on that subject till they two should be secluded together for the night.

CHAPTER V.

THE MILLER.

Mr. Fenwick reached Brattle's mill about two o'clock in the day. During the whole morning, while saying comfortable words to old women, and gently rebuking young maidens, he had been thinking of Sam Brattle and his offences. He had not been in the parish very long, not over five or six years, but he had been there long enough to see Sam grow out of boyhood into manhood; and at his first coming to the parish, for the first two or three years, the lad had been a favourite with him. Young Brattle could run well, leap well, fish well, and do a good turn of work about his father's mill. And he could also read and write, and cast accounts, and was a clever fellow. The parson, though he had tried his hand with energy at making the man, had, perhaps, done something towards marring him; and it may be that some feeling of this was on Mr. Fenwick's conscience. A gentleman's favourite in a country village, when of Sam Brattle's age, is very apt to be spoiled by the kindness that is shown to him. Sam had spent many a long afternoon fishing with the parson, but those fishing days were now more than two years gone by. It had been understood that Sam was to assist his father at the mill; and much good advice as to his trade the lad had received from Mr. Fenwick. There ought to be no more fishing for the young miller, except on special holiday occasions,—no more fishing, at least, during the hours required for milling purposes. So Mr. Fenwick had said frequently. Nevertheless the old miller attributed his son's idleness in great part to the parson's conduct, and he had so told the parson more than once. Of late Sam Brattle had certainly not been a good son, had neglected his work, disobeyed his father, and brought trouble on a household which had much suffering to endure independently of that which he might bring upon it.

Jacob Brattle was a man at this time over sixty-five years of age, and every year of the time had been spent in that mill. He had never known another occupation or another home, and had very rarely slept under another roof. He had married the daughter of a neighbouring farmer, and had had some twelve or fourteen children. There were at this time six still living. He himself had ever been a hardworking, sober, honest man. But he was cross-grained, litigious, moody, and tyrannical. He held his mill and about a hundred acres of adjoining meadow land at a rent in which no account was taken either of the building or of the mill privileges attached to it. He paid simply for the land at a rate per acre, which, as both he and his landlord well knew, would make it acceptable on the same terms to any farmer in the parish; and neither for his mill, nor for his land, had he any lease, nor had his father or his grandfather had leases before him. Though he was a clever man in his way, he hardly knew what a lease was. He doubted whether his landlord could dispossess him as long as he paid his rent, but he was not sure. But of this he thought he was sure,—that were Mr. Gilmore to attempt to do such a thing, all Wiltshire would cry out against the deed, and probably the heavens would fall and crush the doer. He was a man with an unlimited love of justice; but the justice which he loved best was justice to himself. He brooded over injuries done to him,—injuries real or fancied,—till he taught himself to wish that all who hurt him might be crucified for the hurt they did to him. He never forgot, and never wished to forgive. If any prayer came from him, it was a prayer that his own heart might be so hardened that when vengeance came in his way he might take it without stint against the trespasser of the moment. And yet he was not a cruel man. He would almost despise himself, because when the moment for vengeance did come, he would abstain from vengeance. He would dismiss a disobedient servant with curses which would make one's hair stand on end, and would hope within his heart of hearts that before the end of the next week the man with his wife and children might be in the poorhouse. When the end of the next week came, he would send the wife meat, and would give the children bread, and would despise himself for doing so. In matters of religion he was an old Pagan, going to no place of worship, saying no prayer, believing in no creed,—with some vague idea that a supreme power would bring him right at last, if he worked hard, robbed no one, fed his wife and children, and paid his way. To pay his way was the pride of his heart; to be paid on his way was its joy.

In that matter of his quarrel with his landlord he was very bitter. The Squire's father some fifteen years since had given to the miller a verbal promise that the house and mill should be repaired. The old Squire had not been a good man of business, and had gone on with his tenants very much as he had found them, without looking much into the position of each. But he had, no doubt, said something that amounted to a promise on his own account as to these repairs. He had died soon after, and the repairs had not been effected. A year after his death an application,—almost a demand,—was made upon our Squire by the miller, and the miller had been wrathful even when the Squire said that he would look into it. The Squire did look into it, and came to the conclusion that as he received no rent at all for the house and mill, and as his own property would be improved if the house and mill were made to vanish, and as he had no evidence whatever of any undertaking on his father's part, as any such promise on his father's part must simply have been a promise of a gift of money out of his own pocket, and further as the miller was impudent, he would not repair the mill. Ultimately he offered £20 towards the repairs, which the miller indignantly refused. Readers will be able to imagine how pretty a quarrel there would thus be between the landlord and his tenant. When all this was commencing,—at the time, that is, of the old Squire's death,—Brattle had the name of being a substantial person; but misfortune had come upon him; doctors' bills had been very heavy, his children had drained his resources from him, and it was now known that it set him very hard to pay his way. In regard to the house and the mill, some absolutely essential repairs had been done at his own costs; but the £20 had never been taken.

In some respects the man's fortune in life had been good. His wife was one of those loving, patient, self-denying, almost heavenly human beings, one or two of whom may come across one's path, and who, when found, are generally found in that sphere of life to which this woman belonged. Among the rich there is that difficulty of the needle's eye; among the poor there is the difficulty of the hardness of their lives. And the miller loved this woman with a perfect love. He hardly knew that he loved her as he did. He could be harsh to her and tyrannical. He could say cutting words to her. But at any time in his life he would have struck over the head, with his staff, another man who should have said a word to hurt her. They had lost many children; but of the six who remained, there were four of whom they might be proud. The eldest was a farmer, married and away, doing well in a far part of the county, beyond Salisbury, on the borders of Hampshire. The father in his emergencies had almost been tempted to ask his son for money; but hitherto he had refrained. A daughter was married to a tradesman at Warminster, and was also doing well. A second son who had once been sickly and weak, was a scholar in his way, and was now a schoolmaster, also at Warminster, and in great repute with the parson of the parish there. There was a second daughter, Fanny, at home, a girl as good as gold, the glory and joy and mainstay of her mother, whom even the miller could not scold,—whom all Bullhampton loved. But she was a plain girl, brown, and somewhat hard-visaged;—a morsel of fruit as sweet as any in the garden, but one that the eye would not select for its outside grace, colour, and roundness. Then there were the two younger. Of Sam, the youngest of all, who was now twenty-one, something has already been said. Between him and Fanny there was,—perhaps it will be better to say there had been,—another daughter. Of all the flock Carry had been her father's darling. She had not been brown or hard-visaged. She was such a morsel of fruit as men do choose, when allowed to range and pick through the whole length of the garden wall. Fair she had been, with laughing eyes, and floating curls; strong in health, generous in temper, though now and again with something of her father's humour. To her mother's eye she had never been as sweet as Fanny; but to her father she had been as bright and beautiful as the harvest moon. Now she was a thing, somewhere, never to be mentioned! Any man who would have named her to her father's ears, would have encountered instantly the force of his wrath. This was so well known in Bullhampton that there was not one who would dare to suggest to him even that she might be saved. But her mother prayed for her daily, and her father thought of her always. It was a great lump upon him, which he must bear to his grave; and for which there could be no release. He did not know whether it was his mind, his heart, or his body that suffered. He only knew that it was there,—a load that could never be lightened. What comfort was it to him now, that he had beaten a miscreant to death's door—that he, with his old hands, had nearly torn the wretch limb from limb—that he had left him all but lifeless, and had walked off scatheless, nobody daring to put a finger on him? The man had been pieced up by some doctor, and was away in Asia, in Africa, in America—soldiering somewhere. He had been a lieutenant in those days, and was probably a lieutenant still. It was nothing to old Brattle where he was. Had he been able to drink the fellow's blood to the last drop, it would not have lightened his load an ounce. He knew that it was so now. Nothing could lighten it;—not though an angel could come and tell him that his girl was a second Magdalen. The Brattles had ever held up their heads. The women, at least, had always been decent.

Jacob Brattle, himself, was a low, thickset man, with an appearance of great strength, which was now submitting itself, very slowly, to the hand of time. He had sharp green eyes, and shaggy eyebrows, with thin lips, and a square chin, a nose which, though its shape was aquiline, protruded but little from his face. His forehead was low and broad, and he was seldom seen without a flat hat upon his head. His hair and very scanty whiskers were gray; but, then too, he was gray from head to foot. The colour of his trade had so clung to him, that no one could say whether that grayish whiteness of his face came chiefly from meal or from sorrow. He was a silent, sad, meditative man, thinking always of the evil things that had been done to him.

CHAPTER VI.

BRATTLE'S MILL.

When Mr. Fenwick reached the mill, he found old Brattle sitting alone on a fixed bench in front of the house door with a pipe in his mouth. Mary Lowther was quite right in saying that the mill, in spite of its dilapidations,—perhaps by reason of them,—was as pretty as anything in Bullhampton. In the first place it was permeated and surrounded by cool, bright, limpid little streams. One of them ran right through it, as it were, passing between the dwelling-house and the mill, and turning the wheel, which was there placed. This course was, no doubt, artificial, and the water ran more rapidly in it than it did in the neighbouring streamlets. There were sluice-gates, too, by which it could be altogether expelled, or kept up to this or that height; and it was a river absolutely under man's control, in which no water-god could take delight. But there were other natural streams on each side of the building, the one being the main course of the Avon, and the other some offspring of a brooklet, which joined its parent two hundred yards below, and fifty yards from the spot at which the ill-used working water was received back into its mother's idle bosom. Mill and house were thatched, and were very low. There were garrets in the roof, but they were so shaped that they could hardly be said to have walls to them at all, so nearly were they contained by the sloping roof. In front of the building there ran a road,—which after all was no more than a private lane. It crossed the smaller stream and the mill-run by two wooden bridges; but the river itself had been too large for the bridge-maker's efforts, and here there was a ford, with stepping-stones for foot passengers. The banks on every side were lined with leaning willows, which had been pollarded over and over again, and which with their light-green wavy heads gave the place, from a distance, the appearance of a grove. There was a little porch in front of the house, and outside of that a fixed seat, with a high back, on which old Brattle was sitting when the parson accosted him. He did not rise when Mr. Fenwick addressed him; but he intended no want of courtesy by not doing so. He was on his legs at business during nearly the whole of the day, and why should he not rest his old limbs during the few mid-day minutes which he allowed himself for recreation?

"I thought I should catch you idle just at this moment," said the clergyman.

**"I thought I should catch you idle just
at this moment," said the clergyman.**

"Like enough, Muster Fenwick," said the miller; "I be idle at times, no doubt."

"It would be a bad life if you did not,—and a very short one too. It's hot walking, I can tell you, Mr. Brattle. If it goes on like this, I shall want a little idle time myself, I fear. Is Sam here?"

"No, Muster Fenwick, Sam is not here."

"Nor has been this morning, I suppose?"

"He's not here now, if you're wanting him."

This the old man said in a tone that seemed to signify some offence, or at least a readiness to take offence if more were said to him about his son. The clergyman did not sit down, but stood close over the father, looking down upon him; and the miller went on with his pipe gazing into the clear blue sky.

"I do want him, Mr. Brattle." Then he stopped, and there was a pause. The miller puffed his pipe, but said not a word. "I do want him. I fear, Mr. Brattle, he's not coming to much good."

"Who said as he was? I never said so. The lad'd have been well enough if other folks would have let him be."

"I know what you mean, Mr. Brattle."

"I usually intend folks to know what I mean, Muster Fenwick. What's the good o' speaking else? If nobody hadn't a meddled with the lad, he'd been a good lad. But they did, and he ain't. That's all about it."

"You do me a great injustice, but I'm not going to argue that with you now. There would be no use in it. I've come to tell you I fear that Sam was at no good last night."

"That's like enough."

"I had better tell you the truth at once. He was about my place with two ruffians."

"And you wants to take him afore the magistrate?"

"I want nothing of the kind. I would make almost any sacrifice rather. I had him yesterday night by the collar of the coat, and I let him go free."

"If he couldn't shake himself free o' you, Muster Fenwick, without any letting in the matter, he ain't no son of mine."

"I was armed, and he couldn't. But what does that matter? What does matter is this;—that they who were with him were thoroughly bad fellows. Was he at home last night?"

"You'd better ax his mother, Muster Fenwick. The truth is, I don't care much to be talking of him at all. It's time I was in the mill, I believe. There's no one much to help me now, barring the hired man." So saying, he got up and passed into the mill without making the slightest form of salutation.

Mr. Fenwick paused for a minute, looking after the old man, and then went into the house. He knew very well that his treatment from the women would be very different to that which the miller had vouchsafed to him; but on that very account it would be difficult for him to make his communication. He had, however, known all this before he came. Old Brattle would, quite of course, be silent, suspicious, and uncivil. It had become the nature of the man to be so, and there was no help for it. But the two women would be glad to see him,—would accept his visit as a pleasure and a privilege; and on this account he found it to be very hard to say unpleasant words to them. But the unpleasant words must be spoken. Neither in duty nor in kindness could he know what he had learned last night, and be silent on this matter to the young man's family. He entered the house, and turned into the large kitchen or keeping-room on the left, in which the two women were almost always to be found. This was a spacious, square, low apartment, in which there was a long grate with various appurtenances for boiling, roasting, and baking. It was an old-fashioned apparatus, but Mrs. Brattle thought it to be infinitely more commodious than any of the newer-fangled ranges which from time to time she had been taken to see. Opposite to the fire-place there was a small piece of carpet, without which the stone floor would hardly have looked warm and comfortable. On the outer corner of this, half facing the fire, and half on one side of it, was an old oak arm-chair, made of oak throughout, but with a well-worn cushion on the seat of it, in which it was the miller's custom to sit when the work of the day was done. In this chair no one else would ever sit, unless Sam would do so occasionally, in bravado, and as a protest against his father's authority. When he did so his mother would be wretched, and his sister lately had begged him to desist from the sacrilege. Close to this was a little round deal table, on which would be set the miller's single glass of gin and water, which would be made to last out the process of his evening smoking, and the candle, by the light of which, and with the aid of a huge pair of tortoise-shell spectacles, his wife would sit and darn her husband's stockings. She also had her own peculiar chair in this corner, but she had never accustomed herself to the luxury of arms to lean on, and had no cushion for her own comfort. There were various dressers, tables, and sideboards round the room, and a multiplicity of dishes, plates, and bowls, all standing in their proper places. But though the apartment was called a kitchen,—and, in truth, the cookery for the family was done here,— there was behind it, opening out to the rear, another kitchen in which there was a great boiler, and a huge oven never now used. The necessary but unsightly doings of kitchen life were here carried on, out of view. He, indeed, would have been fastidious who would have hesitated, on any score of cleanliness or niceness, to sit and eat at the long board on which the miller's dinner was daily served, or would have found it amiss to sit at that fire and listen to the ticking of the great mahogany-cased clock, which stood in the corner of the room. On the other side of the broad opening passage Mrs. Brattle had her parlour. Doubtless this parlour added something to the few joys of her life; though how it did so, or why she should have rejoiced in it, it would be very difficult to say. She never entered it except for the purpose of cleaning and dusting. But it may be presumed that it was a glory to her to have a room carpeted, with six horsehair chairs, and a round table, and a horsehair sofa, and an old mirror over the fireplace, and a piece of worsted-work done by her daughter and framed like a picture, hanging up on one of the walls. But there must have come from it, we should say, more of regret than of pleasure; for when that room was first furnished, under her own auspices, and when those horsehair chairs were bought with a portion of her own modest dowry, doubtless she had intended that these luxuries should be used by her and hers. But they never had been so used. The day for using them had never come. Her husband never, by any chance, entered the apartment. To him probably, even in his youth, it had been a woman's gewgaw, useless, but allowable as tending to her happiness. Now the door was never even opened before his eye. His last interview with Carry had been in that room,—when he had laid his curse upon her, and bade her begone before his return, so that his decent threshold should be no longer polluted by her vileness.

On this side of the house there was a cross passage, dividing the front rooms from the back. At the end of this, looking to the front so as to have the parlour between it and the house-door, was the chamber in which slept Brattle and his wife. Here all those children had been born who had brought upon the household so many joys and so much sorrow. And behind, looking to the back on to the little plot of vegetables which was called the garden,—a plot in which it seemed that cabbages and gooseberry bushes were made to alternate,—there was a large store-room, and the chamber in which Fanny slept,—now alone, but which she had once shared with four sisters. Carry was the last one that had left her; and now Fanny hardly dared to name the word sister above her breath. She could speak, indeed, of Sister Jay, the wife of the prosperous ironmonger at Warminster; but of sisters by their Christian names no mention was ever made.

Upstairs there were garrets, one of which was inhabited by Sam, when he chose to reside at home; and another by the red-armed country lass, who was maid-of-all-work at Brattle Mill. When it has also been told that below the cabbage-plot there was an orchard, stretching down to the junction of the waters, the description of Brattle Mill will have been made.

CHAPTER VII.

THE MILLER'S WIFE.

When Mr. Fenwick entered the kitchen, Mrs. Brattle was sitting there alone. Her daughter was away, disposing of the remnants and utensils of the dinner-table. The old lady, with her spectacles on her nose, was sitting as usual with a stocking over her left arm. On the round table was a great open Bible, and, lying on the Bible, were sundry large worsted hose, which always seemed to Mr. Fenwick as though they must have undarned themselves as quickly as they were darned. Her Bible and her stockings furnished the whole of Mrs. Brattle's occupation from her dinner to her bed. In the morning, she would still occupy herself in matters of cookery, would peel potatoes, and prepare apples for puddings, and would look into the pot in which the cabbage was being boiled. But her stockings and her Bible shared together the afternoons of her week-days. On the Sundays there would only be the Bible, and then she would pass many hours of the day asleep. On every other Sunday morning she still walked to church and back,—going there always alone. There was no one now to accompany her. Her husband never went,—never had gone,—to church, and her son now had broken away from his good practices. On alternate mornings Fanny went, and also on every Sunday afternoon. Wet or dry, storm or sunshine, she always went; and her father, who was an old Pagan, loved her for her zeal. Mrs. Brattle was a slight-made old woman, with hair almost white peering out modestly from under her clean cap, dressed always in a brown stuff gown that never came down below her ankle. Her features were still pretty, small, and débonnaire, and there was a sweetness in her eyes that no observer could overlook. She was a modest, pure, high-minded woman,—whom we will not call a lady, because of her position in life, and because she darned stockings in a kitchen. In all other respects she deserved the name.

"I heard your voice outside with the master," she said, rising from her chair to answer the parson's salutation, and putting down her stockings first, and then her spectacles upon the book, so that the Bible was completely hidden; "and I knew you would not go without saying a word to the old woman."

"I believe I came mostly to see you to-day, Mrs. Brattle."

"Did you then? It's kind of you, I'm sure, Mr. Fenwick, this hot weather,—and you with so many folk to mind too. Will you take an apple, Mr. Fenwick? I don't know that we've anything else to offer, but the quarantines are rare this year, they say;—though, no doubt, you have them better at the Vicarage?"

Fenwick took a large, red apple from the dresser, and began to munch, it, declaring that they had none such in their orchard. And then, when the apple was finished, he had to begin his story.

"Mrs. Brattle, I'm sorry that I have something to say that will vex you."

"Eh, Mr. Fenwick! Bad news? 'Deed and I think there's but little good news left to us now,—little that comes from the tongues of men. It's bad news that is always coming here. Mr. Fenwick,—what is it, sir?"

Then he repeated the question he had before put to the miller about Sam. Where was Sam last night?—She only shook her head. Did he sleep at home?—She shook her head again. Had he breakfasted at home?

"'Deed no, sir. I haven't set eyes on him since before yesterday."

"But how does he live? His father does not give him money, I suppose?"

"There's little enough to give him, Mr. Fenwick. When he is at the mill his father do pay him a some'at over and above his keep. It isn't much, sir. Young men must have a some'at in their pockets at times."

"He has too much in his pockets, I fear. I wish he had nothing, so that he needs must come home for his meals. He works at the mill, doesn't he?"

"At times, sir; and there isn't a lad in all Bullumpton,"—for so the name was ordinarily pronounced,—"who can do a turn of work to beat him."

"Do he and his father agree pretty well?"

"At times, sir. Times again his father don't say much to him. The master ain't given to much talking in the mill, and Sam, when he's there, works with a will. There's times when his father softens down to him, and then to see 'em, you'd think they was all in all to each other. There's a stroke of the master about Sam hisself, at times, Mr. Fenwick, and the old man's eyes gladden to see it. There's none so near his heart now as poor Sam."

"If he were as honest a man as his father, I could forgive all the rest," said Mr. Fenwick slowly, meaning to imply that he was not there now to complain of church observances neglected, or of small irregularities of life. The paganism of the old miller had often been the subject of converse between the parson and Mrs. Brattle, it being a matter on which she had many an unhappy thought. He, groping darkly among subjects which he hardly dared to touch in her presence lest he should seem to unteach that in private which he taught in public, had subtlely striven to make her believe that though she, through her faith, would be saved, he, the husband, might yet escape that doom of everlasting fire, which to her was so stern a reality that she thought of its fury with a shudder whenever she heard of the world's wickedness. When Parson Fenwick had first made himself intimate at the mill Mrs. Brattle had thought that her husband's habits of life would have been to him as wormwood and gall,—that he would be unable not to chide, and well she knew that her husband would bear no chiding. By degrees she had come to understand that this new parson was one who talked more of life with its sorrows, and vices, and chances of happiness, and possibilities of goodness, than he did of the requirements of his religion. For herself inwardly she had grieved at this, and, possibly, also for him; but, doubtless, there had come to her some comfort, which she did not care to analyse, from the manner in which "the master," as she called him, Pagan as he was, had been treated by her clergyman. She wondered that it should be so, but yet it was a relief to her to know that God's messenger should come to her, and yet say never a word of his message to that hard lord, whom she so feared and so loved, and who was, as she well knew, too stubborn to receive it. And Fenwick had spoken,—still spoke to her, so tenderly of her erring, fallen child, never calling her a castaway, talking of her as Carry, who might yet be worthy of happiness here and of all joy hereafter; that when she thought of him as a minister of God, whose duty it was to pronounce God's threats to erring human beings, she was almost alarmed. She could hardly understand his leniency,—his abstinence from reproof; but entertained a vague, wandering, unformed wish that, as he never opened the vials of his wrath on them, he would pour it out upon her,—on her who would bear it for their sake so meekly. If there was such a wish it was certainly doomed to disappointment. At this moment Fanny came in and curtseyed as she gave her hand to the parson.

"Was Sam at home last night, Fan?" asked the mother, in a sad, low voice.

"Yes, mother. He slept in his bed."

"You are sure?" said the parson.

"Quite sure. I heard him this morning as he went out. It was about five. He spoke to me, and I answered him."

"What did he say?"

"That he must go over to Lavington, and wouldn't be home till nightfall. I told him where he would find bread and cheese, and he took it."

"But you didn't see him last night?"

"No, sir. He comes in at all hours, when he pleases. He was at dinner before yesterday, but I haven't seen him since. He didn't go nigh the mill after dinner that day."

Then Mr. Fenwick considered how much he would tell to the mother and sister, and how much he would keep back. He did not in his heart believe that Sam Brattle had intended to enter his house and rob it; but he did believe that the men with whom Sam was associated were thieves and housebreakers. If these men were prowling about Bullhampton it was certainly his duty to have them arrested if possible, and to prevent probable depredations, for his neighbours' sake as well as for his own. Nor would he be justified in neglecting this duty with the object of saving Sam Brattle. If only he could entice Sam away from them, into his own hands, under the power of his tongue,—there might probably be a chance.

"You think he'll be home to-night?" he asked.

"He said he would," replied Fanny, who knew that she could not answer for her brother's word.

"If he does, bid him come to me. Make him come to me! Tell him that I will do him no harm. God knows how truly it is my object to do him good."

"We are sure of that, sir," said the mother.

"He need not be afraid that I will preach to him. I will only talk to him, as I would to a younger brother."

"But what is it that he has done, sir?"

"He has done nothing that I know. There;—I will tell you the whole. I found him prowling about my garden at near midnight, yesterday. Had he been alone I should have thought nothing of it. He thinks he owes me a grudge for speaking to his father; and had I found him paying it by filling his pockets with fruit, I should only have told him that it would be better that he should come and take it in the morning."

"But he wasn't—stealing?" asked the mother.

"He was doing nothing; neither were the men. But they were blackguards, and he was in bad hands. He could not have been in worse. I had a tussle with one of them, and I am sure the man was hurt. That, however, has nothing to do with it. What I desire is to get a hold of Sam, so that he may be rescued from the hands of such companions. If you can make him come to me, do so."

Fanny promised, and so did the mother; but the promise was given in that tone which seemed to imply that nothing should be expected from its performance. Sam had long been deaf to the voices of the women of his family, and, when his father's anger would be hot against him, he would simply go, and live where and how none of them knew. Among such men and women as the Brattles, parental authority must needs lie much lighter than it does with those who are wont to give much and to receive much. What obedience does the lad owe who at eighteen goes forth and earns his own bread? What is it to him that he has not yet reached man's estate? He has to do a man's work, and the price of it is his own, in his hands, when he has earned it. There is no curse upon the poor heavier than that which comes from the early breach of all ties of duty between fathers and their sons, and mothers and their daughters.

Mr. Fenwick, as he passed out of the miller's house, saw Jacob Brattle at the door of the mill. He was tugging along some load, pulling it in at the door, and prevailing against the weakness of his age by the force of his energy. The parson knew that the miller saw him, but the miller took no notice,—looked rather as though he did not wish to be observed,—and so the parson went on. When at home he postponed his account of what had taken place till he should be alone with his wife; but at night he told her the whole story.

"The long and the short of it is, Master Sam will turn to housebreaking, if somebody doesn't get hold of him."

"To housebreaking, Frank?"

"I believe that he is about it."

"And were they going to break in here?"

"I don't think he was. I don't believe he was so minded then. But he had shown them the way in, and they were looking about on their own scores. Don't you frighten yourself. What with the constable and the life-preserver, we'll be safe. I've a big dog coming, a second Bone'm. Sam Brattle is in more danger, I fear, than the silver forks."

But, in spite of the cheeriness of his speech, the Vicar was anxious, and almost unhappy. After all that occurred in reference to himself and to Sam Brattle,—their former intimacies, the fish they had caught together, the rats they had killed together, the favour which he, the parson of the parish, had shown to this lad, and especially after the evil things which had been said of himself because of this friendship on his part for one so much younger than himself, and so much his inferior in rank,—it would be to him a most grievous misfortune should he be called upon to acknowledge publicly Sam Brattle's iniquity, and more grievous still, if the necessity should be forced upon him of bringing Sam to open punishment. Fenwick knew well that diverse accusations had been made against him in the parish regarding Sam. The Marquis of Trowbridge had said a word. Mr. Puddleham had said many words. The old miller himself had growled. Even Gilmore had expressed disapprobation. The Vicar, in his pride, had turned a deaf ear to them all. He began to fear now that possibly he had been wrong in the favours shown to Sam Brattle.

CHAPTER VIII.

THE LAST DAY.

The parson's visit to the mill was on a Saturday. The next Sunday passed by very quietly, and nothing was seen of Mr. Gilmore at the Vicarage. He was at church, and walked with the two ladies from the porch to their garden gate, but he declined Mrs. Fenwick's invitation to lunch, and was not seen again on that day. The parson had sent word to Fanny Brattle during the service to stop a few minutes for him, and had learned from her that Sam had not been at home last night. He had also learned, before the service that morning, that very early on the Saturday, probably about four o'clock, two men had passed through Paul's Hinton with a huxter's cart and a pony. Now Paul's Hinton, or Hinton Saint Paul's as it should be properly called, was a long straggling village, six miles from Bullhampton, and half-way on the road to Market Lavington, to which latter place Sam had told his sister that he was going. Putting these things together, Mr. Fenwick did not in the least doubt but the two men in the cart were they who had been introduced to his garden by young Brattle.

"I only hope," said the parson, "that there's a good surgeon at Market Lavington. One of the gentlemen in that cart must have wanted him, I take it." Then he thought that it might, perhaps, be worth his while to trot over to Lavington in the course of the week, and make inquiries.

On the Wednesday Mary Lowther was to go back to Loring. This seemed like a partial break-up of their establishment, both to the parson and his wife. Fenwick had made up his mind that Mary was to be his nearest neighbour for life, and had fallen into the way of treating her accordingly, telling her of things in the parish as he might have done to the Squire's wife, presuming the Squire's wife to have been on the best possible terms with him. He now regarded Mary as being almost an impostor. She had taken him in and obtained his confidence under false pretences. It was true that she might still come and fill the place that he had appointed for her. He rather thought that at last she would do so. But he was angry with her because she hesitated. She was creating an unnecessary disturbance among them. She had, he thought, been now wooed long enough, and, as he told his wife more than once, was making an ass of herself. Mrs. Fenwick was not quite so hard in her judgment, but she also was tempted to be a little angry. She loved her friend Mary a great deal better than she loved Mr. Gilmore, but she was thoroughly convinced that Mary could not do better than accept a man whom she owned that she liked,—whom she, at any rate, liked so well that she had not as yet rejected him. Therefore, although Mary was going, they were, both of them, rather savage with her.

The Monday passed by, also very quietly, and Mr. Gilmore did not come to them, but he had sent a note to tell them that he would walk down on the Tuesday evening to say good-bye to Miss Lowther. Early on the Wednesday Mr. Fenwick was to drive her to Westbury, whence the railway would take her round by Chippenham and Swindon to Loring. On the Tuesday morning she was very melancholy. Though she knew that it was right to go away, she greatly regretted that it was necessary. She was angry with herself for not having better known her own mind, and though she was quite sure that were Mr. Gilmore to repeat his offer to her that moment, she would not accept it, nevertheless she thought ill of herself because she would not do so. "I do believe," she said to herself, "that I shall never like any man better." She knew well enough that if she was never brought to love any man, she never ought to marry any man; but she was not quite sure whether Janet was not right in telling her that she had formed erroneous notions of the sort of love she ought to feel for the man whom she should resolve to accept. Perhaps it was true that that kind of adoration which Janet entertained for her husband was a feeling which came after marriage—a feeling which would spring up in her own heart as soon as she was the man's own wife, the mistress of his house, the mother of his children, the one human being for whose welfare he was solicitous beyond that of all others. And this man did love her. She had no doubt about that. And she was unhappy, too, because she felt that she had offended his friends, and that they thought that she was not treating their friend well.

"Janet," she said, as they were again sitting out on the lawn, on that Tuesday afternoon, "I am almost sorry that I came here at all."

"Don't say that, dear."

"I have spent some of the happiest days of my life here, but the visit, on the whole, has been unfortunate. I am going away in disgrace. I feel that so acutely."

"What nonsense! How are you in disgrace?"

"Mr. Fenwick and you think that I have behaved badly. I know you do, and I feel it so strongly! I think so much of him, and believe him to be so good, and so wise, and so understanding,—he knows what people should do, and should be, so well,—that I cannot doubt that I have been wrong if he thinks so."

"He only wishes that you could have made up your mind to marry a most worthy man, who is his friend, and who, by marrying you, would have fixed you close to us. He wishes it still, and so do I."

"But he thinks that I have been—have been mopish, and lack-a-daisical, and—and—almost untrue. I can hear it in the tone of his voice, and see it in his eye. I can tell it from the way he shakes hands with me in the morning. He is such a true man that I know in a moment what he means at all times. I am going away under his displeasure, and I wish I had never come."

"Return as Mrs. Gilmore, and all his displeasure will disappear."

"Yes, because he would forgive me. He would say to himself that, as I had repented, I might be taken back to his grace; but as things are at present he condemns me. And so do you."

"If you ask me, Mary, I must tell the truth. I don't think you know your own mind."

"Suppose I don't, is that disgraceful?"

"But there comes a time when a girl should know her own mind. You are giving this poor fellow an enormous deal of unnecessary trouble."

"I have known my own mind so far as to tell him that I could not marry him."

"As far as I understand, Mary, you have always told him to wait a little longer."

"I have never asked him to wait, Janet;—never. It is he who says that he will wait; and what can I answer when he says so? All the same I don't mean to defend myself. I do believe that I have been wrong, and I wish that I had never come here. It sounds ungrateful, but I do. It is so dreadful to feel that I have incurred the displeasure of people that I love so dearly."

"There is no displeasure, Mary; the word is a good deal too strong. I wonder what you'll think of all this when the parson and his wife come up on future Sundays to dine with the Squire and his lady. I have long since made up my mind that when afternoon service is over, we ought to go up and be made much of at the Privets; and you're putting all this off till I'm an old woman—for a chimera. It's about our Sunday dinners that I'm angry. Flo, my darling, what a face you have got. Do come and sit still for a few minutes, or you'll be in a fever." While Mrs. Fenwick was wiping her girl's brow, and smoothing her ringlets, Mary walked off to the orchard by herself. There was a broad green path which made the circuit of it, and she took the round twice, pausing at the bottom to look at the spot from which she had tumbled into the river. What a trouble she had been to them all! She was thoroughly dissatisfied with herself; especially so because she had fallen into those very difficulties which from early years she had resolved that she would avoid. She had made up her mind that she would not flirt, that she would never give a right to any man—or to any woman—to call her a coquette; that if love and a husband came in her way she would take them thankfully, and that if they did not, she would go on her path quietly, if possible, feeling no uneasiness, and certainly showing none, because the joys of a married life did not belong to her. But now she had gotten herself into a mess, and she could not tell herself that it was not her own fault. Then she resolved again that in future she would go right. It could not but be that a woman could keep herself from floundering in these messes of half-courtship,—of courtship on one side, and doubt on the other,—if she would persistently adhere to some safe rule. Her rejection of Mr. Gilmore ought to have been unhesitating and certain from the first. She was sure of that now. She had been guilty of an absurdity in supposing that because the man had been in earnest, therefore she had been justified in keeping him in suspense, for his own sake. She had been guilty of an absurdity, and also of great self-conceit. She could do nothing now but wait till she should hear from him,—and then answer him steadily. After what had passed she could not go to him and declare that it was all over. He was coming to-night, and she was nearly sure that he would not say a word to her on the subject. If he did,—if he renewed his offer,—then she would speak out. It was hardly possible that he should do so, and therefore the trouble which she had created must remain.

As she thus resolved, she was leaning over the gate looking into the churchyard, not much observing the graves or the monuments or the beautiful old ivy-covered tower, or thinking of the dead that were lying there, or of the living who prayed there; but swearing to herself that for the rest of her life she would keep clear of, what she called, girlish messes. Like other young ladies she had read much poetry and many novels; but her sympathies had never been with young ladies who could not go straight through with their love affairs, from the beginning to the end, without flirtation of either an inward or an outward nature. Of all her heroines, Rosalind was the one she liked the best, because from the first moment of her passion she knew herself and what she was about, and loved her lover right heartily. Of all girls in prose or poetry she declared that Rosalind was the least of a flirt. She meant to have the man, and never had a doubt about it. But with such a one as Flora MacIvor she had no patience;—a girl who did and who didn't, who would and who wouldn't, who could and who couldn't, and who of all flirts was to her the most nauseous! As she was taking herself to task, accusing herself of being a Flora without the poetry and romance to excuse her, Mr. Fenwick came round from Farmer Trumbull's side of the church, and got over the stile into the churchyard.

Mr. Fenwick came round from Farmer Trumbull's side of the church, and got over the stile into the churchyard.

"What, Mary, is that you gazing in so intently among your brethren that were?"

"I was not thinking of them," she said, with a smile. "My mind was intent on some of my brethren that are." Then there came a thought across her, and she made a sudden decision. "Mr. Fenwick," she said, "would you mind walking up and down the churchyard with me once or twice? I have something to say to you, and I can say it now so well." He opened the gate for her, and she joined him. "I want to beg your pardon, and to get you to forgive me. I know you have been angry with me."

"Hardly angry,—but vexed. As you ask me so frankly and prettily, I will forgive you. There is my hand upon it. All evil thoughts against you shall go out of my head. I shall still have my wishes, but I will not be cross with you."

"You are so good, and so clearly honest. I declare I think Janet the happiest woman that I ever heard of."

"Come, come; I didn't bargain for this kind of thing when I allowed myself to be brought in here."

"But it is so. I did not stop you for that, however, but to acknowledge that I have been wrong, and to ask you to pardon me."

"I will. I do. If there has been anything amiss, it shall not be looked on again as amiss. But there has been only one thing amiss."

"And, Mr. Fenwick, will you do this for me? Will you tell him that I was foolish to say that he might wait? Why should he wait? Of course he should not wait. When I am gone, tell him so, and beg him to make an end of it. I had not thought of it properly, or I would not have allowed him to be tormented."

There was a pause after this, during which they walked half the length of the path in silence. "No, Mary," he said, after a while; "I will not tell him that."

"Why not, Mr. Fenwick?"

"Because it will not be for his good, or for mine, or for Janet's, or, as I believe, for yours."

"Indeed, it will, for the good of us all."

"I think, Mary, you do not quite understand. There is not one among us who does not wish that you should come here and be one of us; a real, right down Bullompton 'ooman, as they say in the village. I want you to be my wife's dearest friend, and my own nearest neighbour. There is no man in the world whom I love as I do Harry Gilmore, and I want you to be his wife. I have said to myself and to Janet a score of times that you certainly would be so sooner or later. My wrath has not come from your bidding him to wait, but from your coldness in not taking him without waiting. You should remember that we grow gray very quickly, Mary."

Here was the old story again,—the old story as she had heard it from Harry Gilmore, but told as she had never expected to hear it from the lips of Frank Fenwick. It amounted to this; that even he, Frank Fenwick, bade her wait and try. But she had formed her resolution, and she was not going to be turned aside, even by Frank Fenwick; "I had thought that you would help me," she said, very slowly.

"So I will, with all my heart, towards the keys of the store closets of the Privets, but not a step the other way. It has to be, Mary. He is too much in earnest, and too good, and too fit for the place to which he aspires, to miss his object. Come, we'll go in. Mind, you and I are one again, let it go how it may. I will own that I have been vexed for the last two days,—have been in a humour unbecoming your departure to-morrow. I throw all that behind me. You and I are dear friends,—are we not?"

"I do hope so, Mr. Fenwick?"

"There shall be no feather moulted between us. But as to operating between you and Harry, with the view of keeping you apart, I decline the commission. It is my assured belief that sooner or later he will be your husband. Now we will go up to Janet, who will begin to think herself a Penelope, if we desert her much longer."

Immediately after this Mary went up to dress for dinner. Should she make up her mind to give way, and put on the blue ribbons which he loved so well? She thought that she could tell him at once, if she made up her mind in that direction. It would not, perhaps, be very maidenly, but anything would be better than suspense,—than torment to him. Then she took out her blue ribbons, and tried to go through that ceremony of telling him. It was quite impossible. Were she to do so, she would know no happiness again in this world, or probably in the other. To do the thing, it would be necessary that she should lie to him.

She came down in a simple white dress, without any ribbons, in just the dress which she would have worn had Mr. Gilmore not been coming. At dinner they were very merry. The word of command had gone forth from Frank that Mary was to be forgiven, and Janet of course obeyed. The usual courtesies of society demand that there shall be civility—almost flattering civility—from host to guest, and from guest to host; and yet how often does it occur that in the midst of these courtesies there is something that tells of hatred, of ridicule, or of scorn! How often does it happen that the guest knows that he is disliked, or the host knows that he is a bore! In the last two days Mary had felt that she was not cordially a welcome guest. She had felt also that the reason was one against which she could not contend. Now all that, at least, was over. Frank Fenwick's manner had never been pleasanter to her than it was on this occasion, and Janet followed the suit which her lord led.

They were again on the lawn between eight and nine o'clock when Harry Gilmore came up to them. He was gracious enough in his salutation to Mary Lowther, but no indifferent person would have thought that he was her lover. He talked chiefly to Fenwick, and when they went in to tea did not take a place on the sofa beside Mary. But after a while he said something which told them all of his love.

"What do you think I've been doing to-day, Frank?"

"Getting your wheat down, I should hope."

"We begin that to-morrow. I never like to be quite the earliest at that work, or yet the latest."

"Better be a day too early than a day too late, Harry."

"Never mind about that. I've been down with old Brattle."

"And what have you been doing with him?"

"I'm half ashamed, and yet I fancy I'm right."

As he said this he looked across to Mary Lowther, who no doubt was watching every turn of his face from the corner of her eye. "I've just been and knocked under, and told him that the old place shall be put to rights."

"That's your doing, Mary," said Mrs. Fenwick, injudiciously.

"Oh, no; I'm sure it is not. Mr. Gilmore would only do such a thing as that because it is proper."

"I don't know about it's being proper," said he. "I'm not quite sure whether it is or not. I shall never get any interest for my money."

"Interest for one's money is not everything," said Mrs. Fenwick.

"Nevertheless, when one builds houses for other people to live in, one has to look to it," said the parson.

"People say it's the prettiest spot in the parish," continued Mr. Gilmore, "and as such it shouldn't be let go to ruin." Janet remarked afterwards to her husband that Mary Lowther had certainly declared that it was the prettiest spot in the parish, but that, as far as her knowledge went, nobody else had ever said so. "And then, you see, when I refused to spend money upon it, old Brattle had money of his own, and it was his business to do it."

"He hasn't much now, I fear," said Mr. Fenwick.

"I fear not. His family has been very heavy on him. He paid money to put two of his boys into trade who died afterwards, and then for years he had either doctors or undertakers about the place. So I just went down to him and told him I would do it."

"And how did he take it?"

"Like a bear, as he is. He would hardly speak to me, but went away into the mill, telling me that I might settle it all with his wife. It's going to be done, however. I shall have the estimate next week, and I suppose it will cost me two or three hundred pounds. The mill is worse than the house, I take it."

"I am so glad it is to be done," said Mary. After that Mr. Gilmore did not in the least begrudge his two or three hundred pounds. But he said not a word to Mary, just pressed her hand at parting, and left her subject to a possibility of a reversal of her sentence at the end of the stated period.

On the next morning Mr. Fenwick drove her in his little open phaeton to the station at Westbury. "You are to come back to us, you know," said Mrs. Fenwick, "and remember how anxiously I am waiting for my Sunday dinners." Mary said not a word, but as she was driven round in front of the church she looked up at the dear old tower, telling herself that, in all probability, she would never see it again.

"I have just one thing to say, Mary," said the parson, as he walked up and down the platform with her at Westbury; "you are to remember that, whatever happens, there is always a home for you at Bullhampton when you choose to come to it. I am not speaking of the Privets now, but of the Vicarage."

"How very good you are to me!"

"And so are you to us. Dear friends should be good to each other. God bless you, dear." From thence she made her way home to Loring by herself.

CHAPTER IX.

MISS MARRABLE.

Whatever may be the fact as to the rank and proper calling of Bullhampton, there can be no doubt that Loring is a town. There is a market-place, and a High Street, and a Board of Health, and a Paragon Crescent, and a Town Hall, and two different parish churches, one called St. Peter Lowtown, and the other St. Botolph's Uphill, and there are Uphill Street, and Lowtown Street, and various other streets. I never heard of a mayor of Loring, but, nevertheless, there is no doubt as to its being a town. Nor did it ever return members to Parliament; but there was once, in one of the numerous bills that have been proposed, an idea of grouping it with Cirencester and Lechlade. All the world of course knows that this was never done; but the transient rumour of it gave the Loringites an improved position, and justified that little joke about a live dog being better than a dead lion, with which the parson at Bullhampton regaled Miss Lowther at the time.

All the fashion of Loring dwelt, as a matter of course, at Uphill. Lowtown was vulgar, dirty, devoted to commercial and manufacturing purposes, and hardly owned a single genteel private house. There was the parsonage, indeed, which stood apart from its neighbours, inside great tall slate-coloured gates, and which had a garden of its own. But except the clergyman, who had no choice in the matter, nobody who was anybody lived at Lowtown. There were three or four factories there,—in and out of which troops of girls would be seen passing twice a day, in their ragged, soiled, dirty mill dresses, all of whom would come out on Sunday dressed with a magnificence that would lead one to suppose that trade at Loring was doing very well. Whether trade did well or ill, whether wages were high or low, whether provisions were cheap in price, whether there were peace or war between capital and labour, still there was the Sunday magnificence. What a blessed thing it is for women,—and for men too certainly,—that there should be a positive happiness to the female sex in the possession, and in exhibiting the possession, of bright clothing! It is almost as good for the softening of manners, and the not permitting of them to be ferocious, as is the faithful study of the polite arts. At Loring the manners of the mill hands, as they were called, were upon the whole good,—which I believe was in a great degree to be attributed to their Sunday magnificence.

The real West-end of Loring was understood by all men to lie in Paragon Crescent, at the back of St. Botolph's Church. The whole of this Crescent was built, now some twenty years ago, by Mrs. Fenwick's father, who had been clever enough to see that as mills were made to grow in the low town, houses for wealthy people to live in ought to be made to grow in the high town. He therefore built the Paragon, and a certain small row of very pretty houses near the end of the Paragon, called Balfour Place,—and had done very well, and had made money; and now lay asleep in the vaults below St. Botolph's Church. No inconsiderable proportion of the comfort of Bullhampton parsonage is due to Mr. Balfour's success in that achievement of Paragon Crescent. There were none of the family left at Loring. The widow had gone away to live at Torquay with a sister, and the only other child, another daughter, was married to that distinguished barrister on the Oxford circuit, Mr. Quickenham. Mr. Quickenham and our friend the parson were very good friends; but they did not see a great deal of each other, Mr. Fenwick not going up very often to London, and Mr. Quickenham being unable to use the Vicarage of Bullhampton when on his own circuit. As for the two sisters, they had very strong ideas about their husbands' professions; Sophia Quickenham never hesitating to declare that one was life, and the other stagnation; and Janet Fenwick protesting that the difference to her seemed to be almost that between good and evil. They wrote to each other perhaps once a quarter. But the Balfour family was in truth broken up.

Miss Marrable, Mary Lowther's aunt, lived, of course, at Uphill; but not in the Crescent, nor yet in Balfour Place. She was an old lady with very modest means, whose brother had been rector down at St. Peter's, and she had passed the greatest part of her life within those slate-coloured gates. When he died, and when she, almost exactly at the same time, found that it would be expedient that she should take charge of her niece, Mary, she removed herself up to a small house in Botolph Lane, in which she could live decently on her £300 a year. It must not be surmised that Botolph Lane was a squalid place, vile, or dirty, or even unfashionable. It was narrow and old, having been inhabited by decent people long before the Crescent, or even Mr. Balfour himself, had been in existence; but it was narrow and old, and the rents were cheap, and here Miss Marrable was able to live, and occasionally to give tea-parties, and to provide a comfortable home for her niece, within the limits of her income. Miss Marrable was herself a lady of very good family, the late Sir Gregory Marrable having been her uncle; but her only sister had married a Captain Lowther, whose mother had been first cousin to the Earl of Periwinkle; and therefore on her own account, as well as on that of her niece, Miss Marrable thought a good deal about blood. She was one of those ladies,—now few in number,—who within their heart of hearts conceive that money gives no title to social distinction, let the amount of money be ever so great, and its source ever so stainless. Rank to her was a thing quite assured and ascertained, and she had no more doubt as to her own right to pass out of a room before the wife of a millionaire than she had of the right of a millionaire to spend his own guineas. She always addressed an attorney by letter as Mister, raising up her eyebrows when appealed to on the matter, and explaining that an attorney is not an esquire. She had an idea that the son of a gentleman, if he intended to maintain his rank as a gentleman, should earn his income as a clergyman, or as a barrister, or as a soldier, or as a sailor. Those were the professions intended for gentlemen. She would not absolutely say that a physician was not a gentleman, or even a surgeon; but she would never allow to physic the same absolute privileges which, in her eyes, belonged to law and the church. There might also possibly be a doubt about the Civil Service and Civil Engineering; but she had no doubt whatever that when a man touched trade or commerce in any way he was doing that which was not the work of a gentleman. He might be very respectable, and it might be very necessary that he should do it; but brewers, bankers, and merchants, were not gentlemen, and the world, according to Miss Marrable's theory, was going astray, because people were forgetting their landmarks.

As to Miss Marrable herself nobody could doubt that she was a lady; she looked it in every inch. There were not, indeed, many inches of her, for she was one of the smallest, daintiest, little old women that ever were seen. But now, at seventy, she was very pretty, quite a woman to look at with pleasure. Her feet and hands were exquisitely made, and she was very proud of them. She wore her own grey hair of which she showed very little, but that little was always exquisitely nice. Her caps were the perfection of caps. Her green eyes were bright and sharp, and seemed to say that she knew very well how to take care of herself. Her mouth, and nose, and chin, were all well-formed, small, shapely, and concise, not straggling about her face as do the mouths, noses, and chins of some old ladies—ay, and of some young ladies also. Had it not been that she had lost her teeth, she would hardly have looked to be an old woman. Her health was perfect. She herself would say that she had never yet known a day's illness. She dressed with the greatest care, always wearing silk at and after luncheon. She dressed three times a day, and in the morning would come down in what she called a merino gown. But then, with her, clothes never seemed to wear out. Her motions were so slight and delicate, that the gloss of her dresses would remain on them when the gowns of other women would almost have been worn to rags. She was never seen of an afternoon or evening without gloves, and her gloves were always clean and apparently new. She went to church once on Sundays in winter, and twice in summer, and she had a certain very short period of each day devoted to Bible reading; but at Loring she was not reckoned to be among the religious people. Indeed, there were those who said that she was very worldly-minded, and that at her time of life she ought to devote herself to other books than those which were daily in her hands. Pope, Dryden, Swift, Cowley, Fielding, Richardson, and Goldsmith, were her authors. She read the new novels as they came out, but always with critical comparisons that were hostile to them. Fielding, she said, described life as it was; whereas

Dickens had manufactured a kind of life that never had existed, and never could exist. The pathos of Esmond was very well, but Lady Castlemaine was nothing to Clarissa Harlowe. As for poetry, Tennyson, she said, was all sugar-candy; he had neither the common sense, nor the wit, nor, as she declared, to her ear the melody of Pope. All the poets of the present century, she declared, if put together, could not have written the Rape of the Lock. Pretty as she was, and small, and nice, and lady-like, I think she liked her literature rather strong. It is certain that she had Smollett's novels in a cupboard up-stairs, and it was said that she had been found reading one of Wycherley's plays.

The strongest point in her character was her contempt of money. Not that she had any objection to it, or would at all have turned up her nose at another hundred a year had anybody left to her such an accession of income; but that in real truth she never measured herself by what she possessed, or others by what they possessed. She was as grand a lady to herself, eating her little bit of cold mutton, or dining off a tiny sole, as though she sat at the finest banquet that could be spread. She had no fear of economies, either before her two handmaids or anybody else in the world. She was fond of her tea, and in summer could have cream for twopence; but when cream became dear, she saved money and had a pen'north of milk. She drank two glasses of Marsala every day, and let it be clearly understood that she couldn't afford sherry. But when she gave a tea-party, as she did, perhaps, six or seven times a year, sherry was always handed round with cake before the people went away. There were matters in which she was extravagant. When she went out herself she never took one of the common street flies, but paid eighteen pence extra to get a brougham from the Dragon. And when Mary Lowther,—who had only fifty pounds a year of her own, with which she clothed herself and provided herself with pocket-money,—was going to Bullhampton, Miss Marrable actually proposed to her to take one of the maids with her. Mary, of course, would not hear of it, and said that she should just as soon think of taking the house; but Miss Marrable had thought that it would, perhaps, not be well for a girl so well-born as Miss Lowther to go out visiting without a maid. She herself very rarely left Loring, because she could not afford it; but when, two summers back, she did go to Weston-super-Mare for a fortnight, she took one of the girls with her.

Miss Marrable had heard a great deal about Mr. Gilmore. Mary, indeed, was not inclined to keep secrets from her aunt, and her very long absence,—so much longer than had at first been intended,—could hardly have been sanctioned unless some reason had been given. There had been many letters on the subject, not only between Mary and her aunt, but between Mrs. Fenwick and her very old friend Miss Marrable. Of course these latter letters had spoken loudly the praises of Mr. Gilmore, and Miss Marrable had become quite one of the Gilmore faction. She desired that her niece should marry; but that she should marry a gentleman. She would have infinitely preferred to see Mary an old maid, than to hear that she was going to give herself to any suitor contaminated by trade. Now Mr. Gilmore's position was exactly that which Miss Marrable regarded as being the best in England. He was a country gentleman, living on his own acres, a justice of the peace, whose father and grandfather and great-grandfather had occupied exactly the same position. Such a marriage for Mary would be quite safe; and in those days one did hear so often of girls making, she would not say improper marriages, but marriages which in her eyes were not fitting! Mr. Gilmore, she thought, exactly filled that position which entitled a gentleman to propose marriage to such a lady as Mary Lowther.

"Yes, my dear, I am glad to have you back again. Of course I have been a little lonely, but I bear that kind of thing better than most people. Thank God, my eyes are good."

"You are looking so well, Aunt Sarah!"

"I am well. I don't know how other women get so much amiss; but God has been very good to me."

"And so pretty," said Mary, kissing her.

"My dear, it's a pity you're not a young gentleman."

"You are so fresh and nice, aunt. I wish I could always look as you do."

"What would Mr. Gilmore say?"

"Oh, Mr. Gilmore, Mr. Gilmore, Mr. Gilmore! I am so weary of Mr. Gilmore."

"Weary of him, Mary?"

"Weary of myself because of him—that is what I mean. He has behaved always well, and I am not at all sure that I have. And he is a perfect gentleman. But I shall never be Mrs. Gilmore, Aunt Sarah."

"Janet says that she thinks you will."

"Janet is mistaken. But, dear aunt, don't let us talk about it at once. Of course you shall hear everything in time, but I have had so much of it. Let us see what new books there are. Cast Iron! You don't mean to say you have come to that?"

"I shan't read it."

"But I will, aunt. So it must not go back for a day or two. I do love the Fenwicks, dearly, dearly, both of them. They are almost, if not quite, perfect. And yet I am glad to be at home."

CHAPTER X.

CRUNCH'EM CAN'T BE HAD.

Mr. Fenwick had intended to have come home round by Market Lavington, after having deposited Miss Lowther at the Westbury Station, with the view of making some inquiry respecting the gentleman with the hurt shoulder; but he had found the distance to be too great, and had abandoned the idea. After that there was not a day to spare till the middle of the next week; so that it was nearly a fortnight after the little scene at the corner of the Vicarage garden wall before he called upon the Lavington constable and the Lavington doctor. From the latter he could learn nothing. No such patient had been to him. But the constable, though he had not seen the two men, had heard of them. One was a man who in former days had frequented Lavington, Burrows by name, generally known as Jack the Grinder, who had been in every prison in Wiltshire and Somersetshire, but who had not,—so said the constable,—honoured Lavington for the last two years, till this his last appearance. He had, however, been seen there in company with another man, and had evidently been in a condition very unfit for work. He had slept one night at a low public-house, and had then moved on. The man had complained of a fall from the cart, and had declared that he was black and blue all over; but it seemed to be clear that he had no broken bones. Mr. Fenwick therefore was all but convinced that Jack the Grinder was the gentleman with whom he had had the encounter, and that the grinder's back had withstood that swinging blow from the life-preserver. Of the Grinder's companions nothing could be learned. The two men had taken the Devizes road out of Lavington, and beyond that nothing was known of them. When the parson mentioned Sam Brattle's name in a whisper, the Lavington constable shook his head. He knew all about old Jacob Brattle. A very respectable party was old Mr. Brattle in the constable's opinion. Nevertheless the constable shook his head when Sam Brattle's name was mentioned. Having learned so much, the parson rode home.

Two days after this, on a Friday, Fenwick was sitting after breakfast in his study, at work on his sermon for next Sunday, when he was told that old Mrs. Brattle was waiting to see him. He immediately got up, and found his own wife and the miller's seated in the hall. It was not often that Mrs. Brattle made her way to the Vicarage, but when she did so she was treated with great consideration. It was still August, and the weather was very hot, and she had walked up across the water mead, and was tired. A glass of wine and a biscuit were pressed upon her, and she was encouraged to sit and say a few indifferent words, before she was taken into the study and told to commence the story which had brought her so far. And there was a most inviting topic for conversation. The mill and the mill premises were to be put in order by the landlord. Mrs. Brattle affected to be rather dismayed than otherwise by the coming operations. The mill would have lasted their time, she thought, "and as for them as were to come after them,—well! she didn't know. As things was now, perhaps, it might be that after all Sam would have the mill." But the trouble occasioned by the workmen would be infinite. How were they to live in the mean time, and where were they to go? It soon appeared, however, that all this had been already arranged. Milling must of course be stopped for a month or six weeks. "Indeed, sir, feyther says that there won't be no more grinding much before winter." But the mill was to be repaired first, and then, when it became absolutely necessary to dismantle the house, they were to endeavour to make shift, and live in the big room of the mill itself, till their furniture should be put back again. Mrs. Fenwick, with ready good nature, offered to accommodate Mrs. Brattle and Fanny at the Vicarage; but the old woman declined with many protestations of gratitude. She had never left her old man yet, and would not do so now. The weather would be mild for awhile, and she thought that they could get through. By this time the glass of wine had been sipped to the bottom, and the parson, mindful of his sermon, had led the visitor into his study. She had come to tell that Sam at last had returned home.

"Why didn't you bring him up with you, Mrs. Brattle?" Here was a question to ask of an old lady, whose dominion over her son was absolutely none! Sam had become so frightfully independent that he hardly regarded the word of his father, who was a man pre-eminently capable of maintaining authority, and would no more do a thing because his mother told him than because the wind whistled.

"I axed him to come up, not just with me, but of hisself, Mr. Fenwick; but he said as how you would know where to find him if you wanted him."

"That's just what I don't know. However, if he's there now I'll go to him. It would have been better far that he should have come to me."

"I told 'un so, Mr. Fenwick, I did, indeed."

"It does not signify. I will go to him; only it cannot be to-day, as I have promised to take my wife over to Charlicoats. But I'll come down immediately after breakfast to-morrow. You think he'll be still there?"

"I be sure he will, Mr. Fenwick. He and feyther have taken on again, till it's beautiful to see. There was none of 'em feyther ever loved like he,—only one." Thereupon the poor woman burst out into tears, and covered her face with her handkerchief. "He never makes half so much account of my Fan, that never had a fault belonging to her."

"If Sam will stick to that it will be well for him."

"He's taken up extraordinary with the repairs, Mr. Fenwick. He's in and about and over the place, looking to everything; and feyther says he knows so much about it, he b'lieves the boy could do it all out o' his own head. There's nothing feyther ever liked so much as folks to be strong and clever."

"Perhaps the Squire's tradesmen won't like all that. Is Mitchell going to do it?"

"It ain't a doing in that way, Mr. Fenwick. The Squire is allowing £200, and feyther is to get it done. Mister Mitchell is to see that it's done proper, no doubt."

"And now tell me, Mrs. Brattle, what has Sam been about all the time that he was away?"

"That's just what I cannot tell you, Mr. Fenwick."

"Your husband has asked him, I suppose?"

"If he has, he ain't told me, Mr. Fenwick. I don't care to come between them with hints and jealousies, suspecting like. Our Fan says he's been out working somewhere Lavington way; but I don't know as she knows."

"Was he decent looking when he came home?"

"He wasn't much amiss, Mr. Fenwick. He has that way with him that he most always looks decent;—don't he, sir?"

"Had he any money?"

"He had a some'at, because when he was working, moving the big lumber as though for bare life, he sent one of the boys for beer, and I see'd him give the boy the money."

"I'm sorry for it. I wish he'd come back without a penny, and with hunger like a wolf in his stomach, and with his clothes all rags, so that he might have had a taste of the suffering of a vagabond's life."

"Just like the Prodigal Son, Mr. Fenwick?"

"Just like the Prodigal Son. He would not have come back to his father had he not been driven by his own vices to live with the swine." Then, seeing the tears coming down the poor mother's cheeks, he added in a kinder voice, "Perhaps it may be all well as it is. We will hope so at least, and to-morrow I will come down and see him. You need not tell him that I am coming, unless he should ask where you have been." Then Mrs. Brattle took her leave, and the parson finished his sermon.

That afternoon he drove his wife across the county to visit certain friends at Charlicoats, and, both going and coming, could not keep himself from talking about the Brattles. In the first place, he thought that Gilmore was wrong not to complete the work himself.

"Of course he'll see that the money is spent and all that, and no doubt in this way he may get the job done twenty or thirty pounds cheaper; but the Brattles have not interest enough in the place to justify it."

"I suppose the old man liked it best so."

"The old man shouldn't have been allowed to have his way. I am in an awful state of alarm about Sam. Much as I like him,—or at any rate did like him,—I fear he is going, or perhaps has gone, to the dogs. That those two men were housebreakers is as certain as that you sit there; and I cannot doubt but that he has been with them over at Lavington or Devizes, or somewhere in that country."

"But he may, perhaps, never have joined them in anything of that kind."

"A man is known by his companions. I would not have believed it if I had not found him with the men, and traced him and them about the county together. You see that this fellow whom they call the Grinder was certainly the man I struck. I tracked him to Lavington, and there he was complaining of being sore all over his body. I don't wonder that he was sore. He must be made like a horse to be no worse than sore. Well, then, that man and Sam were certainly in our garden together."

"Give him a chance, Frank."

"Of course, I will give him a chance. I will give him the very best chance I can. I would do anything to save him,—but I can't help knowing what I know."

He had made very little to his wife of the danger of the Vicarage being robbed, but he could not but feel that there was danger. His wife had brought with her, among other plenishing for their household, a considerable amount of handsome plate, more than is, perhaps, generally to be found in country parsonages, and no doubt this fact was known, at any rate, to Sam Brattle. Had the men simply intended to rob the garden, they would not have run the risk of coming so near to the house windows. But then it certainly was true that Sam was not showing them the way. The parson did not quite know what to think about it, but it was clearly his duty to be on his guard.

That same evening he sauntered across the corner of the churchyard to his neighbour the farmer. Looking out warily for Bone'm, he stood leaning upon the farm gate. Bone'm was not to be seen or heard, and therefore he entered, and walked up to the back door, which indeed was the only door for entrance or egress that was ever used. There was a front door opening into a little ragged garden, but this was as much a fixture as the wall. As he was knocking at the back door, it was opened by the farmer himself. Mr. Fenwick had called to inquire whether his friend had secured for him,—as half promised,—the possession of a certain brother of Bone'm's, who was supposed to be of a very pugnacious disposition in the silent watches of the night.

"It's no go, parson."

"Why not, Mr. Trumbull?"

"The truth is, there be such a deal of talk o' thieves about the country, that no one likes to part with such a friend as that. Muster Crickly, over at Imber, he have another big dog it's true, a reg'lar mastiff, but he do say that Crunch'em be better than the mastiff, and he won't let 'un go, parson,—not for love nor money. I wouldn't let Bone'm go, I know; not for nothing." Then Mr. Fenwick walked back to the Vicarage, and was half induced to think that as Crunch'em was not to be had, it would be his duty to sit up at night, and look after the plate box himself.

CHAPTER XI.

DON'T YOU BE AFEARD ABOUT ME.

On the following morning Mr. Fenwick walked down to the mill. There was a path all along the river, and this was the way he took. He passed different points as he went, and he thought of the trout he had caught there, or had wished to catch, and he thought also how often Sam Brattle had been with him as he had stood there delicately throwing his fly. In those days Sam had been very fond of him, had thought it to be a great thing to be allowed to fish with the parson, and had been reasonably obedient. Now Sam would not even come up to the Vicarage when he was asked to do so. For more than a year after the close of those amicable relations the parson had behaved with kindness and almost with affection to the lad. He had interceded with the Squire when Sam was accused of poaching,—had interceded with the old miller when Sam had given offence at home,—and had even interceded with the constable when there was a rumour in the wind of offences something worse than these. Then had come the occasion on which Mr. Fenwick had told the father that unless the son would change his course evil would come of it; and both father and son had taken this amiss. The father had told the parson to his face that he, the parson, had led his son astray; and the son in his revenge had brought housebreakers down upon his old friend's premises.

"One hasn't to do it for thanks," said Mr. Fenwick, as he became a little bitter while thinking of all this. "I'll stick to him as long as I can, if it's only for the old woman's sake,—and for the poor girl whom we used to love." Then he thought of a clear, sweet, young voice that used to be so well known in his village choir, and of the heavy curls, which it was a delight to him to see. It had been a pleasure to him to have such a girl as Carry Brattle in his church, and now Carry Brattle was gone utterly, and would probably never be seen in a church again. These Brattles had suffered much, and he would bear with them, let the task of doing so be ever so hard.

The sound of workmen was to be already heard as he drew near to the mill. There were men there pulling the thatch off the building, and there were carts and horses bringing laths, lime, bricks, and timber, and taking the old rubbish away. As he crossed quickly by the slippery stones he saw old Jacob Brattle standing before the mill looking on, with his hands in his breeches pockets. He was too old to do much at such work as this,—work to which he was not accustomed—and was looking up in a sad melancholy way, as though it were a work of destruction, and not one of reparation.

"We shall have you here as smart as possible before long, Mr. Brattle," said the parson.

"I don't know much about smart, Muster Fenwick. The old place was a'most tumbling down,—but still it would have lasted out my time, I'm thinking. If t' Squire would 'a done it fifteen years ago, I'd 'a thanked un; but I don't know what to say about it now, and this time of year and all, just when the new grist would be coming in. If t' Squire would 'a thought of it in June, now. But things is contrary—a'most allays so." After this speech, which was made in a low, droning voice, bit by bit, the miller took himself off and went into the house.

At the back of the mill, perched on an old projecting beam, in the midst of dust and dirt, assisting with all the energy of youth in the demolition of the roof, Mr. Fenwick saw Sam Brattle. He perceived at once that Sam had seen him; but the young man immediately averted his eyes and went on with his work. The parson did not speak at once, but stepped over the ruins around him till he came immediately under the beam in question. Then he called to the lad, and Sam was constrained to answer "Yes, Mr. Fenwick, I am here;—hard at work, as you see."

"I do see it, and wish you luck with your job. Spare me ten minutes, and come down and speak to me."

"I am in such a muck now, Mr. Fenwick, that I do wish to go on with it, if you'll let me."

But Mr. Fenwick, having taken so much trouble to get at the young man, was not going to be put off in this way. "Never mind your muck for a quarter of an hour," he said. "I have come here on purpose to find you, and I must speak to you."

"Must!" said Sam, looking down with a very angry lower on his face.

"Yes,—must. Don't be a fool now. You know that I do not wish to injure you. You are not such a coward as to be afraid to speak to me. Come down."

"Afeard! Who talks of being afeard? Stop a moment, Mr. Fenwick, and I'll be with you;—not that I think it will do any good." Then slowly he crept back along the beam and came down through the interior of the building. "What is it, Mr. Fenwick? Here I am. I ain't a bit afeard of you at any rate."

"Where have you been the last fortnight, Sam?"

"What right have you to ask me, Mr. Fenwick?"

"I have the right of old friendship, and perhaps also some right from my remembrance of the last place in which I saw you. What has become of that man, Burrows?"

"What Burrows?"

"Jack the Grinder, whom I hit on the back the night I made you prisoner. Do you think that you were doing well in being in my garden about midnight in company with such a fellow as that,—one of the most notorious jailbirds in the county? Do you know that I could have had you arrested and sent to prison at once?"

"I know you couldn't—do nothing of the kind."

"You know this, Sam,—that I've no wish to do it; that nothing would give me more pain than doing it. But you must feel that if we should hear now of any depredation about the county, we couldn't,—I at least could not,—help thinking of you. And I am told that there will be depredations, Sam. Are you concerned in these matters?"

"No, I am not," said Sam, doggedly.

"Are you disposed to tell me why you were in my garden, and why those men were with you?"

"We were down in the churchyard, and the gate was open, and so we walked up;—that was all. If we'd meant to do anything out of the way we shouldn't 'a come like that, nor yet at that hour. Why, it worn't midnight, Mr. Fenwick."

"But why was there such a man as Burrows with you? Do you think he was fit company for you, Sam?"

"I suppose a chap may choose his own company, Mr. Fenwick?"

"Yes, he may, and go to the gallows because he chooses it, as you are doing."

"Very well; if that's all you've got to say to me, I'll go back to my work."

"Stop one moment, Sam. That is not quite all. I caught you the other night where you had no business to be, and for the sake of your father and mother, and for old recollections, I let you go. Perhaps I was wrong, but I don't mean to hark back upon that again."

"You are a-harking back on it, ever so often."

"I shall take no further steps about it."

"There ain't no steps to be taken, Mr. Fenwick."

"But I see that you intend to defy me, and therefore I am bound to tell you that I shall keep my eye upon you."

"Don't you be afeard about me, Mr. Fenwick."

"And if I hear of those fellows, Burrows and the other, being about the place any more, I shall give the police notice that they are associates of yours. I don't think so badly of you yet, Sam, as to believe you would bring your father's grey hairs with sorrow to the grave by turning thief and housebreaker; but when I hear of your being away from home, and nobody knowing where you are, and find that you are living without decent employment, and prowling about at nights with robbers and cut-throats, I cannot but be afraid. Do you know that the Squire recognised you that night as well as I?"

"The Squire ain't nothing to me, and if you've done with me now, Mr. Fenwick, I'll go back to my work." So saying, Sam Brattle again mounted up to the roof, and the parson returned discomfited to the front of the building. He had not intended to see any of the family, but, as he was crossing the little bridge, meaning to go home round by the Privets, he was stopped by Fanny Brattle.

"I hope it will be all right now, Mr. Fenwick," the girl said.

"I hope it will be all right now, Mr. Fenwick," the girl said.

"I hope so too, Fanny. But you and your mother should keep an eye on him, so that he may know that his goings and comings are noticed. I dare say it will be all right as long as the excitement of these changes is going on; but there is nothing so bad as that he should be in and out of the house at nights and not feel that his absence is noticed. It will be better always to ask him, though he be ever so cross. Tell your mother I say so."

CHAPTER XII.

BONE'M AND HIS MASTER.

After leaving the mill Mr. Fenwick went up to the Squire, and, in contradiction, as it were, of all the hard things that he had said to Sam Brattle, spoke to the miller's landlord in the lad's favour. He was hard at work now, at any rate; and seemed inclined to stick to his work. And there had been an independence about him which the parson had half liked, even while he had been offended at it. Gilmore differed altogether from his friend. "What was he doing in your garden? What was he doing hidden in Trumbull's hedge? When I see fellows hiding in ditches at night, I don't suppose that they're after much good." Mr. Fenwick made some lame apology, even for these offences. Sam had, perhaps, not really known the extent of the iniquity of the men with whom he had associated, and had come up the garden probably with a view to the fruit. The matter was discussed at great length, and the Squire at last promised that he would give Sam another chance in regard to his own estimation of the young man's character.

On that same evening,—or, rather, after the evening was over, for it was nearly twelve o'clock at night,—Fenwick walked round the garden and the orchard with his wife. There was no moon now, and the night was very dark. They stopped for a minute at the wicket leading into the churchyard, and it was evident to them that Bone'm, from the farmyard at the other side of the church, had heard them, for he commenced a low growl, with which the parson was by this time well acquainted.

"Good dog, good dog," said the parson, in a low voice. "I wish we had his brother, I know."

"He would only be tearing the maids and biting the children," said Mrs. Fenwick. "I hate having a savage beast about."

"But it would be so nice to catch a burglar and crunch him. I feel almost bloodthirsty since I hit that fellow with the life-preserver, and find that I didn't kill him."

"I know, Frank, you're thinking about these thieves more than you like to tell me."

"I was thinking just then, that if they were to come and take all the silver it wouldn't do much harm. We should have to buy German plate, and nobody would know the difference."

"Suppose they murdered us all?"

"They never do that now. The profession is different from what it used to be. They only go where they know they can find a certain amount of spoil, and where they can get it without much danger. I don't think housebreakers ever cut throats in these days. They're too fond of their own." Then they both agreed that if these rumours of housebreakings were continued, they would send away the plate some day to be locked up in safe keeping at Salisbury. After that they went to bed.

On the next morning, the Sunday morning, at a few minutes before seven, the parson was awakened by his groom at his bedroom door.

"What is it, Roger?" he asked.

"For the love of God, sir, get up! They've been and murdered Mr. Trumbull."

Mrs. Fenwick, who heard the tidings, screamed; and Mr. Fenwick was out of bed and into his trousers in half a minute. In another half minute Mrs. Fenwick, clothed in her dressing-gown, was up-stairs among her children. No doubt she thought that as soon as the poor farmer had been despatched, the murderers would naturally pass on into her nursery. Mr. Fenwick did not believe the tidings. If a man be hurt in the hunting-field, it is always said that he's killed. If the kitchen flue be on fire, it is always said that the house is burned down. Something, however, had probably happened at Farmer Trumbull's; and down went the parson across the garden and orchard, and through the churchyard, as quick as his legs would carry him. In the farmyard he found quite a crowd of men, including the two constables and three or four of the leading tradesmen in the village. The first thing that he saw was the dead body of Bone'm, the dog. He was stiff and stark, and had been poisoned.

"How's Mr. Trumbull?" he asked, of the nearest by-stander.

"Laws, parson, ain't ye heard?" said the man. "They've knocked his skull open with a hammer, and he's as dead—as dead."

Hearing this, the parson turned round, and made his way into the house. There was not a doubt about it. The farmer had been murdered during the night, and his money carried off. Upstairs Mr. Fenwick made his way to the farmer's bedroom, and there lay the body. Mr. Crittenden, the village doctor, was there; and a crowd of men, and an old woman or two. Among the women was Trumbull's sister, the wife of a neighbouring farmer, who, with her husband, a tenant of Mr. Gilmore's, had come over just before the arrival of Mr. Fenwick. The body had been found on the stairs, and it was quite clear that the farmer had fought desperately with the man or men before he had received the blow which despatched him.

"I told 'um how it be,—I did, I did, when he would 'a all that money by 'um." This was the explanation given by Mr. Trumbull's sister, Mrs. Boddle.

It seemed that Trumbull had had in his possession over a hundred and fifty pounds, of which the greater part was in gold, and that he kept this in a money-box in his bedroom. One of the two women who lived in his service,—he himself had been a widower without children,—declared that she had always known that at night he took the box out of his cupboard into bed with him. She had seen it there more than once when she had taken him up drinks when he was unwell. When first interrogated, she declared that she did not remember, at that moment, that she had ever told anybody; she thought she had never told anybody; at last, she would swear that she had never spoken a word about it to a single soul. She was supposed to be a good girl, had come of decent people, and was well known by Mr. Fenwick, of whose congregation she was one. Her name was Agnes Pope. The other servant was an elderly woman, who had been in the house all her life, but was unfortunately deaf. She had known very well about the money, and had always been afraid about it; had very often spoken to her master about it, but never a word to Agnes. She had been woken in the night,—that was, as it turned out, about 2 A.M.,—by the girl who slept with her, and who declared that she had heard a great noise, as of somebody tumbling,—a very great noise indeed, as though there were ever so many people tumbling. For a long time, for perhaps an hour, they had lain still, being afraid to move. Then the elder woman had lighted a candle, and gone down from the garret in which they slept. The first thing she saw was the body of her master, in his shirt, upon the stairs. She had then called up the only other human being who slept on the premises, a shepherd, who had lived for thirty years with Trumbull. This man had thrown open the house, and had gone for assistance, and had found the body of the dead dog in the yard.

Before nine o'clock the facts, as they have been told, were known everywhere, and the Squire was down on the spot. The man,—or, as it was presumed, men,—had entered by the unaccustomed front door, which was so contrived as to afford the easiest possible mode of getting into the house; whereas, the back door, which was used by everybody, had been bolted and barred with all care. The men must probably have entered by the churchyard and the back gate of the farmyard, as that had been found to be unlatched, whereas the gate leading out on to the road had been found closed. The farmer himself had always been very careful to close both these gates when he let out Bone'm before going to bed. Poor Bone'm had been enticed to his death by a piece of poisoned meat, thrown to him probably some considerable time before the attack was made.

Who were the murderers? That of course was the first question. It need hardly be said with how sad a heart Mr. Fenwick discussed this matter with the Squire. Of course inquiry must be made of the manner in which Sam Brattle had passed the night. Heavens! how would it be with that poor family if he had been concerned in such an affair as this! And then there came across the parson's mind a remembrance that Agnes Pope and Sam Brattle had been seen by him together, on more Sundays than one. In his anxiety, and with much imprudence, he went to the girl and questioned her again.

"For your own sake, Agnes, tell me, are you sure you never mentioned about the money-box to—Sam Brattle?"

The girl blushed and hesitated, and then said that she was quite sure she never had. She didn't think she had ever said ten words to Sam since she knew about the box.

"But five words would be sufficient, Agnes."

"Then them five words was never spoke, sir," said the girl. But still she blushed, and the parson thought that her manner was not in her favour.

It was necessary that the parson should attend to his church; but the Squire, who was a magistrate, went down with the two constables to the mill. There they found Sam and his father, with Mrs. Brattle and Fanny. No one went to the church from the mill on that day. The news had reached them of the murder, and they all felt,—though no one of them had so said to any other,—that something might in some way connect them with the deed that had been done. Sam had hardly spoken since he had heard of Mr. Trumbull's death; though when he saw that his father was perfectly silent, as one struck with some sudden dread, he bade the old man hold up his head and fear nothing. Old Brattle, when so addressed, seated himself in his arm-chair, and there remained without a word till the magistrate with the constables were among them.

There were not many at church, and Mr. Fenwick made the service very short. He could not preach the sermon which he had prepared, but said a few words on the terrible catastrophe which had occurred so near to them. This man who was now lying within only a few yards of them, with his brains knocked out, had been alive among them, strong and in good health, yesterday evening! And there had come into their peaceful village miscreants who had been led on from self-indulgence to idleness, and from idleness to theft, and from theft to murder! We all know the kind of words which the parson spoke, and the thrill of attention with which they would be heard. Here was a man who had been close to them, and therefore the murder came home to them all, and filled them with an excitement which, alas! was not probably without some feeling of pleasure. But the sermon, if sermon it could be called, was very short; and when it was over, the parson also hurried down to the mill.

It had already been discovered that Sam Brattle had certainly been out during the night. He had himself denied this at first, saying, that though he had been the last to go to bed, he had gone to bed about eleven, and had not left the mill-house till late in the morning;—but his sister had heard him rise, and had seen his body through the gloom as he passed beneath the window of the room in which she slept. She had not heard him return, but, when she arose at six, had found out that he was then in the house. He manifested no anger against her when she gave this testimony, but acknowledged that he had been out, that he had wandered up to the road, and explained his former denial frankly,—or with well-assumed frankness,—by saying that he would, if possible, for his father's and mother's sake, have concealed the fact that he had been away,—knowing that his absence would give rise to suspicions which would well-nigh break their hearts. He had not, however,—so he said,—been any nearer to Bullhampton than the point of the road opposite to the lodge of Hampton Privets, from whence the lane turned down to the mill. What had he been doing down there? He had done nothing, but sat and smoked on a stile by the road side. Had he seen any strangers? Here he paused, but at last declared that he had seen none, but had heard the sound of wheels and of a pony's feet upon the road. The vehicle, whatever it was, must have passed on towards Bullhampton just before he reached the road. Had he followed the vehicle? No;—he had thought of doing so, but had not. Could he guess who was in the vehicle? By this time many surmises had been made aloud as to Jack the Grinder and his companion, and it had become generally known that the parson had encountered two such men in his own garden some nights previously. Sam, when he was pressed, said that the idea had come into his mind that the vehicle was the Grinder's cart. He had no knowledge, he said, that the man was coming to Bullhampton on that night;—but the man had said in his hearing, that he would like to strip the parson's peaches. He was asked also about Farmer Trumbull's money. He declared that he had never heard that the farmer kept money in the house. He did know that the farmer was accounted to be a very saving man,—but that was all that he knew. He was as much surprised, he said, as any of them at what had occurred. Had the men turned the other way and robbed the parson he would have been less surprised. He acknowledged that he had called the parson a turn-coat and a meddling tell-tale, in the presence of these men.

All this ended of course in Sam's arrest. He had himself seen from the first that it would be so, and had bade his mother take comfort and hold up her head. "It won't be for long, mother. I ain't got any of the money, and they can't bring it nigh me." He was taken away to be locked up at Heytesbury that night, in order that he might be brought before the bench of magistrates which would sit at that place on Tuesday. Squire Gilmore for the present committed him.

The parson remained for some time with the old man and his wife after Sam was gone, but he soon found that he could be of no service by doing so. The miller himself would not speak, and Mrs. Brattle was utterly prostrated by her husband's misery.

"I do not know what to say about it," said Mr. Fenwick to his wife that night. "The suspicion is very strong; but I cannot say that I have an opinion one way or the other." There was no sermon in Bullhampton Church on that Sunday afternoon.

CHAPTER XIII.

CAPTAIN MARRABLE AND HIS FATHER.

Only that it is generally conceived that in such a history as is this the writer of the tale should be able to make his points so clear by words that no further assistance should be needed, I should be tempted here to insert a properly illustrated pedigree tree of the Marrable family. The Marrable family is of very old standing in England, the first baronet having been created by James I., and there having been Marrables,—as is well known by all attentive readers of English history,—engaged in the Wars of the Roses, and again others very conspicuous in the religious persecutions of the children of Henry VIII. I do not know that they always behaved with consistency; but they held their heads up after a fashion, and got themselves talked of, and were people of note in the country. They were cavaliers in the time of Charles I. and of Cromwell,—as became men of blood and gentlemen,—but it is not recorded of them that they sacrificed much in the cause; and when William III. became king they submitted with a good grace to the new order of things. A certain Sir Thomas Marrable was member for his county in the reigns of George I. and George II., and enjoyed a lucrative confidence with Walpole. Then there came a blustering, roystering Sir Thomas, who, together with a fine man and gambler as a heir, brought the property to rather a low ebb; so that when Sir Gregory, the grandfather of our Miss Marrable, came to the title in the early days of George III. he was not a rich man. His two sons, another Sir Gregory and a General Marrable, died long before the days of which we are writing,—Sir Gregory in 1815, and the General in 1820. That Sir Gregory was the second of the name,—the second at least as mentioned in these pages. He had been our Miss Marrable's uncle, and the General had been her father, and the father of Mrs. Lowther,—Mary's mother. A third Sir Gregory was reigning at the time of our story, a very old gentleman with one single son,—a fourth Gregory. Now the residence of Sir Gregory was at Dunripple Park, just on the borders of Warwickshire and Worcestershire, but in the latter county. The property was small,—for a country gentleman with a title,—not much exceeding £3000 a year; and there was no longer any sitting in Parliament, or keeping of race-horses, or indeed any season in town for the present race of Marrables. The existing Sir Gregory was a very quiet man, and his son and only child, a man now about forty years of age, lived mostly at home, and occupied himself with things of antiquity. He was remarkably well read in the history of his own country, and it had been understood for the last twenty years by the Antiquarian, Archæological, and other societies that he was the projector of a new theory about Stonehenge, and that his book on the subject was almost ready. Such were the two surviving members of the present senior branch of the family. But Sir Gregory had two brothers,—the younger of the two being Parson John Marrable, the present rector of St. Peter's Lowtown and the occupier of the house within the heavy slate-coloured gates, where he lived a bachelor life, as had done before him his cousin the late rector;—the elder being a certain Colonel Marrable. The Colonel Marrable again had a son, who was a Captain Walter Marrable,—and after him the confused reader shall be introduced to no more of the Marrable family. The enlightened reader will have by this time perceived that Miss Mary Lowther and Captain Walter Marrable were second cousins; and he will also have perceived, if he has given his mind fully to the study, that the present Parson John Marrable had come into the living after the death of a cousin of the same generation as himself,—but of lower standing in the family. It was so; and by this may be seen how little the Sir Gregory of the present day had been able to do for his brother, and perhaps it may also be imagined from this that the present clergyman at Loring Lowtown had been able to do very little for himself. Nevertheless, he was a kindly-hearted, good, sincere old man,—not very bright, indeed, nor peculiarly fitted for preaching the gospel, but he was much liked, and he kept a curate, though his income out of the living was small. Now it so happened that Captain Marrable,—Walter Marrable,—came to stay with his uncle the parson about the same time that Mary Lowther returned to Loring.

"You remember Walter, do you not?" said Miss Marrable to her niece.

"Not the least in the world. I remember there was a Walter when I was at Dunripple. But that was ten years ago, and boy cousins and girl cousins never fraternise."

"I suppose he was nearly a young man then, and you were a child?"

"He was still at school, though just leaving it. He is seven years older than I am."

"He is coming to stay with Parson John."

"You don't say so, aunt Sarah? What will such a man as Captain Marrable do at Loring?"

Then aunt Sarah explained all that she knew, and perhaps suggested more than she knew. Walter Marrable had quarrelled with his father, the Colonel,—with whom, indeed, everybody of the name of Marrable had always been quarrelling, and who was believed by Miss Marrable to be the very—mischief himself. He was a man always in debt, who had broken his wife's heart, who lived with low company and disgraced the family, who had been more than once arrested, on whose behalf all the family interest had been expended, so that nobody else could get anything, and who gambled and drank and did whatever wicked things a wicked old colonel living at

Portsmouth could do. And indeed, hitherto, Miss Marrable had entertained opinions hardly more charitable respecting the son than she had done in regard to the father. She had disbelieved in this branch of the Marrables altogether. Captain Marrable had lived with his father a good deal,—at least, so she had understood,—and therefore could not but be bad. And, moreover, our Miss Sarah Marrable had, throughout her whole life, been somewhat estranged from the elder branches of the family. Her father, Walter, had been,—so she thought,—injured by his brother Sir Gregory, and there had been some law proceedings, not quite amicable, between her brother the parson, and the present Sir Gregory. She respected Sir Gregory as the head of the family, but she never went now to Dunripple, and knew nothing of Sir Gregory's heir. Of the present Parson John she had thought very little before he had come to Loring. Since he had been living there she had found that blood was thicker than water,—as she would say,—and they two were intimate. When she heard that Captain Marrable was coming, because he had quarrelled with his father, she began to think that perhaps it might be as well that she should allow herself to meet this new cousin.

"What do you think of your cousin, Walter?" the old clergyman said to his nephew, one evening, after the two ladies, who had been dining at the Rectory, had left them. It was the first occasion on which Walter Marrable had met Mary since his coming to Loring.

"I remember her as well as if it were yesterday, at Dunripple. She was a little girl then, and I thought her the most beautiful little girl in the world."

"We all think her very beautiful still."

"So she is; as lovely as ever she can stand. But she does not seem to have much to say for herself. I remember when she was a little girl she never would speak."

"I fancy she can talk when she pleases, Walter. But you mustn't fall in love with her."

"I won't, if I can help it."

"In the first place I think she is as good as engaged to a fellow with a very pretty property in Wiltshire, and in the next place she hasn't got—one shilling."

"There is not much danger. I am not inclined to trouble myself about any girl in my present mood, even if she had the pretty property herself, and wasn't engaged to anybody. I suppose I shall get over it some day, but I feel just at present as though I couldn't say a kind word to a human being."

"Psha! psha! that's nonsense, Walter. Take things coolly. They're more likely to come right, and they won't be so troublesome, even if they don't." Such was the philosophy of Parson John,—for the sake of digesting which the captain lit a cigar, and went out to smoke it, standing at one of the open slate-coloured gates.

It was said in the first chapter of this story that Mr. Gilmore was one of the heroes whose deeds the story undertakes to narrate, and a hint was perhaps expressed that of all the heroes he was the favourite. Captain Marrable is, however, another hero, and, as such, some word or two must be said of him. He was a better-looking man, certainly, than Mr. Gilmore, though perhaps his personal appearance did not at first sight give to the observer so favourable an idea of his character as did that of the other gentleman. Mr. Gilmore was to be read at a glance as an honest, straightforward, well-behaved country squire, whose word might be taken for anything, who might, perhaps, like to have his own way, but who could hardly do a cruel or an unfair thing. He was just such a man to look at as a prudent mother would select as one to whom she might entrust her daughter with safety. Now Walter Marrable's countenance was of a very different die. He had served in India, and the naturally dark colour of his face had thus become very swarthy. His black hair curled round his head, but the curls on his brow were becoming very thin, as though age were already telling on them, and yet he was four or five years younger than Mr. Gilmore. His eyebrows were thick and heavy, and his eyes seemed to be black. They were eyes which were used without much motion; and when they were dead set, as they were not unfrequently, it would seem as though he were defying those on whom he looked. Thus he made many afraid of him, and many who were not afraid of him, disliked him because of a certain ferocity which seemed to characterise his face. He wore no beard beyond a heavy black moustache, which quite covered his upper lip. His nose was long and straight, his mouth large, and his chin square. No doubt he was a handsome man. And he looked to be a tall man, though in truth he lacked two full inches of the normal six feet. He was broad across the chest, strong on his legs, and was altogether such a man to look at that few would care to quarrel with him, and many would think that he was disposed to quarrel. Of his nature he was not quarrelsome; but he was a man who certainly had received much injury. It need not be explained at length how his money affairs had gone wrong with him. He should have inherited, and, indeed, did inherit, a fortune from his mother's family, of which his father had contrived absolutely to rob him. It was only within the last month that he had discovered that his father had succeeded in laying his hands on certainly the bulk of his money, and it might be upon all. Words between them had been very bitter. The father, with a cigar between his teeth, had told his son that this was the fortune of war, that if justice had been done him at his marriage, the money would have been his own, and that by G—— he was very sorry, and couldn't say anything more. The son had called the father a liar and a swindler,—as, indeed, was the truth, though the son was doubtless wrong to say so to the author of his being. The father had threatened the son with his horsewhip; and so they had parted, within ten days of Walter Marrable's return from India.

Walter had written to his two uncles, asking their advice as to saving the wreck, if anything might be saved. Sir Gregory had written back to say that he was an old man, that he was greatly grieved at the misunderstanding, and that Messrs. Block and Curling were the family lawyers. Parson John invited his nephew to come down to Loring Lowtown. Captain Marrable went to Block and Curling, who were by no means consolatory, and accepted his uncle's invitation.

It was but three days after the first meeting between the two cousins, that they were to be seen one evening walking together along the banks of the Lurwell, a little river which at Loring sometimes takes the appearance of a canal, and sometimes of a natural stream. But it is commercial, having connection with the Kennet and Avon navigation; and long, slow, ponderous barges, with heavy, dirty, sleepy bargemen, and rickety, ill-used barge-horses, are common in the neighbourhood. In parts it is very pretty, as it runs under the chalky downs, and there are a multiplicity of locks, and the turf of the sheep-walks comes up to the towing path; but in the close neighbourhood of the town the canal is straight and uninteresting; the ground is level, and there is a scattered community of small, straight-built light-brick houses, which are in themselves so ugly that they are incompatible with anything that is pretty in landscape.

Parson John, always so called to distinguish him from the late parson, his cousin, who had been the Rev. James Marrable, had taken occasion, on behalf of his nephew, to tell the story of his wrong to Miss Marrable, and by Miss Marrable it had been told to Mary. To both these ladies the thing seemed to be so horrible,—the idea that a father should have robbed his son,—that the stern ferocity of the slow-moving eyes was forgiven, and they took him to their hearts, if not for love, at least for pity. Twenty thousand pounds ought to have become the property of Walter Marrable, when some maternal relative had died. It had seemed hard that the father should have none of it, and, on the receipt in India of representations from the Colonel, Walter had signed certain fatal papers, the effect of which was that the father had laid his hands on pretty nearly the whole, if not on the whole, of the money, and had caused it to vanish. There was now a question whether some five thousand pounds might not be saved. If so, Walter would stay in England; if not, he would exchange and go back to India; "or," as he said himself, "to the Devil."

"Don't speak of it in that way," said Mary.

"The worst of it is," said he "that I am ashamed of myself for being so absolutely cut up about money. A man should be able to bear that kind of thing; but this hits one all round."

"I think you bear it very well."

"No, I don't. I didn't bear it well when I called my father a swindler. I didn't bear it well when I swore that I would put him in prison for robbing me. I don't bear it well now, when I think of it every moment. But I do so hate India, and I had so absolutely made up my mind never to return. If it hadn't been that I knew that this fortune was to be mine, I could have saved money, hand over hand."

"Can't you live on your pay here?"

"No!" He answered her almost as though he were angry with her. "If I had been used all my life to the strictest economies, perhaps I might do so. Some men do, no doubt; but I am too old to begin it. There is the choice of two things,—to blow my brains out, or go back."

"You are not such a coward as that."

"I don't know. I ain't sure that it would be cowardice. If there were anybody I could injure by doing it, it would be cowardly."

"The family," suggested Mary.

"What does Sir Gregory care for me? I'll show you his letter to me some day. I don't think it would be cowardly at all to get away from such a lot."

"I am sure you won't do that, Captain Marrable."

"Think what it is to know that your father is a swindler. Perhaps that is the worst of it all. Fancy talking or thinking of one's family after that. I like my uncle John. He is very kind, and has offered to lend me £150, which I'm sure he can't afford to lose, and which I am too honest to take. But even he hardly sees it. He calls it a misfortune, and I've no doubt would shake hands with his brother to-morrow."

"So would you, if he were really sorry."

"No, Mary; nothing on earth shall ever induce me to set my eyes on him again willingly. He has destroyed all the world for me. He should have had half of it without a word. When he used to whine to me in his letters, and say how cruelly he had been treated, I always made up my mind that he should have half the income for life. It was because he should not want till I came home that I enabled him to do what he has done. And now he has robbed me of every cursed shilling! I wonder whether I shall ever get my mind free from it."

"Of course you will."

"It seems now that my heart is wrapped in lead." As they were coming home she put her hand upon his arm, and asked him to promise her to withdraw that threat.

"Why should I withdraw it? Who cares for me?"

"We all care. My aunt cares. I care."

"The threat means nothing, Mary. People who make such threats don't carry them out. Of course I shall go on and endure it. The worst of all is, that the whole thing makes me so unmanly,—makes such a beast of me. But I'll try to get over it."

Mary Lowther thought that, upon the whole, he bore his misfortune very well.

CHAPTER XIV.

COUSINHOOD.

Mary Lowther and her cousin had taken their walk together on Monday evening, and on the next morning she received the following letter from Mrs. Fenwick. When it reached her she had as yet heard nothing of the Bullhampton tragedy.

Vicarage, Monday, Sept. 1, 186—.

DEAREST MARY,

I suppose you will have heard before you get this of the dreadful murder that has taken place here, and which has so startled and horrified us, that we hardly know what we are doing even yet. It is hard to say why a thing should be worse because it is close, but it certainly is so. Had it been in the next parish, or even further off in this parish, I do not think that I should feel it so much, and then we knew the old man so well; and then, again,—which makes it worst of all,—we all of us are unable to get rid of a suspicion that one whom we knew, and was liked, has been a participator in the crime.

It seems that it must have been about two o'clock on Sunday morning that Mr. Trumbull was killed. It was, at any rate, between one and three. As far as they can judge, they think that there must have been three men concerned. You remember how we used to joke about poor Mr. Trumbull's dog. Well, he was poisoned first,—probably an hour before the men got into the house. It has been discovered that the foolish old man kept a large sum of money by him in a box, and that he always took this box into bed with him. The woman, who lived in the house with him, used to see it there. No doubt the thieves had heard of this, and both Frank and Mr. Gilmore think that the girl, Agnes Pope, whom you will remember in the choir, told about it. She lived with Mr. Trumbull, and we all thought her a very good girl,—though she was too fond of that young man, Sam Brattle.

They think that the men did not mean to do the murder, but that the old man fought so hard for his money that they were driven to it. His body was not in the room, but on the top of the stairs, and his temple had been split open with a blow of a hammer. The hammer lay beside him, and was one belonging to the house. Mr. Gilmore says that there was great craft in their using a weapon which they did not bring with them. Of course they cannot be traced by the hammer.

They got off with £150 in the box, and did not touch anything else. Everybody feels quite sure that they knew all about the money, and that when Mr. Gilmore saw them that night down at the churchyard corner, they were prowling about with a view of seeing how they could get into the farmer's house, and not into the Vicarage. Frank thinks that when he afterwards found them in our place, Sam Brattle had brought them in with a kind of wild idea of taking the fruit, but that the men, of their own account, had come round to reconnoitre the house. They both say that there can be no doubt about the men having been the same. Then comes the terrible question whether Sam Brattle, the son of that dear woman at the mill, has been one of the murderers. He had been at home all the previous day working very hard at the works,—which are being done in obedience to your orders, my dear; but he certainly was out on the Saturday night.

It is very hard to get at any man's belief in such matters, but, as far as I can understand them, I don't think that either Frank or Mr. Gilmore do really believe that he was there. Frank says that it will go very hard with him, and Mr. Gilmore has committed him. The magistrates are to sit to-morrow at Heytesbury, and Mr. Gilmore will be there. He has, as you may be sure, behaved as well as possible, and has quite altered in his manner to the old people. I was at the mill this morning. Brattle himself would not speak to me, but I sat for an hour with Mrs. Brattle and Fanny. It makes it almost the more melancholy having all the rubbish and building things about, and yet the work stopped.

Fanny Brattle has behaved so well! It was she who told that her brother had been out at night. Mr. Gilmore says that when the question was asked in his presence, she answered it in her own quiet, simple way, without a moment's doubt; but since that she has never ceased to assert her conviction that her brother has had nothing to do either with the murder or with the robbery. If it had not been for this, Mrs. Brattle would, I think, have sunk under the load. Fanny says the same thing constantly to her father. He scolds her, and bids her hold her tongue; but she goes on, and I think it has some effect even on him. The whole place does look such a picture of ruin! It would break your heart to see it. And then, when one looks at the father and mother, one remembers about that other child, and is almost tempted to ask why such misery should have fallen upon parents who have been honest, sober, and industrious. Can it really be that the man is being punished here on earth because he will not believe? When I hinted this to Frank, he turned upon me, and scolded me, and told me I was measuring the Almighty God with a foot-rule. But men were punished in the Bible because they did not believe. Remember the Baptist's father. But I never dare to go on with Frank on these matters.

I am so full of this affair of poor Mr. Trumbull, and so anxious about Sam Brattle, that I cannot now write about anything else. I can only say that no man ever behaved with greater kindness and propriety than Harry Gilmore, who has had to act as magistrate. Poor Fanny Brattle has to go to Heytesbury to-morrow to give her evidence. At first they said that they must take the father also, but he is to be spared for the present.

I should tell you that Sam himself declares that he got to know these men at a place where he was at work, brickmaking, near Devizes. He had quarrelled with his father, and had got a job there, with high wages. He used to be out at night with them, and acknowledges that he joined one of them, a man named Burrows, in stealing a brood of pea-fowl which some poulterers wanted to buy. He says he looked on it as a joke. Then it seems he had some spite against Trumbull's dog, and that this man, Burrows, came over here on purpose to take the dog away. This, according to his story, is all that he knows of the man; and he says that on that special Saturday night he had not the least idea that Burrows was at Bullhampton, till he heard the sound of a certain cart on the road. I tell you all this, as I am sure you will share our anxiety respecting this unfortunate young man,—because of his mother and sister.

Good-bye, dearest; Frank sends ever so many loves;—and somebody else would send them too, if he thought that I would be the bearer. Try to think so well of Bullhampton as to make you wish to live here.—Give my kindest love to your aunt Sarah.

Your most affectionate friend,

JANET FENWICK.

Mary was obliged to read the letter twice before she completely understood it. Old Mr. Trumbull murdered! Why she had known the old man well, had always been in the habit of speaking to him when she met him either at the one gate or the other of the farmyard,—had joked with him about Bone'm, and had heard him assert his own perfect security against robbers not a week before the night on which he was murdered! As Mrs. Fenwick had said, the truth is so much more real when it comes from things that are near. And then she had so often heard the character of Sam Brattle described,—the man who was now in prison as a murderer! And she herself had given lessons in singing to Agnes Pope, who was now in some sort accused of aiding the thieves. And she herself had asked Agnes whether it was not foolish for her to be hanging about the farmyard, outside her master's premises, with Sam Brattle. It was all brought very near to her!

Before that day was over she was telling the story to Captain Marrable. She had of course told it to her aunt, and they had been discussing it the whole morning. Mr. Gilmore's name had been mentioned to Captain Marrable, but very little more than the name. Aunt Sarah, however, had already begun to think whether it might not be prudent to tell cousin Walter the story of the half-formed engagement. Mary had expressed so much sympathy with her cousin's wrongs, that aunt Sarah had begun to fear that that sympathy might lead to a tenderer feeling, and aunt Sarah was by no means anxious that her niece should fall in love with a gentleman whose chief attraction was the fact that he had been ruined by his own father, even though that gentleman was a Marrable himself. This danger might possibly be lessened if Captain Marrable were made acquainted with the Gilmore affair, and taught to understand how desirable such a match would be for Mary. But aunt Sarah had qualms of conscience on the subject. She doubted whether she had a right to tell the story without leave from Mary; and then there was in truth no real engagement. She knew indeed that Mr. Gilmore had made the offer more than once; but then she knew also that the offer had at any rate not as yet been accepted, and she felt that on Mr. Gilmore's account as well as on Mary's she ought to hold her tongue. It might indeed be admissible to tell to a cousin that which she would not tell to an indifferent young man; but, nevertheless, she could not bring herself to do, even with so good an object, that which she believed to be wrong.

That evening Mary was again walking on the towing-path beside the river with her cousin Walter. She had met him now about five times, and there was already an intimacy between them. The idea of cousinly intimacy to girls is undoubtedly very pleasant; and I do not know whether it is not the fact that the better and the purer is the girl, the sweeter and the pleasanter is the idea. In America a girl may form a friendly intimacy with any young man she fancies, and though she may not be free from little jests and good-humoured joking, there is no injury to her from such intimacy. It is her acknowledged right to enjoy herself after that fashion, and to have what she calls a good time with young men. A dozen such intimacies do not stand in her way when there comes some real adorer who means to marry her and is able to do so. She rides with these friends, walks with them, and corresponds with them. She goes out to balls and picnics with them, and afterwards lets herself in with a latchkey, while her papa and mamma are a-bed and asleep, with perfect security. If there be much to be said against the practice, there is also something to be said for it. Girls on the other hand, on the continent of Europe, do not dream of making friendship with any man. A cousin with them is as much out of the question as the most perfect stranger. In strict families, a girl is hardly allowed to go out with her brother; and I have heard of mothers who thought it indiscreet that a father should be seen alone with his daughter at a theatre. All friendships between the sexes must, under such a social code, be looked forward to as post-nuptial joys. Here in England there is a something betwixt the two. The intercourse between young men and girls is free enough to enable the latter to feel how pleasant it is to be able to forget for awhile conventional restraints, and to acknowledge how joyous a thing it is to indulge in social intercourse in which the simple delight of equal mind meeting equal mind in equal talk is just enhanced by the unconscious remembrance that boys and girls when they meet together may learn to love. There is nothing more sweet in youth than this, nothing more natural, nothing more fitting, nothing, indeed, more essentially necessary for God's purposes with his creatures. Nevertheless, here with us, there is the restriction, and it is seldom that a girl can allow herself the full flow of friendship with a man who is not old enough to be her father, unless he is her lover as well as her friend. But cousinhood does allow some escape from the hardship of this rule. Cousins are Tom, and Jack, and George, and Dick. Cousins probably know all or most of your little family secrets. Cousins, perhaps, have romped with you, and scolded you, and teased you, when you were young. Cousins are almost the same as brothers, and yet they may be lovers. There is certainly a great relief in cousinhood.

Mary Lowther had no brother. She had neither brother nor sister;—had since her earliest infancy hardly known any other relative save her aunt and old Parson John. When first she had heard that Walter Marrable was at Loring, the tidings gave her no pleasure whatever. It never occurred to her to say to herself: "Now I shall have one who may become my friend, and be to me perhaps almost a brother?" What she had hitherto heard of Walter Marrable had not been in his favour. Of his father she had heard all that was bad, and she had joined the father and the son together in what few ideas she had formed respecting them. But now, after five interviews, Walter Marrable was her dear cousin, with whom she sympathised, of whom she was proud, whose misfortunes were in some degree her misfortunes, to whom she thought she could very soon tell this great trouble of her life about Mr. Gilmore, as though he were indeed her brother. And she had learned to like his dark staring eyes, which now always seemed to be fixed on her with something of real regard. She liked them the better, perhaps, because there was in them so much of real admiration; though if it were so, Mary knew nothing of such liking herself. And now at his bidding she called him Walter. He had addressed her by her Christian name at first, as a matter of course, and she had felt grateful to him for doing so. But she had not dared to be so bold with him, till he had bade her do so, and now she felt that he was a cousin indeed. Captain Marrable was at present waiting, not with much patience, for tidings from Block and Curling. Would that £5000 be saved for him, or must he again go out to India and be heard of no more at home in his own England? Mary was not so impatient as the Captain, but she also was intensely interested in the expected letters. On this day, however, their conversation chiefly ran on the news which Mary had that morning heard from Bullhampton.

"I suppose you feel sure," said the Captain, "that young Sam Brattle was one of the murderers?"

"Oh no, Walter."

"Or at least one of the thieves?"

"But both Mr. Fenwick and Mr. Gilmore think that he is innocent."

"I do not gather that from what your friend says. She says that she thinks that they think so. And then it is clear that he was hanging about the place before with the very men who have committed the crime; and that there was a way in which he might have heard and probably had heard of the money; and then he was out and about that very night."

"Still I can't believe it. If you knew the sort of people his father and mother are." Captain Marrable could not but reflect that, if an honest gentleman might have a swindler for his father, an honest miller might have a thief for his son. "And then if you saw the place at which they live! I have a particular interest about it."

"Then the young man, of course, must be innocent."

"Don't laugh at me, Walter."

"Why is the place so interesting to you?"

"I can hardly tell you why. The father and the mother are interesting people, and so is the sister. And in their way they are so good! And they have had great troubles,—very great troubles. And the place is so cool and pretty, all surrounded by streams and old pollard willows, with a thatched roof that comes in places nearly to the ground; and then the sound of the mill wheel is the pleasantest sound I know anywhere."

"I will hope he is innocent, Mary."

"I do so hope he is innocent! And then my friends are so much interested about the family. The Fenwicks are very fond of them, and Mr. Gilmore is their landlord."

"He is the magistrate?"

"Yes, he is the magistrate."

"What sort of fellow is he?"

"A very good sort of fellow; such a sort that he can hardly be better; a perfect gentleman."

"Indeed! And has he a perfect lady for his wife?"

"Mr. Gilmore is not married."

"What age is he?"

"I think he is thirty-three."

"With a nice estate and not married! What a chance you have left behind you, Mary!"

"Do you think, Walter, that a girl ought to wish to marry a man merely because he is a perfect gentleman, and has a nice estate and is not yet married?"

"They say that they generally do;—don't they?"

"I hope you don't think so. Any girl would be very fortunate to marry Mr. Gilmore—if she loved him."

"But you don't?"

"You know I am not talking about myself, and you oughtn't to make personal allusions."

These cousinly walks along the banks of the Lurwell were not probably favourable to Mr. Gilmore's hopes.

CHAPTER XV.

THE POLICE AT FAULT.

The magistrates sat at Heytesbury on the Tuesday, and Sam Brattle was remanded. An attorney thus was employed on his behalf by Mr. Fenwick. The parson on the Monday evening had been down at the mill, and had pressed strongly on the old miller the necessity of getting some legal assistance for his son. At first Mr. Brattle was stern, immovable, and almost dumb. He sat on the bench outside his door, with his eyes fixed on the dismantled mill, and shook his head wearily, as though sick and sore with the words that were being addressed to him. Mrs. Brattle the while stood in the doorway, and listened without uttering a sound. If the parson could not prevail, it would be quite out of the question that any word of hers should do good. There she stood, wiping the tears from her eyes, looking on wishfully, while her husband did not even know that she was there. At last he rose from his seat, and hallooed to her. "Maggie," said he, "Maggie." She stepped forward, and put her hand upon his shoulder. "Bring me down the purse, mother," he said.

"There will be nothing of that kind wanted," said the parson.

"Them gentlemen don't work for such as our boy for nothin'," said the miller. "Bring me the purse, mother, I say. There ar'n't much in it, but there's a few guineas as 'll do for that, perhaps. As well pitch 'em away that way as any other."

Mr. Fenwick, of course, declined to take the money. He would make the lawyer understand that he would be properly paid for his trouble, and that for the present would suffice. Only, as he explained, it was expedient that he should have the father's authority. Should any question on the matter arise, it would be bettor for the young man that he should be defended by his father's aid than by that of a stranger. "I understand, Mr. Fenwick," said the old man,—"I understand; and it's neighbourly of you. But it'd be better that you'd just leave us alone to go out like the snuff of a candle."

"Father," said Fanny, "I won't have you speak in that way, making out our Sam to be guilty before ere a one else has said so."

The miller shook his head again, but said nothing further, and the parson, having received the desired authority, returned to the Vicarage.

The attorney had been employed, and Sam had been remanded. There was no direct evidence against him, and nothing could be done until the other men should be taken, for whom they were seeking. The police had tracked the two men back to a cottage, about fifteen miles distant from Bullhampton, in which lived an old woman, who was the mother of the Grinder. With Mrs. Burrows they found a young woman who had lately come to live there, and who was said in the neighbourhood to be the Grinder's wife.

But nothing more could be learned of the Grinder than that he had been at the cottage on the Sunday morning, and had gone away, according to his wont. The old woman swore that he slept there the whole of Saturday night, but of course the policemen had not believed her statement. When does any policeman ever believe anything? Of the pony and cart the old woman declared she knew nothing. Her son had no pony, and no cart, to her knowing. Then she went on to declare that she knew very little about her son, who never lived with her; and that she had only taken in the young woman out of charity, about two weeks since. The mother did not for a moment pretend that her son was an honest man, getting his bread after an honest fashion. The Grinder's mode of life was too well known for even a mother to attempt to deny it. But she pretended that she was very honest herself, and appealed to sundry brandy-balls and stale biscuits in her window, to prove that she lived after a decent, honest, commercial fashion.

Sam was of course remanded. The head constable of the district asked for a week more to make fresh inquiry, and expressed a very strong opinion that he would have the Grinder and his friend by the heels before the week should be over. The Heytesbury attorney made a feeble request that Sam might be released on bail, as there was not, according to his statement, "the remotest shadow of a tittle of evidence against him." But poor Sam was sent back to gaol, and there remained for that week. On the next Tuesday the same scene was re-enacted. The Grinder had not been taken, and a further remand was necessary. The face of the head constable was longer on this occasion than it had been before, and his voice less confident. The Grinder, he thought, must have caught one of the early Sunday trains, and made his way to Birmingham. It had been ascertained that he had friends at Birmingham. Another remand was asked for a week, with an understanding that at the end of the week it should be renewed if necessary. The policeman seemed to think that by that time, unless the Grinder were below the sod, his presence above it would certainly be proved. On this occasion the Heytesbury attorney made a very loud demand for Sam's liberation, talking of habeas corpus, and the injustice of carceration without evidence of guilt. But the magistrates would not let him go. "When I'm told that the young man was seen hiding in a ditch close to the murdered man's house, only a few days before the murder, is that no evidence against him, Mr. Jones?" said Sir Thomas Charleys, of Charlicoats.

"No evidence at all, Sir Thomas. If I had been found asleep in the ditch, that would have been no evidence against me."

"Yes, it would, very strong evidence; and I would have committed you on it, without hesitation, Mr. Jones."

Mr. Jones made a spirited rejoinder to this; but it was of no use, and poor Sam was sent back to gaol for the third time.

For the first ten days after the murder nothing was done as to the works at the mill. The men who had been employed by Brattle ceased to come, apparently of their own account, and everything was lying there just in the state in which the men had left the place on the Saturday night. There was something inexpressibly sad in this, as the old man could not even make a pretence of going into the mill for employment, and there was absolutely nothing to which he could put his hands, to do it. When ten days were over, Gilmore came down to the mill, and suggested that the works should be carried on and finished by him. If the mill were not kept at work, the old man could not live, and no rent would be paid. At any rate, it would be better that this great sorrow should not be allowed so to cloud everything as to turn industry into idleness, and straitened circumstances into absolute beggary. But the Squire found it very difficult to deal with the miller. At first old Brattle would neither give nor withhold his consent. When told by the Squire that the property could not be left in that way, he expressed himself willing to go out into the road, and lay himself down and die there;—but not until the term of his holding was legally brought to a close. "I don't know that I owe any rent over and beyond this Michaelmas as is coming, and there's the hay on the ground yet." Gilmore, who was very patient, assured him that he had no wish to allude to rent; that there should be no question of rent even when the day came, if at that time money was scarce. But would it not be better that the mill, at least, should be put in order?

"Indeed it will, Squire," said Mrs. Brattle. "It is the idleness that is killing him."

"Hold your jabbering tongue," said the miller, turning round upon her fiercely. "Who asked you? I will see to it myself, Squire, to-morrow or next day."

After two or three further days of inaction at the mill the Squire came again, bringing the parson with him; and they did manage to arrange between them that the repairs should be at once continued. The mill should be completed; but the house should be left till next summer. As to Brattle himself, when he had been once persuaded to yield the point, he did not care how much they pulled down, or how much they built up. "Do it as you will," he said; "I ain't nobody now. The women drives me about my own house as if I hadn't a'most no business there." And so the hammers and trowels were heard again; and old Brattle would sit perfectly silent, gazing at the men as they worked. Once, as he saw two men and a boy shifting a ladder, he turned round, with a little chuckle to his wife, and said, "Sam'd 'a see'd hisself d——d, afore he'd 'a asked another chap to help him with such a job as that."

As Mrs. Brattle told Mrs. Fenwick afterwards, he had one of the two erring children in his thoughts morning, noon, and night. "When I tell 'un of George,"—who was the farmer near Fordingbridge,—"and of Mrs. Jay,"—who was the ironmonger's wife at Warminster,—"he won't take any comfort in them," said Mrs. Brattle. "I don't think he cares for them, just because they can hold their own heads up."

At the end of three weeks the Grinder was still missing; and others besides Mr. Jones, the attorney, were beginning to say that Sam Brattle should be let out of prison. Mr. Fenwick was clearly of opinion that he should not be detained, if bail could be forthcoming. The Squire was more cautious, and said that it might well be that his escape would render it impossible for the police even to get on the track of the real murderers. "No doubt, he knows more than he has told," said Gilmore, "and will probably tell it at last. If he be let out, he will tell nothing." The police were all of opinion that Sam had been present at the murder, and that he should be kept in custody till he was tried. They were very sharp in their manœuvres to get evidence against him. His boot, they had said, fitted a footstep which had been found in the mud in the farm-yard. The measure had been taken on the Sunday. That was evidence. Then they examined Agnes Pope over and over again, and extracted from the poor girl an admission that she loved Sam better than anything in the whole wide world. If he were to be in prison, she would not object to go to prison with him. If he were to be hung, she would wish to be hung with him. She had no secret she would not tell him. But, as a matter of fact,—so she swore over and over again,—she had never told him a word about old Trumbull's box. She did not think she had ever told any one; but she would swear on her death-bed that she had never told Sam Brattle. The head constable declared that he had never met a more stubborn or a more artful young woman. Sir Thomas Charleys was clearly of opinion that no bail should be accepted. Another week of remand was granted with the understanding that, if nothing of importance was elicited by that time, and if neither of the other two suspected men were then in custody, Sam should be allowed to go at large upon bail—a good, substantial bail, himself in £400, and his bailsmen in £200 each.

"Who'll be his bailsmen?" said the Squire, coming away with his friend the parson from Heytesbury.

"There will be no difficulty about that, I should say."

"But who will they be,—his father for one?"

"His brother George, and Jay, at Warminster, who married his sister," said the parson.

"I doubt them both," said the Squire.

"He sha'n't want for bail. I'll be one myself, sooner. He shall have bail. If there's any difficulty, Jones shall bail him; and I'll see Jones safe through it. He sha'n't be persecuted in that way."

"I don't think anybody has attempted to persecute him, Frank."

"He will be persecuted if his own brothers won't come forward to help him. It isn't that they have looked into the matter, and that they think him guilty; but that they go just the way they're told to go, like sheep. The more I think of it, the more I feel that he had nothing to do with the murder."

"I never knew a man change his opinion so often as you do," said Gilmore.

During three weeks the visits made by Head Constable Toffy to the cottage in which Mrs. Burrows lived were much more frequent than were agreeable to that lady. This cottage was about four miles from Devizes, and on the edge of a common, about half a mile from the high road which leads from that town to Marlborough. There is, or was a year or two back, a considerable extent of unenclosed land thereabouts, and on a spot called Pycroft Common there was a small collection of cottages, sufficient to constitute a hamlet of the smallest class. There was no house there of greater pretensions than the very small beershop which provided for the conviviality of the Pycroftians; and of other shops there was none, save a baker's, the owner of which seldom had much bread to sell, and the establishment for brandy-balls, which was kept by Mrs. Burrows. The inhabitants were chiefly labouring men, some of whom were in summer employed in brick making; and there was an idea abroad that Pycroft generally was not sustained by regular labour and sober industry. Rents, however, were paid for the cottages, or the cottagers would have been turned adrift; and Mrs. Burrows had lived in hers for five or six years, and was noted in the neighbourhood for her outward neatness and attention to decency. In the summer there were always half-a-dozen large sunflowers in the patch of ground called a garden, and there was a rose-tree, and a bush of honeysuckle over the door, and an alder stump in a corner, which would still put out leaves and bear berries. When Head Constable Toffy visited her there would be generally a few high words, for Mrs. Burrows was by no means unwilling to let it be known that she objected to morning calls from Mr. Toffy.

It has been already said that at this time Mrs. Burrows did not live alone. Residing with her was a young woman, who was believed by Mr. Toffy to be the wife of Richard Burrows, alias the Grinder. On his first visit to Pycroft no doubt, Mr. Toffy was mainly anxious to ascertain whether anything was known by the old woman as to her son's whereabouts, but the second, third, and fourth visits were made rather to the younger than to the older woman. Toffy had probably learned in his wide experience that a man of the Grinder's nature will generally place more reliance on a young woman than on an old; and that the young woman will, nevertheless, be more likely to betray confidence than the older,—partly from indiscretion, and partly, alas! from treachery. But, if the presumed Mrs. Burrows, junior, knew aught of the Grinder's present doings, she was neither indiscreet nor treacherous. Mr. Toffy could get nothing from her. She was sickly, weak, sullen, and silent. "She didn't think it was her business to say where she had been living before she came to Pycroft. She hadn't been living with any husband, and had got no husband that she knew of. If she had she wasn't going to say so. She hadn't any children, and she didn't know what business he had to ask her. She came from Lunnun. At any rate, she came from there last, and she didn't know what business he had to ask her where she came from. What business was it of his to be asking what her name was? Her name was Anne Burrows, if he liked to call her so. She wouldn't answer him any more questions. No; she wouldn't say what her name was before she was married."

Mr. Toffy had his reasons for interrogating this poor woman, but he did not for a while let any one know what those reasons were. He could not, however, obtain more information than what is contained in the answers above given, which were, for the most part, true. Neither the mother nor the younger woman knew where was to be found, at the present moment, that hero of adventure who was called the Grinder, and all the police of Wiltshire began to fear that they were about to be outwitted.

"You never were at Bullhampton with your husband, I suppose?" asked Mr. Toffy.

"Never," said the supposed Grinder's wife; "but what does it matter to you where I was?"

"Don't answer him never another word," said old Mrs. Burrows.

"I won't," said the other.

"Were you ever at Bullhampton at all?" asked Mr. Toffy.

"Oh dear, oh dear," said the younger woman.

"I think you must have been there once," said Mr. Toffy.

"What business is it of yourn?" demanded Mrs. Burrows, senior. "Drat you; get out of this. You ain't no right here, and you shan't stay here. If you ain't out of this, I'll brain yer. I don't care for perlice nor anything. We ain't done nothing. If he did smash the gen'leman's head, we didn't do it; neither she nor me."

"All the same, I think that Mrs. Burrows has been at Bullhampton," said the policeman.

Not another word after this was said by Mrs. Burrows, junior, so called, and constable Toffy soon took his departure. He was convinced, at any rate, of this;—that wherever the murderers might be, the man or men who had joined Sam Brattle in the murder,—for of Sam's guilt he was quite convinced,—neither the mother, nor the so-called wife knew of their whereabouts. He, in his heart, condemned the constabulary of Warwickshire, of Gloucestershire, of Worcestershire, and of Somersetshire, because the Grinder was not taken. Especially he condemned the constabulary of Warwickshire, feeling almost sure that the Grinder was in Birmingham. If the constabulary in those counties would only do their duty as they in Wiltshire did theirs, the Grinder and his associates would soon be taken. But by him nothing further could be learned, and Mr. Toffy left Pycroft Common with a heavy heart.

CHAPTER XVI.

MISS LOWTHER ASKS FOR ADVICE.

All these searchings for the murderers of Mr. Trumbull, and these remandings of Sam Brattle, took place in the month of September, and during that same month the energy of other men of law was very keenly at work on a widely different subject. Could Messrs. Block and Curling assure Captain Marrable that a portion of his inheritance would be saved for him, or had that graceless father of his in very truth seized upon it all? There was no shadow of doubt but that if aught was spared, it had not been spared through any delicacy on the part of the Colonel. The Colonel had gone to work, paying creditors who were clamorous against him, the moment he had got his hand upon the money, and had gone to work also gambling, and had made assignments of money, and done his very best to spend the whole. But there was a question whether a certain sum of £5000, which seemed to have got into the hands of a certain lady who protested that she wanted it very badly, might not be saved. Messrs. Block and Curling thought that it might, but were by no means certain. It probably might be done, if the Captain would consent to bring the matter before a jury; in which case the whole story of the father's iniquity must, of course, be proved. Or it might be that by threatening to do this, the lady's friends would relax their grasp on receiving a certain present out of the money.

"We would offer them £50, and perhaps they would take £500," said Messrs. Block and Curling.

All this irritated the Captain. He was intensely averse to any law proceedings by which the story should be made public.

"I won't pretend that it is on my father's account," said he to his uncle. Parson John shrugged his shoulders, and shook his head, meaning to imply that it certainly was a bad case, but that as Colonel Marrable was a Marrable, he ought to be spared, if possible. "It is on my own account," continued the Captain, "and partly, perhaps, on that of the family. I would endure anything rather than have the filth of the transaction flooded through the newspapers. I should never be able to join my mess again if I did that."

"Then you'd better let Block and Curling compromise and get what they can," said Parson John, with an indifferent and provoking tone, which clearly indicated that he would regard the matter when so settled as one arranged amicably and pleasantly between all the parties. His uncle's calmness and absence of horror at the thing that had been done was very grievous to Captain Marrable.

"Poor Wat!" the parson had once said, speaking of his wicked brother; "he never could keep two shillings together. It's ever so long since I had to determine that nothing on earth should induce me to let him have half-a-crown. I must say that he did not take it amiss when I told him."

"Why should he have wanted half-a-crown from you?"

"He was always one of those thirsty sandbags that swallow small drops and large alike. He got £10,000 out of poor Gregory about the time that you were born, and Gregory is fretting about it yet."

"What kills me is the disgrace of it," said the young man.

"It would be disagreeable to have it in the newspapers," said Parson John. "And then he was such a pleasant fellow, and so handsome. I always enjoyed his society when once I had buttoned up my breeches' pocket."

Yet this man was a clergyman, preaching honesty and moral conduct, and living fairly well up to his preaching, too, as far as he himself was concerned! The Captain almost thought that the earth and skies should be brought together, and the clouds clap with thunder, and the mountains be riven in twain at the very mention of his father's wickedness. But then sins committed against oneself are so much more sinful than any other sins.

The Captain had much more sympathetic listeners in Uphill Lane; not that either of the ladies there spoke severely against his father, but that they entered more cordially into his own distresses. If he could save even £4500 out of the wreck, the interest on the money would enable him to live at home in his regiment. If he could get £4000 he would do it.

"With £150 per annum," he said, "I could just hold my head up and get along. I should have to give up all manner of things; but I would never cry about that."

Then, again, he would declare that the one thing necessary for his happiness was, that he should get the whole business of the money off his mind. "If I could have it settled, and have done with it," said he, "I should be at ease."

"Quite right, my dear," said the old lady. "My idea about money is this, that whether you have much or little, you should make your arrangements so that it be no matter of thought to you. Your money should be just like counters at a round game with children, and should mean nothing. It comes to that when you once get things on a proper footing."

They thus became very intimate, the two ladies in Uphill Lane and the Captain from his uncle's parsonage in the Lowtown; and the intimacy on his part was quite as strong with the younger as with the elder relative,—quite as strong, and no doubt more pleasant. They walked together constantly, as cousins may walk, and they discussed every turn that took place in the correspondence with Messrs. Block and Curling. Captain Marrable had come to his uncle's house for a week or ten days, but had been pressed to remain on till this business should be concluded. His leave of absence lasted till the end of November, and might be prolonged if he intended to return to India. "Stay here till the end of November," said Parson John. "What's the use of spending your money at a London hotel? Only don't fall in love with cousin Mary." So the Captain did stay, obeying one half of his uncle's advice, and promising obedience to the other half.

Aunt Sarah also had her fears about the falling in love, and spoke a prudent word to Mary. "Mary, dear," she said, "you and Walter are as loving as turtle doves."

"I do like him so much," said Mary, boldly.

"So do I, my dear. He is a gentleman, and clever, and, upon the whole, he bears a great injury well. I like him. But I don't think people ought to fall in love when there is a strong reason against it."

"Certainly not, if they can help it."

"Pshaw! That's missish nonsense, Mary, and you know it. If a girl were to tell me she fell in love because she couldn't help it, I should tell her that she wasn't worth any man's love."

"But what's your reason, Aunt Sarah?"

"Because it wouldn't suit Mr. Gilmore."

"I am not bound to suit Mr. Gilmore."

"I don't know about that. And then, too, it would not suit Walter himself. How could he marry a wife when he has just been robbed of all his fortune?"

"But I have not the slightest idea of falling in love with him. In spite of what I said, I do hope that I can help it. And then I feel to him just as though he were my brother. I've got almost to know what it would be to have a brother."

In this Miss Lowther was probably wrong. She had now known her cousin for just a month. A month is quite long enough to realise the pleasure of a new lover, but it may be doubted whether the intimacy of a brother does not take a very much longer period for its creation.

"I think if I were you," said Miss Marrable, after a pause, "that I would tell him about Mr. Gilmore."

"Would you, Aunt Sarah?"

"I think I would. If he were really your brother you would tell him."

It was probably the case, that when Miss Marrable gave this advice, her opinion of Mr. Gilmore's success was greater than the circumstances warranted. Though there had been much said between the aunt and her niece about Mr. Gilmore and his offers, Mary had never been able quite to explain her own thoughts and feelings. She herself did not believe that she could be brought to accept him, and was now stronger in that opinion than ever. But were she to say so in language that would convince her aunt, her aunt would no doubt ask her, why then had she left the man in doubt? Though she knew that at every moment in which she had been called upon to act, she had struggled to do right, yet there hung over her a half-conviction that she had been weak, and almost selfish. Her dearest friends wrote to her and spoke to her as though she would certainly take Mr. Gilmore at last. Janet Fenwick wrote of it in her letters as of a thing almost fixed; and Aunt Sarah certainly lived as though she expected it. And yet Mary was very nearly sure that it could not be so. Would it not be better that she should write to Mr. Gilmore at once, and not wait till the expiration of the weary six months which he had specified as the time at the end of which he might renew his proposals? Had Aunt Sarah known all this,—had she been aware how very near Mary was to the writing of such a letter,—she would not probably have suggested that her niece should tell her cousin anything about Mr. Gilmore. She did think that the telling of the tale would make Cousin Walter understand that he should not allow himself to become an interloper; but the tale, if told as Mary would tell it, might have a very different effect.

Nevertheless Mary thought that she would tell it. It would be so nice to consult a brother! It would be so pleasant to discuss the matter with some one that would sympathise with her,—with some one who would not wish to drive her into Mr. Gilmore's arms simply because Mr. Gilmore was an excellent gentleman, with a snug property! Even from Janet Fenwick, whom she loved dearly, she had never succeeded in getting the sort of sympathy that she wanted. Janet was the best friend in the world,—was actuated in this matter simply by a desire to do a good turn to two people whom she loved. But there was no sympathy between her and Mary in the matter.

"Marry him," said Janet, "and you will adore him afterwards."

"I want to adore him first," said Mary.

So she resolved that she would tell Walter Marrable what was her position. They were again down on the banks of the Lurwell, sitting together on a slope which had been made to support some hundred yards of a canal, where the river itself rippled down a slightly rapid fall. They were seated between the canal and the river, with their feet towards the latter, and Walter Marrable was just lighting a cigar. It was very easy to bring the conversation round to the affairs of Bullhampton, as Sam was still in prison, and Janet's letters were full of the mystery which shrouded the murder of Mr. Trumbull.

"By the bye," said she, "I have something to tell you about Mr. Gilmore."

"Tell away," said he, as he turned the cigar round in his mouth, to complete the lighting of the edges in the wind.

"Ah, but I shan't, unless you will interest yourself. What I am going to tell you ought to interest you."

"He has made you a proposal of marriage?"

"Yes."

"I knew it."

"How could you know it? Nobody has told you."

"I felt sure of it from the way in which you speak of him. But I thought also that you had refused him. Perhaps I was wrong there?"

"No."

"You have refused him?"

"Yes."

"I don't see that there is very much of a story to be told, Mary."

"Don't be so unkind, Walter. There is a story, and one that troubles me. If it were not so I should not have proposed to tell you. I thought that you would give me advice, and tell me what I ought to do."

"But if you have refused him, you have done so,—no doubt rightly,—without my advice; and I am too late in the field to be of any service."

"You must let me tell my own story, and you must be good to me while I do so. I think I shouldn't tell you if I hadn't almost made up my mind; but I shan't tell you which way, and you must advise me. In the first place, though I did refuse him, the matter is still open, and he is to ask me again, if he pleases."

"He has your permission for that?"

"Well,—yes. I hope it wasn't wrong. I did so try to be right."

"I do not say you were wrong."

"I like him so much, and think him so good, and do really feel that his affection is so great an honour to me, that I could not answer him as though I were quite indifferent to him."

"At any rate, he is to come again?"

"If he pleases."

"Does he really love you?"

"How am I to say? But that is missish and untrue. I am sure he loves me."

"So that he will grieve to lose you?"

"I know he will grieve. I ought not to say so. But I know he will."

"You ought to tell the truth, as you believe it. And you yourself,—do you love him?"

"I don't know. I do love him; but if I heard he was going to marry another girl to-morrow it would make me very happy."

"Then you can't love him?"

"I feel as though I should think the same of any man who wanted to marry me. But let me go on with my story. Everybody I care for wishes me to take him. I know that Aunt Sarah feels quite sure that I shall at last, and that she thinks I ought to do so at once. My friend, Janet Fenwick, cannot understand why I should hesitate, and only forgives me because she is sure that it will come right, in her way, some day. Mr. Fenwick is just the same, and will always talk to me as though it were my fate to live at Bullhampton all my life."

"Is not Bullhampton a nice place?"

"Very nice; I love the place."

"And Mr. Gilmore is rich?"

"He is quite rich enough. Fancy my inquiring about that, with just £1200 for my fortune."

"Then why, in God's name, don't you accept him?"

"You think I ought?"

"Answer my question;—why do you not?"

"Because—I do not love him—as I should hope to love my husband."

After this Captain Marrable, who had been looking her full in the face while he had been asking these questions, turned somewhat away from her, as though the conversation were over. She remained motionless, and was minded so to remain till he should tell her that it was time to move, that they might return home. He had given her no advice; but she presumed she was to take what had passed as the expression of his opinion that it was her duty to accept an offer so favourable and so satisfactory to the family. At any rate, she would say nothing more on the subject till he should address her. Though she loved him dearly as her cousin, yet she was, in some slight degree, afraid of him. And now she was not sure but that he was expressing towards her, by his anger, some amount of displeasure at her weakness and inconsistency. After a while he turned round suddenly, and took her by the hand.

"Well, Mary!" he said.

"Well, Walter!"

"What do you mean to do, after all?"

"What ought I to do?"

"What ought you to do? You know what you ought to do. Would you marry a man for whom you have no more regard than you have for this stick, simply because he is persistent in asking you? No more than you have for this stick, Mary. What sort of a feeling must it be, when you say that you would willingly see him married to any other girl to-morrow? Can that be love?"

"I have never loved any one better."

"And never will?"

"How can I say? It seems to me that I haven't got the feeling that other girls have. I want some one to love me;—I do. I own that. I want to be first with some one; but I have never found the one yet that I cared for."

"You had better wait till you find him," said he, raising himself up on his arm. "Come, let us get up and go home. You have asked me for my advice, and I have given it you. Do not throw yourself away upon a man because other people ask you, and because you think you might as well oblige them and oblige him. If you do, you will soon live to repent it. What would you do, if after marrying this man you found there was some one you could love?"

"I do not think it would come to that, Walter."

"How can you tell? How can you prevent its coming to that, except by loving the man you do marry? You don't care two straws for Mr. Gilmore; and I cannot understand how you can have the courage to think of becoming his wife. Let us go home. You have asked my advice, and you've got it. If you do not take it, I will endeavour to forget that I gave it you."

Of course she would take it. She did not tell him so then; but, of course, he should guide her. With how much more accuracy, with how much more delicacy of feeling had he understood her position, than had her other friends! He had sympathised with her at a word. He spoke to her sternly, severely, almost cruelly. But it was thus that she had longed to be spoken to by some one who would care enough for her, would take sufficient interest in her, to be at the trouble so to advise her. She would trust him as a brother, and his words should be sweet to her, were they ever so severe.

They walked together home in silence, and his very manner was stern to her; but it might be just thus that a loving brother would carry himself who had counselled his sister wisely, and had not as yet been assured that his counsel would be taken.

"Walter," she said, as they neared the town, "I hope you have no doubt about it."

"Doubt about what, Mary?"

"It is quite a matter of course that I shall do as you tell me."

CHAPTER XVII.

THE MARQUIS OF TROWBRIDGE.

By the end of September it had come to be pretty well understood that Sam Brattle must be allowed to go out of prison, unless something in the shape of fresh evidence should be brought up on the next Tuesday. There had arisen a very strong feeling in the county on the subject;—a Brattle feeling, and an anti-Brattle feeling. It might have been called a Bullhampton feeling and an anti-Bullhampton feeling, were it not that the biggest man concerned in Bullhampton, with certain of his hangers-on and dependents, were very clearly of opinion that Sam Brattle had committed the murder, and that he should be kept in prison till the period for hanging him might come round. This very big person was the Marquis of Trowbridge, under whom poor Farmer Trumbull had held his land, and who now seemed to think that a murder committed on one of his tenants was almost as bad as insult to himself. He felt personally angry with Bullhampton, had ideas of stopping his charities to the parish, and did resolve, then and there, that he would have nothing to do with a subscription for the repair of the church, at any rate for the next three years. In making up his mind on which subject he was, perhaps, a little influenced by the opinions and narratives of Mr. Puddleham, the Methodist minister in the village.

It was not only that Mr. Trumbull had been murdered. So great and wise a man as Lord Trowbridge would, no doubt, know very well, that in a free country, such as England, a man could not be specially protected from the hands of murderers, or others, by the fact of his being the tenant, or dependent,—by his being in some sort the possession of a great nobleman. The Marquis's people were all expected to vote for his candidates, and would soon have ceased to be the Marquis's people had they failed to do so. They were constrained, also in many respects, by the terms of their very short leases. They could not kill a head of game on their farms. They could not sell their own hay off the land, nor, indeed, any produce other than their corn or cattle. They were compelled to crop their land in certain rotation; and could take no other lands than those held under the Marquis without his leave. In return for all this, they became the Marquis's people. Each tenant shook hands with the Marquis perhaps once in three years; and twice a year was allowed to get drunk at the Marquis's expense—if such was his taste— provided that he had paid his rent. If the duties were heavy, the privileges were great. So the Marquis himself felt; and he knew that a mantle of security, of a certain thickness, was spread upon the shoulders of each of his people by reason of the tenure which bound them together. But he did not conceive that this mantle would be proof against the bullet of the ordinary assassin, or the hammer of the outside ruffian. But here the case was very different. The hammer had been the hammer of no outside ruffian. To the best of his lordship's belief,—and in that belief he was supported by the constabulary of the whole county,—the hammer had been wielded by a man of Bullhampton,—had been wielded against his tenant by the son of "a person who holds land under a gentleman who has some property in the parish." It was thus the Marquis was accustomed to speak of his neighbour, Mr. Gilmore, who, in the Marquis's eyes, was a man not big enough to have his tenants called his people. That such a man as Sam Brattle should have murdered such a one as Mr. Trumbull, was to the Marquis an insult rather than an injury; and now it was to be enhanced by the release of the man from prison, and that by order of a bench of magistrates on which Mr. Gilmore sat!

And there was more in it even than all this. It was very well known at Turnover Park,—the seat of Lord Trowbridge, near Westbury,—that Mr. Gilmore, the gentleman who held property in his lordship's parish of Bullhampton, and Mr. Fenwick, who was vicar of the same, were another Damon and Pythias. Now the ladies at Turnover, who were much devoted to the Low Church, had heard and doubtless believed, that our friend, Mr. Fenwick, was little better than an infidel. When first he had come into the county, they had been very anxious to make him out to be a High Churchman, and a story or two about a cross and a candlestick were fabricated for their gratification. There was at that time the remnant of a great fight going on between the Trowbridge people and another great family in the neighbourhood on this subject; and it would have suited the Ladies Stowte,—John Augustus Stowte was the Marquis of Trowbridge,—to have enlisted our parson among their enemies of this class; but the accusation fell so plump to the ground, was so impossible of support, that they were obliged to content themselves with knowing that Mr. Fenwick was—an infidel! To do the Marquis justice, we must declare that he would not have troubled himself on this score, if Mr. Fenwick would have submitted himself to become one of his people. The Marquis was master at home, and the Ladies Sophie and Carolina would have been proud to entertain Mr. Fenwick by the week together at Turnover, had he been willing, infidel or believer, to join that faction. But he never joined that faction, and he was not only the bosom friend of the "gentleman who owned some land in the parish;" but he was twice more rebellious than that gentleman himself. He had contradicted the Marquis flat to his face,—so the Marquis said himself,—when they met once about some business in the parish; and again, when, in the Vicar's early days in Bullhampton, some gathering for school-festival purposes was made in the great home field behind Farmer Trumbull's house, Mrs. Fenwick misbehaved herself egregiously.

"Upon my word, she patronised us," said Lady Sophie, laughing. "She did, indeed! And you know what she was. Her father was just a common builder at Loring, who made some money by a speculation in bricks and mortar."

When Lady Sophie said this she was, no doubt, ignorant of the fact that Mr. Balfour had been the younger son of a family much more ancient than her own, that he had taken a double-first at Oxford, had been a member of half the learned societies in Europe, and had belonged to two or three of the best clubs in London.

From all this it will be seen that the Marquis of Trowbridge would be disposed to think ill of whatever might be done in regard to the murder by the Gilmore-Fenwick party in the parish. And then there were tales about for which there was perhaps some foundation, that the Vicar and the murderer had been very dear friends. It was certainly believed at Turnover that the Vicar and Sam Brattle had for years past spent the best part of their Sundays fishing together. There were tales of rat-killing matches in which they had been engaged,—originating in the undeniable fact of a certain campaign against rats at the mill, in which the Vicar had taken an ardent part. Undoubtedly the destruction of vermin, and, in regard to one species, its preservation for the sake of destruction,—and the catching of fish,—and the shooting of birds,—were things lovely in the Vicar's eyes. He, perhaps, did let his pastoral dignity go a little by the board, when he and Sam stooped together, each with a ferret in his hand, grovelling in the dust to get at certain rat-advantages in the mill. Gilmore, who had seen it, had told him of this. "I understand it all, old fellow," Fenwick had said to his friend, "and know very well I have got to choose between two things. I must be called a hypocrite, or else I must be one. I have no doubt that as years go on with me I shall see the advantage of choosing the latter." There were at that time frequent discussions between them on the same subject, for they were friends who could dare to discuss each other's modes of life; but the reader need not be troubled further now with this digression. The position which the Vicar held in the estimation of the Marquis of Trowbridge will probably be sufficiently well understood.

The family at Turnover Park would have thought it a great blessing to have had a clergyman at Bullhampton with whom they could have cordially co-operated; but, failing this, they had taken Mr. Puddleham, the Methodist minister, to their arms. From Mr. Puddleham they learned parish facts and parish fables, which would never have reached them but for his assistance. Mr. Fenwick was well aware of this, and used to declare that he had no objection to it. He would protest that he could not see why Mr. Puddleham should not get along in the parish just as well as himself, he having, and meaning to keep to himself, the slight advantages of the parish church, the vicarage-house, and the small tithes. Of this he was quite sure, that Mr.

Puddleham's religious teaching was better than none at all; and he was by no means convinced,—so he said,—that, for some of his parishioners, Mr. Puddleham was not a better teacher than he himself. He always shook hands with Mr. Puddleham, though Mr. Puddleham would never look him in the face, and was quite determined that Mr. Puddleham should not be a thorn in his side.

In this matter of Sam Brattle's imprisonment and now intended liberation, tidings from the parish were doubtless conveyed by Mr. Puddleham to Turnover,—probably not direct, but still in such a manner that the great people at Turnover knew to whom they were indebted. Now Mr. Gilmore had certainly, from the first, been by no means disposed to view favourably the circumstances attaching to Sam Brattle on that Saturday night. When the great blow fell on the Brattle family, his demeanour to them was changed, and he forgave the miller's contumacy; but he had always thought that Sam had been guilty. The parson had from the first regarded the question with great doubt, but, nevertheless, his opinion too had at first been averse to Sam. Even now, when he was so resolute that Sam should be released, he founded his demand, not on Sam's innocence, but on the absence of any evidence against him.

"He's entitled to fair play, Harry," he would say to Gilmore, "and he is not getting it, because there is a prejudice against him. You hear what that old ass, Sir Thomas, says."

"Sir Thomas is a very good magistrate."

"If he don't take care, he'll find himself in trouble for keeping the lad locked up without authority. Is there a juryman in the country would find him guilty because he was lying in the old man's ditch a week before?" In this way Gilmore also became a favourer of Sam's claim to be released; and at last it came to be understood that on the next Tuesday he would be released, unless further evidence should be forthcoming.

And then it came to pass that a certain very remarkable meeting took place in the parish. Word was brought to Mr. Gilmore on Monday, the 5th October, that the Marquis of Trowbridge was to be at the Church Farm,— poor Trumbull's farm,—on that day at noon, and that his lordship thought that it might be expedient that he and Mr. Gilmore should meet on the occasion. There was no note, but the message was brought by Mr. Packer, a sub-agent, one of the Marquis's people, with whom Mr. Gilmore was very well acquainted.

"I'll walk down about that time, Packer," said Mr. Gilmore, "and shall be very happy to see his lordship."

Now the Marquis never sat as a magistrate at the Heytesbury bench, and had not been present on any of the occasions on which Sam had been examined; nor had Mr. Gilmore seen the Marquis since the murder,—nor, for the matter of that, for the last twelve months. Mr. Gilmore had just finished breakfast when the news was brought to him, and he thought he might as well walk down and see Fenwick first. His interview with the parson ended in a promise that he, Fenwick, would also look in at the farm.

At twelve o'clock the Marquis was seated in the old farmer's arm-chair, in the old farmer's parlour. The house was dark and gloomy, never having been altogether opened since the murder. With the Marquis was Packer, who was standing, and the Marquis was pretending to cast his eye over one or two books which had been brought to him. He had been taken all over the house; had stood looking at the bed where the old man lay when he was attacked, as though he might possibly discover, if he looked long enough, something that would reveal the truth; had gazed awe-struck at the spot on which the body had been found, and had taken occasion to remark to himself that the house was a good deal out of order. The Marquis was a man nearer seventy than sixty, but very hale, and with few signs of age. He was short and plump, with hardly any beard on his face, and short grey hair, of which nothing could be seen when he wore his hat. His countenance would not have been bad, had not the weight of his marquisate always been there; nor would his heart have been bad, had it not been similarly burdened. But he was a silly, weak, ignorant man, whose own capacity would hardly have procured bread for him in any trade or profession, had bread not been so adequately provided for him by his fathers before him.

"Mr. Gilmore said he would be here at twelve, Packer?"

"Yes, my lord."

"And it's past twelve now?"

"One minute, my lord."

Then the peer looked again at poor old Trumbull's books.

"I shall not wait, Packer."

"No, my lord."

"You had better tell them to put the horses to."

"Yes, my lord."

But just as Packer went out into the passage for the sake of giving the order he met Mr. Gilmore, and ushered him into the room.

"Ha! Mr. Gilmore; yes, I am very glad to see you, Mr. Gilmore;" and the Marquis came forward to shake hands with his visitor. "I thought it better that you and I should meet about this sad affair in the parish;—a very sad affair, indeed."

"It certainly is, Lord Trowbridge; and the mystery makes it more so."

"I suppose there is no real mystery, Mr. Gilmore? I suppose there can be no doubt that that unfortunate young man did,—did,—did bear a hand in it at least?"

"I think that there is very much doubt, my lord."

"Do you, indeed? I think there is none,—not the least. And all the police force are of the same opinion. I have considerable experiences of my own in these matters; but I should not venture, perhaps, to express my opinion so confidently, if I were not backed by the police. You are aware, Mr. Gilmore, that the police are—very—seldom wrong?"

"I should be tempted to say that they are very seldom right—except when the circumstances are all under their noses."

"I must say I differ from you entirely, Mr. Gilmore. Now, in this case—" The Marquis was here interrupted by a knock at the door, and, before the summons could be answered, the parson entered the room. And with the parson came Mr. Puddleham. The Marquis had thought that the parson might, perhaps, intrude; and Mr. Puddleham was in waiting as a make-weight, should he be wanting. When Mr. Fenwick had met the minister hanging about the farmyard, he had displayed not the slightest anger. If Mr. Puddleham chose to come in also, and make good his doing so before the Marquis, it was nothing to Mr. Fenwick. The great man looked up, as though he were very much startled and somewhat offended; but he did at last condescend to shake hands, first with one clergyman and then with the other, and to ask them to sit down. He explained that he had come over to make some personal inquiry into the melancholy matter, and then proceeded with his opinion respecting Sam Brattle. "From all that I can hear and see," said his lordship, "I fear there can be no doubt that this murder has been due to the malignity of a near neighbour."

"Do you mean the poor boy that is in prison, my lord?" asked the parson.

"Of course I do, Mr. Fenwick. The constabulary are of opinion—"

"We know that, Lord Trowbridge."

"Perhaps, Mr. Fenwick, you will allow me to express my own ideas. The constabulary, I say, are of opinion that there is no manner of doubt that he was one of those who broke into my tenant's house on that fatal night; and, as I was explaining to Mr. Gilmore when you did us the honour to join us, in the course of a long provincial experience I have seldom known the police to be in error."

"Why, Lord Trowbridge—!"

"If you please, Mr. Fenwick, I will go on. My time here cannot be long, and I have a proposition which I am desirous of making to Mr. Gilmore, as a magistrate acting in this part of the county. Of course, it is not for me to animadvert upon what the magistrates may do at the bench to-morrow."

"I am sure your lordship would make no such animadversion," said Mr. Gilmore.

"I do not intend it, for many reasons. But I may go so far as to say that a demand for the young man's release will be made."

"He is to be released, I presume, as a matter of course," said the parson.

The Marquis made no allusion to this, but went on. "If that be done,—and I must say that I think no such step would be taken by the bench at Westbury,—whither will the young man betake himself?"

"Home to his father, of course," said the parson.

"Back into this parish, with his paramour, to murder more of my tenants."

"My lord, I cannot allow such an unjust statement to be made," said the parson.

"I wish to speak for one moment; and I wish it to be remembered that I am addressing myself especially to your neighbour, Mr. Gilmore, who has done me the honour of waiting upon me here at my request. I do not object to your presence, Mr. Fenwick, or to that of any other gentleman," and the Marquis bowed to Mr. Puddleham, who had stood by hitherto without speaking a word; "but, if you please, I must carry out the purpose that has brought me here. I shall think it very sad indeed, if this young man be allowed to take up his residence in the parish after what has taken place."

"His father has a house here," said Mr. Gilmore.

"I am aware of the fact," said the Marquis. "I believe that the young man's father holds a mill from you, and some few acres of land?"

"He has a very nice farm."

"So be it. We will not quarrel about terms. I believe there is no lease?—though, of course, that is no business of mine."

"I must say that it is not, my lord," said Mr. Gilmore, who was waxing wrothy and becoming very black about the brows.

"I have just said so; but I suppose you will admit that I have some interest in this parish? I presume that these two gentlemen, who are God's ministers here, will acknowledge that it is my duty, as the owner of the greater part of the parish, to interfere?"

"Certainly, my lord," said Mr. Puddleham.

Mr. Fenwick said nothing. He sat, or rather leant, against the edge of a table, and smiled. His brow was not black, like that of his friend; but Gilmore, who knew him, and who looked into his face, began to fear that the Marquis would be addressed before long in terms stronger than he himself, Mr. Gilmore, would approve.

"And when I remember," continued his lordship, "that the unfortunate man who has fallen a victim had been for nearly half a century a tenant of myself and of my family, and that he was foully murdered on my own property,—dragged from his bed in the middle of the night, and ruthlessly slaughtered in this very house in which I am sitting, and that this has been done in a parish of which I own, I think, something over two-thirds—"

"Two thousand and two acres out of two thousand nine hundred and ten," said Mr. Puddleham.

"I suppose so. Well, Mr. Puddleham, you need not have interrupted me."

"I beg pardon, my lord."

"What I mean to say is this, Mr. Gilmore,—that you should take steps to prevent that young man's return among our people. You should explain to the father that it cannot be allowed. From what I hear, it would be no loss if the whole family left the parish. I am told that one of the daughters is a—prostitute."

"It is too true, my lord," said Mr. Puddleham.

The parson turned round and looked at his colleague, but said nothing. It was one of the principles of his life that he wouldn't quarrel with Mr. Puddleham; and at the present moment he certainly did not wish to waste his anger on so weak an enemy.

"I think that you should look to this, Mr. Gilmore," said the Marquis, completing his harangue.

"I cannot conceive, my lord, what right you have to dictate to me in such a matter," said Mr. Gilmore.

"I have not dictated at all; I have simply expressed my opinion," said the Marquis.

"Now, my lord, will you allow me for a moment?" said Mr. Fenwick. "In the first place, if Sam Brattle could not find a home at the mill,—which I hope he will do for many a long year to come,—he should have one at the Vicarage."

"I dare say," said the Marquis.

Mr. Puddleham held up both hands.

"You might as well hold your tongue, Frank," said Gilmore.

"It is a matter on which I wish to say a word or two, Harry. I have been appealed to as one of God's ministers here, and I acknowledge my responsibility. I never in my life heard any proposition more cruel or inhuman than that made by Lord Trowbridge. This young man is to be turned out because a tenant of his lordship has been murdered! He is to be adjudged to be guilty by us, without any trial, in the absence of all evidence, in opposition to the decision of the magistrates—"

"It is not in opposition to the magistrates, sir," said the Marquis.

"And to be forbidden to return to his own home, simply because Lord Trowbridge thinks him guilty! My lord, his father's house is his own, to entertain whom he may please, as much as is yours. And were I to suggest to you to turn out your daughters, it would be no worse an offence than your suggesting to Mr. Brattle that he should turn out his son."

"My daughters!"

"Yes, your daughters, my lord."

"How dare you mention my daughters?"

"How dare you mention my daughters?"

"The ladies, I am well aware, are all that is respectable. I have not the slightest wish that you should ill-use them. But if you desire that your family concerns should be treated with reserve and reticence, you had better learn to treat the family affairs of others in the same way."

The Marquis by this time was on his feet, and was calling for Packer,—was calling for his carriage and horses,—was calling on the very gods to send down their thunder to punish such insolence as this. He had never heard of the like in all his experience. His daughters! And then there came across his dismayed mind an idea that his daughters had been put upon a par with that young murderer, Sam Brattle,—perhaps even on a par with something worse than this. And his daughters were such august persons,—old and ugly, it is true, and almost dowerless in consequence of the nature of the family settlements and family expenditure. It was an injury and an insult that Mr. Fenwick should make the slightest allusion to his daughters; but to talk of them in such a way as this, as though they were mere ordinary human beings, was not to be endured! The Marquis had hitherto had his doubts, but now he was quite sure that Mr. Fenwick was an infidel. "And a very bad sort of infidel, too," as he said to Lady Carolina on his return home. "I never heard of such conduct in all my life," said Lord Trowbridge, walking down to his carriage. "Who can be surprised that there should be murderers and prostitutes in the parish?"

"My lord, they don't sit under me," said Mr. Puddleham.

"I don't care who they sit under," said his lordship.

As they walked away together, Mr. Fenwick had just a word to say to Mr. Puddleham. "My friend," he said, "you were quite right about his lordship's acres."

"Those are the numbers," said Mr. Puddleham.

"I mean that you were quite right to make the observation. Facts are always valuable, and I am sure Lord Trowbridge was obliged to you. But I think you were a little wrong as to another statement."

"What statement, Mr. Fenwick?"

"What you said about poor Carry Brattle. You don't know it as a fact."

"Everybody says so."

"How do you know she has not married, and become an honest woman?"

"It is possible, of course. Though as for that,—when a young woman has once gone astray—"

"As did Mary Magdalene, for instance!"

"Mr. Fenwick, it was a very bad case."

"And isn't my case very bad,—and yours? Are we not in a bad way,—unless we believe and repent? Have we not all so sinned as to deserve eternal punishment?"

"Certainly, Mr. Fenwick."

"Then there can't be much difference between her and us. She can't deserve more than eternal punishment. If she believes and repents, all her sins will be white as snow."

"Certainly, Mr. Fenwick."

"Then speak of her as you would of any other sister or brother,—not as a thing that must be always vile because she has fallen once. Women will so speak,—and other men. One sees something of a reason for it. But you and I, as Christian ministers, should never allow ourselves to speak so thoughtlessly of sinners. Good morning, Mr. Puddleham."

CHAPTER XVIII.

BLANK PAPER.

Early in October Captain Marrable was called up to town by letters from Messrs. Block and Curling, and according to promise wrote various letters to Mary Lowther, telling her of the manner in which his business progressed. All of these letters were shown to Aunt Sarah,—and would have been shown to Parson John were it not that Parson John declined to read them. But though the letters were purely cousinly,—just such letters as a brother might write,—yet Miss Marrable thought that they were dangerous. She did not say so; but she thought that they were dangerous. Of late Mary had spoken no word of Mr. Gilmore; and Aunt Sarah, through all this silence, was able to discover that Mr. Gilmore's prospects were not becoming brighter. Mary herself, having quite made up her mind that Mr. Gilmore's prospects, so far as she was concerned, were all over, could not decide how and when she should communicate the resolve to her lover. According to her present agreement with him, she was to write to him at once should she accept any other offer; and was to wait for six months if this should not be the case. Certainly, there was no rival in the field, and therefore she did not quite know whether she ought or ought not to write at once in her present circumstances of assured determination. She soon told herself that in this respect also she would go to her new-found brother for advice. She would ask him, and do just as he might bid her. Had he not already proved how fit a person he was to give advice on such a subject?

After an absence of ten days he came home, and nothing could exceed Mary's anxiety as to the tidings which he should bring with him. She endeavoured not to be selfish about the matter; but she could not but acknowledge that, even as regarded herself, the difference between his going to India or staying at home was so great as to affect the whole colour of her life. There was, perhaps, something of the feeling of being subject to desertion about her, as she remembered that in giving up Mr. Gilmore she must also give up the Fenwicks. She could not hope to go to Bullhampton again, at least for many a long day. She would be very much alone if her new brother were to leave her now. On the morning after his arrival he came up to them at Uphill, and told them that the matter was almost settled. Messrs. Block and Curling had declared that it was as good as settled; the money would be saved, and there would be, out of the £20,000 which he had inherited, something over £4000 for him; so that he need not return to India. He was in very high spirits, and did not speak a word of his father's iniquities.

"Oh, Walter, what a joy!" said Mary, with the tears streaming from her eyes.

He took her by both her hands, and kissed her forehead. At that moment Aunt Sarah was not in the room.

"I am so very, very happy," she said, pressing her little hands against his.

Why should he not kiss her? Was he not her brother? And then, before he went, she remembered she had something special to tell him;—something to ask him. Would he not walk with her that evening? Of course he would walk with her.

"Mary, dear," said her aunt, putting her little arm round her niece's waist, and embracing her, "don't fall in love with Walter."

"How can you say anything so foolish, Aunt Sarah?"

"It would be very foolish to do so."

"You don't understand how completely different it is. Do you think I could be so intimate with him as I am if anything of the kind were possible?"

"I do not know how that may be."

"Do not begrudge it me because I have found a cousin that I can love almost as I would a brother. There has never been anybody yet for whom I could have that sort of feeling."

Aunt Sarah, whatever she might think, had not the heart to repeat her caution; and Mary, quite happy and contented with herself, put on her hat to run down the hill and meet her cousin at the great gates of the Lowtown Rectory. Why should he be dragged up the hill, to escort a cousin down again? This arrangement had, therefore, been made between them.

For the first mile or two the talk was all about Messrs. Block and Curling and the money. Captain Marrable was so full of his own purposes, and so well contented that so much should be saved to him out of the fortune he had lost, that he had, perhaps, forgotten that Mary required more advice. But when they had come to the spot on which they had before sat, she bade him stop and seat himself.

"And now what is it?" he said, as he rolled himself comfortably close to her side. She told her story, and explained her doubts, and asked for the revelations of his wisdom. "Are you quite sure about the propriety of this, Mary?" he said.

"The propriety of what, Walter?"

"Giving up a man who loves you so well, and who has so much to offer?"

"What was it you said yourself? Sure! Of course I am sure. I am quite sure. I do not love him. Did I not tell you that there could be no doubt after what you said?"

"I did not mean that my words should be so powerful."

"They were powerful; but, independently of that, I am quite sure now. If I could do it myself, I should be false to him. I know that I do not love him." He was not looking at her where he was lying, but was playing with a cigar-case which he had taken out, as though he were about to resume his smoking. But he did not open the case, or look towards her, or say a word to her. Two minutes had perhaps passed before she spoke again. "I suppose it would be best that I should write to him at once?"

"There is no one else, then, you care for, Mary?" he asked.

"No one," she said, as though the question were nothing.

"It is all blank paper with you?"

"It is all blank paper with you?"

"Quite blank," she said, and laughed. "Do you know, I almost think it always will be blank."

"By G———! it is not blank with me," he said, springing up and jumping to his feet. She stared at him, not in the least understanding what he meant, not dreaming even that he was about to tell her his love secrets in reference to another. "I wonder what you think I'm made of, Mary;—whether you imagine I have any affection to bestow?"

"I do not in the least understand."

"Look here, dear," and he knelt down beside her as he spoke, "it is simply this, that you have become to me more than all the world;—that I love you better than my own soul;—that your beauty and sweetness, and soft, darling touch, are everything to me. And then you come to me for advice! I can only give you one bit of advice now, Mary."

"And what is that?"

"Love me."

"I do love you."

"Ay, but love me and be my wife."

She had to think of it; but she knew from the first moment that the thinking of it was a delight to her. She did not quite understand at first that her chosen brother might become her lover, with no other feeling than that of joy and triumph; and yet there was a consciousness that no other answer but one was possible. In the first place, to refuse him anything, asked in love, would be impossible. She could not say No to him. She had struggled often in reference to Mr. Gilmore, and had found it impossible to say Yes. There was now the same sort of impossibility in regard to the No. She couldn't blacken herself with such a lie. And yet, though she was sure of this, she was so astounded by his declaration, so carried off her legs by the alteration in her position, so hard at work within herself with her new endeavour to change the aspect in which she must look at the man, that she could not even bring herself to think of answering him. If he would only sit down near her for awhile,—very near,—and not speak to her, she thought that she would be happy. Everything else was forgotten. Aunt Sarah's caution, Janet Fenwick's anger, poor Gilmore's sorrow,—of all these she thought not at all, or only allowed her mind to dwell on them as surrounding trifles, of which it would be necessary that she, that they—they two who were now all in all to each other—must dispose; as they must, also, of questions of income, and such like little things. She was without a doubt. The man was her master, and had her in his keeping, and of course she would obey him. But she must settle her voice, and let her pulses become calm, and remember herself before she could tell him so. "Sit down again, Walter," she said at last.

"Why should I sit?"

"Because I ask you. Sit down, Walter."

"No. I understand how wise you will be, and how cold; and I understand, too, what a fool I have been."

"Walter, will you not come when I ask you?"

"Why should I sit?"

"That I may try to tell you how dearly I love you."

He did not sit, but he threw himself at her feet, and buried his face upon her lap. There were but few more words spoken then. When it comes to this, that a pair of lovers are content to sit and rub their feathers together like two birds, there is not much more need of talking. Before they had arisen, her fingers had been playing through his curly hair, and he had kissed her lips and cheeks as well as her forehead. She had begun to feel what it was to have a lover and to love him. She could already talk to him almost as though he were a part of herself, could whisper to him little words of nonsense, could feel that everything of hers was his, and everything of his was hers. She knew more clearly now even than she had done before that she had never loved Mr. Gilmore, and never could have loved him. And that other doubt had been solved for her. "Do you know," she had said, not yet an hour ago, "that I think it always will be blank." And now every spot of the canvas was covered.

"We must go home now," she said at last.

"And tell Aunt Sarah," he replied, laughing.

"Yes, and tell Aunt Sarah;—but not to-night. I can do nothing to-night but think about it. Oh, Walter, I am so happy!"

CHAPTER XIX.

SAM BRATTLE RETURNS HOME.

The Tuesday's magistrates' meeting had come off at Heytesbury, and Sam Brattle had been discharged. Mr. Jones had on this occasion indignantly demanded that his client should be set free without bail; but to this the magistrates would not assent. The attorney attempted to demonstrate to them that they could not require bail for the reappearance of an accused person, when that accused person was discharged simply because there was no evidence against him. But to this exposition of the law Sir Thomas and his brother magistrates would not listen. "If the other persons should at last be taken, and Brattle should not then be forthcoming, justice would suffer," said Sir Thomas. County magistrates, as a rule, are more conspicuous for common sense and good instincts than for sound law; and Mr. Jones may, perhaps, have been right in his view of the case. Nevertheless bail was demanded, and was not forthcoming without considerable trouble. Mr. Jay, the ironmonger at Warminster, declined. When spoken to on the subject by Mr. Fenwick, he declared that the feeling among the gentry was so strong against his brother-in-law, that he could not bring himself to put himself forward. He couldn't do it for the sake of his family. When Fenwick promised to make good the money risk, Jay declared that the difficulty did not lie there. "There's the Marquis, and Sir Thomas, and Squire Greenthorne, and our parson, all say, sir, as how he shouldn't be bailed at all. And then, sir, if one has a misfortune belonging to one, one doesn't want to flaunt it in everybody's face, sir." And there was trouble, too, with George Brattle from Fordingbridge. George Brattle was a prudent, hard-headed, hard-working man, not troubled with much sentiment, and caring very little what any one could say of him as long as his rent was paid; but he had taken it into his head that Sam was guilty, that he was at any rate a thoroughly bad fellow who should be turned out of the Brattle nest, and that no kindness was due to him. With the farmer, however, Mr. Fenwick did prevail, and then the parson became the other bondsman himself. He had been strongly advised,—by Gilmore, by Gilmore's uncle, the prebendary at Salisbury, and by others,—not to put himself forward in this position. The favour which he had shown to the young man had not borne good results either for the young man or for himself; and it would be unwise,—so said his friends,—to subject his own name to more remark than was necessary. He had so far assented as to promise not to come forward himself, if other bailsmen could be procured. But, when the difficulty came, he offered himself, and was, of necessity, accepted.

When Sam was released, he was like a caged animal who, when liberty is first offered to him, does not know how to use it. He looked about him in the hall of the Court House, and did not at first seem disposed to leave it. The constable had asked him whether he had means of getting home, to which he replied, that "it wasn't no more than a walk." Dinner was offered to him by the constable, but this he refused, and then he stood glaring about him. After a while Gilmore and Fenwick came up to him, and the Squire was the first to speak. "Brattle," he said, "I hope you will now go home, and remain there working with your father for the present."

"I don't know nothing about that," said the lad, not deigning to look at the Squire.

"Sam, pray go home at once," said the parson. "We have done what we could for you, and you should not oppose us."

"Mr. Fenwick, if you tells me to go to—to—to,"—he was going to mention some very bad place, but was restrained by the parson's presence,—"if you tells me to go anywheres, I'll go."

"That's right. Then I tell you to go to the mill."

"I don't know as father'll let me in," said he, almost breaking into sobs as he spoke.

"That he will, heartily. Do you tell him that you had a word or two with me here, and that I'll come up and call on him to-morrow." Then he put his hand into his pocket, and whispering something, offered the lad money. But Sam turned away, and shook his head, and walked off. "I don't believe that that fellow had any more to do with it than you or I," said Fenwick.

"I don't know what to believe," said Gilmore. "Have you heard that the Marquis is in the town? Greenthorne just told me so."

"Then I had better get out of it, for Heytesbury isn't big enough for the two of us. Come, you've done here, and we might as well jog home."

Gilmore dined at the Vicarage that evening, and of course the day's work was discussed. The quarrel, too, which had taken place at the farmhouse had only yet been in part described to Mrs. Fenwick. "Do you know I feel half triumphant and half frightened," Mrs. Fenwick said to the Squire. "I know that the Marquis is an old fool, imperious, conceited, and altogether unendurable when he attempts to interfere. And yet I have a kind of feeling that because he is a Marquis, and because he owns two thousand and so many acres in the parish, and because he lives at Turnover Park, one ought to hold him in awe."

"Frank didn't hold him in awe yesterday," said the Squire.

"He holds nothing in awe," said the wife.

"You wrong me there, Janet. I hold you in great awe, and every lady in Wiltshire more or less;—and I think I may say every woman. And I would hold him in a sort of awe, too, if he didn't drive me beyond myself by his mixture of folly and pride."

"He can do us a great deal of mischief, you know," said Mrs. Fenwick.

"What he can do, he will do," said the parson. "He even gave me a bad name, no doubt; but I fancy he was generous enough to me in that way before yesterday. He will now declare that I am the Evil One himself, and people won't believe that. A continued persistent enmity, always at work, but kept within moderate bounds, is more dangerous now-a-days, than a hot fever of revengeful wrath. The Marquis can't send out his men-at-arms and have me knocked on the head, or cast into a dungeon. He can only throw mud at me, and the more he throws at once, the less will reach me."

As to Sam, they were agreed that, whether he were innocent or guilty, the old miller should be induced to regard him as innocent, as far as their joint exertion in that direction might avail.

"He is innocent before the law till he has been proved to be guilty," said the Squire.

"Then of course there can be nothing wrong in telling his father that he is innocent," said the lady.

The Squire did not quite admit this, and the parson smiled as he heard the argument; but they both acknowledged that it would be right to let it be considered throughout the parish that Sam was to be regarded as blameless for that night's transaction. Nevertheless, Mr. Gilmore's mind on the subject was not changed.

"Have you heard from Loring?" the Squire asked Mrs. Fenwick as he got up to leave the Vicarage.

"Oh, yes,—constantly. She is quite well, Mr. Gilmore."

"I sometimes think that I'll go off and have a look at her."

"I'm sure both she and her aunt would be glad to see you."

"But would it be wise?"

"If you ask me, I am bound to say that I think it would not be wise. If I were you, I would leave her for awhile. Mary is as good as gold, but she is a woman; and, like other women, the more she is sought, the more difficult she will be."

"It always seems to me," said Mr. Gilmore, "that to be successful in love, a man should not be in love at all; or, at any rate, he should hide it." Then he went off home alone, feeling on his heart that pernicious load of a burden which comes from the unrestrained longing for some good thing which cannot be attained. It seemed to him now that nothing in life would be worth a thought if Mary Lowther should continue to say him nay; and it seemed to him, too, that unless the yea were said very quickly, all his aptitudes for enjoyment would be worn out of him.

On the next morning, immediately after breakfast, Mr. and Mrs. Fenwick walked down to the mill together. They went through the village, and thence by a pathway down to a little foot-bridge, and so along the river side. It was a beautiful October morning, the 7th of October, and Fenwick talked of the pheasants. Gilmore, though he was a sportsman, and shot rabbits and partridges about his own property, and went occasionally to shooting-parties at a distance, preserved no game. There had been some old unpleasantness about the Marquis's pheasants, and he had given it up. There could be no doubt that his property in the parish being chiefly low lying lands and water meads unfit for coverts, was not well disposed for preserving pheasants, and that in shooting he would more likely shoot Lord Trowbridge's birds than his own. But it was equally certain that Lord Trowbridge's pheasants made no scruple of feeding on his land. Nevertheless, he had thought it right to give up all idea of keeping up a head of game for his own use in Bullhampton.

"Upon my word, if I were you, Gilmore," said the parson, as a bird rose from the ground close at their feet, "I should cease to be nice about the shooting after what happened yesterday."

"You don't mean that you would retaliate, Frank?"

"I think I should."

"Is that good parson's law?"

"It's very good squire's law. And as for that doctrine of non-retaliation, a man should be very sure of his own motives before he submits to it. If a man be quite certain that he is really actuated by a Christian's desire to forgive, it may be all very well; but if there be any admixture of base alloy in his gold, if he allows himself to think that he may avoid the evils of pugnacity, and have things go smooth for him here, and become a good Christian by the same process, why then I think he is likely to fall to the ground between two stools." Had Lord Trowbridge heard him, his lordship would now have been quite sure that Mr. Fenwick was an infidel.

They had both doubted whether Sam would be found at the mill; but there he was, hard at work among the skeleton timbers, when his friends reached the place.

"I am glad to see you at home again, Sam," said Mrs. Fenwick, with something, however, of an inner feeling that perhaps she might be saluting a murderer.

Sam touched his cap, but did not utter a word, or look away from his work. They passed on amidst the heaps in front of the mill, and came to the porch before the cottage. Here, as had been his wont in all these idle days, the miller was sitting with a pipe in his mouth. When he saw the lady he got up and ducked his head, and then sat down again. "If your wife is here, I'll just step in, Mr. Brattle," said Mrs. Fenwick.

"She be there, ma'am," said the miller, pointing towards the kitchen window with his head. So Mrs. Fenwick lifted the latch and entered. The parson sat himself down by the miller's side.

"I am heartily glad, Mr. Brattle, that Sam is back with you here once again."

"He be there, at work among the rest o' 'em," said the miller.

"I saw him as I came along. I hope he will remain here now."

"I can't say, Muster Fenwick."

"But he intends to do so?"

"I can't say, Muster Fenwick."

"Would it not be well that you should ask him?"

"Not as I knows on, Muster Fenwick."

It was manifest enough that the old man had not spoken to his son on the subject of the murder, and that there was no confidence,—at least, no confidence that had been expressed,—between the father and the son. No one had as yet heard the miller utter any opinion as to Sam's innocence or his guilt. This of itself seemed to the clergyman to be a very terrible condition for two persons who were so closely united, and who were to live together, work together, eat together, and have mutual interests.

"I hope, Mr. Brattle," he said, "that you give Sam the full benefit of his discharge."

"He'll get his vittles and his bed, and a trifle of wages if he works for 'em."

"I didn't mean that. I'm quite sure you wouldn't see him want a comfortable home, as long as you have one to give him."

"There ain't much comfort about it now."

"I was speaking of your own opinion of the deed that was done. My own opinion is that Sam had nothing to do with it."

"I'm sure I can't say, Muster Fenwick."

"But it would be a comfort to you to think that he is innocent."

"I ain't no comfort in talking about it,—not at all,—and I'd rayther not, if it's all one to you, Muster Fenwick."

"I will not ask another question, but I'll repeat my own opinion, Mr. Brattle. I don't believe that he had anything more to do with the robbery or the murder, than I had."

"I hope not, Muster Fenwick. Murder is a terrible crime. And now, if you'll tell me how much it was you paid the lawyer at Heytesbury—"

"I cannot say as yet. It will be some trifle. You need not trouble yourself about that."

"But I mean to pay 'un, Muster Fenwick. I can pay my way as yet, though it's hard enough at times." The parson was obliged to promise that Mr. Jones's bill of charges should be sent to him, and then he called his wife, and they left the mill. Sam was still up among the timbers, and had not once come down while the visitors were in the cottage. Mrs. Fenwick had been more successful with the women than the parson had been with the father. She had taken upon herself to say that she thoroughly believed Sam to be innocent, and they had thanked her with many protestations of gratitude.

They did not go back by the way they had come, but went up to the road, which they crossed, and thence to some outlying cottages which were not very far from Hampton Privets House. From these cottages there was a path across the fields back to Bullhampton, which led by the side of a small wood belonging to the Marquis. There was a good deal of woodland just here, and this special copse, called Hampton bushes, was known to be one of the best pheasant coverts in that part of the country. Whom should they meet, standing on the path, armed with his gun, and with his keeper behind him armed with another, than the Marquis of Trowbridge himself. They had heard a shot or two, but they had thought nothing of it, or they would have gone back to the road. "Don't speak," said the parson, as he walked on quickly with his wife on his arm. The Marquis stood and scowled; but he had the breeding of a gentleman, and when Mrs. Fenwick was close to him, he raised his hat. The parson also raised his, the lady bowed, and then they passed on without a word. "I had no excuse for doing so, or I would certainly have told him that Sam Brattle was comfortably at home with his father," said the parson.

"How you do like a fight, Frank!"

"If it's stand up, and all fair, I don't dislike it."

CHAPTER XX.

I HAVE A JUPITER OF MY OWN NOW.

When Mary Lowther returned home from the last walk with her cousin that has been mentioned, she was quite determined that she would not disturb her happiness on that night by the task of telling her engagement to her aunt. It must, of course, be told, and that at once; and it must be told also to Parson John; and a letter must be written to Janet; and another, which would be very difficult in the writing, to Mr. Gilmore; and she must be prepared to bear a certain amount of opposition from all her friends; but for the present moment, she would free herself from these troubles. To-morrow, after breakfast, she would tell her aunt. To-morrow, at lunch-time, Walter would come up to the lane as her accepted lover. And then, after lunch, after due consultation with him and with Aunt Sarah, the letter should be written.

She had solved, at any rate, one doubt, and had investigated one mystery. While conscious of her own coldness towards Mr. Gilmore, she had doubted whether she was capable of loving a man, of loving him as Janet Fenwick loved her husband. Now she would not admit to herself that any woman that ever lived adored a man more thoroughly than she adored Walter Marrable. It was sweet to her to see and to remember the motions of his body. When walking by his side she could hardly forbear to touch him with her shoulder. When parting from him it was a regret to her to take her hand from his. And she told herself that all this had come to her in the course of one morning's walk, and wondered at it,—that her heart should be a thing capable of being given away so quickly. It had, in truth, been given away quickly enough, though the work had not been done in that one morning's walk. She had been truly honest, to herself and to others, when she said that her cousin Walter was and should be a brother to her; but had her new brother, in his brotherly confidence, told her that his heart was devoted to some other woman, she would have suffered a blow, though she would never have confessed even to herself that she suffered. On that evening, when she reached home, she said very little.

She was so tired. Might she go to bed? "What, at nine o'clock?" asked Aunt Sarah.

"I'll stay up, if you wish it," said Mary.

But before ten she was alone in her own chamber, sitting in her own chair, with her arms folded, feeling, rather than thinking, how divine a thing it was to be in love. What could she not do for him? What would she not endure to have the privilege of living with him? What other good fortune in life could be equal to this good fortune? Then she thought of her relations with Mr. Gilmore, and shuddered as she remembered how near she had been to accepting him. "It would have been so wrong. And yet I did not see it! With him I am sure that it is right, for I feel that in going to him I can be every bit his own."

So she thought, and so she dreamed; and then the morning came, and she had to go down to her aunt. She ate her breakfast almost in silence, having resolved that she would tell her story the moment breakfast was over. She had, over night, and while she was in bed, studiously endeavoured not to con any mode of telling it. Up to the moment at which she rose her happiness was, if possible, to be untroubled. But while she dressed herself, she endeavoured to arrange her plans. She at last came to the conclusion that she could do it best without any plan.

As soon as Aunt Sarah had finished her breakfast, and just as she was about to proceed, according to her morning custom, down-stairs to the kitchen, Mary spoke. "Aunt Sarah, I have something to tell you. I may as well bring it out at once. I am engaged to marry Walter Marrable." Aunt Sarah immediately let fall the sugar-tongs, and stood speechless. "Dear aunt, do not look as if you were displeased. Say a kind word to me. I am sure you do not think that I have intended to deceive you."

"No; I do not think that," said Aunt Sarah.

"And is that all?"

"I am very much surprised. It was yesterday that you told me, when I hinted at this, that he was no more to you than a cousin,—or a brother."

"And so I thought; indeed I did. But when he told me how it was with him, I knew at once that I had only one answer to give. No other answer was possible. I love him better than anyone else in all the world. I feel that I can promise to be his wife without the least reserve or fear. I don't know why it should be so; but it is. I know I am right in this." Aunt Sarah still stood silent, meditating. "Don't you think I was right, feeling as I do, to tell him so? I had before become certain, quite, quite certain that it was impossible to give any other answer but one to Mr. Gilmore. Dearest aunt, do speak to me."

"I do not know what you will have to live upon."

"It is settled, you know, that he will save four or five thousand pounds out of his money, and I have got twelve hundred. It is not much, but it will be just something. Of course he will remain in the army, and I shall be a soldier's wife. I shall think nothing of going out to India, if he wishes it; but I don't think he means that. Dear Aunt Sarah, do say one word of congratulation."

Aunt Sarah did not know how to congratulate her niece. It seemed to her that any congratulation must be false and hypocritical. To her thinking, it would be a most unfitting match. It seemed to her that such an engagement had been most foolish. She was astonished at Mary's weakness, and was indignant with Walter Marrable. As regarded Mary, though she had twice uttered a word or two, intended as a caution, yet she had never thought it possible that a girl so steady in her ordinary demeanour, so utterly averse to all flirtation, so little given to the weakness of feminine susceptibility, would fall at once into such a quagmire of indiscreet love-troubles. The caution had been intended, rather in regard to outward appearances, and perhaps with the view of preventing the possibility of some slight heart-scratches, than with the idea that danger of this nature was to be dreaded. As Mr. Gilmore was there as an acknowledged suitor,—a suitor, as to whose ultimate success Aunt Sarah had her strong opinions,—it would be well those cousinly-brotherly associations and confidences should not become so close as to create possible embarrassment. Such had been the nature of Aunt Sarah's caution; and now,—in the course of a week or two,—when the young people were in truth still strangers to each other,—when Mr. Gilmore was still waiting for his answer,—Mary came to her, and told her that the engagement was a thing completed! How could she utter a word of congratulation?

"You mean, then, to say that you disapprove of it?" said Mary, almost sternly.

"I cannot say that I think it wise."

"I am not speaking of wisdom. Of course, Mr. Gilmore is very much richer, and all that."

"You know, Mary, that I would not counsel you to marry a man because he was rich."

"That is what you mean when you tell me I am not wise. I tried it,—with all the power of thought and calculation that I could give to it, and I found that I could not marry Mr. Gilmore."

"I am not speaking about that now."

"You mean that Walter is so poor, that he never should be allowed to marry."

"I don't care twopence about Walter."

"But I do, Aunt Sarah. I care more about him than all the world beside. I had to think for him."

"You did not take much time to think."

"Hardly a minute—and yet it was sufficient." Then she paused, waiting for her aunt; but it seemed that her aunt had nothing further to say. "Well," continued Mary, "if it must be so, it must. If you cannot wish me joy—"

"Dearest, you know well enough that I wish you all happiness."

"This is my happiness." It seemed to the bewildered old lady that the whole nature of the girl was altered. Mary was speaking now as might have spoken some enthusiastic young female who had at last succeeded in obtaining for herself the possession,—more or less permanent,—of a young man, after having fed her imagination on novels for the last five years; whereas Mary Lowther had hitherto, in all moods of her life, been completely opposite to such feminine ways and doings. "Very well," continued Mary; "we will say nothing more about it at present. I am greatly grieved that I have incurred your displeasure; but I cannot wish it otherwise."

"I have said nothing of displeasure."

"Walter is to be up after lunch, and I will only ask that he may not be received with black looks. If it must be visited as a sin, let it be visited on me."

"Mary, that is unkind and ungenerous."

"If you knew, Aunt Sarah, how I have longed during the night for your kind voice,—for your sympathy and approval!"

Aunt Sarah paused again for a moment, and then went down to her domestic duties without another word.

In the afternoon Walter came, but Aunt Sarah did not see him. When Mary went to her the old lady declared that, for the present, it would be better so. "I do not know what to say to him at present. I must think of it, and speak to his uncle, and try to find out what had best be done."

She was sitting as she said this up in her own room, without even a book in her hand; in very truth, passing an hour in an endeavour to decide what, in the present emergency, she ought to say or do. Mary stooped over her and kissed her, and the aunt returned her niece's caresses.

"Do not let you and me quarrel, at any rate," said Miss Marrable. "Who else is there that I care for? Whose happiness is anything to me except yours?"

"Then come to him, and tell him that he also shall be dear to you."

"No; at any rate, not now. Of course you can marry, Mary, without any sanction from me. I do not pretend that you owe to me that obedience which would be due to a mother. But I cannot say,—at least, not yet,—that such sanction as I have to give can be given to this engagement. I have a dread that it will come to no good. It grieves me. I do not forbid you to receive him; but for the present it would be better that I should not see him."

"What is her objection?" demanded Walter, with grave indignation.

"She thinks we shall be poor."

"Shall we ask her for anything? Of course we shall be poor. For the present there will be but £300 a year, or thereabouts, beyond my professional income. A few years back, if so much had been secured, friends would have thought that everything necessary had been done. If you are afraid, Mary—"

"You know I am not afraid."

"What is it to her, then? Of course we shall be poor,—very poor. But we can live."

There did come upon Mary Lowther a feeling that Walter spoke of the necessity of a comfortable income in a manner very different from that in which he had of late been discussing the same subject ever since she had known him. He had declared that it was impossible that he should exist in England as a bachelor on his professional income, and yet surely he would be poorer as a married man with that £300 a year added to it, than he would have been without it, and also without a wife. But what girl that loves a man can be angry with him for such imprudence and such inconsistency? She had already told him that she would be ready, if it were necessary, to go with him to India. She had said so before she went up to her aunt's room. He had replied that he hoped no such sacrifice would be demanded from her. "There can be no sacrifice on my part," she had replied, "unless I am required to give up you." Of course he had taken her in his arms and kissed her. There are moments in one's life in which not to be imprudent, not to be utterly, childishly forgetful of all worldly wisdom, would be to be brutal, inhuman, and devilish. "Had he told Parson John?" she asked.

"Oh, yes!"

"And what does he say?"

"Just nothing. He raised his eyebrows, and suggested 'that I had changed my ideas of life.' 'So I have,' I said. 'All right!' he replied. 'I hope that Block and Curling won't have made any mistake about the £5000.' That was all he said. No doubt he thinks we're two fools; but then one's folly won't embarrass him."

"Nor will it embarrass Aunt Sarah," said Mary.

"But there is this difference. If we come to grief, Parson John will eat his dinner without the slightest interference with his appetite from our misfortunes; but Aunt Sarah would suffer on your account."

"She would, certainly," said Mary.

"But we will not come to grief. At any rate, darling, we cannot consent to be made wise by the prospect of her possible sorrows on our behalf."

It was agreed that on that afternoon Mary should write both to Mr. Gilmore and to Janet Fenwick. She offered to keep her letters, and show them, when written, to her lover; but he declared that he would prefer not to see them. "It is enough for me that I triumph," he said, as he left her. When he had gone, she at once told her aunt that she would write the letters, and bring that to Mr. Gilmore to be read by her when they were finished.

"I would postpone it for awhile, if I were you," said Aunt Sarah.

But Mary declared that any such delay would be unfair to Mr. Gilmore. She did write the letters before dinner, and they were as follows:—

> My dear Mr. Gilmore,
>
> When last you came down to the Vicarage to see me I promised you, as you may perhaps remember, that if it should come to pass that I should engage myself to any other man, I would at once let you know that it was so. I little thought then that I should so soon be called upon to keep my promise. I will not pretend that the writing of this letter is not very painful to me; but I know that it is my duty to write it, and to put an end to a suspense which you have been good enough to feel on my account. You have, I think, heard the name of my cousin, Captain Walter Marrable, who returned from India two or three months ago. I found him staying here with his uncle, the clergyman, and now I am engaged to be his wife.
>
> Perhaps it would be better that I should say nothing more than this, and that I should leave myself and my character and name to your future kindness,—or unkindness,—without any attempt to win the former or to decry the latter; but you have been to me ever so good and noble that I cannot bring myself to be so cold and short. I have always felt that your preference for me has been a great honour to me. I have appreciated your esteem most highly, and have valued your approbation more than I have been able to say. If it could be possible that I should in future have your friendship, I should value it more than that of any other person. God bless you, Mr. Gilmore. I shall always hope that you may be happy, and I shall hear with delight any tidings which may seem to show that you are so.
>
> Pray believe that I am
> Your most sincere friend,

Mary Lowther.

I have thought it best to tell Janet Fenwick what I have done.

Loring, Thursday.

Dearest Janet,

I wonder what you will say to my news? But you must not scold me. Pray do not scold me. It could never, never have been as you wanted. I have engaged myself to marry my cousin, Captain Walter Marrable, who is a nephew of Sir Gregory Marrable, and a son of Colonel Marrable. We shall be very poor, having not more than £300 a-year above his pay as a captain; but if he had nothing, I think I should do the same. Do you remember how I used to doubt whether I should ever have that sort of love for a man for which I used to envy you? I don't envy you any longer, and I don't regard Mr. Fenwick as being nearly so divine as I used to do. I have a Jupiter of my own now, and need envy no woman the reality of her love.

I have written to Mr. Gilmore by the same post as will take this, and have just told him the bare truth. What else could I tell him? I have said something horribly stilted about esteem and friendship, which I would have left out, only that my letter seemed to be heartless without it. He has been to me as good as a man could be; but was it my fault that I could not love him? If you knew how I tried,—how I tried to make believe to myself that I loved him; how I tried to teach myself that that sort of very chill approbation was the nearest approach to love that I could ever reach; and how I did this because you bade me;—if you could understand all this, then you would not scold me. And I did almost believe that it was so. But now—! Oh, dear! how would it have been if I had engaged myself to Mr. Gilmore, and that then Walter Marrable had come to me! I get sick when I think how near I was to saying that I would love a man whom I never could have loved.

Of course I used to ask myself what I should do with myself. I suppose every woman living has to ask and to answer that question. I used to try to think that it would be well not to think of the outer crust of myself. What did it matter whether things were soft to me or not? I could do my duty. And as this man was good, and a gentleman, and endowed with high qualities and appropriate tastes, why should he not have the wife he wanted? I thought that I could pretend to love him, till, after some fashion, I should love him; but as I think of it now, all this seems to be so horrid! I know now what to do with myself. To be his from head to foot! To feel that nothing done for him would be mean or distasteful! To stand at a washtub and wash his clothes, if it were wanted. Oh, Janet, I used to dread the time in which he would have to put his arm round me and kiss me! I cannot tell you what I feel now about that other he.

I know well how provoked you will be,—and it will all come of love for me; but you cannot but own that I am right. If you have any justice in you, write to me and tell me that I am right.

Only that Mr. Gilmore is your great friend, and that, therefore, just at first, Walter will not be your friend, I would tell you more about him,—how handsome he is, how manly, and how clever. And then his voice is like the music of the spheres. You won't feel like being his friend at first, but you must look forward to his being your friend; you must love him—as I do Mr. Fenwick; and you must tell Mr. Fenwick that he must open his heart for the man who is to be my husband. Alas, alas! I fear it will be long before I can go to Bullhampton. How I do wish that he would find some nice wife to suit him!

Good bye, dearest Janet. If you are really good, you will write me a sweet, kind, loving letter, wishing me joy. You must know all. Aunt Sarah has refused to congratulate me, because the income is so small. Nevertheless, we have not quarrelled. But the income will be nothing to you, and I do look forward to a kind word. When everything is settled, of course I will tell you.

Your most affectionate friend,

MARY LOWTHER.

The former letter of the two was shown to Miss Marrable. That lady was of opinion that it should not be sent; but would not say that, if to be sent, it could be altered for the better.

CHAPTER XXI.

WHAT PARSON JOHN THINKS ABOUT IT.

On that same Thursday, the Thursday on which Mary Lowther wrote her two despatches to Bullhampton, Miss Marrable sent a note down to Parson John, requesting that she might have an interview with him. If he were at home and disengaged, she would go down to him that evening, or he might, if he pleased, come to her. The former she thought would be preferable. Parson John assented, and very soon after dinner the private brougham came round from the Dragon, and conveyed Miss Marrable down to the rectory at Lowtown.

"I am going down to Parson John," said she to Mary. "I think it best to speak to him about the engagement."

Mary received the information with a nod of her head that was intended to be gracious, and Aunt Sarah proceeded on her way. She found her cousin alone in his study, and immediately opened the subject which had brought her down the hill. "Walter, I believe, has told you about this engagement, Mr. Marrable."

"Never was so astonished in my life! He told me last night. I had begun to think that he was getting very fond of her, but I didn't suppose it would come to this."

"Don't you think it very imprudent?"

"Of course it's imprudent, Sarah. It don't require any thinking to be aware of that. It's downright stupid;—two cousins with nothing a year between them, when no doubt each of them might do very well. They're well-born, and well-looking, and clever, and all that. It's absurd, and I don't suppose it will ever come to anything."

"Did you tell Walter what you thought?"

"Why should I tell him? He knows what I think without my telling him; and he wouldn't care a pinch of snuff for my opinion. I tell you because you ask me."

"But ought not something to be done to prevent it?"

"What can we do? I might tell him that I wouldn't have him here any more, but I shouldn't like to do that. Perhaps she'll do your bidding."

"I fear not, Mr. Marrable."

"Then you may be quite sure he won't do mine. He'll go away and forget her. That'll be the end of it. It'll be as good as a year gone out of her life, and she'll lose this other lover of hers at—what's the name of the place? It's a pity, but that's what she'll have to go through."

"Is he so light as that?" asked Aunt Sarah, shocked.

"He's about the same as other men, I take it; and she'll be the same as other girls. They like to have their bit of fun now, and there'd be no great harm,—only such fun costs the lady so plaguy dear. As for their being married, I don't think Walter will ever be such a fool as that."

There was something in this that was quite terrible to Aunt Sarah. Her Mary Lowther was to be treated in this way;—to be played with as a plaything, and then to be turned off when the time for playing came to an end! And this little game was to be played for Walter Marrable's delectation, though the result of it would be the ruin of Mary's prospects in life!

"I think," said she, "that if I believed him to be so base as that, I would send him out of the house."

"He does not mean to be base at all. He's just like the rest of 'em," said Parson John.

Aunt Sarah used every argument in her power to show that something should be done; but all to no purpose. She thought that if Sir Gregory were brought to interfere, that perhaps might have an effect; but the old clergyman laughed at this. What did Captain Walter Marrable, who had been in the army all his life, and who had no special favour to expect from his uncle, care about Sir Gregory? Head of the family, indeed! What was the head of the family to him? If a girl would be a fool, the girl must take the result of her folly. That was Parson John's doctrine,—that and a confirmed assurance that this engagement, such as it was, would lead to nothing. He was really very sorry for Mary, in whose praise he said ever so many good-natured things; but she had not been the first fool, and she would not be the last. It was not his business, and he could do no good by interfering. At last, however, he did promise that he would himself speak to Walter. Nothing would come of it, but, as his cousin asked him, he would speak to his nephew.

He waited for four-and-twenty hours before he spoke, and during that time was subject to none of those terrors which were now making Miss Marrable's life a burden to her. In his opinion it was almost a pity that a young fellow like Walter should be interrupted in his amusement. According to his view of life, very much wisdom was not expected from ladies, young or old. They, for the most part, had their bread found for them; and were not required to do anything, whether they were rich or poor. Let them be ever so poor, the disgrace of poverty did not fall upon them as it did upon men. But then, if they would run their heads into trouble, trouble came harder upon them than on men; and for that they had nobody to blame but themselves. Of course it was a very nice thing to be in love. Verses and pretty speeches and easy-spoken romance were pleasant enough in their way. Parson John had no doubt tried them himself in early life, and had found how far they were efficacious for his own happiness. But young women were so apt to want too much of the excitement! A young man at Bullhampton was not enough without another young man at Loring. That, we fear, was the mode in which Parson John looked at the subject,—which mode of looking at it, had he ever ventured to explain it to Mary Lowther, would have brought down upon his head from that young woman an amount of indignant scorn which would have been very disagreeable to Parson John. But then he was a great deal too wise to open his mind on such a subject to Mary Lowther.

"I think, sir, I'd better go up and see Curling again next week," said the Captain.

"I dare say. Is anything not going right?"

"I suppose I shall get the money, but I shall like to know when. I am very anxious, of course, to fix a day for my marriage."

"I should not be over quick about that, if I were you," said Parson John.

"Why not? Situated as I am, I must be quick. I must make up my mind at any rate where we're to live."

"You'll go back to your regiment, I suppose, next month?"

"Yes, sir. I shall go back to my regiment next month, unless we may make up our minds to go out to India."

"What, you and Mary?"

"Yes, I and Mary."

"As man and wife?" said Parson John, with a smile.

"How else should we go?"

"Well, no. If she goes with you, she must go as Mrs. Captain Marrable, of course. But if I were you, I would not think of anything so horrible."

"It would be horrible," said Walter Marrable.

"I should think it would. India may be very well when a man is quite young, and if he can keep himself from beer and wine; but to go back there at your time of life with a wife, and to look forward to a dozen children there, must be an unpleasant prospect, I should say."

Walter Marrable sat silent and black.

"I should give up all idea of India," continued his uncle.

"What the deuce is a man to do?" asked the Captain.

The parson shrugged his shoulders.

"I'll tell you what I've been thinking of," said the Captain. "If I could get a farm of four or five hundred acres—"

"A farm!" exclaimed the parson.

"Why not a farm? I know that a man can do nothing with a farm unless he has capital. He should have £10 or £12 an acre for his land, I suppose. I should have that and some trifle of an income besides if I sold out. I suppose my uncle would let me have a farm under him?"

"He'd see you—further first."

"Why shouldn't I do as well with a farm as another?"

"Why not turn shoemaker? Because you have not learned the business. Farmer, indeed! You'd never get the farm, and if you did, you would not keep it for three years. You've been in the army too long to be fit for anything else, Walter."

Captain Marrable looked black and angry at being so counselled; but he believed what was said to him, and had no answer to make to it.

"You must stick to the army," continued the old man; "and if you'll take my advice, you'll do so without the impediment of a wife."

"That's quite out of the question."

"Why is it out of the question?"

"How can you ask me, Uncle John? Would you have me go back from an engagement after I have made it?"

"I would have you go back from anything that was silly."

"And tell a girl, after I have asked her to be my wife, that I don't want to have anything more to do with her?"

"I should not tell her that; but I should make her understand, both for her own sake and for mine, that we had been too fast, and that the sooner we gave up our folly the better for both of us. You can't marry her, that's the truth of it."

"You'll see if I can't."

"If you choose to wait ten years, you may."

"I won't wait ten months, nor, if I can have my own way, ten weeks." What a pity that Mary could not have heard him. "Half the fellows in the army are married without anything beyond their pay; and I'm to be told that we can't get along with £300 a year? At any rate, we'll try."

"Marry in haste, and repent at leisure," said Uncle John.

"According to the doctrines that are going now-a-days," said the Captain, "it will be held soon that a gentleman can't marry unless he has got £3000 a year. It is the most heartless, damnable teaching that ever came up. It spoils the men, and makes women, when they do marry, expect ever so many things that they ought never to want."

"And you mean to teach them better, Walter?"

"I mean to act for myself, and not be frightened out of doing what I think right, because the world says this and that."

As he so spoke, the angry Captain got up to leave the room.

"All the same," rejoined the parson, firing the last shot; "I'd think twice about it, if I were you, before I married Mary Lowther."

"He's more of an ass, and twice as headstrong as I thought him," said Parson John to Miss Marrable the next day; "but still I don't think it will come to anything. As far as I can observe, three of these engagements are broken off for one that goes on. And when he comes to look at things he'll get tired of it. He's going up to London next week, and I shan't press him to come back. If he does come I can't help it. If I were you, I wouldn't ask him up the hill, and I should tell Miss Mary a bit of my mind pretty plainly."

Hitherto, as far as words went, Aunt Sarah had told very little of her mind to Mary Lowther on the subject of her engagement, but she had spoken as yet no word of congratulation; and Mary knew that the manner in which she proposed to bestow herself was not received with favour by any of her relatives at Loring.

CHAPTER XXII.

WHAT THE FENWICKS THOUGHT ABOUT IT.

Bullhampton unfortunately was at the end of the postman's walk, and as the man came all the way from Lavington, letters were seldom received much before eleven o'clock. Now this was a most pernicious arrangement, in respect to which Mr. Fenwick carried on a perpetual feud with the Post-office authorities, having put forward a great postal doctrine that letters ought to be rained from heaven on to everybody's breakfast-table exactly as the hot water is brought in for tea. He, being an energetic man, carried on a long and angry correspondence with the authorities aforesaid; but the old man from Lavington continued to toddle into the village just at eleven o'clock. It was acknowledged that ten was his time; but, as he argued with himself, ten and eleven were pretty much of a muchness. The consequence of this was, that Mary Lowther's letters to Mrs. Fenwick had been read by her two or three hours before she had an opportunity of speaking on the subject to her husband. At last, however, he returned, and she flew at him with the letter in her hand. "Frank," she said, "Frank, what do you think has happened?"

"The Bank of England must have stopped, from the look of your face."

"I wish it had, with all my heart, sooner than this. Mary has gone and engaged herself to her cousin, Walter Marrable."

"Mary Lowther!"

"Yes; Mary Lowther! Our Mary! And from what I remember hearing about him, he is anything but nice."

"He had a lot of money left to him the other day."

"It can't have been much, because Mary owns that they will be very poor. Here is her letter. I am so unhappy about it. Don't you remember hearing about that Colonel Marrable who was in a horrible scrape about somebody's wife?"

"You shouldn't judge the son from the father."

"They've been in the army together, and they're both alike. I hate the army. They are almost always no better than they should be."

"That's true, my dear, certainly of all services, unless it be the army of martyrs; and there may be a doubt on the subject even as to them. May I read it?"

"Oh, yes; she has been half ashamed of herself every word she has written. I know her so well. To think that Mary Lowther should have engaged herself to any man after two days' acquaintance!"

Mr. Fenwick read the letter through attentively, and then handed it back.

"It's a good letter," he said.

"You mean that it's well written?"

"I mean that it's true. There are no touches put in to make effect. She does love the one man, and she doesn't love the other. All I can say is, that I'm very sorry for it. It will drive Gilmore out of the place."

"Do you mean it?"

"I do, indeed. I never knew a man to be at the same time so strong and so weak in such a matter. One would say that the intensity of his affection would be the best pledge of his future happiness if he were to marry the girl; but seeing that he is not to marry her, one cannot but feel that a man shouldn't stake his happiness on a thing beyond his reach."

"You think it is all up, then;—that she really will marry this man?"

"What else can I think?"

"These things do go off sometimes. There can't be much money, because, you see, old Miss Marrable opposes the whole thing on account of there not being income enough. She is anything but rich herself, and is the last person of all the world to make a fuss about money. If it could be broken off—."

"If I understand Mary Lowther," said Mr. Fenwick, "she is not the woman to have her match broken off for her by any person. Of course I know nothing about the man; but if he is firm, she'll be as firm."

"And then she has written to Mr. Gilmore," said Mrs. Fenwick.

"It's all up with Harry as far as this goes," said Mr. Fenwick.

The Vicar had another matter of moment to discuss with his wife. Sam Brattle, after having remained hard at work at the mill for nearly a fortnight,—so hard at work as to induce his father to declare that he'd bet a guinea there wasn't a man in the three parishes who could come nigh his Sam for a right down day's work;—after all this, Sam had disappeared, had been gone for two days, and was said by the constable to have been seen at night on the Devizes side, from whence was supposed to come the Grinder, and all manner of Grinder's iniquities. Up to this time no further arrest had been made on account of Mr. Trumbull's murder, nor had any trace been found of the Grinder, or of that other man who had been his companion. The leading policeman, who still had charge of the case, expressed himself as sure that the old woman at Pycroft Common knew nothing of her son's whereabouts; but he had always declared, and still continued to declare, that Sam Brattle could tell them the whole story of the murder if he pleased, and there had been a certain amount of watching kept on the young man, much to his own disgust, and to that of his father. Sam had sworn aloud in the village—so much aloud that he had shown his determination to be heard by all men—that he would go to America, and see whether anyone would dare to stop him. He had been told of his bail, and had replied that he would demand to be relieved of his bail;—that his bail was illegal, and that he would have it all tried in a court of law. Mr. Fenwick had heard of this, and had replied that as far as he was concerned he was not in the least afraid. He believed that the bail was illegal, and he believed also that Sam would stay where he was. But now Sam was gone, and the Bullhampton constable was clearly of opinion that he had gone to join the Grinder. "At any rate, he's off somewhere," said Mr. Fenwick, "and his mother doesn't know where he's gone. Old Brattle, of course, won't say a word."

"And will it hurt you?"

"Not unless they get hold of those other fellows and require Sam's appearance. I don't doubt but that he'd turn up in that case."

"Then it does not signify?"

"It signifies for him. I've an idea that I know where he's gone, and I think I shall go after him."

"Is it far, Frank?"

"Something short of Australia, luckily."

"Oh, Frank!"

"I'll tell you the truth. It's my belief that Carry Brattle is living about twenty miles off, and that he's gone to see his sister."

"Carry Brattle!—down here!"

"I don't know it, and I don't want to hear it mentioned; but I fancy it is so. At any rate, I shall go and see."

"Poor, dear, bright little Carry! But how is she living, Frank?"

"She's not one of the army of martyrs, you may be sure. I daresay she's no better than she should be."

"You'll tell me if you see her?"

"Oh, yes."

"Shall I send her anything?"

"The only thing to send her is money. If she is in want, I'll relieve her,—with a very sparing hand."

"Will you bring her back,—here?"

"Ah, who can say? I should tell her mother, and I suppose we should have to ask her father to receive her. I know what his answer will be."

"He'll refuse to see her."

"No doubt. Then we should have to put our heads together, and the chances are that the poor girl will be off in the meantime,—back to London and the Devil. It is not easy to set crooked things straight."

In spite, however, of this interruption, Mary Lowther and her engagement to Captain Marrable was the subject of greatest interest at the Vicarage that day and through the night. Mrs. Fenwick half expected that Gilmore would come down in the evening; but the Vicar declared that his friend would be unwilling to show himself after the blow which he would have received. They knew that he would know that they had received the news, and that therefore he could not come either to tell it, or with the intention of asking questions without telling it. If he came at all, he must come like a beaten cur with his tail between his legs. And then there arose the question whether it would not be better that Mary's letter should be answered before Mr. Gilmore was seen. Mrs. Fenwick, whose fingers were itching for pen and paper, declared at last that she would write at once; and did write, as follows, before she went to bed:—

The Vicarage, Friday.

DEAREST MARY,

> I do not know how to answer your letter. You tell me to write pleasantly, and to congratulate you; but how is one to do that so utterly in opposition to one's own interests and wishes? Oh dear, oh dear! how I do so wish you had stayed at Bullhampton! I know you will be angry with me for saying so, but how can I say anything else? I cannot picture you to myself going about from town to town and living in country-quarters. And as I never saw Captain Marrable, to the best of my belief, I cannot interest myself about him as I do about one whom I know and love and esteem. I feel that this is not a nice way of writing to you, and indeed I would be nice if I could. Of course I wish you to be full of joy;—of course I wish with all my heart that you may be happy if you marry your cousin; but the

> thing has come so suddenly that we cannot bring ourselves to look upon it as a reality.

"You should speak for yourself, Janet," said Mr. Fenwick, when he came to this part of the letter. He did not, however, require that the sentence should be altered.

> You talk so much of doing what is right! Nobody has ever doubted that you were right both in morals and sentiment. The only regret has been that such a course should be right, and that the other thing should be wrong. Poor man! we have not seen him yet, nor heard from him. Frank says that he will take it very badly. I suppose that men do always get over that kind of thing much quicker than women do. Many women never can get over it at all; and Harry Gilmore, though there is so little about him that seems to be soft, is in this respect more like a woman than a man. Had he been otherwise, and had only half cared for you, and asked you to be his wife as though your taking him were a thing he didn't much care about, and were quite a matter of course, I believe you would have been up at Hampton Privets this moment, instead of going soldiering with a captain.
>
> Frank bids me send you his kindest love and his best wishes for your happiness. Those are his very words, and they seem to be kinder than mine. Of course you have my love and my best wishes; but I do not know how to write as though I could rejoice with you. Your husband will always be dear to us, whoever he may be, if he be good to you. At present I feel very, very angry with Captain Marrable; as though I wish he had had his head blown off in battle. However, if he is to be the happy man, I will open my heart to him;— that is, if he be good.
>
> I know this is not nice, but I cannot make it nicer now. God bless you, dearest Mary.
>
> Ever your most affectionate friend,
>
> JANET FENWICK.

The letter was not posted till the hour for despatch on the following day; but, up to that hour, nothing had been seen at the Vicarage of Mr. Gilmore.

CHAPTER XXIII.

WHAT MR. GILMORE THOUGHT ABOUT IT.

Mr. Gilmore was standing on the doorsteps of his own house when Mary's letter was brought to him. It was a modest-sized country gentleman's residence, built of variegated uneven stones, black and grey and white, which seemed to be chiefly flint; but the corners and settings of the windows and of the door-ways, and the chimneys, were of brick. There was something sombre about it, and many perhaps might call it dull of aspect; but it was substantial, comfortable, and unassuming. It was entered by broad stone steps, with iron balustrades curving outwards as they descended, and there was an open area round the house, showing that the offices were in the basement. In these days it was a quiet house enough, as Mr. Gilmore was a man not much given to the loudness of bachelor parties. He entertained his neighbours at dinner perhaps once a month, and occasionally had a few guests staying with him. His uncle, the prebendary from Salisbury, was often with him, and occasionally a brother who was in the army. For the present, however, he was much more inclined, when in want of society, to walk off to the Vicarage than to provide it for himself at home. When Mary's letter was handed to him with his "Times" and other correspondence, he looked, as everybody does, at the address, and at once knew that it came from Mary Lowther. He had never hitherto received a letter from her, but yet he knew her handwriting well. Without waiting a moment, he turned upon his heel, and went back into his house, and through the hall to the library. When there, he first opened three other letters, two from tradesmen in London, and one from his uncle, offering to come to him on the next Monday. Then he opened the "Times," and cut it, and put it down on the table. Mary's letter meanwhile was in his hand, and anyone standing by might have thought that he had forgotten it. But he had not forgotten it, nor was it out of his mind for a moment. While looking at the other letters, while cutting the paper, while attempting, as he did, to read the news, he was suffering under the dread of the blow that was coming. He was there for twenty minutes before he dared to break the envelope; and though during the whole of that time he pretended to deceive himself by some employment, he knew that he was simply postponing an evil thing that was coming to him. At last he cut the letter open, and stood for some moments looking for courage to read it. He did read it, and then sat himself down in his chair, telling himself that the thing was over, and that he would bear it as a man. He took up his newspaper, and began to study it. It was the time of the year when newspapers are not very interesting, but he made a rush at the leading articles, and went through two of them. Then he turned over to the police reports. He sat there for an hour, and read hard during the whole time. Then he got up and shook himself, and knew that he was a crippled man, with every function out of order, disabled in every limb. He walked from the library into the hall, and thence to the dining-room, and so, backwards and forwards, for a quarter of an hour. At last he could walk no longer, and, closing the door of the library behind him, he threw himself on a sofa and cried like a woman.

What was it that he wanted, and why did he want it? Were there not other women whom the world would say were as good? Was it ever known that a man had died, or become irretrievably broken and destroyed by disappointed love? Was it not one of those things that a man should shake off from him, and have done with it? He asked himself these, and many such-like questions, and tried to philosophise with himself on the matter. Had he no will of his own, by which he might conquer this enemy? No; he had no will of his own, and the enemy would not be conquered. He had to tell himself that he was so poor a thing that he could not stand up against the evil that had fallen on him.

He walked out round his shrubberies and paddocks, and tried to take an interest in the bullocks and the horses. He knew that if every bullock and horse about the place had been struck dead it would not enhance his misery. He had not had much hope before, but now he would have seen the house of Hampton Privets in flames, just for the chance that had been his yesterday. It was not only that he wanted her, or that he regretted the absence of some recognised joys which she would have brought to him; but that the final decision on her part seemed to take from him all vitality, all power of enjoyment, all that inward elasticity which is necessary for an interest in worldly affairs.

He had as yet hardly thought of anything but himself;—had hardly observed the name of his successful rival, or paid any attention to aught but the fact that she had told him that it was all over. He had not attempted to make up his mind whether anything could still be done, whether he might yet have a chance, whether it would be well for him to quarrel with the man; whether he should be indignant with her, or remonstrate once again in regard to her cruelty. He had thought only of the blow, and of his inability to support it. Would it not be best that he should go forth, and blow out his brains, and have done with it?

He did not look at the letter again till he had returned to the library. Then he took it from his pocket, and read it very carefully. Yes, she had been quick about it. Why; how long had it been since she had left their parish? It was still October, and she had been there just before the murder—only the other day! Captain Walter Marrable! No; he didn't think he had ever heard of him. Some fellow with a moustache and a military strut—just the man that he had always hated; one of a class which, with nothing real to recommend it, is always interfering with the happiness of everybody. It was in some such light as this that Mr. Gilmore at present regarded Captain Marrable. How could such a man make a woman happy,—a fellow who probably had no house nor home in which to make her comfortable? Staying with his uncle the clergyman! Poor Gilmore expressed a wish that the uncle the clergyman had been choked before he had entertained such a guest. Then he read the concluding sentence of poor Mary's letter, in which she expressed a hope that they might be friends. Was there ever such cold-blooded trash? Friends indeed! What sort of friendship could there be between two persons, one of whom had made the other so wretched,—so dead as was he at present!

For some half-hour he tried to comfort himself with an idea that he could get hold of Captain Marrable and maul him; that it would be a thing permissible for him, a magistrate, to go forth with a whip and flog the man, and then perhaps shoot him, because the man had been fortunate in love where he had been unfortunate. But he knew the world in which he lived too well to allow himself long to think that this could really be done. It might be that it would be a better world were such revenge practicable in it; but, as he well knew, it was not practicable now, and if Mary Lowther chose to give herself to this accursed Captain, he could not help it. There was nothing that he could do but to go away and chafe at his suffering in some part of the world in which nobody would know that he was chafing.

When the evening came, and he found that his solitude was terribly oppressive to him, he thought that he would go down to the Vicarage. He had been told by that false one that her tidings had been sent to her friend. He took his hat and sauntered out across the fields, and did walk as far as the churchyard gate close to poor Mr. Trumbull's farm, the very spot on which he had last seen Mary Lowther; but when he was there he could not endure to go through to the Vicarage. There is something mean to a man in the want of success in love. If a man lose a venture of money he can tell his friend; or if he be unsuccessful in trying for a seat in parliament; or be thrown out of a run in the hunting-field; or even if he be blackballed for a club; but a man can hardly bring himself to tell his dearest comrade that his Mary has preferred another man to himself. This wretched fact the Fenwicks already knew as to poor Gilmore's Mary; and yet, though he had come down there, hoping for some comfort, he did not dare to face them. He went back all alone, and tumbled and tossed and fretted through the miserable night.

And the next morning was as bad. He hung about the place till about four, utterly crushed by his burden. It was a Saturday, and when the postman called no letter had yet been even written in answer to his uncle's proposition. He was moping about the grounds, with his hands in his pockets, thinking of this, when suddenly Mrs. Fenwick appeared in the path before him. There had been another consultation that morning between herself and her husband, and this visit was the result of it. He dashed at the matter immediately.

"You have come," he said, "to talk to me about Mary Lowther."

"I have come to say a word, if I can, to comfort you. Frank bade me to come."

"I have come to say a word, if I can, to comfort you."

"There isn't any comfort," he replied.

"We knew that it would be hard to bear, my friend," she said, putting her hand within his arm; "but there is comfort."

"There can be none for me. I had set my heart upon it so that I cannot forget it."

"I know you had, and so had we. Of course there will be sorrow, but it will wear off." He shook his head without speaking. "God is too good," she continued, "to let such troubles remain with us long."

"You think, then," he said, "that there is no chance?"

What could she say to him? How, under the circumstances of Mary's engagement, could she encourage his love for her friend?

"I know that there is none," he continued. "I feel, Mrs. Fenwick, that I do not know what to do with myself or how to hold myself. Of course it is nonsense to talk about dying, but I do feel as though if I didn't die I should go crazy. I can't settle my mind to a single thing."

"It is fresh with you yet, Harry," she said. She had never called him Harry before, though her husband did so always, and now she used the name in sheer tenderness.

"I don't know why such a thing should be different with me than with other people," he said; "only perhaps I am weaker. But I've known from the very first that I have staked everything upon her. I have never questioned to myself that I was going for all or nothing. I have seen it before me all along, and now it has come. Oh, Mrs. Fenwick, if God would strike me dead this moment, it would be a mercy!" And then he threw himself on the ground at her feet. He was not there a moment before he was up again. "If you knew how I despise myself for all this, how I hate myself!"

She would not leave him, but stayed there till he consented to come down with her to the Vicarage. He should dine there, and Frank should walk back with him at night. As to that question of Mr. Chamberlaine's visit, respecting which Mrs. Fenwick did not feel herself competent to give advice herself, it should become matter of debate between them and Frank, and then a man and horse could be sent to Salisbury on Sunday morning. As he walked down to the Vicarage with that pretty woman at his elbow, things perhaps were a little better with him.

CHAPTER XXIV.

THE REV. HENRY FITZACKERLEY CHAMBERLAINE.

It was decided that evening at the Vicarage that it would be better for all parties that the reverend uncle from Salisbury should be told to make his visit, and spend the next week at Hampton Privets; that is, that he should come on the Monday and stay till the Saturday. The letter was written down at the Vicarage, as Fenwick feared that it would never be written if the writing of it were left to the unassisted energy of the Squire. The letter was written, and the Vicar, who walked back to Hampton Privets with his friend, took care that it was given to a servant on that night.

On the Sunday nothing was seen of Mr. Gilmore. He did not come to church, nor would he dine at the Vicarage. He remained the whole day in his own house, pretending to write, trying to read, with accounts before him, with a magazine in his hand, even with a volume of sermons open on the table before him. But neither the accounts, nor the magazines, nor the sermons, could arrest his attention for a moment. He had staked everything on obtaining a certain object, and that object was now beyond his reach. Men fail often in other things, in the pursuit of honour, fortune, or power, and when they fail they can begin again. There was no beginning again for him. When Mary Lowther should have married this captain, she would be a thing lost to him for ever;—and was she not as bad as married to this man already? He could do nothing to stop her marriage.

Early in the afternoon of Monday the Rev. Henry Fitzackerley Chamberlaine reached Hampton Privets. He came with his own carriage and a pair of post-horses, as befitted a prebendary of the good old times. Not that Mr. Chamberlaine was a very old man, but that it suited his tastes and tone of mind to adhere to the well-bred ceremonies of life, so many of which went out of fashion when railroads came in. Mr. Chamberlaine was a gentleman of about fifty-five years of age, unmarried, possessed of a comfortable private independence, the incumbent of a living in the fens of Cambridgeshire, which he never visited,—his health forbidding him to do so,—on which subject there had been a considerable amount of correspondence between him and a certain right rev. prelate, in which the prebendary had so far got the better in the argument as not to be disturbed in his manner of life; and he was, as has been before said, the owner of a stall in Salisbury Cathedral. His lines had certainly fallen to him in very pleasant places. As to that living in the fens, there was not much to prick his conscience, as he gave up the parsonage house and two-thirds of the income to his curate, expending the other third on local charities. Perhaps the argument which had most weight in silencing the bishop was contained in a short postscript to one of his letters. "By-the-by," said the postscript, "perhaps I ought to inform your lordship that I have never drawn a penny of income out of Hardbedloe since I ceased to live there." "It's a bishop's living," said the happy holder of it, "to one or two clerical friends, and Dr. —— thinks the patronage would be better in his hands than in mine. I disagree with him, and he'll have to write a great many letters before he succeeds." But his stall was worth £800 a year and a house, and Mr. Chamberlaine, in regard to his money matters, was quite in clover.

He was a very handsome man, about six feet high, with large light grey eyes, a straight nose, and a well cut chin. His lips were thin, but his teeth were perfect,—only that they had been supplied by a dentist. His grey hair encircled his head, coming round upon his forehead in little wavy curls, in a manner that had conquered the hearts of spinsters by the dozen in the cathedral. It was whispered, indeed, that married ladies would sometimes succumb, and rave about the beauty, and the dignity, and the white hands, and the deep rolling voice of the Rev. Henry Fitzackerley Chamberlaine. Indeed, his voice was very fine when it would be heard from the far-off end of the choir during the communion service, altogether trumping the exertion of the other second-rate clergyman who would be associated with him at the altar. And he had, too, great gifts of preaching, which he would exercise once a week during thirteen weeks of the year. He never exceeded twenty-five minutes; every word was audible throughout the whole choir, and there was a grace about it that was better than any doctrine. When he was to be heard the cathedral was always full, and he was perhaps justified in regarding himself as one of the ecclesiastical stars of the day. Many applications were made to him to preach here and there, but he always refused. Stories were told of how he had declined to preach before the Queen at St. James's, averring that if Her Majesty would please to visit Salisbury, every accommodation should be provided for her. As to preaching at Whitehall, Westminster, and St. Paul's, it was not doubted that he had over and over again declared that his appointed place was in his own stall, and that he did not consider that he was called to holding forth in the market-place. He was usually abroad during the early autumn months, and would make sundry prolonged visits to friends; but his only home was his prebendal residence in the Close. It was not much of a house to look at from the outside, being built with the plainest possible construction of brick; but within it was very pleasant. All that curtains, and carpets, and armchairs, and books, and ornaments could do, had been done lavishly, and the cellar was known to be the best in the city. He always used post-horses, but he had his own carriage. He never talked very much, but when he did speak people listened to him. His appetite was excellent, but he was a feeder not very easy to please; it was understood well by the ladies of Salisbury that if Mr. Chamberlaine was expected to dinner, something special must be done in the way of entertainment. He was always exceedingly well dressed. What he did with his hours nobody knew, but he was supposed to be a man well educated at all points. That he was such a judge of all works of art, that not another like him was to be found in Wiltshire, nobody doubted. It was considered that he was almost as big as the bishop, and not a soul in Salisbury would have thought of comparing the dean to him. But the dean had seven children, and Mr. Chamberlaine was quite unencumbered.

Henry Gilmore was a little afraid of his uncle, but would always declare that he was not so. "If he chooses to come over here he is welcome," the nephew would say; "but he must live just as I do." Nevertheless, though there was but little left of the '47 Lafitte in the cellar of Hampton Privets, a bottle was always brought up when Mr. Chamberlaine was there, and Mrs. Bunker, the cook, did not pretend but that she was in a state of dismay from the hour of his coming to that of his going. And yet, Mrs. Bunker and the other servants liked him to be there. His presence honoured the Privets. Even the boy who blacked his boots felt that he was blacking the boots of a great man. It was acknowledged throughout the household that the Squire having such an uncle, was more of a Squire than he would have been without him. The clergyman, being such as he was, was greater than the country gentleman. And yet Mr. Chamberlaine was only a prebendary, was the son of a country clergyman who had happened to marry a wife with money, and had absolutely never done anything useful in the whole course of his life. It is often very curious to trace the sources of greatness. With Mr. Chamberlaine, I think it came from the whiteness of his hands, and from a certain knack he had of looking as though he could say a great deal, though it suited him better to be silent, and say nothing. Of outside deportment, no doubt, he was a master.

Mr. Fenwick always declared that he was very fond of Mr. Chamberlaine, and greatly admired him. "He is the most perfect philosopher I ever met," Fenwick would say, "and has gone to the very centre depth of contemplation. In another ten years he will be the great Akinetos. He will eat and drink, and listen, and be at ease, and desire nothing. As it is, no man that I know disturbs other people so little." On the other hand, Mr. Chamberlaine did not profess any great admiration for Mr. Fenwick, who he designated as one of the smart "windbag tribe, clever, no doubt, and perhaps conscientious, but shallow and perhaps a little conceited." The Squire, who was not clever and not conceited, understood them both, and much preferred his friend the Vicar to his uncle the prebendary.

Gilmore had once consulted his uncle,—once in an evil moment, as he now felt,—whether it would not be well for him to marry Miss Lowther. The uncle had expressed himself as very adverse to the marriage, and would now, on this occasion, be sure to ask some question about it. When the great man arrived the Squire was out, still wandering round among the bullocks and sheep; but the evening after dinner would be very long. On the following day Mr. and Mrs. Fenwick, with Mr. and Mrs. Greenthorne, were to dine at the Privets. If this first evening were only through, Gilmore thought that he could get some comfort, even from his uncle. As he came near the house, he went into the yard, and saw the Prebendary's grand carriage, which was being washed. No; as far as the groom knew, Mr. Chamberlaine had not gone out; but was in the house then. So Gilmore entered, and found his uncle in the library.

His first questions were about the murder. "You did catch one man, and let him go?" said the Prebendary.

"Yes; a tenant of mine; but there was no evidence against him. He was not the man."

"I would not have let him go," said Mr. Chamberlaine.

"You would not have kept a man that was innocent?" said Gilmore.

"I would not have let the young man go."

"But the law would not support us in detaining him."

"Nevertheless, I would not have let him go," said Mr. Chamberlaine. "I heard all about it."

"From whom did you hear?"

"From Lord Trowbridge. I certainly would not have let him go." It appeared, however, that Lord Trowbridge's opinion had been given to the Prebendary prior to that fatal meeting which had taken place in the house of the murdered man.

The uncle drank his claret in silence on this evening. He said nothing, at least, about Mary Lowther.

"I don't know where you got it, Harry, but that is not a bad glass of wine."

"We think there's none better in the country, sir," said Harry.

"I should be very sorry to commit myself so far; but it is a good glass of wine. By the bye, I hope your chef has learned to make a cup of coffee since I was here in the spring. I think we will try it now." The coffee was brought, and the Prebendary shook his head,—the least shake in the world,—and smiled blandly.

"Coffee is the very devil in the country," said Harry Gilmore, who did not dare to say that the mixture was good in opposition to his uncle's opinion.

After the coffee, which was served in the library, the two men sat silent together for half an hour, and Gilmore was endeavouring to think what it was that made his uncle come to Bullhampton. At last, before he had arrived at any decision on this subject, there came first a little nod, then a start and a sweet smile, then another nod and a start without the smile, and, after that, a soft murmuring of a musical snore, which gradually increased in deepness till it became evident that the Prebendary was extremely happy. Then it occurred to Gilmore that perhaps Mr. Chamberlaine might become tired of going to sleep in his own house, and that he had come to the Privets, as he could not do so with comfortable self-satisfaction in the houses of indifferent friends. For the benefit of such a change it might perhaps be worth the great man's while to undergo the penalty of a bad cup of coffee.

And could not he, too, go to sleep,—he, Gilmore? Could he not fall asleep,—not only for a few moments on such an occasion as this,—but altogether, after the Akinetos fashion, as explained by his friend Fenwick? Could he not become an immoveable one, as was this divine uncle of his? No Mary Lowther had ever disturbed that man's happiness. A good dinner, a pretty ring, an easy chair, a china tea-cup, might all be procured with certainty, as long as money lasted. Here was a man before him superbly comfortable, absolutely happy, with no greater suffering than what might come to him from a chance cup of bad coffee, while he, Harry Gilmore himself, was as miserable a devil as might be found between the four seas, because a certain young woman wouldn't come to him and take half of all that he owned! If there were any curative philosophy to be found, why could not he find it? The world might say that the philosophy was a low philosophy; but what did that matter, if it would take away out of his breast that horrid load which was more than he could bear? He declared to himself that he would sell his heart with all its privileges for half-a-farthing, if he could find anybody to take it with all its burden. Here, then, was a man who had no burden. He was snoring with almost harmonious cadence,—slowly, discreetly,—one might say, artistically, quite like a gentleman; and the man who so snored could not but be happy. "Oh, d——n it!" said Gilmore, in a private whisper, getting up and leaving the room; but there was more of envy than of anger in the exclamation.

"Ah! you've been out," said Mr. Chamberlaine, when his nephew returned.

"Been to look at the horses made up."

"I never can see the use of that; but I believe a great many men do it. I suppose it's an excuse for smoking generally." Now, Mr. Chamberlaine did not smoke.

"Well; I did light my pipe."

"There's not the slightest necessity for telling me so, Harry. Let us see if Mrs. Bunker's tea is better than her coffee." Then the bell was rung, and Mr. Chamberlaine desired that he might have a cup of black tea, not strong, but made with a good deal of tea, and poured out rapidly, without much decoction. "If it be strong and harsh I can't sleep a wink," he said. The tea was brought, and sipped very leisurely. There was then a word or two said about certain German baths from which Mr. Chamberlaine had just returned; and Mr. Gilmore began to believe that he should not be asked to say anything about Mary Lowther that night.

But the Fates were not so kind. The Prebendary had arisen with the intention of retiring for the night, and was already standing before the fire, with his bedroom candle in his hand, when something,—the happiness probably of his own position in life, which allowed him to seek the blessings of an undivided couch,—brought to his memory the fact that his nephew had spoken to him about some young woman, some young woman who had possessed not even the merit of a dowry.

"By the bye," said he, "what has become of that flame of yours, Harry?" Harry Gilmore became black and glum. He did not like to hear Mary spoken of as a flame. He was standing at this moment with his back to his uncle, and so remained, without answering him. "Do you mean to say that you did not ask her, after all?" asked the uncle. "If there be any scrape, Harry, you had better let me hear it."

"I don't know what you call a scrape," said Harry. "She's not going to marry me."

"Thank God, my boy!" Gilmore turned round, but his uncle did not probably see his face. "I can assure you," continued Mr. Chamberlaine, "that the idea made me quite uncomfortable. I set some inquiries on foot, and she was not the sort of girl that you should marry."

"By G——," said Gilmore, "I'd give every acre I have in the world, and every shilling, and every friend, and twenty years of my life, if I could only be allowed at this moment to think it possible that she would ever marry me!"

"Good heavens!" said Mr. Chamberlaine. While he was saying it, Harry Gilmore walked off, and did not show himself to his uncle again that night.

CHAPTER XXV.

CARRY BRATTLE.

On the day after the dinner-party at Hampton Privets Mr. Fenwick made his little excursion out in the direction towards Devizes, of which he had spoken to his wife. The dinner had gone off very quietly, and there was considerable improvement in the coffee. There was some gentle sparring between the two clergymen, if that can be called sparring in which all the active pugnacity was on one side. Mr. Fenwick endeavoured to entrap Mr. Chamberlaine into arguments, but the Prebendary escaped with a degree of skill,—without the shame of sullen refusal,—that excited the admiration of Mr. Fenwick's wife. "After all, he is a clever man," she said, as she went home, "or he could never slip about as he does, like an eel, and that with so very little motion."

On the next morning the Vicar started alone in his gig. He had at first said that he would take with him a nondescript boy, who was partly groom, partly gardener, and partly shoeblack, and who consequently did half the work of the house; but at last he decided that he would go alone. "Peter is very silent, and most meritoriously uninterested in everything," he said to his wife. "He wouldn't tell much, but even he might tell something." So he got himself into his gig, and drove off alone. He took the Devizes road, and passed through Lavington without asking a question; but when he was half way between that place and Devizes, he stopped his horse at a lane that led away to the right. He had been on the road before, but he did not know that lane. He waited awhile till an old woman whom he saw coming to him, reached him, and asked her whether the lane would take him across to the Marlborough Road. The old woman knew nothing of the Marlborough Road, and looked as though she had never heard of Marlborough. Then he asked the way to Pycroft Common. Yes; the lane would take him to Pycroft Common. Would it take him to the Bald-faced Stag? The old woman said it would take him to Rump End Corner, "but she didn't know nowt o' t'other place." He took the lane, however, and without much difficulty made his way to the Bald-faced Stag,—which, in the days of the glory of that branch of the Western Road, used to supply beer to at least a dozen coaches a-day, but which now, alas! could slake no drowth but that of the rural aborigines. At the Bald-faced Stag, however, he found that he could get a feed of corn, and here he put up his horse,—and saw the corn eaten.

Pycroft Common was a mile from him, and to Pycroft Common he walked. He took the road towards Marlborough for half a mile, and then broke off across the open ground to the left. There was no difficulty in finding this place, and now it was his object to discover the cottage of Mrs. Burrows without asking the neighbours for her by name. He had obtained a certain amount of information, and thought that he could act on it. He walked on to the middle of the common, and looked for his points of bearing. There was the beer-house, and there was the lane that led away to Pewsey, and there were the two brick cottages standing together. Mrs. Burrows lived in the little white cottage just behind. He walked straight up to the door, between the sunflowers and the rose-bush, and, pausing for a few moments to think whether or no he would enter the cottage unannounced, knocked at the door. A policeman would have entered without doing so,—and so would a poacher knock over a hare on its form; but whatever creature a gentleman or a sportsman be hunting, he will always give it a chance. He rapped, and immediately heard that there were sounds within. He rapped again, and in about a minute was told to enter. Then he opened the door, and found but one person within. It was a young woman, and he stood for a moment looking at her before he spoke.

"Carry Brattle," he said, "I am glad that I have found you."

"Laws, Mr. Fenwick!"

"Carry, I am so glad to see you;"—and then he put out his hand to her.

"Oh, Mr. Fenwick, I ain't fit for the likes of you to touch," she said. But as his hand was still stretched out she put her own into it, and he held it in his grasp for a few seconds. She was a poor, sickly-looking thing now, but there were the remains of great beauty in the face,—or rather, the presence of beauty, but of beauty obscured by flushes of riotous living and periods of want, by ill-health, harsh usage, and, worst of all, by the sharp agonies of an intermittent conscience. It was a pale, gentle face, on which there were still streaks of pink,—a soft, laughing face it had been once, and still there was a gleam of light in the eyes that told of past merriment, and almost promised mirth to come, if only some great evil might be cured. Her long flaxen curls still hung down her face, but they were larger, and, as Fenwick thought, more tawdry than of yore; and her cheeks were thin, and her eyes were hollow; and then there had come across her mouth that look of boldness which the use of bad, sharp words, half-wicked and half-witty, will always give. She was dressed decently, and was sitting in a low chair, with a torn, disreputable-looking old novel in her hand. Fenwick knew that the book had been taken up on the spur of the moment, as there had certainly been someone there when he had knocked at the door.

And yet, though vice had laid its heavy hand upon her, the glory and the brightness, and the sweet outward flavour of innocence, had not altogether departed from her. Though her mouth was bold, her eyes were soft and womanly, and she looked up into the face of the clergyman with a gentle, tamed, beseeching gaze, which softened and won his heart at once. Not that his heart had ever been hard against her. Perhaps it was a fault with him that he never hardened his heart against a sinner, unless the sin implied pretence and falsehood. At this moment, remembering the little Carry Brattle of old, who had sometimes been so sweetly obedient, and sometimes so wilful, under his hands, whom he had petted, and caressed, and scolded, and loved,—whom he had loved undoubtedly in part because she had been so pretty,—whom he had hoped that he might live to marry to some good farmer, in whose kitchen he would ever be welcome, and whose children he would christen;—remembering all this, he would now, at this moment, have taken her in his arms and embraced her, if he dared, showing her that he did not account her to be vile, begging her to become more good, and planning some course for her future life.

"I have come across from Bullhampton, Carry, to find you," he said.

"It's a poor place you're come to, Mr. Fenwick. I suppose the police told you of my being here?"

"I had heard of it. Tell me, Carry, what do you know of Sam?"

"Of Sam?"

"Yes—of Sam. Don't tell me an untruth. You need tell me nothing, you know, unless you like. I don't come to ask as having any authority, only as a friend of his, and of yours."

She paused a moment before she replied. "Sam hasn't done any harm to nobody," she said.

"I don't say he has. I only want to know where he is. You can understand, Carry, that it would be best that he should be at home."

She paused again, and then she blurted out her answer. "He went out o' that back door, Mr. Fenwick, when you came in at t'other." The Vicar immediately went to the back door, but Sam, of course, was not to be seen.

"Why should he be hiding if he has done no harm?" said the Vicar.

"He thought it was one of them police. They do be coming here a'most every day, till one's heart faints at seeing 'em. I'd go away if I'd e'er a place to go to."

"Have you no place at home, Carry?"

"No, sir; no place."

This was so true that he couldn't tell himself why he had asked the question. She certainly had no place at home till her father's heart should be changed towards her.

"Carry," said he, speaking very slowly, "they tell me that you are married. Is that true?"

She made him no answer.

"I wish you would tell me, if you can. The state of a married woman is honest at any rate, let her husband be who he may."

"My state is not honest."

"You are not married, then?"

"No, sir."

He hardly knew how to go on with this interrogation, or to ask questions about her past and present life, without expressing a degree of censure which, at any rate for the present, he wished to repress.

"You are living here, I believe, with old Mrs. Burrows?" he said.

"Yes, sir."

"I was told that you were married to her son."

"They told you untrue, sir. I know nothing of her son, except just to have see'd him."

"Is that true, Carry?"

"It is true. It wasn't he at all."

"Who was it, Carry?"

"Not her son;—but what does it signify? He's gone away, and I shall see un no more. He wasn't no good, Mr. Fenwick, and if you please we won't talk about un."

"He was not your husband?"

"No, Mr. Fenwick; I never had a husband, nor never shall, I suppose. What man would take the likes of me? I have just got one thing to do, and that's all."

"What thing is that, Carry?"

"To die and have done with it," she said, bursting out into loud sobs. "What's the use o' living? Nobody 'll see me, or speak to me. Ain't I just so bad that they'd hang me if they knew how to catch me?"

"What do you mean, girl?" said Fenwick, thinking for the moment that from her words she, too, might have had some part in the murder.

"Ain't the police coming here after me a'most every day? And when they hauls about the place, and me too, what can I say to 'em? I have got that low that a'most everybody can say what they please to me. And where can I go out o' this? I don't want to be living here always with that old woman."

"Who is the old woman, Carry?"

"I suppose you knows, Mr. Fenwick?"

"Mrs. Burrows, is it?" She nodded her head. "She is the mother of the man they call the Grinder?" Again she nodded her head. "It is he whom they accuse of the murder?" Yet again she nodded her head. "There was another man?" She nodded it again. "And they say that there was a third," he said,— "your brother Sam."

"Then they lie," she shouted, jumping up from her seat. "They lie like devils. They are devils; and they'll go, oh, down into the fiery furnace for ever and ever." In spite of the tragedy of the moment, Mr. Fenwick could not help joining this terribly earnest threat and the Marquis of Trowbridge together in his imagination. "Sam hadn't no more to do with it than you had, Mr. Fenwick."

"I don't believe he had," said Mr. Fenwick.

"Yes; because you're good, and kind, and don't think ill of poor folk when they're a bit down. But as for them, they're devils."

"I did not come here, however, to talk about the murder, Carry. If I thought you knew who did it, I shouldn't ask you. That is business for the police, not for me. I came here partly to look after Sam. He ought to be at home. Why has he left his home and his work while his name is thus in people's mouths?"

"It ain't for me to answer for him, Mr. Fenwick. Let 'em say what they will, they can't make the white of his eye black. But as for me, I ain't no business to speak of nobody. How should I know why he comes and why he goes? If I said as how he'd come to see his sister, it wouldn't sound true, would it, sir, she being what she is?"

He got up and went to the front door, and opened it, and looked about him. But he was looking for nothing. His eyes were full of tears, and he didn't care to wipe the drops away in her presence.

"Carry," he said, coming back to her, "it wasn't all for him that I came."

"Carry," he said, coming back to her, "it wasn't all for him that I came."

"For who else, then?"

"Do you remember how we loved you when you were young, Carry? Do you remember my wife, and how you used to come and play with the children on the lawn? Do you remember, Carry, where you sat in church, and the singing, and what trouble we had together with the chaunts? There are one or two at Bullhampton who never will forget it?"

"Nobody loves me now," she said, talking at him over her shoulder, which was turned to him.

He thought for a moment that he would tell her that the Lord loved her; but there was something human at his heart, something perhaps too human, which made him feel that were he down low upon the ground, some love that was nearer to him, some love that was more easily intelligible, which had been more palpably felt, would in his frailty and his wickedness be of more immediate avail to him than the love even of the Lord God.

"Why should you think that, Carry?"

"Because I am bad."

"If we were to love only the good, we should love very few. I love you, Carry, truly. My wife loves you dearly."

"Does she?" said the girl, breaking into low sobs. "No, she don't. I know she don't. The likes of her couldn't love the likes of me. She wouldn't speak to me. She wouldn't touch me."

"Come and try, Carry."

"Father would kill me," she said.

"Your father is full of wrath, no doubt. You have done that which must make a father angry."

"Oh, Mr. Fenwick, I wouldn't dare to stand before his eye for a minute. The sound of his voice would kill me straight. How could I go back?"

"It isn't easy to make crooked things straight, Carry, but we may try; and they do become straighter if one tries in earnest. Will you answer me one question more?"

"Anything about myself, Mr. Fenwick?"

"Are you living in sin now, Carry?" She sat silent, not that she would not answer him, but that she did not comprehend the extent of the meaning of his question. "If it be so, and if you will not abandon it, no honest person can love you. You must change yourself, and then you will be loved."

"I have got the money which he gave me, if you mean that," she said.

Then he asked no further questions about herself, but reverted to the subject of her brother. Could she bring him in to say a few words to his old friend? But she declared that he was gone, and that she did not know whither; that he might probably return this very day to the mill, having told her that it was his purpose to do so soon. When he expressed a hope that Sam held no consort with those bad men who had murdered and robbed Mr. Trumbull, she answered him with such naïve assurance that any such consorting was out of the question, that he became at once convinced that the murderers were far away, and that she knew that such was the case. As far as he could learn from her, Sam had really been over to Pycroft with the view of seeing his sister, taking probably a holiday of a day or two on the way. Then he again reverted to herself, having as he thought obtained a favourable answer to that vital question which he had asked her.

"Have you nothing to ask of your mother?" he said.

"Sam has told me of her and of Fan."

"And would you not care to see her?"

"Care, Mr. Fenwick! Wouldn't I give my eyes to see her? But how can I see her? And what could she say to me? Father 'd kill her if she spoke to me. Sometimes I think I'll walk there all the day, and so get there at night, and just look about the old place, only I know I'd drown myself in the millstream. I wish I had. I wish it was done. I've seed an old poem in which they thought much of a poor girl after she was drowned, though nobody wouldn't think nothing at all about her before."

"Don't drown yourself, Carry, and I'll care for you. Keep your hands clean. You know what I mean, and I will not rest till I find some spot for your weary feet. Will you promise me?" She made him no answer. "I will not ask you for a spoken promise, but make it yourself, Carry, and ask God to help you to keep it. Do you say your prayers, Carry?"

"Never a prayer, sir."

"But you don't forget them. You can begin again. And now I must ask for a promise. If I send for you will you come?"

"What—to Bull'ompton?"

"Wheresoever I may send for you? Do you think that I would have you harmed?"

"Perhaps it'd be—for a prison; or to live along with a lot of others. Oh, Mr. Fenwick, I could not stand that."

He did not dare to proceed any further lest he should be tempted to make promises which he himself could not perform; but she did give him an assurance before he went that if she left her present abode within a month, she would let him know whither she was going.

He went to the Bald-faced Stag and got his gig; and on his way home, just as he was leaving the village of Lavington, he overtook Sam Brattle. He stopped and spoke to the lad, asking him whether he was returning home, and offering him a seat in the gig. Sam declined the seat, but said that he was going straight to the mill.

"It is very hard to make crooked things straight," said Mr. Fenwick to himself as he drove up to his own hall-door.

CHAPTER XXVI.

THE TURNOVER CORRESPONDENCE.

It is hoped that the reader will remember that the Marquis of Trowbridge was subjected to very great insolence from Mr. Fenwick during the discussion which took place in poor old farmer Trumbull's parlour respecting the murder. Our friend, the Vicar, did not content himself with personal invective, but made allusion to the Marquis's daughters. The Marquis, as he was driven home in his carriage, came to sundry conclusions about Mr. Fenwick. That the man was an infidel he had now no matter of doubt whatever; and if an infidel, then also a hypocrite, and a liar, and a traitor, and a thief. Was he not robbing the parish of the tithes, and all the while entrapping the souls of men and women? Was it not to be expected that with such a pastor there should be such as Sam Brattle and Carry Brattle in the parish? It was true that as yet this full blown iniquity had spread itself only among the comparatively small number of tenants belonging to the objectionable "person," who unfortunately owned a small number of acres in his lordship's parish;—but his lordship's tenant had been murdered! And with such a pastor in the parish, and such an objectionable person, owning acres, to back the pastor, might it not be expected that all his tenants would be murdered? Many applications had already been made to the Marquis for the Church Farm; but as it happened that the applicant whom the Marquis intended to favour, had declared that he did not wish to live in the house because of the murder, the Marquis felt himself justified in concluding that if everything about the parish were not changed very shortly, no decent person would be found willing to live in any of his houses. And now, when they had been talking of murderers, and worse than murderers, as the Marquis said to himself, shaking his head with horror in the carriage as he thought of such iniquity, this infidel clergyman had dared to allude to his lordship's daughters! Such a man had no right even to think of women so exalted. The existence of the Ladies Stowte must no doubt be known to such men, and among themselves probably some allusion in the way of faint guesses might be made as to their modes of life, as men guess at kings and queens, and even at gods and goddesses. But to have an illustration, and a very base illustration, drawn from his own daughters in his own presence, made with the object of confuting himself,—this was more than the Marquis could endure. He could not horsewhip Mr. Fenwick; nor could he send out his retainers to do so; but, thank God, there was a bishop! He did not quite see his way, but he thought that Mr. Fenwick might be made at least to leave that parish. "Turn my daughters out of my house, because—oh, oh!" He almost put his fist through the carriage window in the energy of his action as he thought of it.

As it happened, the Marquis of Trowbridge had never sat in the House of Commons, but he had a son who sat there now. Lord St. George was member for another county in which Lord Trowbridge had an estate, and was a man of the world. His father admired him much, and trusted him a good deal, but still had an idea that his son hardly estimated in the proper light the position in the world which he was called to fill. Lord St. George was now at home at the Castle, and in the course of that evening the father, as a matter of course, consulted the son. He considered that it would be his duty to write to the bishop, but he would like to hear St. George's idea on the subject. He began, of course, by saying that he did not doubt but that St. George would agree with him.

"I shouldn't make any fuss about it," said the son.

"What! pass it over?"

"Yes; I think so."

"Do you understand the kind of allusion that was made to your sisters?"

"It won't hurt them, my lord; and people make allusion to everything now-a-days. The bishop can't do anything. For aught you know he and Fenwick may be bosom friends."

"The bishop, St. George, is a most right-thinking man."

"No doubt. The bishops, I believe, are all right-thinking men, and it is well for them that they are so very seldom called on to go beyond thinking. No doubt he'll think that this fellow was indiscreet; but he can't go beyond thinking. You'll only be raising a blister for yourself."

"Raising a what?"

"A blister, my lord. The longer I live the more convinced I become that a man shouldn't keep his own sores open."

There was something in the tone of his son's conversation which pained the Marquis much; but his son was known to be a wise and prudent man, and one who was rising in the political world. The Marquis sighed, and shook his head, and murmured something as to the duty which lay upon the great to bear the troubles incident to their greatness;—by which he meant that sores and blisters should be kept open, if the exigencies of rank so required. But he ended the discussion at last by declaring that he would rest upon the matter for forty-eight hours. Unfortunately before those forty-eight hours were over Lord St. George had gone from Turnover Castle, and the Marquis was left to his own lights. In the meantime, the father and son and one or two friends, had been shooting over at Bullhampton; so that no further steps of warfare had been taken when Mr. and Mrs. Fenwick met the Marquis on the pathway.

On the following day his lordship sat in his own private room thinking of his grievance. He had thought of it and of little else for now nearly sixty hours. "Suggest to me to turn out my daughters! Heaven and earth! My daughters!" He was well aware that, though he and his son often differed, he could never so safely keep himself out of trouble as by following his son's advice. But surely this was a matter per se, standing altogether on its own bottom, very different from those ordinary details of life on which he and his son were wont to disagree. His daughters! The Ladies Sophie and Carolina Stowte! It had been suggested to him to turn them out of his house because— Oh! oh! The insult was so great that no human marquis could stand it. He longed to be writing a letter to the bishop. He was proud of his letters. Pen and paper were at hand, and he did write.

>RIGHT REV. AND DEAR LORD BISHOP,
>
>I think it right to represent to your lordship the conduct,— I believe I may be justified in saying the misconduct,—of the Reverend —— Fenwick, the vicar of Bullhampton.

He knew our friend's Christian name very well, but he did not choose to have it appear that his august memory had been laden with a thing so trifling.

>You may have heard that there has been a most horrid murder committed in the parish on one of my tenants; and that suspicion is rife that the murder was committed in part by a young man, the son of a miller who lives under a person who owns some land in the parish. The family is very bad, one of the daughters being, as I understand, a prostitute. The other day I thought it right to visit the parish with the view of preventing, if possible, the sojourn there among my people of these objectionable characters. When there I was encountered by Mr. Fenwick, not only in a most unchristian spirit, but in a bearing so little gentlemanlike, that I cannot describe it to you. He had obtruded himself into my presence, into one of my own houses, the very house of the murdered man, and there, when I was consulting with the person to whom I have alluded as to the expediency of ridding ourselves of these objectionable characters, he met me with ribaldry and personal insolence. When I tell your lordship that he made insinuations about

my own daughters, so gross that I cannot repeat them to you, I am sure that I need go no further. There were present at this meeting Mr. Puddleham, the Methodist minister, and Mr. Henry Gilmore, the landlord of the persons in question.

Your lordship has probably heard the character, in a religious point of view, of this gentleman. It is not for me to express an opinion of the motives which can induce such a one to retain his position as an incumbent of a parish. But I do believe that I have a right to ask from your lordship for some inquiry into the scene which I have attempted to describe, and to expect some protection for the future. I do not for a moment doubt that your lordship will do what is right in the matter.

I have the honour to be,
Right Reverend and dear Lord Bishop,
Your most obedient and faithful Servant,

TROWBRIDGE.

He read this over thrice, and became so much in love with the composition, that on the third reading he had not the slightest doubt as to the expediency of sending it. Nor had he much doubt but that the bishop would do something to Mr. Fenwick, which would make the parish too hot to hold that disgrace to the Church of England.

When Fenwick came home from Pycroft Common he found a letter from the bishop awaiting him. He had driven forty miles on that day, and was rather late for dinner. His wife, however, came upstairs with him in order that she might hear something of his story, and brought his letters with her. He did not open that from the bishop till he was half dressed, and then burst out into loud laughter as he read it.

"What is it, Frank?" asked his wife, through the open door of her own room.

"Here's such a game," said he. "Never mind; let's have dinner, and then you shall see it." The reader, however, may be quite sure that Mrs. Fenwick did not wait till dinner was served before she knew the nature of the game.

The bishop's letter to the Vicar was very short and very rational, and it was not that which made the Vicar laugh; but inside the bishop's letter was that from the Marquis. "My dear Mr. Fenwick," said the bishop,

after a good deal of consideration, I have determined to send you the enclosed. I do so because I have made it a rule never to receive an accusation against one of my clergy without sending it to the person accused. You will, of course, perceive that it alludes to some matter which lies outside of my control and right of inquiry; but perhaps you will allow me, as a friend, to suggest to you that it is always well for a parish clergyman to avoid controversy and quarrel with his neighbours; and that it is especially expedient that he should be on good terms with those who have influence in his parish. Perhaps you will forgive me if I add that a spirit of pugnacity, though no doubt it may lead to much that is good, has its bad tendencies if not watched closely.

Pray remember that Lord Trowbridge is a worthy man, doing his duty on the whole well; and that his position, though it be entitled to no veneration, is entitled to much respect. If you can tell me that you will feel no grudge against him for what has taken place, I shall be very happy.

You will observe that I have been careful that this letter shall have no official character.

Yours very faithfully,

&c., &c., &c.

The letter was answered that evening, but before the answer was written, the Marquis of Trowbridge was discussed between the husband and wife, not in complimentary terms. Mrs. Fenwick on the occasion was more pugnacious than her husband. She could not forgive the man who had hinted to the bishop that her husband held his living from unworthy motives, and that he was a bad clergyman.

"My dear girl," said Fenwick, "what can you expect from an ass but his ears?"

"I don't expect downright slander from such a man as the Marquis of Trowbridge, and if I were you I should tell the bishop so."

"I shall tell him nothing of the kind. I shall write about the Marquis with the kindliest feelings."

"But you don't feel kindly?"

"Yes, I do. The poor old idiot has nobody to keep him right, and does the best he can according to his lights. I have no doubt he thinks that I am everything that is horrid. I am not a bit angry with him, and would be as civil to him to-morrow as my nature would allow me, if he would only be civil to me."

Then he wrote his letter which will complete the correspondence, and which he dated for the following day:—

Bullhampton Vicarage, Oct. 23, 186—.

MY DEAR LORD BISHOP,

I return the Marquis's letter with many thanks. I can assure you that I take in proper spirit your little hints as to my pugnacity of disposition, and will endeavour to profit by them. My wife tells me that I am given to combativeness, and I have no doubt that she is right.

As to Lord Trowbridge, I can assure your lordship that I will not bear any malice against him, or even think ill of him because of his complaint. He and I probably differ in opinion about almost everything, and he is one of those who pity the condition of all who are so blinded as to differ from him. The next time that I am thrown into his company I shall act exactly as though no such letter had been written, and as if no such meeting had taken place as that which he describes.

I hope I may be allowed to assure your lordship, without any reference to my motives for keeping it, that I shall be very slow to give up a living in your lordship's diocese. As your letter to me is unofficial,—and I thank you heartily for sending it in such form,—I have ventured to reply in the same strain.

I am, my dear Lord Bishop,
Your very faithful servant,

FRANCIS FENWICK.

"There," said he, as he folded it, and handed it to his wife, "I shall never see the remainder of the series. I would give a shilling to know how the bishop gets out of it in writing to the Marquis, and half-a-crown to see the Marquis's rejoinder." The reader shall be troubled with neither, as he would hardly price them so high as did the Vicar. The bishop's letter really contained little beyond an assurance on his part that Mr. Fenwick had not meant anything wrong, and that the matter was one with which he, the bishop, had no concern; all which was worded with most complete episcopal courtesy. The rejoinder of the Marquis was long, elaborate, and very pompous. He did not exactly scold the bishop, but he expressed very plainly his opinion that the

Church of England was going to the dogs, because a bishop had not the power of utterly abolishing any clergyman who might be guilty of an offence against so distinguished a person as the Marquis of Trowbridge.

But what was to be done about Carry Brattle? Mrs. Fenwick, when she had expressed her anger against the Marquis, was quite ready to own that the matter of Carry's position was to them of much greater moment than the wrath of the peer. How were they to put out their hands and save that brand from the burning? Fenwick, in his ill-considered zeal, suggested that she might be brought to the Vicarage; but his wife at once knew that such a step would be dangerous in every way. How could she live, and what would she do? And what would the other servants think of it?

"Why would the other servants mind it?" asked Fenwick. But his wife on such a matter could have a way of her own, and that project was soon knocked on the head. No doubt her father's house was the proper place for her, but then her father was so dour a man.

"Upon my word," said the Vicar, "he is the only person in the world of whom I believe myself to be afraid. When I get at him I do not speak to him as I would to another; and of course he knows it."

Nevertheless, if anything was to be done for Carry Brattle, it seemed as though it must be done by her father's permission and assistance. "There can be no doubt that it is his duty," said Mrs. Fenwick.

"I will not say that as a certainty," said the husband. "There is a point at which, I presume, a father may be justified in disowning a child. The possession of such a power, no doubt, keeps others from going wrong. What one wants is that a father should be presumed to have the power; but that when the time comes, he should never use it. It is the comfortable doctrine which we are all of us teaching;—wrath, and abomination of the sinner, before the sin; pardon and love after it. If you were to run away from me, Janet—"

"Frank, do not dare to speak of anything so horrible."

"I should say now probably that were you to do so, I would never blast my eyes by looking at you again; but I know that I should run after you, and implore you to come back to me."

"You wouldn't do anything of the kind; and it isn't proper to talk about it; and I shall go to bed."

"It is very difficult to make crooked things straight," said the Vicar, as he walked about the room after his wife had left him. "I suppose she ought to go into a reformatory. But I know she wouldn't; and I shouldn't like to ask her after what she said."

It is probably the case that Mr. Fenwick would have been able to do his duty better, had some harsher feeling towards the sinner been mixed with his charity.

CHAPTER XXVII.

"I NEVER SHAMED NONE OF THEM."

"Something must be done about Carry Brattle at once." The Vicar felt that he had pledged himself to take some steps for her welfare, and it seemed to him, as he thought of the matter, that there were only two steps possible. He might intercede with her father, or he might use his influence to have her received into some house of correction, some retreat, in which she might be kept from evil and disciplined for good. He knew that the latter would be the safer plan, if it could be brought to bear; and it would certainly be the easier for himself. But he thought that he had almost pledged himself to the girl not to attempt it, and he felt sure that she would not accede to it. In his doubt he went up to his friend Gilmore, intending to obtain the light of his friend's wisdom. He found the Squire and the Prebendary together, and at once started his subject.

"You'll do no good, Mr. Fenwick," said Mr. Chamberlaine, after the two younger men had been discussing the matter for half an hour.

"Do you mean that I ought not to try to do any good?"

"I mean that such efforts never come to anything."

"All the unfortunate creatures in the world, then, should be left to go to destruction in their own way."

"It is useless, I think, to treat special cases in an exceptional manner. When such is done, it is done from enthusiasm, and enthusiasm is never useful."

"What ought a man to do, then, for the assistance of such fellow-creatures as this poor girl?" asked the Vicar.

"There are penitentiaries and reformatories, and it is well, no doubt, to subscribe to them," said the Prebendary. "The subject is so full of difficulty that one should not touch it rashly. Henry, where is the last Quarterly?"

"I never take it, sir."

"I ought to have remembered," said Mr. Chamberlaine, smiling blandly. Then he took up the Saturday Review, and endeavoured to content himself with that.

Gilmore and Fenwick walked down to the mill together, it being understood that the Squire was not to show himself there. Fenwick's difficult task, if it were to be done at all, must be done by himself alone. He must beard the lion in his den, and make the attack without any assistant. Gilmore had upon the whole been disposed to think that no such attack should be made. "He'll only turn upon you with violence, and no good will be done," said he. "He can't eat me," Fenwick had replied, acknowledging, however, that he approached the undertaking with fear and trembling. Before they were far from the house Gilmore had changed the conversation and fallen back upon his own sorrows. He had not answered Mary's letter, and now declared that he did not intend to do so. What could he say to her? He could not write and profess friendship; he could not offer her his congratulations; he could not belie his heart by affecting indifference. She had thrown him over, and now he knew it. Of what use would it be to write to her and tell her that she had made him miserable for ever? "I shall break up the house and get away," said he.

"Don't do that rashly, Harry. There can be no spot in the world in which you can be so useful as you are here."

"All my usefulness has been dragged out of me. I don't care about the place or about the people. I am ill already, and shall become worse. I think I will go abroad for four or five years. I've an idea I shall go to the States."

"You'll become tired of that, I should think."

"Of course I shall. Everything is tiresome to me. I don't think anything else can be so tiresome as my uncle, and yet I dread his leaving me,—when I shall be alone. I suppose if one was out among the Rocky Mountains, one wouldn't think so much about it."

"Atra Cura sits behind the horseman," said the Vicar. "I don't know that travelling will do it. One thing certainly will do it."

"And what is that?"

"Hard work. Some doctor told his patient that if he'd live on half-a-crown a day and earn it, he'd soon be well. I'm sure that the same prescription holds good for all maladies of the mind. You can't earn the half-crown a day, but you may work as hard as though you did."

"What shall I do?"

"Read, dig, shoot, look after the farm, and say your prayers. Don't allow yourself time for thinking."

"It's a fine philosophy," said Gilmore, "but I don't think any man ever made himself happy by it. I'll leave you now."

"I'd go and dig, if I were you," said the Vicar.

"Perhaps I will. Do you know, I've half an idea that I'll go to Loring."

"What good will that do?"

"I'll find out whether this man is a blackguard. I believe he is. My uncle knows something about his father, and says that a bigger scamp never lived."

"I don't see what good you can do, Harry," said the Vicar. And so they parted.

Fenwick was about half a mile from the mill when Gilmore left him, and he wished that it were a mile and a half. He knew well that an edict had gone forth at the mill that no one should speak to the old man about his daughter. With the mother the Vicar had often spoken of her lost child, and had learned from her how sad it was to her that she could never dare to mention Carry's name to her husband. He had cursed his child, and had sworn that she should never more have part in him or his. She had brought sorrow and shame upon him, and he had cut her off with a steady resolve that there should be no weak backsliding on his part. Those who knew him best declared that the miller would certainly keep his word, and hitherto no one had dared to speak of the lost one in her father's hearing. All this Mr. Fenwick knew, and he knew also that the man was one who could be very fierce in his anger. He had told his wife that old Brattle was the only man in the world before whom he would be afraid to speak his mind openly, and in so saying he had expressed a feeling that was very general throughout all Bullhampton. Mr. Puddleham was a very meddlesome man, and he had once ventured out to the mill to say a word, not indeed about Carry, but touching some youthful iniquity of which Sam was supposed to have been guilty. He never went near the mill again, but would shudder and lift up his hands and his eyes when the miller's name was mentioned. It was not that Brattle used rough language, or became violently angry when accosted; but there was a sullen sternness about the man, and a capability of asserting his own mastery and personal authority, which reduced those who attacked him to the condition of vanquished combatants, and repulsed them, so that they would retreat as beaten dogs. Mr. Fenwick, indeed, had always been well received at the mill. The women of the family loved him dearly, and took great comfort in his visits. From his first arrival in the parish he had been on intimate terms with them, though the old man had never once entered his church. Brattle himself would bear with him more kindly than he would with his own landlord, who might at any day have turned him out of his holding. But even Fenwick had been so answered more than once as to have been forced to retreat with that feeling of having his tail, like a cur, between his legs. "He can't eat me," he said to himself, as the low willows round the mill came in sight. When a man is reduced to that consolation, as many a man often is, he may be nearly sure that he will be eaten.

When he got over the stile into the lane close to the mill-door, he found that the mill was going. Gilmore had told him that it might probably be so, as he had heard that the repairs were nearly finished. Fenwick was sure that after so long a period of enforced idleness Brattle would be in the mill, but he went at first into the house and there found Mrs. Brattle and Fanny. Even with them he hardly felt himself to be at home, but after a while managed to ask a few questions about Sam. Sam had come back, and was now at work, but he had had some terribly hard words with his father. The old man had desired to know where his son had been. Sam had declined to tell, and had declared that if he was to be cross-questioned about his comings and goings he would leave the mill altogether. His father had told him that he had better go. Sam had not gone, but the two had been working on together since without interchanging a word. "I want to see him especially," said Mr. Fenwick.

"You mean Sam, sir?" asked the mother.

"No; his father. I will go out into the lane, and perhaps Fanny will ask him to come to me." Mrs. Brattle immediately became dismayed by a troop of fears, and looked up into his face with soft, supplicating, tearful eyes. So much of sorrow had come to her of late! "There is nothing wrong, Mrs. Brattle," he said.

"I thought perhaps you had heard something of Sam."

"Nothing but what has made me surer than ever that he had no part in what was done at Mr. Trumbull's farm."

"Thank God for that!" said the mother, taking him by the hand. Then Fanny went into the mill, and the Vicar followed her out of the house, on to the lane. He stood leaning against a tree till the old man came to him. He then shook the miller's hand, and made some remark about the mill. They had begun again that morning, the miller said. Sam had been off again, or they might have been at work on yesterday forenoon.

"Do not be angry with him; he has been on a good work," said the Vicar.

"Good or bad, I know nowt of it," said the miller.

"I know, and if you wish I will tell you; but there is another thing I must say first. Come a little way down the lane with me, Mr. Brattle."

The Vicar had assumed a tone which was almost one of rebuke,—not intending it, but falling into it from want of histrionic power in his attempt to be bold and solemn at the same time. The miller at once resented it. "Why should I come down the lane?" said he. "You're axing me to come out at a very busy moment, Muster Fenwick."

"Nothing can be so important as that which I have to say. For the love of God, Mr. Brattle,—for the love you bear your wife and children, endure with me for ten minutes." Then he paused, and walked on, and Mr. Brattle was still at his elbow. "My friend, I have seen your daughter."

"Which daughter?" said the miller, arresting his step.

"Your daughter Carry, Mr. Brattle." Then the old man turned round and would have hurried back to the mill without a word; but the Vicar held him by his coat. "If I have ever been a friend to you or yours listen to me now one minute."

"Do I come to your house and tell you of your sorrows and your shame? Let me go!"

"Mr. Brattle, if you will stretch forth your hand, you may save her. She is your own child—your flesh and blood. Think how easy it is for a poor girl to fall,—how great is the temptation and how quick, and how it comes without knowledge of the evil that is to follow! How small is the sin, and how terrible the punishment! Your friends, Mr. Brattle, have forgiven you worse sins than ever she has committed."

"I never shamed none of them," said he, struggling on his way back to the mill.

"It is that, then;—your own misfortune and not the girl's sin that would harden your heart against your own child? You will let her perish in the streets, not because she has fallen, but because she has hurt you in her fall! Is that to be a father? Is that to be a man? Mr. Brattle, think better of yourself, and dare to obey the instincts of your heart."

But by this time the miller had escaped, and was striding off in furious silence to the mill. The Vicar, oppressed by a sense of utter failure, feeling that his interference had been absolutely valueless, that the man's wrath and constancy were things altogether beyond his reach, stood where he had been left, hardly daring to return to the mill and say a word or two to the women there. But at last he did go back. He knew well that Brattle himself would not be seen in the house till his present mood was over. After any encounter of words he would go and work in silence for half a day, and would seldom or never refer again to what had taken place; he would never, so thought the Vicar, refer to the encounter which had just taken place; but he would remember it always, and it might be that he would never again speak in friendship to a man who had offended him so deeply.

After a moment's thought he determined to tell the wife, and informed her and Fanny that he had seen Carry over at Pycroft Common. The mother's questions as to what her child was doing, how she was living, whether she were ill or well, and, alas! whether she were happy or miserable, who cannot imagine?

"She is anything but happy, I fear," said Mr. Fenwick.

"My poor Carry!"

"I should not wish that she should be happy till she be brought back to the decencies of life. What shall we do to bring her back?"

"Would she come if she were let to come?" asked Fanny.

"I believe she would. I feel sure that she would."

"And what did he say, Mr. Fenwick?" asked the mother. The Vicar only shook his head. "He's very good; to me he's ever been good as gold. But, oh, Mr. Fenwick, he is so hard."

"He will not let you speak of her?"

"Never a word, Mr. Fenwick. He'd look at you, sir, so that the gleam of his eyes would fall on you like a blow. I wouldn't dare;—nor yet wouldn't Fanny, who dares more with him than any of us."

"If it'd serve her, I'd speak," said Fanny.

"But couldn't I see her, Mr. Fenwick? Couldn't you take me in the gig with you, sir? I'd slip out arter breakfast up the road, and he wouldn't be no wiser, at least till I war back again. He wouldn't ax no questions then, I'm thinking. Would he, Fan?"

"He'd ask at dinner; but if I said you were out for the day along with Mr. Fenwick, he wouldn't say any more, maybe. He'd know well enough where you was gone to."

Mr. Fenwick said that he would think of it, and let Fanny know on the following Sunday. He would not make a promise now, and at any rate he could not go before Sunday. He did not like to pledge himself suddenly to such an adventure, knowing that it would be best that he should first have his wife's ideas on the matter. Then he took his leave, and as he went out of the house he saw the miller standing at the door of the mill. He raised his hand and said, "Good-bye," but the miller quickly turned his back to him and retreated into his mill.

As he walked up to his house through the village he met Mr. Puddleham. "So Sam Brattle is off again, sir," said the minister.

"Off what, Mr. Puddleham?"

"Gone clean away. Out of the country."

"Who has told you that, Mr. Puddleham?"

"Isn't it true, sir? You ought to know, Mr. Fenwick, as you're one of the bailsmen."

"I've just been at the mill, and I didn't see him."

"I don't think you'll ever see him at the mill again, Mr. Fenwick; nor yet in Bullhampton, unless the police have to bring him here."

"As I was saying, I didn't see him at the mill, Mr. Puddleham, because I didn't go in; but he's working there at this moment, and has been all the day. He's all right, Mr. Puddleham. You go and have a few words with him, or with his father, and you'll find they're quite comfortable at the mill now."

"Constable Hicks told me that he was out of the country," said Mr. Puddleham, walking away in considerable disgust.

Mrs. Fenwick's opinion was, upon the whole, rather in favour of the second expedition to Pycroft Common, as she declared that the mother should at any rate be allowed to see her child. She indeed would not submit to the idea of the miller's indomitable powers. If she were Mrs. Brattle, she said, she'd pull the old man's ears, and make him give way.

"You go and try," said the Vicar.

On the Sunday morning following, Fanny was told that on Wednesday Mr. Fenwick would drive her mother over to Pycroft Common. He had no doubt, he said, but that Carry would still be found living with Mrs. Burrows. He explained that the old woman had luckily been absent during his visit, but would probably be there when they went again. As to that they must take their chance. And the whole plan was arranged. Mr. Fenwick was to be on the road in his gig at Mr. Gilmore's gate at ten o'clock, and Mrs. Brattle was to meet him there at that hour.

CHAPTER XXVIII.

MRS. BRATTLE'S JOURNEY.

Mrs. Brattle was waiting at the stile opposite to Mr. Gilmore's gate as Mr. Fenwick drove up to the spot. No doubt the dear old woman had been there for the last half-hour, thinking that the walk would take her twice as long as it did, and fearing that she might keep the Vicar waiting. She had put on her Sunday clothes and her Sunday bonnet, and when she climbed up into the vacant place beside her friend she found her position to be so strange that for a while she could hardly speak. He said a few words to her, but pressed her with no questions, understanding the cause of her embarrassment. He could not but think that of all his parishioners no two were so unlike each other as were the miller and his wife. The one was so hard and invincible;— the other so soft and submissive! Nevertheless it had always been said that Brattle had been a tender and affectionate husband. By degrees the woman's awe at the horse and gig and strangeness of her position wore off, and she began to talk of her daughter. She had brought a little bundle with her, thinking that she might supply feminine wants, and had apologised humbly for venturing to come so laden. Fenwick, who remembered what Carry had said about money that she still had, and who was nearly sure that the murderers had gone to Pycroft Common after the murder had been committed, had found a difficulty in explaining to Mrs. Brattle that her child was probably not in want. The son had been accused of the murder of the man, and now the Vicar had but little doubt that the daughter was living on the proceeds of the robbery. "It's a hard life she must be living, Mr. Fenwick, with an old 'ooman the likes of that," said Mrs. Brattle. "Perhaps if I'd brought a morsel of some'at to eat—"

"I don't think they're pressed in that way, Mrs. Brattle."

"Ain't they now? But it's a'most worse, Mr. Fenwick, when one thinks where it's to come from. The Lord have mercy on her, and bring her out of it!"

"Amen," said the Vicar.

"And is she bright at all, and simple still? She was the brightest, simplest lass in all Bull'ompton, I used to think. I suppose her old ways have a'most left her, Mr. Fenwick?"

"I thought her very like what she used to be."

"'Deed now, did you, Mr. Fenwick? And she wasn't mopish and slatternly like?"

"She was tidy enough. You wouldn't wish me to say that she was happy?"

"I suppose not, Mr. Fenwick. I shouldn't ought;—ought I, now? But, Mr. Fenwick, I'd give my left hand she should be happy and gay once more. I suppose none but a mother feels it, but the sound of her voice through the house was ever the sweetest music I know'd on. It'll never have the same ring again, Mr. Fenwick."

He could not tell her that it would. That sainted sinner of whom he had reminded Mr. Puddleham, though she had attained to the joy of the Lord,—even she had never regained the mirth of her young innocence. There is a bloom on the flower which may rest there till the flower has utterly perished, if the handling of it be sufficiently delicate;—but no care, nothing that can be done by friends on earth, or even by better friendship from above, can replace that when once displaced. The sound of which the mother was thinking could never be heard again from Carry Brattle's voice. "If we could only get her home once more," said the Vicar, "she might be a good daughter to you still."

"I'd be a good mother to her, Mr. Fenwick;—but I'm thinking he'll never have it so. I never knew him to change on a thing like that, Mr. Fenwick. He felt it that keenly, it nigh killed 'im. Only that he took it out o' hisself in thrashing that wicked man, I a'most think he'd a' died o' it."

Again the Vicar drove to the Bald-faced Stag, and again he walked along the road and over the common. He offered his arm to the old woman, but she wouldn't accept it; nor would she upon any entreaty allow him to carry her bundle. She assured him that his doing so would make her utterly wretched, and at last he gave up the point. She declared that she suffered nothing from fatigue, and that her two miles' walk would not be more than her Sunday journey to church and back. But as she drew near to the house she became uneasy, and once asked to be allowed to pause for a moment. "May be, then," said she, "after all, my girl'd rather that I wouldn't trouble her." He took her by the arm and led her along, and comforted her,—assuring her that if she would take her child in her arms Carry would for the moment be in a heaven of happiness. "Take her into my arms, Mr. Fenwick? Why,—isn't she in my very heart of hearts at this moment? And I won't say not a word sharp to her;—not now, Mr. Fenwick. And why would I say sharp words at all? I suppose she understands it all."

"I think she does, Mrs. Brattle."

They had now reached the door, and the Vicar knocked. No answer came at once; but such had been the case when he knocked before. He had learned to understand that in such a household it might not be wise to admit all comers without consideration. So he knocked again,—and then again. But still there came no answer. Then he tried the door, and found that it was locked. "May be she's seen me coming," said the mother, "and now she won't let me in." The Vicar then went round the cottage, and found that the back door also was closed. Then he looked in at one of the front windows, and became aware that no one was sitting, at least in the kitchen. There was an upstairs room, but of that the window was closed.

"I begin to fear," he said, "that neither of them is at home."

At this moment he heard the voice of a woman calling to him from the door of the nearest cottage,—one of the two brick tenements which stood together,—and from her he learned that Mrs. Burrows had gone into Devizes, and would not probably be home till the evening. Then he asked after Carry, not mentioning her name, but speaking of her as the young woman who lived with Mrs. Burrows. "Her young man come and took her up to Lon'on o' Saturday," said the woman.

Fenwick heard the words, but Mrs. Brattle did not hear them. It did not occur to him not to believe the woman's statement, and all his hopes about the poor creature were at once dashed to the ground. His first feeling was no doubt one of resentment, that she had broken her word to him. She had said that she would not go within a month without letting him know that she was going; and there is no fault, no vice, that strikes any of us so strongly as falsehood or injustice against ourselves. And then the nature of the statement was so terrible! She had gone back into utter degradation and iniquity. And who was the young man? As far as he could obtain a clue, through the information which had reached him from various sources, this young man must be the companion of the Grinder in the murder and robbery of Mr. Trumbull. "She has gone away, Mrs. Brattle," said he, with as sad a voice as ever a man used.

"And where be she gone to, Mr. Fenwick? Cannot I go arter her?" He simply shook his head and took her by the arm to lead her away. "Do they know nothing of her, Mr. Fenwick?"

"She has gone away; probably to London. We must think no more about her, Mrs. Brattle—at any rate for the present. I can only say that I am very, very sorry that I brought you here."

The drive back to Bullhampton was very silent and very sad. Mrs. Brattle had before her the difficulty of explaining her journey to her husband, together with the feeling that the difficulty had been incurred altogether for nothing. As for Fenwick, he was angry with himself for his own past enthusiasm about the girl. After all, Mr. Chamberlaine had shown himself to be the wiser man of the two. He had declared it to be no good to take up special cases, and the Vicar as he drove himself home notified to himself his assent with the Prebendary's doctrine. The girl had gone off the moment she had ascertained that her friends were aware of her presence and situation. What to her had been the kindness of her clerical friend, or the stories brought to her from her early home, or the dirt and squalor of the life which she was leading? The moment that there was a question of bringing her back to the decencies of the world, she escaped from her friends and hurried back to the pollution which, no doubt, had charms for her. He had allowed himself to think that in spite of her impurity, she might again be almost pure, and this was his reward! He deposited the poor woman at the spot at which he had taken her up, almost without a word, and then drove himself home with a heavy heart. "I believe it will be best to be like her father, and never to name her again," said he to his wife.

"But what has she done, Frank?"

"Gone back to the life which I suppose she likes best. Let us say no more about it,—at any rate for the present. I'm sick at heart when I think of it."

Mrs. Brattle, when she got over the stile close to her own home, saw her husband standing at the mill door. Her heart sank within her, if that could be said to sink which was already so low. He did not move, but stood there with his eyes fixed upon her. She had hoped that she might get into the house unobserved by him, and learn from Fanny what had taken place; but she felt so like a culprit that she hardly dared to enter the door. Would it not be best to go to him at once, and ask his pardon for what she had done? When he spoke to her, which he did at last, his voice was a relief to her. "Where hast been, Maggie?" he asked. She went up to him, put her hand on the lappet of his coat and shook her head. "Best go in and sit easy, and hear what God sends," he said. "What's the use of scouring about the country here and there?"

"There has been no use in it to-day, feyther," she said.

"There arn't no use in it,—not never," he said; and after that there was no more about it. She went into the house and handed the bundle to Fanny, and sat down on the bed and cried. On the following morning Frank Fenwick received the following letter:—

London, Sunday.

> HONOURED SIR,
>
> I told you that I would write if it came as I was going away, but I've been forced to go without writing. There was nothing to write with at the cottage. Mrs. Burrows and me had words, and I thought as she would rob me, and perhaps worse. She is a bad woman, and I could stand it no longer, so I just come up here, as there was nowhere else for me to find a place to lie down in. I thought I'd just write and tell you, because of my word; but I know it isn't no use.
>
> I'd send my respects and love to father and mother, if I dared. I did think of going over; but I know he'd kill me, and so he ought. I'd send my respects to Mrs. Fenwick, only that I isn't fit to name her;—and my love to sister Fanny. I've come away here, and must just wait till I die.
>
> Yours humbly, and most unfortunate,
>
> CARRY.
>
> If it's any good to be sorry, nobody can be more sorry than me, and nobody more unhappy. I did try to pray when you was gone, but it only made me more ashamed. If there was only anywhere to go to, I'd go.

CHAPTER XXIX.

THE BULL AT LORING.

Gilmore had told his friend that he would do two things,—that he would start off and travel for four or five years, and that he would pay a visit to Loring. Fenwick had advised him to do neither, but to stay at home and dig and say his prayers. But in such emergencies no man takes his friend's advice; and when Mr. Chamberlaine had left him, Gilmore had made up his mind that he would at any rate go to Loring. He went to church on the Sunday morning, and was half resolved to tell Mrs. Fenwick of his purpose; but chance delayed her in the church, and he sauntered away home without having mentioned it. He let half the next week pass by without stirring beyond his own ground. During those three days he changed his mind half a dozen times; but at last, on the Thursday, he had his portmanteau packed and started on his journey. As he was preparing to leave the house he wrote one line to Fenwick in pencil. "I am this moment off to Loring.—H. G." This he left in the village as he drove through to the Westbury station.

He had formed no idea in his own mind of any definite purpose in going. He did not know what he should do or what say when he got to Loring. He had told himself a hundred times that any persecution of the girl on his part would be mean and unworthy of him. And he was also aware that no condition in which a man could place himself was more open to contempt than that of a whining, pining, unsuccessful lover. A man is bound to take a woman's decision against him, bear it as he may, and say as little against it as possible. He is bound to do so when he is convinced that a woman's decision is final; and there can be no stronger proof of such finality than the fact that she has declared a preference for some other man. All this Gilmore knew, but he would not divest himself of the idea that there might still be some turn in the wheel of fortune. He had heard a vague rumour that Captain Marrable, his rival, was a very dangerous man. His uncle was quite sure that the Captain's father was thoroughly bad, and had thrown out hints against the son, which Gilmore in his anxiety magnified till he felt convinced that the girl whom he loved with all his heart was going to throw herself into the arms of a thorough scamp. Could he not do something, if not for his own sake, then for hers? Might it not be possible for him to deliver her from her danger? What, if he should discover some great iniquity;—would she not then in her gratitude be softened towards him? It was on the cards that this reprobate was married already, and was about to commit bigamy. It was quite probable that such a man should be deeply in debt. As for the fortune that had been left to him, Mr. Chamberlaine had already ascertained that that amounted to nothing. It had been consumed to the last shilling in paying the joint debts of the father and son. Men such as Mr. Chamberlaine have sources of information which are marvellous to the minds of those who are more secluded, and not the less marvellous because the information is invariably false. Gilmore in this way almost came to a conviction that Mary Lowther was about to sacrifice herself to a man utterly unworthy of her, and he taught himself, not to think,—but to believe it to be possible that he might save her. Those who knew him would have said that he was the last man in the world to be carried away by a romantic notion;—but he had his own idea of romance as plainly developed in his mind as was ever the case with a knight of old, who went forth for the relief of a distressed damsel. If he could do anything towards saving her, he would do it, or try to do it, though he should be brought to ruin in the attempt. Might it not be that at last he would have the reward which other knights always attained? The chance in his favour was doubtless small, but the world was nothing to him without this chance.

He had never been at Loring before, but he had learned the way. He went to Chippenham and Swindon, and then by the train to Loring. He had no very definite plan formed for himself. He rather thought that he would call at Miss Marrable's house,—call if possible when Mary Lowther was not there,—and learn from the elder lady something of the facts of the case. He had been well aware for many weeks past, from early days in the summer, that old Miss Marrable had been in favour of his claim. He had heard too that there had been family quarrels among the Marrables, and a word had been dropped in his hearing by Mrs. Fenwick, which had implied that Miss Marrable was by no means pleased with the match which her niece Mary Lowther was proposing to herself. Everything seemed to show that Captain Marrable was a most undesirable person.

When he reached the station at Loring it was incumbent on him to go somewhither at once. He must provide for himself for the night. He found two omnibuses at the station, and two inn servants competing with great ardour for his carpet bag. There were the Dragon and the Bull fighting for him. The Bull in the Lowtown was commercial and prosperous. The Dragon at Uphill was aristocratic, devoted to county purposes, and rather hard set to keep its jaws open and its tail flying. Prosperity is always becoming more prosperous, and the allurements of the Bull prevailed. "Are you a going to rob the gent of his walise?" said the indignant Boots of the Bull as he rescued Mr. Gilmore's property from the hands of his natural enemy, as soon as he had secured the entrance of Mr. Gilmore into his own vehicle. Had Mr. Gilmore known that the Dragon was next door but one to Miss Marrable's house, and that the Bull was nearly equally contiguous to that in which Captain Marrable was residing, his choice probably would not have been altered. In such cases, the knight who is to be the deliverer desires above all things that he may be near to his enemy.

He was shown up to a bedroom, and then ushered into the commercial room of the house. Loring, though it does a very pretty trade as a small town, and now has for some years been regarded as a thriving place in its degree, is not of such importance in the way of business as to support a commercial inn of the first class. At such houses the commercial room is as much closed against the uninitiated as is a first-class club in London. In such rooms a non-commercial man would be almost as much astray as is a non-broker in Capel Court, or an attorney in a bar mess-room. At the Bull things were a little mixed. The very fact that the words "Commercial Room" were painted on the door proved to those who understood such matters that there was a doubt in the case. They had no coffee room at the Bull, and strangers who came that way were of necessity shown into that in which the gentlemen of the road were wont to relax themselves. Certain commercial laws are maintained in such apartments. Cigars are not allowed before nine o'clock, except upon some distinct arrangement with the waiter. There is not, as a rule, a regular daily commercial repast; but when three or more gentlemen dine together at five o'clock, the dinner becomes a commercial dinner, and the commercial laws as to wine, &c., are enforced, with more or less restriction as circumstances may seem to demand. At the present time there was but one occupant of the chamber to greet Mr. Gilmore when he entered, and this greeting was made with all the full honours of commercial courtesy. The commercial gentleman is of his nature gregarious, and although he be exclusive to a strong degree, more so probably than almost any other man in regard to the sacred hour of dinner, when in the full glory of his confraternity, he will condescend, when the circumstances of his profession have separated him from his professional brethren, to be festive with almost any gentleman whom chance may throw in his way. Mr. Cockey had been alone for a whole day when Gilmore arrived, having reached Loring just twenty-four hours in advance of our friend, and was contemplating the sadly diminished joys of a second solitary dinner at the Bull, when fortune threw this stranger in his way. The waiter, looking at the matter in a somewhat similar light, and aware that a combined meal would be for the advantage of all parties, very soon assisted Mr. Cockey in making his arrangements for the evening. Mr. Gilmore would no doubt want to dine. Dinner would be served at five o'clock. Mr. Cockey was going to dine, and Mr. Gilmore, the waiter thought, would probably be glad to join him. Mr. Cockey expressed himself as delighted, and would only be too happy. Now men in love, let their case be ever so bad, must dine or die. So much no doubt is not admitted by the chroniclers of the old knights who went forth after their ladies; but the old chroniclers, if they soared somewhat higher than do those of the present day, are admitted to have been on the whole less circumstantially truthful. Our knight was very sad at heart, and would have done according to his prowess as much as any Orlando of them all for the lady whom he loved,—but nevertheless he was an hungered; the mention of dinner was pleasant to him, and he accepted the joint courtesies of Mr. Cockey and the waiter with gratitude.

The codfish and beefsteak, though somewhat woolly and tough, were wholesome; and the pint of sherry which at Mr. Cockey's suggestion was supplied to them, if not of itself wholesome, was innocent by reason of its dimensions. Mr. Cockey himself was pleasant and communicative, and told Mr. Gilmore a good deal about Loring. Our friend was afraid to ask any leading questions as to the persons in the place who interested himself, feeling conscious that his own subject was one which would not bear touch from a rough hand. He did at last venture to make inquiry about the clergyman of the parish. Mr. Cockey, with some merriment at his own wit, declared that the church was a house of business at which he did not often call for orders. Though he had been coming to Loring now for four years, he had never heard anything of the clergyman; but the waiter no doubt would tell them. Gilmore rather hesitated, and protested that he cared little for the matter; but the waiter was called in and questioned, and was soon full of stories about old Mr. Marrable. He was a good sort of man in his way, the waiter thought, but not much of a preacher. The people liked him because he never interfered with them. "He don't go poking his nose into people's 'ouses like some of 'em," said the waiter, who then began to tell of the pertinacity in that respect of a younger clergyman at Uphill. Yes; Parson Marrable had a relation living at Uphill; an old lady. "No; not his grandmother." This was in answer to a joke on the part of Mr. Cockey. Nor yet a daughter. The waiter thought she was some kind of a cousin, though he did not know what kind. A very grand lady was Miss Marrable, according to his showing, and much thought of by the quality. There was a young lady living with her, though the waiter did not know the young lady's name.

"Does the Rev. Mr. Marrable live alone?" asked Gilmore. "Well, yes; for the most part quite alone. But just at present he had a visitor." Then the waiter told all that he knew about the Captain. The most material part of this was that the Captain had returned from London that very evening;—had come in by the Express while the two "gents" were at dinner, and had been taken to the Lowtown parsonage by the Bull 'bus. "Quite the gentleman," was the Captain, according to the waiter, and one of the "handsomest gents as ever he'd set his eyes upon." "D—— him," said poor Harry Gilmore to himself. Then he ventured upon another question. Did the waiter know anything of Captain Marrable's father? The waiter only knew that the Captain's father was "a military gent, and was high up in the army." From all which the only information which Gilmore received was the fact that the match between

Marrable and Mary Lowther had not as yet become the talk of the town. After dinner Mr. Cockey proposed a glass of toddy and a cigar, remarking that he would move a bill for dispensing with the smoking rule for that night only, and to this also Gilmore assented. Now that he was at Loring he did not know what to do with himself better than drinking toddy with Mr. Cockey. Mr. Cockey declared the bill to be carried nem. con., and the cigars and toddy were produced. Mr. Cockey remarked that he had heard of Sir Gregory Marrable, of Dunripple Park. He travelled in Warwickshire, and was in the habit, as he said, of fishing up little facts. Sir Gregory wasn't much of a man, according to his account. The estate was small and, as Mr. Cockey fancied, a little out at elbows. Mr. Cockey thought it all very well to be a country gentleman and a "barrow knight," as he called it, as long as you had an estate to follow; but he thought very little of a title without plenty of stuff. Commerce, according to his notions, was the back bone of the nation;—and that the corps of travelling commercial gentlemen was the back bone of trade, every child knew. Mr. Cockey became warm and friendly as he drank his toddy. "Now, I don't know what you are, sir," said he.

"I'm not very much of anything," said Gilmore.

"Perhaps not, sir. Let that be as it may. But a man, sir, that feels that he's one of the supports of the commercial supremacy of this nation ain't got much reason to be ashamed of himself."

"Not on that account, certainly."

"Nor yet on no other account, as long as he's true to his employers. Now you talk of country gentlemen."

"I didn't talk of them," said Gilmore.

"Well,—no,—you didn't; but they do, you know. What does a country gentleman know, and what does he do? What's the country the better of him? He 'unts, and he shoots, and he goes to bed with his skin full of wine, and then he gets up and he 'unts and he shoots again, and 'as his skin full once more. That's about all."

"Sometimes he's a magistrate."

"Yes, justices' justice! we know all about that. Put an old man in prison for a week because he looks into his 'ay-field on a Sunday; or send a young one to the treadmill for two months because he knocks over a 'are! All them cases ought to be tried in the towns, and there should be beaks paid as there is in London. I don't see the good of a country gentleman. Buying and selling;—that's what the world has to go by."

"They buy and sell land."

"No; they don't. They buy a bit now and then when they're screws, and they sell a bit now and then when the eating and drinking has gone too fast. But as for capital and investment, they know nothing about it. After all, they ain't getting above two-and-a-half per cent. for their money. We all know what that must come to."

Mr. Cockey had been so mild before the pint of sherry and the glass of toddy, that Mr. Gilmore was somewhat dismayed by the change. Mr. Cockey, however, in his altered aspect seemed to be so much the less gracious, that Gilmore left him and strolled out into the town. He climbed up the hill and walked round the church and looked up at the windows of Miss Marrable's house, of which he had learned the site; but he had no adventure, saw nothing that interested him, and at half-past nine took himself wearily to bed.

That same day Captain Marrable had run down from London to Loring laden with terrible news. The money on which he had counted was all gone! "What do you mean?" said his uncle; "have the lawyers been deceiving you all through?"

"What is it to me?" said the ruined man. "It is all gone. They have satisfied me that nothing more can be done." Parson John whistled with a long-drawn note of wonder. "The people they were dealing with would be willing enough to give up the money, but it's all gone. It's spent, and there's no trace of it."

"Poor fellow!"

Parson John and Walter Marrable.

"I've seen my father, uncle John."

"And what passed?"

"I told him that he was a scoundrel, and then I left him. I didn't strike him."

"I should hope not that, Walter."

"I kept my hands off him; but when a man has ruined you as he has me, it doesn't much matter who he is. Your father and any other man are much the same to you then. He was worn, and old, and pale, or I should have felled him to the ground."

"And what will you do now?"

"Just go to that hell upon earth on the other side of the globe. There's nothing else to be done. I've applied for extension of leave, and told them why."

Nothing more was said that night between the uncle and nephew, and no word had been spoken about Mary Lowther. On the next morning the breakfast at the parsonage passed by in silence. Parson John had been thinking a good deal of Mary, but had resolved that it was best that he should hold his tongue for the present. From the moment in which he had first heard of the engagement, he had made up his mind that his nephew and Mary Lowther would never be married. Seeing what his nephew was—or rather seeing that which he fancied his nephew to be,—he was sure that he would not sacrifice himself by such a marriage. There was always a way out of things, and Walter Marrable would be sure to find it. The way out of it had been found now with a vengeance. Immediately after breakfast the Captain took his hat without a word, and walked steadily up the hill to Uphill Lane. As he passed the door of the Bull he saw, but took no notice of, a gentleman who was standing under the covered entrance to the inn, and who had watched him coming out from the parsonage gate; but Gilmore, the moment that his eyes fell upon the Captain, declared to himself that that was his rival. Captain Marrable walked straight up the hill and knocked at Miss Marrable's door. Was Miss Lowther at home? Of course Miss Lowther was at home at such an hour. The girl said that Miss Mary was alone in the breakfast parlour. Miss Marrable had already gone down to the kitchen. Without waiting for another word, he walked into the little back room, and there he found his love. "Walter," she said, jumping up and running to him; "how good of you to come so soon! We didn't expect you these two days." She had thrown herself into his arms, but, though he embraced her, he did not kiss her. "There is something the matter!" she said. "What is it?" As she spoke she drew away from him and looked up into his face. He smiled and shook his head, still holding her by the waist. "Tell me, Walter; I know there is something wrong."

"It is only that dirty money. My father has succeeded in getting it all."

"All, Walter?" said she, again drawing herself away.

"Every shilling," said he, dropping his arm.

"That will be very bad."

"Not a doubt of it. I felt it just as you do."

"And all our pretty plans are gone."

"Yes;—all our pretty plans."

"And what shall you do now?"

"There is only one thing. I shall go to India again. Of course it is just the same to me as though I were told that sentence of death had gone against me;—only it will not be so soon over."

"Don't say that, Walter."

"Why not say it, my dear, when I feel it?"

"But you don't feel it. I know it must be bad for you, but it is not quite that. I will not think that you have nothing left worth living for."

"I can't ask you to go with me to that happy Paradise."

"But I can ask you to take me," she said;—"though perhaps it will be better that I should not."

"My darling!—my own darling!" Then she came back to him and laid her head upon his shoulders, and lifted his hand till it came again round her waist. And he kissed her forehead, and smoothed her hair. "Swear to me," she said, "that whatever happens you will not put me away from you."

"Put you away, dearest! A man doesn't put away the only morsel he has to keep him from starving. But yet as I came up here this morning I resolved that I would put you away."

"Walter!"

"And even now I know that they will tell me that I should do so. How can I take you out there to such a life as that without having the means of keeping a house over your head?"

"Officers do marry without fortunes."

"Yes;—and what sort of a time do their wives have? Oh, Mary, my own, my own, my own!—it is very bad! You cannot understand it all at once, but it is very bad."

"If it be better for you, Walter,—" she said, again drawing herself away.

"It is not that, and do not say that it is. Let us at any rate trust each other."

She gave herself a little shake before she answered him. "I will trust you in everything;—as God is my judge, in everything. What you tell me to do, I will do. But, Walter, I will say one thing first. I can look forward to nothing but absolute misery in any life that will separate me from you. I know the difference between comfort and discomfort in money matters, but all that is as a feather in the balance. You are my god upon earth, and to you I must cling. Whether you be away from me or with me, I must cling to you the same. If I am to be separated from you for a time, I can do it with hope. If I am to be separated from you for ever, I shall still do so,—with despair. And now I will trust you, and I will do whatever you tell me. If you forbid me to call you mine any longer,—I will obey, and will never reproach you."

"I will always be yours," he said, taking her again to his heart.

"Then, dearest, you shall not find me wanting for anything you may ask of me. Of course you can't decide at present."

"I have decided that I must go to India. I have asked for the exchange."

"Yes;—I understand; but about our marriage. It may be that you should go out first. I would not be unmaidenly, Walter; but remember this—the sooner the better, if I can be a comfort to you;—but I can bear any delay rather than be a clog upon you."

Marrable, as he had walked up the hill,—and during all his thoughts, indeed, since he had been convinced that the money was gone from him,—had been disposed to think that his duty to Mary required him to give her up. He had asked her to be his wife when he believed his circumstances to be other than they were; and now he knew that the life he had to offer to her was one of extreme discomfort. He had endeavoured to shake off any idea that as he must go back to India it would be more comfortable for himself to return without than with a wife. He wanted to make the sacrifice of himself, and had determined that he would do so. Now, at any rate for the moment, all his resolves were thrown to the wind. His own love was so strong and was so gratified by her love, that half his misery was carried away in an enthusiasm of romantic devotion. Let the worst come to the worst, the man that was so loved by such a woman could not be of all men the most miserable.

He left the house, giving to her the charge of telling the bad news to Miss Marrable; and as he went he saw in the street before the house the man whom he had seen standing an hour before under the gateway of the inn. And Gilmore saw him too, and well knew where he had been.

CHAPTER XXX.

THE AUNT AND THE UNCLE.

Miss Marrable heard the story of the Captain's loss in perfect silence. Mary told it craftily, with a smile on her face, as though she were but slightly affected by it, and did not think very much on the change it might effect in her plans and those of her lover. "He has been ill-treated; has he not?" she said.

"Very badly treated. I can't understand it, but it seems to me that he has been most shamefully treated."

"He tried to explain it all to me; but I don't know that he succeeded."

"Why did the lawyers deceive him?"

"I think he was a little rash there. He took what they told him for more than it was worth. There was some woman who said that she would resign her claim; but when they came to look into it, she too had signed some papers and the money was all gone. He could recover it from his father by law, only that his father has got nothing."

"And that is to be the end of it."

"That is the end of our five thousand pounds," said Mary, forcing a little laugh. Miss Marrable for a few moments made no reply. She sat fidgety in her seat, feeling that it was her duty to explain to Mary what must, in her opinion, be the inevitable result of this misfortune, and yet not knowing how to begin her task. Mary was partly aware of what was coming, and had fortified herself to reject all advice, to assert her right to do as she pleased with herself, and to protest that she cared nothing for the prudent views of worldly-minded people. But she was afraid of what was coming. She knew that arguments would be used which she would find it very difficult to answer; and, although she had settled upon certain strong words which she would speak, she felt that she would be driven at last to quarrel with her aunt. On one thing she was quite resolved. Nothing should induce her to give up her engagement,—short of the expression of a wish to that effect from Walter Marrable himself.

"How will this affect you, dear?" said Miss Marrable at last.

"I should have been a poor man's wife any how. Now I shall be the wife of a very poor man. I suppose that will be the effect."

"What will he do?"

"He has, aunt, made up his mind to go to India."

"Has he made up his mind to anything else?"

"Of course, I know what you mean, aunt?"

"Why should you not know? I mean, that a man going out to India, and intending to live there as an officer on his pay, cannot be in want of a wife."

"You speak of a wife as if she were the same as a coach-and-four, or a box at the opera,—a sort of luxury for rich men. Marriage, aunt, is like death, common to all."

"In our position in life, Mary, marriage cannot be made so common as to be undertaken without foresight for the morrow. A poor gentleman is further removed from marriage than any other man."

"One knows, of course, that there will be difficulties."

"What I mean, Mary, is, that you will have to give it up."

"Never, Aunt Sarah. I shall never give it up."

"Do you mean that you will marry him now, at once, and go out to India with him, as a dead weight round his neck?"

"I mean that he shall choose about that."

"It is for you to choose, Mary. Don't be angry. I am bound to tell you what I think. You can, of course, act as you please; but I think that you ought to listen to me. He cannot go back from his engagement without laying himself open to imputation of bad conduct."

"Nor can I."

"Pardon me, dear. That depends, I think, upon what passes between you. It is at any rate for you to propose the release to him,—not to fix him with the burthen of proposing it." Mary's heart quailed as she heard this, but she did not show her feeling by any expression on her face. "For a man, placed as he is, about to return to such a climate as that of India, with such work before him as I suppose men have there,—the burden of a wife, without the means of maintaining her according to his views of life and hers—"

"We have no views of life. We know that we shall be poor."

"It is the old story of love and a cottage,—only under the most unfavourable circumstances. A woman's view of it is, of course, different from that of a man. He has seen more of the world, and knows better than she does what poverty and a wife and family mean."

"There is no reason why we should be married at once."

"A long engagement for you would be absolutely disastrous."

"Of course, there is disaster," said Mary. "The loss of Walter's money is disastrous. One has to put up with disaster. But the worst of all disasters would be to be separated. I can stand anything but that."

"It seems to me, Mary, that within the last few weeks your character has become altogether altered."

"Of course it has."

"You used to think so much more of other people than yourself."

"Don't I think of him, Aunt Sarah?"

"As of a thing of your own. Two months ago you did not know him, and now you are a millstone round his neck."

"I will never be a millstone round anybody's neck," said Mary, walking out of the room. She felt that her aunt had been very cruel to her,—had attacked her in her misery without mercy; and yet she knew that every word that had been uttered had been spoken in pure affection. She did not believe that her aunt's chief purpose had been to save Walter from the fruits of an imprudent marriage. Had she so believed, the words would have had more effect on her. She saw, or thought that she saw, that her aunt was trying to save herself against her own will, and at this she was indignant. She was determined to persevere; and this endeavour to make her feel that her perseverance would be disastrous to the man she loved was, she thought, very cruel. She stalked upstairs with unruffled demeanour; but when there, she threw herself on her bed and sobbed bitterly. Could it be that it was her duty, for his sake, to tell him that the whole thing should be at an end? It was impossible for her to do so now, because she had sworn to him that she would be guided altogether by him in his present troubles. She must keep her word to him, whatever happened; but of this she was quite sure,—that if he should show the slightest sign of a wish to be free from his engagement, she would make him free—at once. She would make him free, and would never allow herself to think for a moment that he had been wrong. She had told him what her own feelings were very plainly,—perhaps, in her enthusiasm, too plainly,—and now he must judge for himself and for her. In respect to her aunt, she would endeavour to avoid any further conversation on the subject till her lover should have decided finally what would be best for both of them. If he should choose to say that everything between them should be over, she would acquiesce,—and all the world should be over for her at the same time.

While this was going on in Uphill Lane something of the same kind was taking place at the Lowtown Parsonage. Parson John became aware that his nephew had been with the ladies at Uphill, and when the young man came in for lunch, he asked some question which introduced the subject. "You've told them of this fresh trouble, no doubt."

"I didn't see Miss Marrable," said the Captain.

"I don't know that Miss Marrable much signifies. You haven't asked Miss Marrable to be your wife."

"I saw Mary, and I told her."

"I hope you made no bones about it."

"I don't know what you mean, sir."

"I hope you told her that you two had had your little game of play, like two children, and that there must be an end of it."

"No; I didn't tell her that."

"That's what you have got to tell her in some kind of language, and the sooner you do it the better. Of course you can't marry her. You couldn't have done it if this money had been all right, and it's out of the question now. Bless my soul! how you would hate each other before six months were over. I can understand that for a strong fellow like you, when he's used to it, India may be a jolly place enough."

"It's a great deal more than I can understand."

"But for a poor man with a wife and family;—oh dear! it must be very bad indeed. And neither of you have ever been used to that kind of thing."

"I have not," said the Captain.

"Nor has she. That old lady up there is not rich, but she is as proud as Lucifer, and always lives as though the whole place belonged to her. She's a good manager, and she don't run in debt;—but Mary Lowther knows no more of roughing it than a duchess."

"I hope I may never have to teach her."

"I trust you never may. It's a very bad lesson for a young man to have to teach a young woman. Some women die in the learning. Some won't learn it at all. Others do, and become dirty and rough themselves. Now, you are very particular about women."

"I like to see them well turned out."

"What would you think of your own wife, nursing perhaps a couple of babies, dressed nohow when she gets up in the morning, and going on in the same way till night? That's the kind of life with officers who marry on their pay. I don't say anything against it. If the man likes it,—or rather if he's able to put up with it,—it may be all very well; but you couldn't put up with it. Mary's very nice now, but you'd come to be so sick of her, that you'd feel half like cutting her throat,—or your own."

"It would be the latter for choice, sir."

"I dare say it would. But even that isn't a pleasant thing to look forward to. I'll tell you the truth about it, my boy. When you first came to me and told me that you were going to marry Mary Lowther, I knew it could not be. It was no business of mine; but I knew it could not be. Such engagements always get themselves broken off somehow. Now and again there are a pair of fools who go through with it;—but for the most part it's a matter of kissing and lovers' vows for a week or two."

"You seem to know all about it, Uncle John."

"I haven't lived to be seventy without knowing something, I suppose. And now here you are without a shilling. I dare say, if the truth were known, you've a few debts here and there."

"I may owe three or four hundred pounds or so."

"As much as a year's income;—and you talk of marrying a girl without a farthing."

"She has twelve hundred pounds."

"Just enough to pay your own debts, and take you out to India,—so that you may start without a penny. Is that the sort of career that will suit you, Walter? Can you trust yourself to that kind of thing, with a wife under your arm? If you were a man of fortune, no doubt Mary would make a very nice wife; but, as it is,—you must give it up."

Whereupon Captain Marrable lit a pipe and took himself into the parson's garden, thence into the stables and stable-yard, and again back to the garden, thinking of all this. There was not a word spoken by Parson John which Walter did not know to be true. He had already come to the conclusion that he must go out to India before he married. As for marrying Mary at once and taking her with him this winter, that was impossible. He must go and look about him;—and as he thought of this he was forced to acknowledge to himself that he regarded the delay as a reprieve. The sooner the better had been Mary's view with him. Though he was loath enough to entertain the idea of giving her up, he was obliged to confess that, like the condemned man, he desired a long day. There was nothing happy before him in the whole prospect of his life. Of course he loved Mary. He loved her very dearly. He loved her so dearly, that to have her taken from him would be to have his heart plucked asunder. So he swore to himself;—and yet he was in doubt whether it would not be better that his heart should be plucked asunder, than that she should be made to live in accordance with those distasteful pictures which his uncle had drawn for him. Of himself he would not think at all. Everything must be bad for him. What happiness could a man expect who had been misused, cheated, and mined by his own father? For himself it did not much matter what became of him; but he began to doubt whether for Mary's sake it would not be well that they should be separated. And then Mary had thrust upon him the whole responsibility of a decision!

CHAPTER XXXI.

MARY LOWTHER FEELS HER WAY.

That afternoon there came down to the parsonage a note from Mary to the Captain, asking her lover to meet her, and walk with her before dinner. He met her, and they took their accustomed stroll along the towing-path and into the fields. Mary had thought much of her aunt's words before the note was written, and had a fixed purpose of her own in view. It was true enough that though she loved this man with all her heart and soul, so loved him that she could not look forward to life apart from him without seeing that such life would be a great blank, yet she was aware that she hardly knew him. We are apt to suppose that love should follow personal acquaintance; and yet love at third sight is probably as common as any love at all, and it takes a great many sights before one human being can know another. Years are wanted to make a friendship, but days suffice for men and women to get married. Mary was, after a fashion, aware that she had been too quick in giving away her heart, and that now, when the gift had been made in full, it became her business to learn what sort of man was he to whom she had given it. And it was not only his nature as it affected her, but his nature as it affected himself that she must study. She did not doubt but that he was good, and true, and noble-minded; but it might be possible that a man good, true, and noble-minded, might have lived with so many indulgences around him as to be unable to achieve the constancy of heart which would be necessary for such a life as that which would be now before them if they married. She had told him that he should decide for himself and for her also,—thus throwing upon him the responsibility, and throwing upon him also, very probably, the necessity of a sacrifice. She had meant to be generous and trusting; but it might be that of all courses that which she had adopted was the least generous. In order that she might put this wrong right, if there were a wrong, she had asked him to come and walk with her. They met at the usual spot, and she put her hand through his arm with her accustomed smile, leaning upon him somewhat heavily for a minute, as girls do when they want to show that they claim the arm that they lean on as their own.

"Have you told Parson John?" said Mary.

"Oh, yes."

"And what does he say?"

"Just what a crabbed, crafty, selfish old bachelor of seventy would be sure to say."

"You mean that he has told you to give up all idea of comforting yourself with a wife."

"Just that."

"And Aunt Sarah has been saying exactly the same to me. You can't think how eloquent Aunt Sarah has been. And her energy has quite surprised me."

"I don't think Aunt Sarah was ever much of a friend of mine," said the Captain.

"Not in the way of matrimony; in other respects she approves of you highly, and is rather proud of you as a Marrable. If you were only heir to the title, or something of that kind, she would think you the finest fellow going."

"I wish I could gratify her, with all my heart."

"She is such a dear old creature! You don't know her in the least, Walter. I am told she was ever so pretty when she was a girl; but she had no fortune of her own at that time, and she didn't care to marry beneath her position. You mustn't abuse her."

"I've not abused her."

"What she has been saying I am sure is very true; and I dare say Parson John has been saying the same thing."

"If she has caused you to change your mind, say so at once, Mary. I shan't complain."

Mary pressed his arm involuntarily, and loved him so dearly for the little burst of wrath. Was it really true that he, too, had set his heart upon it?—that all that the crafty old uncle had said had been of no avail?—that he also loved so well that he was willing to change the whole course of his life and become another person for the sake of her? If it were so, she would not say a word that could by possibility make him think that she was afraid. She would feel her way carefully, so that he might not be led by a chance phrase to imagine that what she was about to say was said on her own behalf. She would be very careful, but at the same time she would be so explicit that there should be no doubt on his mind but that he had her full permission to retire from the engagement if he thought it best to do so. She was quite ready to share the burthens of life with him, let them be what they might; but she would not be a mill-stone round his neck. At any rate, he should not be weighted with the mill-stone, if he himself looked upon a loving wife in that light.

"She has not caused me to change my mind at all, Walter. Of course I know that all this is very serious. I knew that without Aunt Sarah's telling me. After all, Aunt Sarah can't be so wise as you ought to be, who have seen India and who know it well."

"India is not a nice place to live in—especially for women."

"I don't know that Loring is very nice;—but one has to take that as it comes. Of course it would be nicer if you could live at home and have plenty of money. I wish I had a fortune of my own. I never cared for it before, but I do now."

"Things don't come by wishing, Mary."

"No; but things do come by resolving and struggling. I have no doubt but that you will live yet to do something and to be somebody. I have that faith in you. But I can well understand that a wife may be a great impediment in your way."

"I don't want to think of myself at all."

"But you must think of yourself. For a woman, after all, it doesn't matter much. She isn't expected to do anything particular. A man of course must look to his own career, and take care that he does nothing to mar it."

"I don't quite understand what you're driving at," said the Captain.

"Well;—I'm driving at this: that I think that you are bound to decide upon doing that which you feel to be wisest without reference to my feelings. Of course I love you better than anything in the world. I can't be so false as to say it isn't so. Indeed, to tell the truth, I don't know that I really ever loved anybody else. But if it is proper that we should be separated, I shall get over it,—in a way."

"You mean you'd marry somebody else in the process of time."

"No, Walter; I don't mean that. Women shouldn't make protestations; but I don't think I ever should. But a woman can live and get on very well without being married, and I should always have you in my heart, and I should try to comfort myself with remembering that you had loved me."

"I am quite sure that I shall never marry anyone else," said the Captain.

"You know what I'm driving at now;—eh, Walter?"

"Partly."

"I want you to know wholly. I told you this morning that I should leave it to you to decide. I still say the same. I consider myself for the present as much bound to obey you as though I were your wife already. But after saying that, and after hearing Aunt Mary's sermon, I felt that I ought to make you understand that I am quite aware that it may be impossible for you to keep to your engagement. You understand all that better than I do. Our engagement was made when you thought you had money, and even then you felt that there was little enough."

"It was very little."

"And now there is none. I don't profess to be afraid of poverty myself, because I don't quite know what it means."

"It means something very unpleasant."

"No doubt; and it would be unpleasant to be parted;—wouldn't it?"

"It would be horrible."

She pressed his arm again as she went on. "You must judge between the two. What I want you to understand is this, that whatever you may judge to be right and best, I will agree to it, and will think that it is right and best. If you say that we will get ourselves married and try it, I shall feel that not to get ourselves married and not to try it is a manifest impossibility; and if you say that we should be wrong to get married and try it, then I will feel that to have done so was quite a manifest impossibility."

"Mary," said he, "you're an angel."

"No; but I'm a woman who loves well enough to be determined not to hurt the man she loves if she can help it."

"There is one thing on which I think we must decide."

"What is that?"

"I must at any rate go out before we are married." Mary Lowther felt this to be a decision in her favour,—to be a decision which for the time made her happy and light-hearted. She had so dreaded a positive and permanent separation, that the delay seemed to her to be hardly an evil.

CHAPTER XXXII.

MR. GILMORE'S SUCCESS.

Harry Gilmore, the prosperous country gentleman, the county magistrate, the man of acres, the nephew of Mr. Chamberlaine, respected by all who knew him,—with the single exception of the Marquis of Trowbridge,—was now so much reduced that he felt himself to be an inferior being to Mr. Cockey, with whom he breakfasted. He had come to Loring, and now he was there he did not know what to do with himself. He had come there, in truth, not because he really thought he could do any good, but driven out of his home by sheer misery. He was a man altogether upset, and verging on to a species of insanity. He was so uneasy in his mind that he could read nothing. He was half-ashamed of being looked at by those who knew him; and had felt some relief in the society of Mr. Cockey till Mr. Cockey had become jovial with wine, simply because Mr. Cockey was so poor a creature that he felt no fear of him. But as he had come to Loring, it was necessary that he should do something. He could not come to Loring and go back again without saying a word to anybody. Fenwick would ask him questions, and the truth would come out. There came upon him this morning an idea that he would not go back home;—that he would leave Loring and go away without giving any reason to any one. He was his own master. No one would be injured by anything that he might do. He had a right to spend his income as he pleased. Everything was distasteful that reminded him of Bullhampton. But still he knew that this was no more than a madman's idea;—that it would ill become him so to act. He had duties to perform, and he must perform them, let them be ever so distasteful. It was only an idea, made to be rejected; but, nevertheless, he thought of it.

To do something, however, was incumbent on him. After breakfast he sauntered up the hill and saw Captain Marrable enter the house in which Mary Lowther lived. He felt thoroughly ashamed of himself in thus creeping about, and spying things out,—and, in truth, he had not intended thus to watch his rival. He wandered into the churchyard, sat there sometime on the tombstones, and then again went down to the inn. Mr. Cockey was going to Gloucester by an afternoon train, and invited him to join an early dinner at two. He assented, though by this time he had come to hate Mr. Cockey. Mr. Cockey assumed an air of superiority, and gave his opinions about matters political and social as though his companion were considerably below him in intelligence and general information. He dictated to poor Gilmore, and laid down the law as to eating onions with beefsteaks in a manner that was quite offensive. Nevertheless, the unfortunate man bore with his tormentor, and felt desolate when he was left alone in the commercial room, Cockey having gone out to complete his last round of visits to his customers. "Orders first and money afterwards," Cockey had said, and Cockey had now gone out to look after his money.

Gilmore sat for some half-hour helpless over the fire; and then starting up, snatched his hat, and hurried out of the house. He walked as quickly as he could up the hill, and rang the bell at Miss Marrable's house. Had he been there ten minutes sooner, he would have seen Mary Lowther tripping down the side path to meet her lover. He rang the bell, and in a few minutes found himself in Miss Marrable's drawing-room. He had asked for Miss Marrable, had given his name, and had been shown upstairs. There he remained alone for a few minutes which seemed to him to be interminable. During these minutes Miss Marrable was standing in her little parlour downstairs, trying to think what she would say to Mr. Gilmore,—trying also to think why Mr. Gilmore should have come to Loring.

After a few words of greeting Miss Marrable said that Miss Lowther was out walking. "She will be very glad, I'm sure, to hear good news from her friends at Bullhampton."

"They're all very well," said Mr. Gilmore.

"I've heard a great deal of Mr. Fenwick," said Miss Marrable; "so much that I seem almost to be acquainted with him."

"No doubt," said Mr. Gilmore.

"Your parish has become painfully known to the public by that horrible murder," said Miss Marrable.

"Yes, indeed," said Mr. Gilmore.

"I fear that they will hardly catch the perpetrator of it," said Miss Marrable.

"I fear not," said Mr. Gilmore.

At this period of the conversation Miss Marrable found herself in great difficulty. If anything was to be said about Mary Lowther, she could not begin to say it. She had heard a great deal in favour of Mr. Gilmore. Mrs. Fenwick had written to her about the man; and Mary, though she would not love him, had always spoken very highly of his qualities. She knew well that he had gone through Oxford with credit, that he was a reading man,—so reputed, that he was a magistrate, and in all respects a gentleman. Indeed, she had formed an idea of him as quite a pearl among men. Now that she saw him, she could not repress a feeling of disappointment. He was badly dressed, and bore a sad, depressed, downtrodden aspect. His whole appearance was what the world now calls seedy. And he seemed to be almost unable to speak. Miss Marrable knew that Mr. Gilmore was a man disappointed in his love, but she did not conceive that love had done him all these injuries. Love, however, had done them all. "Are you going to stay long in this neighbourhood?" asked Miss Marrable, almost in despair for a subject.

Then the man's mouth was opened. "No; I suppose not," he said. "I don't know what should keep me here, and I hardly know why I'm come. Of course you have heard of my suit to your niece." Miss Marrable bowed her courtly little head in token of assent. "When Miss Lowther left us, she gave me some hope that I might be successful. At least, she consented that I should ask her once more. She has now written to tell me that she is engaged to her cousin."

"There is something of the kind," said Miss Marrable.

"Something of the kind! I suppose it is settled; isn't it?"

Miss Marrable was a sensible woman, one not easily led away by appearances. Nevertheless, it is probable that had Mr. Gilmore been less lugubrious, more sleek, less "seedy," she would have been more prone than she now was to have made instant use of Captain Marrable's loss of fortune on behalf of this other suitor. She would immediately have felt that perhaps something might be done, and she would have been tempted to tell him the whole story openly. As it was she could not so sympathise with the man before her, as to take him into her confidence. No doubt he was Mr. Gilmore, the favoured friend of the Fenwicks, the owner of the Privets, and the man of whom Mary had often said that there was no fault to be found with him. But there was nothing bright about him, and she did not know how to encourage him as a lover. "As Mary has told you," she said, "I suppose there can be no harm in my repeating that they are engaged," said Miss Marrable.

"Of course they are. I am aware of that. I believe the gentleman is related to you."

"He is a cousin,—not very near."

"And I suppose he has your good will?"

"As to that, Mr. Gilmore, I don't know that I can do any good by speaking. Young ladies in these days don't marry in accordance with the wishes of their old aunts."

"But Miss Lowther thinks so much of you! I don't want to ask any questions that ought not to be asked. If this match is so settled that it must go on, why there's an end of it. I'll just tell you the truth openly, Miss Marrable. I have loved,—I do love your niece with all my heart. When I received her letter it upset me altogether, and every hour since has made the feeling worse. I have come here just to learn whether there may still possibly be a chance. You will not quarrel with me because I have loved her so well?"

"Indeed no," said Miss Marrable, whose heart was gradually becoming soft, and who was learning to forget the mud on Mr. Gilmore's boots and trousers.

"I heard that Captain Marrable was,—at any rate, not a very rich man; that he could hardly afford to marry his cousin. I did hear, also, that the match might in other respects not be suitable."

"There is no other objection, Mr. Gilmore."

"It is the case, Miss Marrable, that these things sometimes come on suddenly and go off suddenly. I won't deny that if I could have gained Miss Lowther's heart without the interference of any interloper, it would have been to me a brighter joy than anything that can now be possible. A man cannot be proud of his position who seeks to win a woman who owns a preference for another man." Miss Marrable's heart had now become very soft, and she began to perceive, of her own knowledge, that Mr. Gilmore was at any rate a gentleman. "But I would take her in any way that I could get her. Perhaps—that is to say, it might be—" And then he stopped.

Should she tell him everything? She had a strong idea that it was her first duty to be true to her own sex and to her own niece. But were she to tell the man the whole story it would do her niece no harm. She still believed that the match with Captain Marrable must be broken off. Even were this done it would be very long, she thought, before Mary would bring herself to listen with patience to another suitor. But of course it would be best for them all that this episode in Mary's life should be forgotten and put out of sight as soon as possible. Had not this dangerous captain come up, Mary, no doubt,—so thought Miss Marrable,—would at last have complied with her friends' advice, and have accepted a marriage which was in all respects advantageous. If the episode could only get itself forgotten and put out of sight, she might do so still. But there must be delay. Miss Marrable, after waiting for half a minute to consider, determined that she would tell him something. "No doubt," she said, "Captain Marrable's income is so small that the match is one that Mary's friends cannot approve."

"I don't think much of money," he said.

"Still it is essential to comfort, Mr. Gilmore."

"What I mean to say is, that I am the last man in the world to insist upon that kind of thing, or to appear to triumph because my income is larger than another man's." Miss Marrable was now quite sure that Mr. Gilmore was a gentleman. "But if the match is to be broken off—"

"I cannot say that it will be broken off."

"But it may be?"

"Certainly it is possible. There are difficulties which may necessarily separate them."

"If it be so, my feelings will be the same as they have always been since I first knew her. That is all that I have got to say."

Then she told him pretty nearly everything. She said nothing of the money which Walter Marrable would have inherited had it not been for Colonel Marrable's iniquity; but she did tell him that the young people would have no income except the Captain's pay, and poor Mary's little fifty pounds a-year; and she went on to explain that, as far as she was concerned, and as far as her cousin the clergyman was concerned, everything would be done to prevent a marriage so disastrous as that in question, and the prospect of a life with so little of allurement as that of the wife of a poor soldier in India. At the same time she bade him remember that Mary Lowther was a girl very apt to follow her own judgment, and that she was for the present absolutely devoted to her cousin. "I think it will be broken off," she said. "That is my opinion. I don't think it can go on. But it is he that will do it; and for a time she will suffer greatly."

"Then I will wait," said Mr. Gilmore. "I will go home, and wait again. If there be a chance, I can live and hope."

"God grant that you may not hope in vain!"

"I would do my best to make her happy. I will leave you now, and am very thankful for your kindness. There would be no good in my seeing Mary?"

"I think not, Mr. Gilmore."

"I suppose not. She would only feel that I was teasing her. You will not tell her of my being here, I suppose?"

"It would do no good, I think."

"None in the least. I'll just go home and wait. If there should be anything to tell me—"

"If the match be broken off, I will take care that you shall hear it. I will write to Janet Fenwick. I know that she is your friend."

Then Mr. Gilmore left the house, descended the hill without seeing Mary, packed up his things, and returned by the night train to Westbury. At seven o'clock in the morning he reached home in a Westbury gig, very cold, but upon the whole, a much more comfortable man than when he had left it. He had almost brought himself to think that even yet he would succeed at last.

CHAPTER XXXIII.

FAREWELL.

Christmas came, and a month beyond Christmas, and by the end of January Captain Marrable and Miss Lowther had agreed to regard all their autumn work as null and void,—to look back upon the love-making as a thing that had not been, and to part as friends. Both of them suffered much in this arrangement,—the man being the louder in the objurgations which he made against his ill-fortune, and in his assurances to himself and others that he was ruined for life. And, indeed, no man could have been much more unhappy than was Walter Marrable in these days. To him was added the trouble, which he did not endeavour to hide from himself or Mary, that all this misery came to him from his own father. Before the end of November, sundry renewed efforts were made to save a portion of the money, and the lawyers descended so low as to make an offer to take £2000. They might have saved themselves the humiliation, for neither £2000 nor £200 could have been made to be forthcoming. Walter Marrable, when the time came, was painfully anxious to fight somebody; but he was told very clearly by Messrs. Block and Curling, that there was nobody whom he could fight but his father, and that even by fighting his father, he would never obtain a penny. "My belief," said Mr. Curling, "is, that you could put your father in prison, but that probably is not your object." Marrable was forced to own that that was not his object; but he did so in a tone which seemed to imply that a prison, were it even for life, would be the best place for his father. Block and Curling had been solicitors to the Marrables for ever so many years; and though they did not personally love the Colonel, they had a professional feeling that the blackness of a black sheep of a family should not be made public, at any rate by the family itself or by the family solicitors. Almost every family has a black sheep, and it is the especial duty of a family solicitor to keep the family black sheep from being dragged into the front and visible ranks of the family. The Captain had been fatally wrong in signing the paper which he had signed, and must take the consequences. "I don't think, Captain Marrable, that you would save yourself in any way by proceeding against the Colonel," said Mr. Curling. "I have not the slightest intention of proceeding against him," said the Captain, in great dudgeon,—and then he left the office and shook the dust off his feet, as against Block and Curling as well as against his father.

After this,—immediately after it,—he had one other interview with his father. As he told his uncle, the devil prompted him to go down to Portsmouth to see the man to whom his interests should have been dearer than to all the world beside, and who had robbed him so ruthlessly. There was nothing to be gained by such a visit. Neither money nor counsel, nor even consolation would be forthcoming from Colonel Marrable. Probably Walter Marrable felt in his anger that it would be unjust that his father should escape without a word to remind him from his son's mouth of all that he had done for his son. The Colonel held some staff office at Portsmouth, and his son came upon him in his lodgings one evening as he was dressing to go out to dinner. "Is that you, Walter?" said the battered old reprobate, appearing at the door of his bed-room; "I am very glad to see you."

"I don't believe it," said the son.

"Well;—what would you have me say? If you'll only behave decently, I shall be glad to see you."

"You've given me an example in that way, sir; have you not? Decency indeed!"

"Now, Walter, if you're going to talk about that horrid money, I tell you at once, that I won't listen to you."

"That's kind of you, sir."

"I've been unfortunate. As soon as I can repay it, or a part of it, I will. Since you've been back, I've done everything in my power to get a portion of it for you,—and should have got it, but for those stupid people in Bedford Row. After all, the money ought to have been mine, and that's what I suppose you felt when you enabled me to draw it."

"By heavens, that's cool!"

"I mean to be cool;—I'm always cool. The cab will be here to take me to dinner in a very few minutes. I hope you will not think I am running away from you?"

"I don't mean you to go till you've heard what I've got to say," said the Captain.

"Then, pray say it quickly." Upon this, the Colonel stood still and faced his son; not exactly with a look of anger, but assuming an appearance as though he were the person injured. He was a thin old man, who wore padded coats, and painted his beard and his eyebrows, and had false teeth, and who, in spite of chronic absence of means, always was possessed of clothes apparently just new from the hands of a West-end tailor. He was one of those men who, through their long, useless, ill-flavoured lives, always contrive to live well, to eat and drink of the best, to lie softly, and to go about in purple and fine linen,—and yet, never have any money. Among a certain set Colonel Marrable, though well known, was still popular. He was good-tempered, well-mannered, sprightly in conversation, and had not a scruple in the world. He was over seventy, had lived hard, and must have known that there was not much more of it for him. But yet he had no qualms, and no fears. It may be doubted whether he knew that he was a bad man,—he, than whom you could find none worse though you were to search the country from one end to another. To lie, to steal,—not out of tills or pockets, because he knew the danger; to cheat—not at the card-table, because he had never come in the way of learning the lesson; to indulge every passion, though the cost to others might be ruin for life; to know no gods but his own bodily senses, and no duty but that which he owed to those gods; to eat all, and produce nothing; to love no one but himself; to have learned nothing but how to sit at table like a gentleman; to care not at all for his country, or even for his profession; to have no creed, no party, no friend, no conscience, to be troubled with nothing that touched his heart;—such had been, was, and was to be the life of Colonel Marrable. Perhaps it was accounted to him as a merit by some that he did not quail at any coming fate. When his doctor warned him that he must go soon, unless he would refrain from this and that and the other,—so wording his caution that the Colonel could not but know and did know, that let him refrain as he would he must go soon,—he resolved that he would refrain, thinking that the charms of his wretched life were sweet enough to be worth such sacrifice; but in no other respect did the caution affect him. He never asked himself whether he had aught even to regret before he died, or to fear afterwards.

There are many Colonel Marrables about in the world, known well to be so at clubs, in drawing-rooms, and by the tradesmen who supply them. Men give them dinners and women smile upon them. The best of coats and boots are supplied to them. They never lack cigars nor champagne. They have horses to ride, and servants to wait upon them more obsequious than the servants of other people. And men will lend them money too,—well knowing that there is no chance of repayment. Now and then one hears a horrid tale of some young girl who surrenders herself to such a one, absolutely for love! Upon the whole the Colonel Marrables are popular. It is hard to follow such a man quite to the end and to ascertain whether or no he does go out softly at last, like the snuff of a candle,—just with a little stink.

"I will say it as quickly as I can," said the Captain. "I can gain nothing I know by staying here in your company."

"Not while you are so very uncivil."

"Civil, indeed! I have to-day made up my mind, not for your sake, but for that of the family, that I will not prosecute you as a criminal for the gross robbery which you have perpetrated."

"That is nonsense, Walter, and you know it as well as I do."

"I am going back to India in a few weeks, and I trust I may never be called upon to see you again. I will not, if I can help it. It may be a toss-up which of us may die first, but this will be our last meeting. I hope you may remember on your death-bed that you have utterly ruined your son in every relation of life. I was engaged to marry a girl,—whom I loved; but it is all over, because of you."

"I had heard of that, Walter, and I really congratulate you on your escape."

"I can't strike you—"

"No; don't do that."

"Because of your age, and because you are my father. I suppose you have no heart, and that I cannot make you feel it."

"My dear boy, I have an appetite, and I must go and satisfy it." So saying the Colonel escaped, and the Captain allowed his father to make his way down the stairs and into the cab before he followed.

Though he had thus spoken to his father of his blasted hopes in regard to Mary Lowther, he had not as yet signified his consent to the measure by which their engagement was to be brought altogether to an end. The question had come to be discussed widely among their friends, as is the custom with such questions in such circumstances, and Mary had been told from all sides that she was bound to give it up,—that she was bound to give it up for her own sake, and more especially for his; that the engagement, if continued, would never lead to a marriage, and that it would in the meantime be absolutely ruinous to her,—and to him. Parson John came up and spoke to her with a strength for which she had not hitherto given Parson John credit. Her Aunt Sarah was very gentle with her, but never veered from her opinion that the engagement must of necessity be abandoned. Mr. Fenwick wrote to her a letter full of love and advice, and Mrs. Fenwick made a journey to Loring to discuss the matter with her. The discussion between them was very long. "If you are saying this on my account," said Mary, "it is quite useless."

"On what other account? Mr. Gilmore? Indeed, indeed, I am not thinking of him. He is out of my mind altogether. I say it because I know it is impossible that you and your cousin should be married, and because such an engagement is destructive to both the parties."

"For myself," said Mary, "it can make no difference."

"It will make the greatest difference. It would wear you to pieces with a deferred hope. There is nothing so killing, so terrible, so much to be avoided. And then for him!— How is a man, thrown about on the world as he will be, to live in such a condition."

The upshot of it all was that Mary wrote a letter to her cousin proposing to surrender her engagement, and declaring that it would be best for them both that he should agree to accept her surrender. That plan which she had adopted before, of leaving all the responsibility to him, would not suffice. She had come to perceive during these weary discussions that if a way out of his bondage was to be given to Walter Marrable it must come from her action and not from his. She had intended to be generous when she left everything to him; but it was explained to her, both by her aunt and Mrs. Fenwick, that her generosity was of a kind which he could not use. It was for her to take the responsibility upon herself; it was for her to make the move; it was, in short, for her to say that the engagement should be over.

The very day that Mrs. Fenwick left her she wrote the letter, and Captain Marrable had it in his pocket when he went down to bid a last farewell to his father. It had been a sad, weary, tear-laden performance,—the writing of that letter. She had resolved that no sign of a tear should be on the paper, and she had rubbed the moisture away from her eyes a dozen times during the work lest it should fall. There was but little of intended pathos in it; there were no expressions of love till she told him at the end that she would always love him dearly; there was no repining,—no mention of her own misery. She used all the arguments which others had used to her, and then drew her conclusion. She remembered that were she to tell him that she would still be true to him, she would in fact be asking for some such pledge back from him; and she said not a word of any such constancy on her own part. It was best for both of them that the engagement should be broken off; and, therefore, broken off it was, and should be now and for ever. That was the upshot of Mary Lowther's letter.

Mary Lowther writes to Walter Marrable.

Captain Marrable when he received it, though he acknowledged the truth of all the arguments, loved the girl far too well to feel that this release gave him any comfort. He had doubtless felt that the engagement was a burthen on him,—that he would not have entered into it had he not felt sure of his diminished fortune, and that there was a fearful probability that it might never result in their being married; but not the less did the breaking up of it make him very wretched. An engagement for marriage can never be so much to a man as it is to a woman,—marriage itself can never be so much, can never be so great a change, produce such utter misery, or of itself be efficient for such perfect happiness,—but his love was true and steadfast, and when he learned that she was not to be his, he was as a man who had been robbed of his treasure. Her letter was long and argumentative. His reply was short and passionate;—and the reader shall see it.

Duke Street, January, 186—.

Dearest Mary,

I suppose you are right. Everybody tells me so, and no doubt everybody tells you the same. The chances are that I shall get bowled over; and as for getting back again, I don't know when I can hope for it. In such a condition it would I believe be very wrong and selfish were I to go and leave you to think of me as your future husband. You would be waiting for that which would never come.

As for me, I shall never care for any other woman. A soldier can get on very well without a wife, and I shall always regard myself now as one of those useless but common animals who are called "not marrying men." I shall never marry. I shall always carry your picture in my heart, and shall not think that I am sinning against you or any one else when I do so after hearing that you are married.

I need not tell you that I am very wretched. It is not only that I am separated from you, my own dear, dearest girl, but that I cannot refrain from thinking how it has come to pass that it is so. I went down to see my father yesterday. I did see him, and you may imagine of what nature was the interview. I sometimes think, when I lie in bed, that no man was ever so ill-treated as I have been.

Dearest love, good-bye. I could not have brought myself to say what you have said, but I know that you are right. It has not been my fault, dear. I did love you, and do love you as truly as any man ever loved a woman.

Yours with all my heart,

Walter Marrable.

I should like to see you once more before I start. Is there any harm in this? I must run down to my uncle's, but I will not go up to you if you think it better not. If you can bring yourself to see me, pray, pray do.

In answer to this Mary wrote to him to say that she would certainly see him when he came. She knew no reason, she said, why they should not meet. When she had written her note she asked her aunt's opinion. Aunt Sarah would not take upon herself to say that no such meeting ought to take place, but it was very evident that she thought that it would be dangerous.

Captain Marrable did come down to Loring about the end of January, and the meeting did take place. Mary had stipulated that she should be alone when he called. He had suggested that they should walk out together, as had been their wont; but this she had declined, telling him that the sadness of such a walk would be too much for her, and saying to her aunt with a smile that were she once again out with him on the towing-path, there would be no chance of their ever coming home. "I could not ask him to turn back," she said, "when I should know that it would be for the last time." It was arranged, therefore, that the meeting should take place in the drawing-room at Uphill Lane.

He came into the room with a quick, uneasy step, and when he reached her he put his arm round her and kissed her. She had formed certain little resolutions on this subject. He should kiss her, if he pleased, once again when he went,—and only once. And now, almost without a motion on her part that was perceptible, she took herself out of his arms. There should be no word about that if she could help it,—but she was bound to remember that he was nothing to her now but a distant cousin. He must cease to be her lover, though she loved him. Nay,—he had so ceased already. There must be no more laying of her head upon his shoulder, no more twisting of her fingers through his locks, no more looking into his eyes, no more amorous pressing of her lips against his own. Much as she loved him she must remember now that such outward signs of love as these would not befit her. "Walter," she said, "I am so glad to see you! And yet I do not know but what it would have been better that you should have stayed away."

"Why should it have been better? It would have been unnatural not to have met each other."

"So I thought. Why should not friends endure to say good-bye, even though their friendship be as dear as ours? I told Aunt Sarah that I should be angry with myself afterwards if I feared to tell you to come."

"There is nothing to fear,—only that it is so wretched an ending," said he.

"In one way I will not look on it as an ending. You and I cannot be married, Walter; but I shall always have your career to look to, and shall think of you as my dearest friend. I shall expect you to write to me;—not at first, but after a year or so. You will be able to write to me then as though you were my brother."

"I shall never be able to do that."

"Oh yes;—that is, if you will make the effort for my sake. I do not believe but what people can manage and mould their own wills if they will struggle hard enough. You must not be unhappy, Walter."

"I am not so wise or self-confident as you, Mary. I shall be unhappy. I should be deceiving myself if I were to tell myself otherwise. There is nothing before me to make me happy. When I came home there was very little that I cared for, though I had the prospect of this money and thought that my cares in that respect were over. Then I met you, and the whole world seemed altered. I was happy even when I found how badly I had been treated. Now all that has gone, and I cannot think that I shall be happy again."

"I mean to be happy, Walter."

"I hope you may, dear."

"There are gradations in happiness. The highest I ever came to yet was when you told me that you loved me." When she said that, he attempted to take her hand, but she withdrew from him, almost without a sign that she was doing so. "I have not quite lost that yet," she continued, "and I do not mean to lose it altogether. I shall always remember that you loved me; and you will not forget that I too loved you."

"Forget it?—no, I don't exactly think that I shall forget it."

"I don't know why it should make us altogether unhappy. For a time, I suppose, we shall be down-hearted."

"I shall, I know. I can't pretend to such strength as to say that I can lose what I want, and not feel it."

"We shall both feel it, Walter;—but I do not know that we must be miserable. When do you leave England?"

"Nothing is settled. I have not had the heart to think of it. It will not be for a month or two yet. I suppose I shall stay out my regular Indian time."

"And what shall you do with yourself?"

"I have no plans at all, Mary. Sir Gregory has asked me to Dunripple, and I shall remain there probably till I am tired of it. It will be so pleasant, talking to my uncle of my father."

"Do not talk of him at all, Walter. You will best forgive him by not talking of him. We shall hear, I suppose, of what you do from Parson John."

She had seated herself a little away from him, and he did not attempt to draw near to her again till at her bidding he rose to leave her. He sat there for nearly an hour, and during that time much more was said by her than by him. She endeavoured to make him understand that he was as free as air, and that she would hope some day to hear that he was married. In reply to this, he asserted very loudly that he would never call any woman his wife, unless unexpected circumstances should enable him to return and again ask for her hand. "Not that you are to wait for me, Mary," he said. She smiled, but made no definite answer to this. She had told herself that it would not be for his welfare that she should allude to the possibility of a renewed engagement, and she did not allude to it.

"God bless you, Walter," she said at last, coming to him and offering him her hand.

"God bless you, for ever and ever, dearest Mary," he said, taking her in his arms and kissing her again and again. It was to be the last, and she did not seem to shun him. Then he left her, went as far as the door,—and returned again. "Dearest, dearest Mary. You will give me one more kiss?"

"It shall be the last, Walter," she said. Then she did kiss him, as she would have kissed her brother that was going from her, and escaping from his arms she left the room.

He had come to Loring late on the previous evening, and on that same day he returned to London. No doubt he dined at his club, drank a pint of wine and smoked a cigar or two, though he did it all after a lugubrious fashion. Men knew that he had fallen into great trouble in the matter of his inheritance, and did not expect him to be joyful and of pleasant countenance. "By George!" said little Captain Boodle, "if it was my governor, I'd go very near being hung for him; I would, by George!" Which remark obtained a good deal of general sympathy in the billiard-room of that military club. In the meantime Mary Lowther at Loring had resolved that she would not be lugubrious, and she sat down to dinner opposite to her aunt with a pleasant smile on her face. Before the evening was over, however, she had in some degree broken down. "I fear I can't get along with novels, Aunt Sarah," she said. "Don't you think I could find something to do." Then the old lady came round the room and kissed her niece;—but she made no other reply.

CHAPTER XXXIV.

BULLHAMPTON NEWS.

When the matter was quite settled at Loring,—when Miss Marrable not only knew that the engagement had been surrendered on both sides, but that it had been so surrendered as to be incapable of being again patched up, she bethought herself of her promise to Mr. Gilmore. This did not take place for a fortnight after the farewell which was spoken in the last chapter,—at which time Walter Marrable was staying with his uncle, Sir Gregory, at Dunripple. Miss Marrable had undertaken that Mr. Gilmore should be informed as soon as the engagement was brought to an end, and had been told that this information should reach him through Mrs. Fenwick. When a fortnight had passed, Miss Marrable was aware that Mary had not herself written to her friend at Bullhampton; and though she felt herself to be shy of the subject, though she entertained a repugnance to make any communication based on a hope that Mary might after a while receive her old lover graciously,—for time must of course be needed before such grace could be accorded,—she did write a few lines to Mrs. Fenwick. She explained that Captain Marrable was to return to India, and that he was to go as a free man. Mary, she said, bore her burden well. Of course, it must be some time before the remembrance of her cousin would cease to be a burden to her; but she went about her heavy task with a good will,—so said Miss Marrable,—and would no doubt conquer her own unhappiness after a time by the strength of her personal character. Not a word was spoken of Mr. Gilmore, but Mrs. Fenwick understood it all. The letter, she knew well, was a message to Mr. Gilmore;—a message which it would be her duty to give as soon as possible, that he might extract from it such comfort as it would contain for him,— though it would be his duty not to act upon it for, at any rate, many months to come. "And it will be a comfort to him," said her husband when he read Miss Marrable's letter.

"Of all the men I know, he is the most constant," said Mrs. Fenwick, "and best deserves that his constancy should be rewarded."

"It is the man's nature," said the parson. "Of course, he will get her at last; and when he has got her, he will be quite contented with the manner in which he has won her. There's nothing like going on with a thing. I believe I might be a bishop if I set my heart on it."

"Why don't you, then?"

"I am not sure that the beauty of the thing is so well-defined to me as is Mary Lowther's to poor Harry. In perseverance and success of that kind the man's mind should admit of no doubt. Harry is quite clear of this,—that in spite of Mary's preference for her cousin, it would be the grandest thing in the world to him that she should marry him. The certainty of his condition will pull him through at last."

Two days after this Mrs. Fenwick put Miss Marrable's letter into Mr. Gilmore's hand,—having perceived that it was specially written that it might be so treated. She kept it in her pocket till she should chance to see him, and at last handed it to him as she met him walking on his own grounds. "I have a letter from Loring," she said.

"From Mary?"

"No;—from Mary's aunt. I have it here, and I think you had better read it. To tell you the truth, Harry, I have been looking for you ever since I got it. Only you must not make too much of it."

Then he read the letter. "What do you mean," he asked, "by making too much of it?"

"You must not suppose that Mary is the same as before she saw this cousin of hers."

"But she is the same."

"Well;—yes, in body and in soul, no doubt. But such an experience leaves a mark which cannot be rubbed out quite at once."

"You mean that I must wait before I ask her again."

"Of course you must wait. The mark must be rubbed out first, you know."

"I will wait; but as for the rubbing out of the mark, I take it that will be altogether beyond me. Do you think, Mrs. Fenwick, that no woman should ever, under any circumstances, marry one man when she loves another?"

She could not bring herself to tell him that in her opinion Mary Lowther would of all women be the least likely to do so. "That is one of those questions," she said, "which it is almost impossible for a person to answer. In the first place, before answering it, we should have a clear definition of love."

"You know what I mean well enough."

"I do know what you mean, but I hardly do know how to answer you. If you went to Mary Lowther now, she would take it almost as an insult; and she would feel it in that light, because she is aware that you know of this story of her cousin."

"Of course I shall not go to her at once."

"She will never forget him altogether."

"Such things cannot be forgotten," said Gilmore.

"Nevertheless," said Mrs. Fenwick, "it is probable that Mary will be married some day. These wounds get themselves cured as do others."

"I shall never be cured of mine," said he, laughing. "As for Mary, I hardly know what to think. I suppose girls do marry without caring very much for the men they take. One sees it every day; and then afterwards, they love their husbands. It isn't very romantic, but it seems to me that it is so."

"Don't think of it too much, Harry," said Mrs. Fenwick. "If you still are devoted to her—"

"Indeed I am."

"Then wait awhile, and we will have her at Bullhampton again. You know at any rate what our wishes are."

Everything had been very quiet at Bullhampton during the last three months. The mill was again in regular work, and Sam had remained at home with fair average regularity. The Vicar had heard nothing more of Carry Brattle, and had been unable to trace her or to learn where she was living. He had taken various occasions to mention her name to her mother, but Mrs. Brattle knew nothing of her, and believed that Sam was equally ignorant with herself. Both she and the Vicar found it impossible to speak to Sam on the subject, though they knew that he had been with his sister more than once when she was living at Pycroft Common. As for the miller himself, no one had mentioned Carry's name to him since the day on which the Vicar had made his attempt. And from that day to the present there had been, if not ill blood, at least cold blood between Mr. Fenwick and old Brattle. The Vicar had gone down to the mill as often as usual, having determined that what had occurred should make no difference with him; and the intercourse with Mrs. Brattle and Fanny had been as kind on each side as usual;—but the miller had kept out of his way, retreating from him openly, going from the house to the mill as soon as he appeared, never speaking to him, and taking no other notice of him beyond a slight touch of the hat. "Your husband is still angry with me," he said one day to Mrs. Brattle. She shook her head and smiled sadly, and said that it would pass over some day,—only that Jacob was so persistent. With Sam, the Vicar held little or no communication. Sam in these days never went to church, and though he worked at the mill pretty constantly, he would absent himself from the village occasionally for a day or two together, and tell no one where he had been.

The strangest and most important piece of business going on at this time in Bullhampton was the building of a new chapel or tabernacle,—the people called it a Salem,—for Mr. Puddleham. The first word as to the erection reached Mr. Fenwick's ears from Grimes, the builder and carpenter, who, meeting him in Bullhampton Street, pointed out to him a bit of spare ground just opposite the vicarage gates,—a morsel of a green on which no building had ever yet stood, and told him that the Marquis had given it for a chapel. "Indeed," said Fenwick. "I hope it may be convenient and large enough for them. All the same, I wish it had been a little farther from my gate." This he said in a cheery tone, showing thereby considerable presence of mind. That such a building should be so placed was a trial to him, and he knew at once that the spot must have been selected to annoy him. Doubtless, the land in question was the property of the Marquis of Trowbridge. When he came to think of it, he had no doubt on the matter. Nevertheless, the small semi-circular piece of grass immediately opposite to his own swinging gate, looked to all the world as though it were an appendage of the Vicarage. A cottage built there would have been offensive; but a staring brick Methodist chapel, with the word Salem inserted in large letters over the door, would, as he was aware, flout him every time he left or entered his garden. He had always been specially careful to avoid any semblance of a quarrel with the Methodist minister, and had in every way shown his willingness to regard Mr. Puddleham's flock as being equal to his own in the general gifts of civilisation. To Mr. Puddleham himself, he had been very civil, sending him fruit and vegetables out of the Vicarage garden, and lending him newspapers. When the little Puddlehams were born, Mrs. Fenwick always inquired after the mother and infant. The greatest possible care had been exercised at the Vicarage since Mr. Fenwick's coming to show that the Established Church did not despise the dissenting congregation. For the last three years there had been talk of a new chapel, and Mr. Fenwick had himself discussed the site with Mr. Puddleham. A large and commodious spot of ground, remote from the vicarage, had, as he believed, been chosen. When he heard those tidings, and saw what would be the effect of the building, it seemed to him almost impossible that a Marquis could condescend to such revenge. He went at once to Mr. Puddleham, and learned from him that Grimes' story was true. This had been in December. After Christmas, the foundations were to be begun at once, said Mr. Puddleham, so that the brickwork might go on as soon as the frosts were over. Mr. Puddleham was in high spirits, and expressed a hope that he should be in his new chapel by next August. When the Vicar asked why the change of site was made, being careful to show no chagrin by the tone of his voice, Mr. Puddleham remarked that the Marquis's agent thought that it would be an improvement, "in which opinion I quite coincide," said Mr. Puddleham, looking very stern,—showing his teeth, as it were, and displaying an inclination for a parish quarrel. Fenwick, still prudent, made no objection to the change, and dropped no word of displeasure in Mr. Puddleham's hearing.

"I don't believe he can do it," said Mrs. Fenwick, boiling with passion.

"He can, no doubt," said the Vicar.

"Do you mean to say the street is his;—to do what he likes with it?"

"The street is the Queen's highway,—which means that it belongs to the public; but this is not the street. I take it that all the land in the village belongs to the Marquis. I never knew of any common right, and I don't believe there is any."

"It is the meanest thing I ever heard of in my life," said Mrs. Fenwick.

"There I agree with you." Later in the day, when he had been thinking of it for hours, he again spoke to his wife. "I shall write to the Marquis and remonstrate. It will probably be of no avail; but I think I ought to do so for the sake of those who come after me. I shall be able to bother him a good deal, if I can do nothing else," he added, laughing. "I feel, too, that I must quarrel with somebody, and I won't quarrel with dear old Puddleham, if I can help it."

CHAPTER XXXV.

MR. PUDDLEHAM'S NEW CHAPEL.

The Vicar devoted a week to the consideration of his grievance about the chapel, and then did write to the Marquis. Indeed, there was no time to be lost if he intended to do anything, as on the second day after his interview with Mr. Grimes, Grimes himself, with two men to assist him, began their measuring on the devoted spot, sticking in little marks for the corners of the projected building, and turning up a sod here and there. Mr. Grimes was a staunch Churchman; and though in the way of business he was very glad to have the building of a Methodist chapel,—or of a Pagan temple, if such might come in his way,—yet, even though he possibly might give some offence to the great man's shadow in Bullhampton, he was willing to postpone his work for two or three days at the Vicar's request. "Grimes," the Vicar said, "I'm not quite sure that I like this."

Site of Mr. Puddleham's new chapel.

"Well, sir;—no, sir. I was thinking myself, sir, that maybe you might take it unkind in the Marquis."

"I think I shall write to him. Perhaps you wouldn't mind giving over for a day or two." Grimes yielded at once, and took his spade and measurements away, although Mr. Puddleham fretted a good deal. Mr. Puddleham had been much elated by the prospect of his new Bethel, and had, it must be confessed, received into his mind an idea that it would be a good thing to quarrel with the Vicar under the auspices of the landlord. Fenwick's character had hitherto been too strong for him, and he had been forced into parochial quiescence and religious amity almost in spite of his conscience. He was a much older man than Mr. Fenwick, having been for thirty years in the ministry, and he had always previously enjoyed the privilege of being on bad terms with the clergyman of the Establishment. It had been his glory to be a poacher on another man's manor, to filch souls, as it were, out of the keeping of a pastor of a higher grade than himself, to say severe things of the short comings of an endowed clergyman, and to obtain recognition of his position by the activity of his operations in the guise of a blister. Our Vicar, understanding something of this, had, with some malice towards the gentleman himself, determined to rob Mr. Puddleham of his blistering powers. There is no doubt a certain pleasure in poaching which does not belong to the licit following of game; but a man can't poach if the right of shooting be accorded to him. Mr. Puddleham had not been quite happy in his mind amidst the ease and amiable relations which Mr. Fenwick enforced upon him, and had long since begun to feel that a few cabbages and peaches did not repay him for the loss of those pleasant and bitter things, which it would have been his to say in his daily walks and from the pulpit of his Salem, had he not been thus hampered, confined, and dominated. Hitherto he had hardly gained a single soul from under Mr. Fenwick's grasp,—had indeed on the balance lost his grasp on souls, and was beginning to be aware that this was so because of the cabbages and the peaches. He told himself that though he had not hankered after these flesh-pots, that though he would have preferred to be without the flesh-pots, he had submitted to them. He was painfully conscious of the guile of this young man, who had, as it were, cheated him out of that appropriate acerbity of religion, without which a proselyting sect can hardly maintain its ground beneath the shadow of an endowed and domineering Church. War was necessary to Mr. Puddleham. He had come to be hardly anybody at all, because he was at peace with the vicar of the parish in which he was established. His eyes had been becoming gradually open to all this for years; and when he had been present at the bitter quarrel between the Vicar and the Marquis, he had at once told himself that now was his opportunity. He had intended to express a clear opinion to Mr. Fenwick that he, Mr. Fenwick, had been very wrong in speaking to the Marquis as he had spoken, and as he was walking out of the farm-house he was preparing some words as to the respect due to those in authority. It happened, however, that at that moment the wind was taken out of his sails by a strange comparison which the Vicar made to him between the sins of them two, ministers of God as they were, and the sins of Carry Brattle. Mr. Puddleham at the moment had been cowed and quelled. He was not quite able to carry himself in the Vicar's presence as though he were the Vicar's equal. But the desire for a quarrel remained, and when it was suggested to him by Mr. Packer, the Marquis's man of business, that the green opposite to the Vicarage gate would be a convenient site for his chapel, and that the Marquis was ready to double his before-proffered subscription, then he saw plainly that the moment had come, and that it was fitting that he should gird up his loins and return all future cabbages to the proud donor.

Mr. Puddleham had his eye keenly set on the scene of his future ministration, and was aware of Grimes's default almost as soon as that man with his myrmidons had left the ground. He at once went to Grimes with heavy denunciations, with threats of the Marquis, and with urgent explanation as to the necessity of instant work. But Grimes was obdurate. The Vicar had asked him to leave the work for a day or two, and of course he must do what the Vicar asked. If he couldn't be allowed to do as much as that for the Vicar of the parish, Bullhampton wouldn't be, in Mr. Grimes's opinion, any place for anybody to live in. Mr. Puddleham argued the matter out, but he argued in vain. Mr. Grimes declared that there was time enough, and that he would have the work finished by the time fixed,—unless, indeed, the Marquis should change his mind. Mr. Puddleham regarded this as a most improbable supposition. "The Marquis doesn't change his mind, Mr. Grimes," he said; and then he walked forth from Mr. Grimes's house with much offence.

By this time all Bullhampton knew of the quarrel,—knew of it, although Mr. Fenwick had been so very careful to guard himself from any quarrelling at all. He had not spoken a word in anger on the subject to anyone but his wife; and in making his request to Grimes had done so with hypocritical good humour. But, nevertheless, he was aware that the parish was becoming hot about it; and when he sat down to write his letter to the Marquis he was almost minded to give up the idea of writing, to return to Grimes, and to allow the measuring and sod-turning to be continued. Why should a place of worship opposite to his gate be considered by him as an injury? Why should the psalm-singing of Christian brethren hurt his ears as he walked about his garden? And if, through the infirmity of his nature, his eyes and his ears were hurt, what was that to the great purport for which he had been sent into the parish? Was he not about to create enmity by his opposition; and was it not his special duty to foster love and goodwill among his people? After all he, within his own Vicarage grounds, had all that it was intended that he should possess; and that he held very firmly. Poor Mr. Puddleham had no such firm holding; and why should he quarrel with Mr. Puddleham because that ill-paid preacher sought to strengthen the ground on which his Salem stood?

As he paused, however, to think of all this, there came upon him the conviction that in this thing that was to be done the Marquis was determined to punish him personally, and he could not resist the temptation of fighting the Marquis. And then, if he succumbed easily in this matter, would it not follow almost as a matter of course that the battle against him would be carried on elsewhere? If he yielded now, resolving to ignore altogether any idea of his own comfort or his own taste, would he thereby maintain that tranquillity in his parish which he thought so desirable? He had already seen that in Mr. Puddleham's manner to himself which made him sure that Mr. Puddleham was ambitious to be a sword in the right hand of the Marquis. Personally the Vicar was himself pugnacious. Few men, perhaps, were more so. If there must be a fight let them come on, and he would do his best. Turning the matter thus backwards and forwards in his mind, he came at last to the conclusion that there must be a fight, and consequently he wrote the following letter to the Marquis;—

Bullhampton Vicarage, January 3, 186—.

MY LORD MARQUIS,

I learned by chance the other day in the village that a new chapel for the use of the Methodist congregation of the parish was to be built on the little open green immediately opposite the Vicarage gate, and that this special spot of ground had been selected and given by your lordship for this purpose. I do not at all know what truth there may be in this,—except that Mr. Grimes, the carpenter here, has received orders from your agent about the work. It may probably be the case that the site has been chosen by Mr. Packer, and not by your lordship. As no real delay to the building can at this time of the year arise from a short postponement of the beginning, I have asked Mr. Grimes to desist till I shall have written to you on the subject.

I can assure your lordship, in the first place, that no clergyman of the Established Church in the kingdom can be less unwilling than I am that they who dissent from my teaching in the parish should have a commodious place of worship. If land belonged to me in the place I would give it myself for such a purpose; and were there no other available site than that chosen, I would not for a moment remonstrate against it. I had heard, with satisfaction, from Mr. Puddleham himself that another spot was chosen near the cross roads in the village, on which there is more space, to which as I believe there is no objection, and which would certainly be nearer than that now selected to the majority of the congregation.

But of course it would not be for me to trouble your lordship as to the ground on which a Methodist chapel should be built, unless I had reason to show why the site now chosen is objectionable. I do not for a moment question your lordship's right to give the site. There is something less than a quarter of an acre in the patch in question; and though hitherto I have always regarded it as belonging in some sort to the Vicarage,—as being a part, as it were, of the entrance,—I feel convinced that you, as landlord of the ground, would not entertain the idea of bestowing it for any purpose without being sure of your right to do so. I raise no question on this point, believing that there is none to be raised; but I respectfully submit to your lordship, whether such an erection as that contemplated by you will not be a lasting injury to the Vicarage of Bullhampton, and whether you would wish to inflict a lasting and gratuitous injury on the vicar of a parish, the greatest portion of which belongs to yourself.

No doubt life will be very possible to me and my wife, and to succeeding vicars and their wives, with a red-brick chapel built as a kind of watch-tower over the Vicarage gate. So would life be possible at Turnover Park with a similar edifice immediately before your lordship's hall-door. Knowing very well that the reasonable wants of the Methodists cannot make such a building on such a spot necessary, you no doubt would not consent to it; and I now venture to ask you to put a stop to this building here for the same reason. Were there no other site in the parish equally commodious I would not say a word.

I have the honour to be,
Your lordship's most obedient servant,

FRANCIS FENWICK.

Lord Trowbridge, when he received this letter,—when he had only partially read it, and had not at all digested it, was disposed to yield the point. He was a silly man, thinking much too highly of his own position, believing himself entitled to unlimited deference from all those who in any way came within the rays of his magnificence, and easily made angry by opposition; but he was not naturally prone to inflict evil, and did in some degree recognise it as a duty attached to his splendour that he should be beneficent to the inferiors with whom he was connected. Great as was his wrath against the present Vicar of Bullhampton, and thoroughly as he conceived it to be expedient that so evil-minded a pastor should be driven out of the parish, nevertheless he felt some scruple at taking a step which would be injurious to the parish vicar, let the parish vicar be who he might. Packer was the sinner who had originated the new plan for punishing Mr. Fenwick,—Packer, with the assistance of Mr. Puddleham; and the Marquis, though he had in some sort authorised the plan, had in truth thought very little about it. When the Vicar spoke of the lasting injury to the Vicarage, and when Lord Trowbridge remembered that he owned two thousand and two acres within the parish,—as Mr. Puddleham had told him,—he began to think that the chapel had better be built elsewhere. The Vicar was a pestilent man to whom punishment was due, but the punishment should be made to attach itself to the man, rather than to the man's office. So was working the Marquis's mind, till the Marquis came upon that horrid passage in the Vicar's letter, in which it was suggested that the building of a Methodist chapel in his own park, immediately in front of his own august hall-door might under certain circumstances be expedient. The remark was almost as pernicious and unpardonable as that which had been made about his lordship's daughters. It was manifest to him that the Vicar intended to declare that marquises were no more than other people,—and that the declaration was made and insisted on with the determination of insulting him. Had this apostate priest been capable of feeling any proper appreciation of his own position and that of the Marquis, he would have said nothing of Turnover Park. When the Marquis had read the letter a second time and had digested it he perceived that its whole tenour was bad, that the writer was evil-minded, and that no request made by him should be granted. Even though the obnoxious chapel should have to be pulled down for the benefit of another vicar, it should be put up for the punishment of this vicar. A man who wants to have a favour done for him, can hardly hope to be successful if he asks for the favour with insolence. So the heart of the Marquis was hardened, and he was strengthened to do that which misbecame him both as a gentleman and a landlord.

He did not answer the letter for some time; but he saw Packer, saw his head agent, and got out the map of the property. The map of the property was not very clear in the matter, but he remembered the space well, and convinced himself that no other place in all Bullhampton could be so appropriate for a Methodist chapel. At the end of a week he caused a reply to be written to Mr. Fenwick. He would not demean himself by writing with his own hand, but he gave his orders to the head agent. The head agent merely informed the Vicar that it was considered that the spot of ground in question was the most appropriate in the village for the purpose in hand.

Mrs. Fenwick when she heard the reply burst out into tears. She was a woman by no means over devoted to things of this world, who thought much of her duties and did them, who would have sacrificed anything for her husband and children, who had learned the fact that both little troubles and great, if borne with patience, may be borne with ease; but she did think much of her house, was proud of her garden, and rejoiced in the external prettiness of her surroundings. It was gall to her that this hideous building should be so placed as to destroy the comeliness of that side of her abode. "We shall hear their singing and ranting whenever we open our front windows," she said.

"Then we won't open them," said the Vicar.

"We can't help ourselves. Just see what it will be whenever we go in and out. We might just as well have it inside the house at once."

"You speak as though Mr. Puddleham were always in his pulpit."

"They're always doing something,—and then the building will be there whether it's open or shut. It will alter the parish altogether, and I really think it will be better that you should get an exchange."

"And run away from my enemy?"

"It would be running away from an intolerable nuisance."

"I won't do that," said the Vicar. "If there were no other reason for staying, I won't put it in the power of the Marquis of Trowbridge to say that he has turned me out of my parish, and so punished me because I have not submitted myself to him. I have not sought the quarrel. He has been overbearing and insolent, and now is meanly desirous to injure me because I will not suffer his insolence. No doubt, placed as he is, he can do much; but he cannot turn me out of Bullhampton."

"What is the good of staying, Frank, if we are to be made wretched?"

"We won't be made wretched. What! be wretched because there is an ugly building opposite to your outside gate? It is almost wicked to say so. I don't like it. I like the doing of the thing less even than the thing itself. If it can be stopped, I will stop it. If it could be prevented by any amount of fighting, I should think myself right to fight in such a cause. If I can see my way to doing anything to oppose the Marquis, it shall be done. But I won't run away." Mrs. Fenwick said nothing more on the subject at that moment, but she felt that the glory and joy of the Vicarage were gone from it.

CHAPTER XXXVI.

SAM BRATTLE GOES OFF AGAIN.

Mr. Grimes had suggested to the Vicar in a very low whisper that the new chapel might perhaps be put down as a nuisance. "It ain't for me to say, of course," said Mr. Grimes, "and in the way of business one building is as good as another as long as you see your money. But buildings is stopped because they're nuisances." This occurred a day or two after the receipt of the agent's letter from Turnover, and the communication was occasioned by orders given to Mr. Grimes to go on with the building instantly, unless he intended to withdraw from the job. "I don't think, Grimes, that I can call a place of Christian worship a nuisance," said the Vicar. To this Grimes rejoined that he had known a nunnery bell to be stopped because it was a nuisance, and that he didn't see why a Methodist chapel bell was not as bad as a nunnery bell. Fenwick had declared that he would fight if he could find a leg to stand upon, and he thanked Grimes, saying that he would think of the suggestion. But when he thought of it, he did not see that any remedy was open to him on that side. In the meantime Mr. Puddleham attacked Grimes with great severity because the work was not continued. Mr. Puddleham, feeling that he had the Marquis at his back, was eager for the fight. He had already received in the street a salutation from the Vicar, cordial as usual, with the very slightest bend of his neck, and the sourest expression of his mouth. Mrs. Puddleham had already taught the little Puddlehams that the Vicarage cabbages were bitter with the wormwood of an endowed Establishment, and ought no longer to be eaten by the free children of an open Church. Mr. Puddleham had already raised up his voice in his existing tabernacle, as to the injury which was being done to his flock, and had been very touching on the subject of the little vineyard which the wicked king coveted. When he described himself as Naboth, it could not but be supposed that Ahab and Jezebel were both in Bullhampton. It went forth through the village that Mr. Puddleham had described Mrs. Fenwick as Jezebel, and the torch of discord had been thrown down, and war was raging through the parish.

There had come to be very high words indeed between Mr. Grimes and Mr. Puddleham, and some went so far as to declare that they had heard the builder threaten to punch the minister's head. This Mr. Grimes denied stoutly, as the Methodist party were making much of it in consequence of Mr. Puddleham's cloth and advanced years. "There's no lies is too hot for them," said Mr. Grimes, in his energy, and "no lawlessness too heavy." Then he absolutely refused to put his hand to a spade or a trowel. He had his time named in his contract, he said, and nobody had a right to drive him. This was ended by the appearance on a certain Monday morning of a Baptist builder from Salisbury, with all the appurtenances of his trade, and with a declaration on Mr. Grimes' part, that he would have the law on the two leading members of the Puddleham congregation, from whom he had received his original order. In truth, however, there had been no contract, and Mr. Grimes had gone to work upon a verbal order which, according to the Puddleham theory, he had already vitiated by refusing compliance with its terms. He, however, was hot upon his lawsuit, and thus the whole parish was by the ears.

It may be easily understood how much Mr. Fenwick would suffer from all this. It had been specially his pride that his parish had been at peace, and he had plumed himself on the way in which he had continued to clip the claws with which nature had provided the Methodist minister. Though he was fond of a fight himself, he had taught himself to know that in no way could he do the business of his life more highly or more usefully than as a peacemaker; and as a peacemaker he had done it. He had never put his hand within Mr. Puddleham's arm, and whispered a little parochial nothing into his neighbour's ear, without taking some credit to himself for his cleverness. He had called his peaches angels of peace, and had spoken of his cabbages as being dove-winged. All this was now over, and there was hardly one in Bullhampton who was not busy hating and abusing somebody else.

And then there came another trouble on the Vicar. Just at the end of January, Sam Brattle came up to the Vicarage and told Mr. Fenwick that he was going to leave the mill. Sam was dressed very decently; but he was attired in an un-Bullhampton fashion, which was not pleasant to Mr. Fenwick's eyes; and there was about him an air which seemed to tell of filial disobedience and personal independence.

"But you mean to come back again, Sam?" said the Vicar.

"Well, sir; I don't know as I do. Father and I has had words."

"And that is to be a reason why you should leave him? You speak of your father as though he were no more to you than another man."

"I wouldn't a' borne not a tenth of it from no other man, Mr. Fenwick."

"Well—and what of that? Is there any measure of what is due by you to your father? Remember, Sam, I know your father well."

"You do, sir."

"He is a very just man, and he is very fond of you. You are the apple of his eye, and now you would bring his gray hairs with sorrow to the grave."

"You ask mother, sir, and she'll tell you how it is. I just said a word to him,— a word as was right to be said, and he turned upon me, and bade me go away and come back no more."

"Do you mean that he has banished you from the mill?"

"He said what I tells you. He told mother afterwards, that if so as I would promise never to mention that thing again, I might come and go as I pleased. But I wasn't going to make no such promise. I up and told him so; and then he—cursed me."

For a moment or two the Vicar was silent, thinking whether in this affair Sam had been most wrong, or the old man. Of course he was hearing but one side of the question. "What was it, Sam, that he forbade you to mention?"

"It don't matter now, sir; only I thought I'd better come and tell you, along of your being the bail, sir."

"Do you mean that you are going to leave Bullhampton altogether?"

"To leave it altogether, Mr. Fenwick. I ain't doing no good here."

"And why shouldn't you do good? Where can you do more good?"

"It can't be good to be having words with father day after day."

"But, Sam, I don't think you can go away. You are bound by the magistrates' orders. I don't speak for myself, but I fear the police would be after you."

"And is it to go on allays,—that a chap can't move to better hisself, because them fellows can't catch the men as murdered old Trumbull? That can't be law,—nor yet justice." Upon this there arose a discussion in which the Vicar endeavoured to explain to the young man that as he had evidently consorted with the men who were, on the strongest possible grounds, suspected to be the murderers, and as he had certainly been with those men where he had no business to be,—namely, in Mr. Fenwick's own garden at night,—he had no just cause of complaint at finding his own liberty more crippled than that of other people. No doubt Sam understood this well enough, as he was sharp and intelligent; but he fought his own battle, declaring that as the Vicar had not prosecuted him for being in the garden, nobody could be entitled to punish him for that offence; and that as it had been admitted that there was no evidence connecting him with the murder, no policeman could have a right to confine him to one parish. He argued the matter so well, that Mr. Fenwick was left without much to say. He was unwilling to press his own responsibility in the matter of the bail, and therefore allowed the question to fall through,—tacitly admitting that if Sam chose to leave the parish, there was nothing in the affair of the murder to hinder him. He went back, therefore, to the inexpediency of the young man's departure, telling him that he would rush right into the Devil's jaws. "May be so, Mr. Fenwick," said Sam, "but I'm sure I'll never be out of 'em as long as I stays here in Bullhampton."

"But what is it all about, Sam?" The Vicar, as he asked the question had a very distinct idea in his own head as to the cause of the quarrel, and was aware that his sympathies were with the son rather than with the father. Sam answered never a word, and the Vicar repeated his question. "You have quarrelled with your father before this, and have made it up. Why should not you make up this quarrel?"

"Because he cursed me," said Sam.

"An idle word, spoken in wrath! Don't you know your father well enough to take that for what it is worth? What was it about?"

"It was about Carry, then."

"What had you said?"

"I said as how she ought to be let come home again, and that if I was to stay there at the mill, I'd fetch her. Then he struck at me with one of the mill-bolts. But I didn't think much o' that."

"Was it then he—cursed you?"

"No; mother came up, and I went aside with her. I told her as I'd go on speaking to the old man about Carry;—and so I did."

"And where is Carry?" Sam made no reply to this whatever. "You know where she can be found, Sam?" Sam shook his head, but didn't speak. "You couldn't have said that you would fetch her, if you didn't know where to find her."

"I wouldn't stop till I did find her, if the old man would take her back again. She's bad enough, no doubt, but there's others worse nor her."

"When did you see her last?"

"Over at Pycroft."

"And whither did she go from Pycroft, Sam?"

"She went to Lon'on, I suppose, Mr. Fenwick."

"And what is her address in London?" In reply to this Sam again shook his head. "Do you mean to seek her now?"

"What's the use of seeking her if I ain't got nowhere to put her into. Father's got a house and plenty of room in it. Where could I put her?"

"Sam, if you'll find her, and bring her to any place for me to see her, I'll find a home for her somewhere. I will, indeed. Or, if I knew where she was, I'd go up to London to her myself. She's not my sister—!"

"No, sir, she ain't. The likes of you won't likely have a sister the likes of her. She's a—"

"Sam, stop. Don't say a bitter word of her. You love her."

"Yes;—I do. That don't make her not a bad 'un."

"So do I love her. And as for being bad, which of us isn't bad? The world is very hard on her offence."

"Down on it, like a dog on a rat."

"It is not for me to make light of her sin;—but her sin can be washed away as well as other sin. I love her too. She was the brightest, kindest, sauciest little lass in all the parish, when I came here."

"Father was proud enough of her then, Mr. Fenwick."

"You find her and let me know where she is, and I will make out a home for her somewhere;—that is, if she will be tractable. I'm afraid your father won't take her at the mill."

"He'll never set eyes on her again, if he can help it. As for you, Mr. Fenwick, if there was only a few more like you about, the world wouldn't be so bad to get on in. Good-bye, Mr. Fenwick."

"Good-bye, Sam;—if it must be so."

"And don't you be afeared about me, Mr. Fenwick. If the hue-and-cry is out anyways again me, I'll turn up. That I will,—though it was to be hung afterwards,—sooner than you'd be hurt by anything I'd been a doing."

So they parted, as friends rather than as enemies, though the Vicar knew very well that the young man was wrong to go and leave his father and mother, and that in all probability he would fall at once into some bad mode of living. But the conversation about Carry Brattle had so softened their hearts to each other, that Mr. Fenwick found it impossible to be severe. And he knew, moreover, that no severity of expression would have been of avail. He couldn't have stopped Sam from going had he preached to him for an hour.

After that the building of the chapel went on apace, the large tradesman from Salisbury being quicker in his work than could have been the small tradesman belonging to Bullhampton. In February there came a hard frost, and still the bricklayers were at work. It was said in Bullhampton that walls built as those walls were being built could never stand. But then it might be that these reports were spread by Mr. Grimes, that the fanatical ardour of the Salisbury Baptist lent something to the rapidity of his operations, and that the Bullhampton feeling in favour of Mr. Fenwick and the Church Establishment added something to the bitterness of the prevailing criticisms.

At any rate, the walls of the new chapel were mounting higher and higher all through February, and by the end of the first week in March there stood immediately opposite to the Vicarage gate a hideously ugly building, roofless, doorless, windowless;—with those horrid words,—"New Salem, 186—" legibly inscribed on a visible stone inserted above the doorway, a thing altogether as objectionable to the eyes of a Church of England parish clergyman as the imagination of any friend or enemy could devise. We all know the abominable adjuncts of a new building,—the squalid half-used heaps of bad mortar, the eradicated grass, the truculent mud, the scattered brickbats, the remnants of timber, the debris of the workmen's dinners, the morsels of paper scattered through the dirt! There had from time to time been actual encroachments on the Vicarage grounds, and Mrs. Fenwick, having discovered that the paint had been injured on the Vicarage gate, had sent an angry message to the Salisbury Baptist. The Salisbury Baptist had apologised to Mr. Fenwick, saying that such things would happen in the building of houses, &c., and Mr. Fenwick had assured him that the matter was of no consequence. He was not going to descend into the arena with the Salisbury Baptist. In this affair the Marquis of Trowbridge was his enemy, and with the Marquis he would fight, if there was to be any fight at all. He would stand at his gate and watch the work, and speak good-naturedly to the workmen; but he was in truth sick at heart. The thing, horrible as it was to him, so fascinated him that he could not keep his mind from it. During all this time it made his wife miserable. She had literally grown thin under the infliction of the new chapel. For more than a fortnight she had refused to visit the front gate of her own house. To and from church she always went by the garden wicket; but in going to the school, she had to make a long round to avoid the chapel,—and this round she made day after day. Fenwick himself, still hoping that there might be some power of fighting, had written to an enthusiastic archdeacon, a friend of his, who lived not very far distant. The Archdeacon had consulted the Bishop,—really troubled deeply about the matter,—and the Bishop had taken upon himself, with his own hands, to write words of mild remonstrance to the Marquis. "For the welfare of the parish generally," said the Bishop, "I venture to make this suggestion to your lordship, feeling sure that you will do anything that may not be unreasonable to promote the comfort of the parishioners." In this letter he made no allusion to his late correspondence with the Marquis as to the sins of the Vicar. Nor did the Marquis in his reply allude to the former correspondence. He expressed an opinion that the erection of a place of Christian worship on an open space outside the bounds of a clergyman's domain ought not to be held to be objectionable by that clergyman;—and that as he had already given the spot, he could not retract the gift. These letters, however, had been written before the first brick had been laid, and the world in that part of the country was of opinion that the Marquis might have retracted his gift. After this Mr. Fenwick found no ground whatever on which he could fight his battle. He could only stand at his gateway, and look at the thing as it rose above the ground, fascinated by its ugliness.

He was standing there once, about a month or five weeks after his interview with Sam Brattle, just at the beginning of March, when he was accosted by the Squire. Mr. Gilmore, through the winter,—ever since he had heard that Mary Lowther's engagement with Walter Marrable had been broken off,— had lived very much alone. He had been pressed to come to the Vicarage, but had come but seldom, waiting patiently till the time should come when he might again ask Mary to be his wife. He was not so gloomy as he had been during the time the engagement had lasted, but still he was a man much altered from his former self. Now he came across the road, and spoke a word or two to his friend. "If I were you, Frank, I should not think so much about it."

"Yes, you would, old boy, if it touched you as it does me. It isn't that the chapel should be there. I could have built a chapel for them with my own hands on the same spot, if it had been necessary."

"I don't see what there is to annoy you."

"This annoys me,—that after all my endeavours, there should be people here, and many people, who find a gratification in doing that which they think I shall look upon as an annoyance. The sting is in their desire to sting, and in my inability to show them their error, either by stopping what they are doing, or by proving myself indifferent to it. It isn't the building itself, but the double disgrace of the building."

CHAPTER XXXVII.

FEMALE MARTYRDOM.

Early in February Captain Marrable went to Dunripple to stay with his uncle, Sir Gregory, and there he still was when the middle of March had come. News of his doings reached the ladies at Loring, but it reached them through hands which were not held to be worthy of a perfect belief,—at any rate, on Mary Lowther's part. Dunripple Park is in Warwickshire, and lies in the middle of a good hunting country. Now, according to Parson John, from whom these tidings came, Walter Marrable was hunting three days a week; and, as Sir Gregory himself did not keep hunters, Walter must have hired his horses,—so said Parson John, deploring that a nephew so poor in purse should have allowed himself to be led into such heavy expense. "He brought home a little ready money with him," said the parson; "and I suppose he thinks he may have his fling as long as that lasts." No doubt Parson John, in saying this, was desirous of proving to Mary that Walter Marrable was not dying of love, and was, upon the whole, leading a jolly life, in spite of the little misfortune that had happened to him. But Mary understood all this quite as well as did Parson John himself; and simply declined to believe the hunting three days a week. She said not a word about it, however, either to him or to her aunt. If Walter could amuse himself, so much the better; but she was quite sure that, at such a period of his life as this, he would not spend his money recklessly. The truth lay between Parson John's stories and poor Mary's belief. Walter Marrable was hunting,—perhaps twice a week, hiring a horse occasionally, but generally mounted by his uncle, Sir Gregory. He hunted; but did so after a lugubrious fashion, as became a man with a broken heart, who was laden with many sorrows, and had just been separated from his lady love for ever and ever. But still, when there came anything good, in the way of a run, and when our Captain could get near to hounds, he enjoyed the fun, and forgot his troubles for a while. Is a man to know no joy because he has an ache at his heart?

In this matter of disappointed and, as it were, disjointed affection, men are very different from women, and for the most part, much more happily circumstanced. Such sorrow a woman feeds;—but a man starves it. Many will say that a woman feeds it, because she cannot but feed it; and that a man starves it, because his heart is of the starving kind. But, in truth, the difference comes not so much from the inner heart, as from the outer life. It is easier to feed a sorrow upon needle-and-thread and novels, than it is upon lawyers' papers, or even the out-a-door occupations of a soldier home upon leave who has no work to do. Walter Marrable told himself again and again that he was very unhappy about his cousin, but he certainly did not suffer in that matter as Mary suffered. He had that other sorrow, arising from his father's cruel usage of him, to divide his thoughts, and probably thought quite as much of the manner in which he had been robbed, as he did of the loss of his love.

But poor Mary was, in truth, very wretched. When a girl asks herself that question,—what shall she do with her life? it is so natural that she should answer it by saying that she will get married, and give her life to somebody else. It is a woman's one career—let women rebel against the edict as they may; and though there may be word-rebellion here and there, women learn the truth early in their lives. And women know it later in life when they think of their girls; and men know it, too, when they have to deal with their daughters. Girls, too, now acknowledge aloud that they have learned the lesson; and Saturday Reviewers and others blame them for their lack of modesty in doing so,—most unreasonably, most uselessly, and, as far as the influence of such censors may go, most perniciously. Nature prompts the desire, the world acknowledges its ubiquity, circumstances show that it is reasonable, the whole theory of creation requires it; but it is required that the person most concerned should falsely repudiate it, in order that a mock modesty may be maintained, in which no human being can believe! Such is the theory of the censors who deal heavily with our Englishwomen of the present day. Our daughters should be educated to be wives, but, forsooth, they should never wish to be wooed! The very idea is but a remnant of the tawdry sentimentality of an age in which the mawkish insipidity of the women was the reaction from the vice of that preceding it. That our girls are in quest of husbands, and know well in what way their lines in life should be laid, is a fact which none can dispute. Let men be taught to recognise the same truth as regards themselves, and we shall cease to hear of the necessity of a new career for women.

Mary Lowther, though she had never encountered condemnation as a husband-hunter, had learned all this, and was well aware that for her there was but one future mode of life that could be really blessed. She had eyes, and could see; and ears, and could hear. She could make,—indeed, she could not fail to make,—comparisons between her aunt and her dear friend, Mrs. Fenwick. She saw, and could not fail to see, that the life of the one was a starved, thin, poor life,—which, good as it was in its nature, reached but to few persons, and admitted but of few sympathies; whereas the other woman, by means of her position as a wife and a mother, increased her roots and spread out her branches, so that there was shade, and fruit, and beauty, and a place in which the birds might build their nests. Mary Lowther had longed to be a wife,—as do all girls healthy in mind and body; but she had found it to be necessary to her to love the man who was to become her husband. There had come to her a suitor recommended to her by all her friends,—

recommended to her also by all outward circumstances,—and she had found that she did not love him! For a while she had been sorely perplexed, hardly knowing what it might be her duty to do, not understanding how it was that the man was indifferent to her, doubting whether, after all, the love of which she had dreamt was not a passion which might come after marriage, rather than before it,—but still fearing to run so great a hazard. She had doubted, feared, and had hitherto declined,—when that other lover had fallen in her way. Mr. Gilmore had wooed her for months without touching her heart. Then Walter Marrable had come and had conquered her almost in an hour. She had never felt herself disposed to play with Mr. Gilmore's hair, to lean against his shoulder, to be touched by his fingers,—never disposed to wait for his coming, or to regret his going. But she had hardly become acquainted with her cousin before his presence was a pleasure to her; and no sooner had he spoken to her of his love, than everything that concerned him was dear to her. The atmosphere that surrounded him was sweeter to her than the air elsewhere. All those little aids which a man gives to a woman were delightful to her when they came to her from his hands. She told herself that she had found the second half that was needed to make herself one whole; that she had become round and entire in joining herself to him; and she thought that she understood well why it had been that Mr. Gilmore had been nothing to her. As Mr. Fenwick was manifestly the husband appointed for his wife, so had Walter Marrable been appointed for her. And so there had come upon her a dreamy conviction that marriages are made in heaven. That question, whether they were to be poor or rich, to have enough or much less than enough for the comforts of life, was, no doubt, one of much importance; but, in the few happy days of her assured engagement, it was not allowed by her to interfere for a moment with the fact that she and Walter were intended, each to be the companion of the other, as long as they two might live.

Then by degrees,—by degrees, though the process had been quick,—had fallen upon her that other conviction, that it was her duty to him to save him from the burdens of that life to which she herself had looked forward so fondly. At first she had said that he should judge of the necessity; swearing to herself that his judgment, let it be what it might, should be right to her. Then she had perceived that this was not sufficient;—that in this way there would be no escape for him;—that she herself must make the decision, and proclaim it. Very tenderly and very cautiously had she gone about her task; feeling her way to the fact that this separation, if it came from her, would be deemed expedient by him. That she would be right in all this, was her great resolve; that she might after all be wrong, her constant fear. She, too, had heard of public censors, of the girl of the period, and of the forward indelicacy with which women of the age were charged. She knew not why, but it seemed to her that the laws of the world around her demanded more of such rectitude from a woman than from a man, and, if it might be possible to her, she would comply with these laws. She had convinced herself, forming her judgment from every tone of his voice, from every glance of his eye, from every word that fell from his lips, that this separation would be expedient for him. And then, assuring herself that the task should be hers, and not his, she had done it. She had done it, and, counting up the cost afterwards, she had found herself to be broken in pieces. That wholeness and roundness, in which she had rejoiced, had gone from her altogether. She would try to persuade herself that she could live as her aunt had lived, and yet be whole and round. She tried, but knew that she failed. The life to which she had looked forward had been the life of a married woman; and now, as that was taken from her, she could be but a thing broken, a fragment of humanity, created for use, but never to be used.

She bore all this well, for a while,—and indeed never ceased to bear it well, to the eyes of those around her. When Parson John told her of Walter's hunting, she laughed, and said that she hoped he would distinguish himself. When her aunt on one occasion congratulated her, telling her that she had done well and nobly, she bore the congratulation with a smile and a kind word. But she thought about it much, and within the chambers of her own bosom there were complaints made that the play which had been played between him and her during the last few months should for her have been such a very tragedy, while for him the matter was no more than a melodrama, touched with a pleasing melancholy. He had not been made a waif upon the waters by the misfortune of a few weeks, by the error of a lawyer, by a mistaken calculation,—not even by the crime of his father. His manhood was, at any rate, perfect to him. Though he might be a poor man, he was still a man with his hands free, and with something before him which he could do. She understood, too, that the rough work of his life would be such that it would rub away, perhaps too quickly, the impression of his late love, and enable him hereafter to love another. But for her,—for her there could be nothing but memory, regrets, and a life which would simply be a waiting for death. But she had done nothing wrong,—and she must console herself with that, if consolation could then be found.

Then there came to her a letter from Mrs. Fenwick which moved her much. It was the second which she had received from her friend since she had made it known that she was no longer engaged to her cousin. In her former letter Mrs. Fenwick had simply expressed her opinion that Mary had done rightly, and had, at the same time, promised that she would write again, more at length, when the passing by of a few weeks should have so far healed the first agony of the wound, as to make it possible for her to speak of the future. Mary, dreading this second letter, had done nothing to elicit it; but at last it came. And as it had some effect on Mary Lowther's future conduct, it shall be given to the reader:—

Bullhampton Vicarage, March 12, 186—.

DEAREST MARY,

I do so wish you were here, if it were only to share our misery with us. I did not think that so small a thing as the building of a wretched chapel could have put me out so much, and made me so uncomfortable as this has done. Frank says that it is simply the feeling of being beaten,—the insult not the injury, which is the grievance; but they both rankle with me. I hear the click of the trowel every hour, and though I never go near the front gate, yet I know that it is all muddy and foul with brickbats and mortar. I don't think that anything so cruel and unjust was ever done before; and the worst of it is that Frank, though he hates it just as much as I do, does preach such sermons to me about the wickedness of caring for small evils. 'Suppose you had to go to it every Sunday yourself,' he said the other day, trying to make me understand what a real depth of misery there is in the world. 'I shouldn't mind that half so much,' I answered. Then he bade me try it,—which wasn't fair because he knows I can't. However, they say it will all tumble down because it has been built so badly.

I have been waiting to hear from you, but I can understand why you should not write. You do not wish to speak of your cousin, or to write without speaking of him. Your aunt has written to me twice, as doubtless you know, and has told me that you are well, only more silent than heretofore. Dearest Mary, do write to me, and tell me what is in your heart. I will not ask you to come to us,—not yet,—because of our neighbour; but I do think that if you were here I could do you good. I know so well, or fancy that I know so well, the current in which your thoughts are running! You have had a wound, and think that therefore you must be a cripple for life. But it is not so; and such thoughts, if not wicked, are at least wrong. I would that it had been otherwise. I would that you had not met your cousin.—

"So would not I," said Mary to herself; but as she said it she knew that she was wrong. Of course it would be for her welfare, and for his too, if his heart was as hers, that she should never have seen him.—

But because you have met him, and have fancied that you and he would be all in all together, you will be wrong indeed if you let that fancy ruin your future life. Or if you encourage yourself to feel that, because you have loved one man from whom you are necessarily parted, therefore you should never allow yourself to become attached to another, you will indeed be teaching yourself an evil lesson. I think I can understand the arguments with which you may perhaps endeavour to persuade your heart that its work of loving has been done, and should not be renewed; but I am quite sure that they are false and inhuman. The Indian, indeed, allows herself to be burned through a false idea of personal devotion; and if that idea be false in a widow, how much falser is it in one who has never been a wife.

You know what have ever been our wishes. They are the same now as heretofore; and his constancy is of that nature, that nothing will ever change it. I am persuaded that it would have been unchanged, even if you had married your cousin, though in that case he would have been studious to keep out of your way. I do not mean to press his claims at present. I have told him that he should be patient, and that if the thing be to him as important as he makes it, he should be content to wait. He replied that he would wait. I ask for no word from you at present on this subject. It will be much better that there should be no word. But it is right that you should know that there is one who loves you with a devotion which nothing can alter.

I will only add to this my urgent prayer that you will not make too much to yourself of your own misfortune, or allow yourself to think that because this and that have taken place, therefore everything must be over. It is hard to say who makes the greatest mistakes, women who treat their own selves with too great a reverence, or they who do so with too little.

Frank sends his kindest love. Write to me at once, if only to condole with me about the chapel.

Most affectionately yours,

JANET FENWICK.

My sister and Mr. Quickenham are coming here for Easter week, and I have still some hopes of getting my brother-in-law to put us up to some way of fighting the Marquis and his myrmidons. I have always heard it said that there was no case in which Mr. Quickenham couldn't make a fight.

Mary Lowther understood well the whole purport of this letter,—all that was meant as well as all that was written. She had told herself again and again that there had been that between her and the lover she had lost,—tender embraces, warm kisses, a bird-like pressure of the plumage,—which alone should make her deem it unfit that she should be to another man as she had been to him, even should her heart allow it. It was against this doctrine that her friend had preached, with more or less of explicitness in her sermon. And how was the truth? If she could take a lesson on that subject from any human being in the world, she would take it from her friend Janet Fenwick. But she rebelled against the preaching, and declared to herself that her friend had never been tried, and therefore did not understand the case. Must she not be guided by her own feelings, and did she not feel that she could never lay her head on the shoulder of another lover without blushing at her memories of the past?

And yet how hard was it all! It was not the joys of young love that she regretted in her present mood, not the loss of those soft delights of which she had suddenly found herself to be so capable; but that all the world should be dark and dreary before her! And he could hunt, could dance, could work,—no doubt could love again! How happy would it be for her if her reason would allow her to be a Roman Catholic, and a nun!

CHAPTER XXXVIII.

A LOVER'S MADNESS.

The letter from Mrs. Fenwick, which the reader has just seen, was the immediate effect of a special visit which Mr. Gilmore had made to her. On the 10th of March he had come to her with a settled purpose, pointing out to her that he had now waited a certain number of months since he had heard of the rupture between Mary and her cousin, naming the exact period which Mrs. Fenwick had bade him wait before he should move again in the matter, and asking her whether he might not now venture to take some step. Mrs. Fenwick had felt it to be unfair that her very words should be quoted against her, as to the three or four months, feeling that she had said three or four instead of six or seven to soften the matter to her friend; but, nevertheless, she had been induced to write to Mary Lowther.

"I was thinking that perhaps you might ask her to come to you again," Mr. Gilmore had said when Mrs. Fenwick rebuked him for his impatience. "If you did that, the thing might come on naturally."

"But she wouldn't come if I did ask her."

"Because she hates me so much that she will not venture to come near me?"

"What nonsense that is, Harry. It has nothing to do with hating. If I thought that she even disliked you, I should tell you so, believing that it would be for the best. But of course if I asked her here just at present, she could not but remember that you are our nearest neighbour, and feel that she was pressed to come with some reference to your hopes."

"And therefore she would not come?"

"Exactly; and if you will think of it, how could it be otherwise? Wait till he is in India. Wait at any rate till the summer, and then Frank and I will do our best to get her here."

"I will wait," said Mr. Gilmore, and immediately took his leave, as though there were no other subject of conversation now possible to him.

Since his return from Loring, Mr. Gilmore's life at his own house had been quite secluded. Even the Fenwicks had hardly seen him, though they lived so near to him. He had rarely been at church, had seen no company at home since his uncle, the prebendary, had left him, and had not dined even at the Vicarage more than once or twice. All this had of course been frequently discussed between Mr. and Mrs. Fenwick, and had made the Vicar very unhappy. He had expressed a fear that his friend would be driven half crazy by a foolish indulgence in a hopeless passion, and had suggested that it might perhaps be for the best that Gilmore should let his place and travel abroad for two or three years, so that, in that way, his disappointment might be forgotten. But Mrs. Fenwick still hoped better things than this. She probably thought more of Mary Lowther than she did of Harry Gilmore, and still believed that a cure for both their sorrows might be found, if one would only be patient, and the other would not despair.

Mr. Gilmore had promised that he would wait, and then Mrs. Fenwick had written her letter. To this there came a very quick answer. In respect to the trouble about the chapel, Mary Lowther was sympathetic and droll, as she would have been had there been upon her the weight of no love misfortune. "She had trust," she said, "in Mr. Quickenham, who no doubt would succeed in harassing the enemy, even though he might be unable to obtain ultimate conquest. And then there seemed to be a fair prospect that the building would fall of itself, which surely would be a great triumph. And, after all, might it not fairly be hoped that the pleasantness of the Vicarage garden, which Mr. Puddleham must see every time he visited his chapel, might be quite as galling and as vexatious to him as would be the ugliness of the Methodist building to the Fenwicks?

"You should take comfort in the reflection that his sides will be quite as full of thorns as your own," said Mary; "and perhaps there may come some blessed opportunity for crushing him altogether by heaping hot coals of fire on his head. Offer him the use of the Vicarage lawn for one of his school tea-parties, and that, I should think, would about finish him."

This was all very well, and was written on purpose to show to Mrs. Fenwick that Mary could still be funny in spite of her troubles; but the pith of the letter, as Mrs. Fenwick well understood, lay in the few words of the last paragraph.

"Don't suppose, dear, that I am going to die of a broken heart. I mean to live and to be as happy as any of you. But you must let me go on in my own way. I am not at all sure that being married is not more trouble than it is worth."

That she was deceiving herself in saying this Mary knew well enough; and Mrs. Fenwick, too, guessed that it was so. Nevertheless, it was plain enough that nothing more could be said about Mr. Gilmore just at present.

"You ought to blow him up, and make him come to us," Mrs. Fenwick said to her husband.

"It is all very well to say that, but one man can't blow another up, as women do. Men don't talk to each other about the things that concern them nearly,—unless it be about money."

"What do they talk about, then?"

"About matters that don't concern them nearly;—game, politics, and the state of the weather. If I were to mention Mary's name to him, he would feel it to be an impertinence. You can say what you please."

Soon after this, Gilmore came again to the Vicarage; but he was careful to come when the Vicar would not be there. He sauntered into the garden by the little gate from the churchyard, and showed himself at the drawing-room window, without going round to the front door. "I never go to the front now," said Mrs. Fenwick; "I have only once been through the gate since they began to build."

"Is not that very inconvenient?"

"Of course it is. When we came home from dining at Sir Thomas's the other day, I had myself put down at the church gate, and walked all the way round, though it was nearly pitch dark. Do come in, Harry."

"Do come in, Harry."

Then Mr. Gilmore came in, and seated himself before the fire. Mrs. Fenwick understood his moods so well, that she would not say a word to hurry him. If he chose to talk about Mary Lowther, she knew very well what she would say to him; but she would not herself introduce the subject. She spoke for awhile about the Brattles, saying that the old man had suffered much since his son had gone from him. Sam had left Bullhampton at the end of January, never having returned to the mill after his visit to the Vicar, and had not been heard of since. Gilmore, however, had not been to see his tenant; and though he expressed an interest about the Brattles, had manifestly come to the Vicarage with the object of talking upon matters more closely interesting to himself.

"Did you write to Loring, Mrs. Fenwick?" he asked at last.

"I wrote to Mary soon after you were last here."

"And has she answered you?"

"Yes; she wrote again almost at once. She could not but write, as I had said so much to her about the chapel."

"She did not allude to—anything else, then?"

"I can't quite say that, Harry. I had written to her out of a very full heart, telling her what I thought as to her future life generally, and just alluding to our wishes respecting you."

"Well?"

"She said just what might have been expected,—that for the present she would rather be let alone."

"I have let her alone. I have neither spoken to her nor written to her. She does not mean to say that I have troubled her?"

"Of course you have not troubled her,—but she knows what we all mean."

"I have waited all the winter, Mrs. Fenwick, and have said not a word. How long was it that she knew her cousin before she was engaged to him?"

"What has that to do with it? You know what our wishes are; but, indeed, indeed, nothing can be done by hurrying her."

"She was engaged to that man, and the engagement broken off all within a month. It was no more than a dream."

"But the remembrance of such dreams will not fade away quickly. Let us hope that hereafter it may be as a dream;—but time must be allowed to efface the idea of its reality."

"Time;—yes; but cannot we arrange some plan for the future? Cannot something be done? I thought you said you would ask her to come here?"

"So I did,—but not yet."

"Why shouldn't she come now? You needn't ask because I am here. There is no saying whom she may meet, and then my chance will be gone again."

"Is that all you know about women, Harry? Do you think that the girl whom you love so dearly will take up with one man after another in that fashion?"

"Who can say? She was not very long in taking up, as you call it, with Captain Marrable. I should be happier if she were here, even if I did not see her."

"Of course you would see her, and of course you would propose again,—and of course she would refuse you."

"Then there is no hope?"

"I do not say that. Wait till the summer comes; and then, if I can influence her, we will have her here. If you find that remaining at the Privets all alone is wearisome to you—"

"Of course it is wearisome."

"Then go up to London—or abroad—or anywhere for a change. Take some occupation in hand and stick to it."

"That is so easily said, Mrs. Fenwick."

"No man ever did anything by moping; and you mope. I know I am speaking plainly, and you may be angry with me, if you please."

"I am not at all angry with you; but I think you hardly understand."

"I do understand," said Mrs. Fenwick, speaking with all the energy she could command; "and I am most anxious to do all that you wish. But it cannot be done in a day. If I were to ask her now, she would not come; and if she came it would not be for your good. Wait till the summer. You may be sure that no harm will be done by a little patience."

Then he went away, declaring again that he would wait with patience; but saying, at the same time, that he would remain at home. "As for going to London," he said, "I should do nothing there. When I find that there is no chance left, then probably I shall go abroad."

"It is my belief," said the Vicar, that evening, when his wife told him what had occurred, "that she will never have him; not because she does not like him, or could not learn to like him if he were as other men are, but simply because he is so unreasonably unhappy about her. No woman was ever got by that sort of puling and whining love. If it were not that I think him crazy, I should say that it was unmanly."

"But he is crazy."

"And will be still worse before he has done with it. Anything would be good now which would take him away from Bullhampton. It would be a mercy that his house should be burned down, or that some great loss should fall upon him. He sits there at home, and does nothing. He will not even look after the farm. He pretends to read, but I don't believe that he does even that."

"And all because he is really in love, Frank."

"I am very glad that I have never been in love with the same reality."

"You never had any need, sir. The plums fell into your mouth too easily."

"Plums shouldn't be too difficult," said the Vicar, "or they lose their sweetness."

A few days after this Mr. Fenwick was standing at his own gate, watching the building of the chapel and talking to the men, when Fanny Brattle from the mill came up to him. He would stand there by the hour at a time, and had made quite a friendship with the foreman of the builder from Salisbury, although the foreman, like his master, was a Dissenter, and had come into the parish as an enemy. All Bullhampton knew how infinite was the disgust of the Vicar at what was being done; and that Mrs. Fenwick felt it so strongly, that she would not even go in and out of her own gate. All Bullhampton was aware that Mr. Puddleham spoke openly of the Vicar as his enemy,—in spite of the peaches and cabbages on which the young Puddlehams had been nourished; and that the Methodist minister had, more than once within the last month or two, denounced his brother of the Established Church from his own pulpit. All Bullhampton was talking of the building of the chapel,—some abusing the Marquis and Mr. Puddleham and the Salisbury builder; others, on the other hand, declaring that it was very good that the Establishment should have a fall. Nevertheless there Mr. Fenwick would stand and chat with the men, fascinated after a fashion by the misfortune which had come upon him. Mr. Packer, the Marquis's steward, had seen him there, and had endeavoured to slink away unobserved,—for Mr. Packer was somewhat ashamed of the share he had had in the matter,—but Mr. Fenwick had called to him, and had spoken to him of the progress of the building.

"Grimes never could have done it so fast," said the Vicar.

"Well,—not so fast, Mr. Fenwick, certainly."

"I suppose it won't signify about the frost?" said the Vicar. "I should be inclined to think that the mortar will want repointing."

Mr. Packer had nothing to say to this. He was not responsible for the building. He endeavoured to explain that the Marquis had nothing to do with the work, and had simply given the land.

"Which was all that he could do," said the Vicar, laughing.

It was on the same day and while Packer was still standing close to him, that Fanny Brattle accosted him. When he had greeted the young woman and perceived that she wished to speak to him, he withdrew within his own gate, and asked her whether there was anything that he could do for her. She had a letter in her hand, and after a little hesitation she asked him to read it. It was from her brother, and had reached her by private means. A young man had brought it to her when her father was in the mill, and had then gone off, declining to wait for any answer.

"Father, sir, knows nothing about it as yet," she said.

Mr. Fenwick took the letter and read it. It was as follows:—

DEAR SISTER,

I want you to help me a little, for things is very bad with me. And it is not for me neither, or I'd sooner starve nor ax for a sixpence from the mill. But Carry is bad too, and if you've got a trifle or so, I think you'd be of a mind to send it. But don't tell father, on no account. I looks to you not to tell father. Tell mother, if you will; but I looks to her not to mention it to father. If it be so you have two pounds by you, send it to me in a letter, to the care of

Muster Thomas Craddock,
Number 5, Crooked Arm Yard,
Cowcross Street,
City of London.

My duty to mother, but don't say a word to father, whatever you do. Carry don't live nowhere there, nor they don't know her.

Your affectionate brother,

SAM BRATTLE.

"Have you told your father, Fanny?"

"Not a word, sir."

"Nor your mother?"

"Oh yes, sir. She has read the letter, and thinks I had better come to you to ask what we should do."

"Have you got the money, Fanny?"

Fanny Brattle explained that she had in her pocket something over the sum named, but that money was so scarce with them now at the mill, that she could hardly send it without her father's knowledge. She would not, she said, be afraid to send it and then to tell her father afterwards. The Vicar considered the matter for some time, standing with the open letter in his hand, and then he gave his advice.

"Come into the house, Fanny," he said, "and write a line to your brother, and then get a money order at the post-office for four pounds, and send it to your brother; and tell him that I lend it to him till times shall be better with him. Do not give him your father's money without your father's leave. Sam will pay me some day, unless I be mistaken in him."

Then Fanny Brattle with many grateful thanks did as the Vicar bade her.

CHAPTER XXXIX.

THE THREE HONEST MEN.

The Vicar of Bullhampton was—a "good sort of fellow." In praise of him to this extent it is hoped that the reader will cordially agree. But it cannot be denied that he was the most imprudent of men. He had done very much that was imprudent in respect to the Marquis of Trowbridge; and since he had been at Bullhampton had been imprudent in nearly everything that he had done regarding the Brattles. He was well aware that the bold words which he had spoken to the Marquis had been dragon's teeth sown by himself, and that they had sprung up from the ground in the shape of the odious brick building which now stood immediately in face of his own Vicarage gate. Though he would smile and be droll, and talk to the workmen, he hated that building quite as bitterly as did his wife. And now, in regard to the Brattles, there came upon him a great trouble. About a week after he had lent the four pounds to Fanny on Sam's behalf, there came to him a dirty note from Salisbury, written by Sam himself, in which he was told that Carry Brattle was now at the Three Honest Men, a public-house in one of the suburbs of the city, waiting there till Mr. Fenwick should find a home for her,—in accordance with his promise given to her brother. Sam, in his letter, had gone on to explain that it would be well that Mr. Fenwick should visit the Three Honest Men speedily, as otherwise there would be a bill there which neither Carry nor Sam would be able to defray. Poor Sam's letter was bald, and they who did not understand his position might have called it bold. He wrote to the Vicar as though the Vicar's coming to Salisbury for the required purpose was a matter of course; and demanded a home for his sister without any reference to her future mode of life, or power of earning her bread, as though it was the Vicar's manifest duty to provide such home. And then that caution in regard to the bill was rather a threat than anything else. If you don't take her quickly from the Three Honest Men there'll be the very mischief of a bill for you to pay. That was the meaning of the caution, and so the Vicar understood it.

But Mr. Fenwick, though he was imprudent, was neither unreasonable nor unintelligent. He had told Sam Brattle that he would provide a home for Carry, if Sam would find his sister and induce her to accept the offer. Sam had gone to work, and had done his part. Having done it, he was right to claim from the Vicar his share of the performance. And then, was it not a matter of course that Carry, when found, should be without means to pay her own expenses? Was it to be supposed that a girl in her position would have money by her. And had not Mr. Fenwick known the truth about their poverty when he had given those four pounds to Fanny Brattle to be sent up to Sam in London? Mr. Fenwick was both reasonable and intelligent as to all this; and, though he felt that he was in trouble, did not for a moment think of denying his responsibility, or evading the performance of his promise. He must find a home for poor Carry, and pay any bill at the Three Honest Men which he might find standing there in her name.

Of course he told his trouble to his wife; and of course he was scolded for the promise he had given. "But, my dear Frank, if for her, why not for others; and how is it possible?"

"For her and not for others, because she is an old friend, a neighbour's child, and one of the parish." That question was easily answered.

"But how is it possible, Frank? Of course one would do anything that it is possible to save her. What I mean is, that one would do it for all of them, if only it were possible."

"If you can do it for one, will not even that be much?"

"But what is to be done? Who will take her? Will she go into a reformatory?"

"I fear not."

"There are so many, and I do not know how they are to be treated except in a body. Where can you find a home for her?"

"She has a married sister, Janet."

"Who would not speak to her, or let her inside the door of her house! Surely, Frank, you know the unforgiving nature of women of that class for such sin as poor Carry Brattle's?"

"I wonder whether they ever say their prayers," said the Vicar.

"Of course they do. Mrs. Jay, no doubt, is a religious woman. But it is permitted to them not to forgive that sin."

"By what law?"

"By the law of custom. It is all very well, Frank, but you can't fight against it. At any rate, you can't ignore it till it has been fought against and conquered. And it is useful. It keeps women from going astray."

"You think, then, that nothing should be done for this poor creature, who fell so piteously, with so small a sin?"

"I have not said so. But when you promised her a home, where did you think of finding one for her? Her only fitting home is with her mother, and you know that her father will not take her there."

Mr. Fenwick said nothing more at that moment, not having clearly made up his mind as to what he might best do; but he had before his eyes, dimly, a plan by which he thought it possible that he might force Carry Brattle on her father's heart. If this plan might be carried out, he would take her to the mill-house and seat her in the room in which the family lived, and then bring the old man in from his work. It might be that Jacob Brattle, in his wrath, would turn with violence upon the man who had dared thus to interfere in the affairs of his family; but he would certainly offer no rough usage to the poor girl. Fenwick knew the man well enough to be sure that he would not lay his hands in anger upon a woman.

But something must be done at once,—something before any such plan as that which was running through his brain could be matured and carried into execution. There was Carry at the Three Honest Men, and, for aught the Vicar knew, her brother staying with her,—with his, the Vicar's credit, pledged for their maintenance. It was quite clear that something must be done. He had applied to his wife, and his wife did not know how to help him. He had suggested the wife of the ironmonger at Warminster as the proper guardian for the poor child, and his own wife had at once made him understand that this was impractical. Indeed, how was it possible that such a one as Carry Brattle should be kept out of sight and stowed away in an open hardware-shop in a provincial town? The properest place for her would be in the country, on some farm; and, so thinking, he determined to apply to the girl's eldest brother.

George Brattle was a prosperous man, living on a large farm near Fordingbridge, ten or twelve miles the other side of Salisbury. Of him the Vicar knew very little, and of his wife nothing. That the man had been married fourteen or fifteen years, and had a family growing up, the Vicar did know; and, knowing it, feared that Mrs. Brattle of Startup, as their farm was called, would not be willing to receive this proposed new inmate. But he would try. He would go on to Startup after having seen Carry at the Three Honest Men, and use what eloquence he could command for the occasion.

He drove himself over on the next day to meet an early train, and was in Salisbury by nine o'clock. He had to ask his way to the Three Honest Men, and at last had some difficulty in finding the house. It was a small beershop, in a lane on the very outskirts of the city, and certainly seemed to him, as he looked at it, to be as disreputable a house, in regard to its outward appearance, as ever he had proposed to enter. It was a brick building of two stories, with a door in the middle of it which stood open, and a red curtain hanging across the window on the left-hand side. Three men dressed like navvies were leaning against the door-posts. There is no sign, perhaps, which gives to a house of this class so disreputable an appearance as red curtains hung across the window; and yet there is no other colour for pot-house curtains that has any popularity. The one fact probably explains the other. A drinking-room with a blue or a brown curtain would offer no attraction to the thirsty navvy who likes to have his thirst indulged without criticism. But, in spite of the red curtain, Fenwick entered the house, and asked the uncomely woman at the bar after Sam Brattle. Was there a man named Sam Brattle staying there;—a man with a sister?

Then were let loose against the unfortunate clergyman the floodgates of a drunken woman's angry tongue. It was not only that the landlady of the Three Honest Men was very drunk, but also that she was very angry. Sam Brattle and his sister had been there, but they had been turned out of the house. There had manifestly been some great row, and Carry Brattle was spoken of with all the worst terms of reproach which one woman can heap upon the name of another. The mistress of the Three Honest Men was a married woman,—and, as far as that went, respectable; whereas poor Carry was not married, and certainly not respectable. Something of her past history had been known. She had been called names which she could not repudiate, and the truth of which even her brother on her behalf could not deny; and then she had been turned into the street. So much Mr. Fenwick learned from the drunken woman, and nothing more he could learn. When he asked after Carry's present address the woman jeered at him, and accused him of base purposes in coming after such a one. She stood with arms akimbo in the passage, and said she would raise the neighbourhood on him. She was drunk, and dirty, as foul a thing as the eye could look upon; every other word was an oath, and no phrase used by the lowest of men in their lowest moments was too hot or too bad for her woman's tongue; and yet there was the indignation of outraged virtue in her demeanour and in her language, because this stranger had come to her door asking after a girl who had been led astray. Our Vicar cared nothing for the neighbourhood, and, indeed, cared very little for the woman at all,—except in so far as she disgusted him; but he did care much at finding that he could obtain no clue to her whom he was seeking. The woman would not even tell him when the girl had left her house, or give him any assistance towards finding her. He had at first endeavoured to mollify the virago by offering to pay the amount of any expenses which might have been left unsettled; but even on this score he could obtain no consideration. She continued to revile him, and he was obliged to leave her,—which he did, at last, with a hurried step to avoid a quart pot which the woman had taken up to hurl at his head, upon some comparison which he most indiscreetly made between herself and poor Carry Brattle.

What should he do now? The only chance of finding the girl was, as he thought, to go to the police-office. He was still in the lane, making his way back to the street which would take him into the city, when he was accosted by a little child. "You be the parson," said the child. Mr. Fenwick owned that he was a parson. "Parson from Bull'umpton?" said the child, inquiringly. Mr. Fenwick acknowledged the fact. "Then you be to come with me." Whereupon Mr. Fenwick followed the child, and was led into a miserable little court in which population was squalid, thick, and juvenile. "She be here, at Mrs. Stiggs's," said the child. Then the Vicar understood that he had been watched, and that he was being taken to the place where she whom he was seeking had found shelter.

CHAPTER XL.

TROTTER'S BUILDINGS.

In the back room up-stairs of Mr. Stiggs's house in Trotter's Buildings the Vicar did find Carry Brattle, and he found also that since her coming thither on the preceding evening,—for only on the preceding evening had she been turned away from the Three Honest Men,—one of Mrs. Stiggs's children had been on the look-out in the lane.

"I thought that you would come to me, sir," said Carry Brattle.

"Of course I should come. Did I not promise that I would come? And where is your brother?"

But Sam had left her as soon as he had placed her in Mrs. Stiggs's house, and Carry could not say whither he had gone. He had brought her to Salisbury, and had remained with her two days at the Three Honest Men, during which time the remainder of their four pounds had been spent; and then there had been a row. Some visitors to the house recognised poor Carry, or knew something of her tale, and evil words were spoken. There had been a fight and Sam had thrashed some man,—or some half-dozen men, if all that Carry said was true. She had fled from the house in sad tears, and after a while her brother had joined her,—bloody, with his lip cut and a black eye. It seemed that he had had some previous knowledge of this woman who lived in Trotter's Buildings,—had known her or her husband,—and there he had found shelter for his sister, having explained that a clergyman would call for her and pay for her modest wants, and then take her away. She supposed that Sam had gone back to London; but he had been so bruised and mauled in the fight that he had determined that Mr. Fenwick should not see him. This was the story as Carry told it; and Mr. Fenwick did not for a moment doubt its truth.

"And now, Carry," said he, "what is it that you would do?"

She looked up into his face, and yet not wholly into his face,—as though she were afraid to raise her eyes so high,—and was silent. His were intently fixed upon her, as he stood over her, and he thought that he had never seen a sight more sad to look at. And yet she was very pretty,—prettier, perhaps, than she had been in the days when she would come up the aisle of his church, to take her place among the singers, with red cheeks and bright flowing clusters of hair. She was pale now, and he could see that her cheeks were rough,—from paint, perhaps, and late hours, and an ill-life; but the girl had become a woman, and the lines of her countenance were fixed, and were very lovely, and there was a pleading eloquence about her mouth for which there had been no need in her happy days at Bullhampton. He had asked her what she would do! But had she not come there, at her brother's instigation, that he might tell her what she should do? Had he not promised that he would find her a home if she would leave her evil ways? How was it possible that she should have a plan for her future life? She answered him not a word; but tried to look into his face and failed.

Nor had he any formed plan. That idea, indeed, of going to Startup had come across his brain,—of going to Startup, and of asking assistance from the prosperous elder brother. But so diffident was he of success that he hardly dared to mention it to the poor girl.

"It is hard to say what you should do," he said.

"Very hard, sir."

His heart was so tender towards her that he could not bring himself to propose to her the cold and unpleasant safety of a Reformatory. He knew, as a clergyman and as a man of common sense, that to place her in such an establishment would, in truth, be the greatest kindness that he could do her. But he could not do it. He satisfied his own conscience by telling himself that he knew that she would accept no such refuge. He thought that he had half promised not to ask her to go to any such place. At any rate, he had not meant that when he had made his rash promise to her brother; and though that promise was rash, he was not the less bound to keep it. She was very pretty, and still soft, and he had loved her well. Was it a fault in him that he was tender to her because of her prettiness, and because he had loved her as a child? We must own that it was a fault. The crooked places of the world, if they are to be made straight at all, must be made straight after a sterner and a juster fashion.

"Perhaps you could stay here for a day or two?" he said.

"Only that I've got no money."

"I will see to that,—for a few days, you know. And I was thinking that I would go to your brother George."

"My brother George?"

"Yes;—why not? Was he not always good to you?"

"He was never bad, sir; only—"

"Only what?"

"I've been so bad, sir, that I don't think he'd speak to me, or notice me, or do anything for me. And he has got a wife, too."

"But a woman doesn't always become hard-hearted as soon as she is married. There must be some of them that will take pity on you, Carry." She only shook her head. "I shall tell him that it is his duty, and if he be an honest, God-fearing man, he will do it."

"And should I have to go there?"

"If he will take you—certainly. What better could you wish? Your father is hard, and though he loves you still, he cannot bring himself to forget."

"How can any of them forget, Mr. Fenwick?"

"I will go out at once to Startup, and as I return through Salisbury I will let you know what your brother says." She again shook her head. "At any rate, we must try, Carry. When things are difficult, they cannot be mended by people sitting down and crying. I will ask your brother; and if he refuses, I will endeavour to think of something else. Next to your father and mother, he is certainly the first that should be asked to look to you." Then he said much to her as to her condition, preached to her the little sermon with which he had come prepared; was as stern to her as his nature and love would allow,—though, indeed, his words were tender enough. He strove to make her understand that she could have no escape from the dirt and vileness and depth of misery into which she had fallen, without the penalty of a hard, laborious life, in which she must submit to be regarded as one whose place in the world was very low. He asked her whether she did not hate the disgrace and the ignominy and the vile wickedness of her late condition. "Yes, indeed, sir," she answered, with her eyes still only half-raised towards him. What other answer could she make? He would fain have drawn from her some deep and passionate expression of repentance, some fervid promise of future rectitude, some eager offer to bear all other hardships, so that she might be saved from a renewal of the past misery. But he knew that no such eloquence, no such energy, no such ecstacy, would be forthcoming. And he knew, also, that humble, contrite, and wretched as was the girl now, the nature within her bosom was not changed. Were he to place her in a reformatory, she would not stay there. Were he to make arrangements with Mrs. Stiggs, who in her way seemed to be a decent, hard-working woman,—to make arrangements for her board and lodging, with some collateral regulations as to occupation, needle-work, and the like,—she would not adhere to them. The change from a life of fevered, though most miserable, excitement, to one of dull, pleasureless, and utterly uninteresting propriety, is one that can hardly be made without the assistance of binding control. Could she have been sent to the mill, and made subject to her mother's softness as well as to her mother's care, there might have been room for confident hope. And then, too,—but let not the reader read this amiss,—because she was pretty and might be made bright again, and because he was young, and because he loved her, he longed, were it possible, to make her paths pleasant for her. Her fall, her first fall had been piteous to him, rather than odious. He, too, would have liked to get hold of the man and to have left him without a sound limb within his skin,—to have left him pretty nearly without a skin at all; but that work had fallen into the miller's hands, who had done it fairly well. And, moreover, it would hardly have fitted the Vicar. But, as regarded Carry herself, when he thought of her in his solitary rambles, he would build little castles in the air on her behalf, in which her life should be anything but one of sackcloth and ashes. He would find for her some loving husband, who should know and should have forgiven the sin which had hardly been a sin, and she should be a loving wife with loving children. Perhaps, too, he would add to this, as he built his castles, the sweet smiles of affectionate gratitude with which he himself would be received when he visited her happy hearth. But he knew that these were castles in the air, and he endeavoured to throw them all behind him as he preached his sermon. Nevertheless, he was very tender with her, and treated her not at all as he would have done an ugly young parishioner who had turned thief upon his hands.

"And now, Carry," he said, as he left her, "I will get a gig in the town, and will drive over to your brother. We can but try it. I am clear as to this, that the best thing for you will be to be among your own people."

"I suppose it would, sir; but I don't think she'll ever be brought to have me."

"We will try, at any rate. And if she will have you, you must remember that you must not eat the bread of idleness. You must be prepared to work for your living."

"I don't want to be idle, sir." Then he took her by the hand, and pressed it, and bade God bless her, and gave her a little money in order that she might make some first payment to Mrs. Stiggs. "I'm sure I don't know why you should do all this for the likes of me, sir," said the girl, bursting into tears. The Vicar did not tell her that he did it because she was gracious in his eyes, and perhaps was not aware of the fact himself.

He went to the Dragon of Wantley, and there procured a gig. He had a contest in the inn-yard before they would let him have the gig without a man to drive him; but he managed it at last, fearing that the driver might learn something of his errand. He had never been at Startup Farm before; and knew very little of the man he was going to see on so very delicate a mission; but he did know that George Brattle was prosperous, and that in early life he had been a good son. His last interview with the farmer had had reference to the matter of bail required for Sam, and on that occasion the brother had, with some persuasion, done as he was asked. George Brattle had contrived to win for himself a wife from the Fordingbridge side of the country, who had had a little money; and as he, too, had carried away from the mill a little money in his father's prosperous days, he had done very well. He paid his rent to the day, owed no man anything, and went to church every other Sunday, eschewing the bad example set to him by his father in matters of religion. He was hard-fisted, ignorant, and self-confident, knowing much about corn and the grinding of it, knowing something of sheep and the shearing of them, knowing also how to get the worth of his ten or eleven shillings a week out of the bones of the rural labourers;—but knowing very little else. Of all this Fenwick was aware; and, in spite of that church-going twice a month, rated the son as inferior to the father; for about the old miller there was a stubborn constancy which almost amounted to heroism. With such a man as was this George Brattle, how was he to preach a doctrine of true human charity with any chance of success? But the man was one who was pervious to ideas of duty, and might be probably pervious to feelings of family respect. And he had been good to his father and mother, regarding with something of true veneration the nest from which he had sprung. The Vicar did not like the task before him, dreading the disappointment which failure would produce; but he was not the man to shrink from any work which he had resolved to undertake, and drove gallantly into the farmyard, though he saw both the farmer and his wife standing at the back-door of the house.

CHAPTER XLI.

STARTUP FARM.

Farmer Brattle, who was a stout man about thirty-eight years of age but looking as though he were nearly ten years older, came up to the Vicar, touching his hat, and then putting his hand out in greeting.

"This be a pleasure something like, Muster Fenwick, to see thee here at Startup. This be my wife. Molly, thou has never seen Muster Fenwick from Bull'umpton. This be our Vicar, as mother and Fanny says is the pick of all the parsons in Wiltshire."

Then Mr. Fenwick got down, and walked into the spacious kitchen, where he was cordially welcomed by the stout mistress of Startup Farm.

He was very anxious to begin his story to the brother alone. Indeed, as to that, his mind was quite made up; but Mrs. Brattle, who within the doors of that house held a position at any rate equal to that of her husband, did not seem disposed to give him the opportunity. She understood well enough that Mr. Fenwick had not come over from Bullhampton to shake hands with her husband, and to say a few civil words. He must have business, and that business must be about the Brattle family. Old Brattle was supposed to be in money difficulties, and was not this an embassy in search of money? Now Mrs. George Brattle, who had been born a Huggins, was very desirous that none of the Huggins money should be sent into the parish of Bullhampton. When, therefore, Mr. Fenwick asked the farmer to step out with him for a moment, Mrs. George Brattle looked very grave, and took her husband apart and whispered a word of caution into his ear.

"It's about the mill, George; and don't you do nothing till you've spoke to me."

Then there came a solid look, almost of grief, upon George's face. There had been a word or two before this between him and the wife of his bosom as to the affairs of the mill.

"I've just been seeing somebody at Salisbury," began the Vicar, abruptly, as soon as they had crossed from the yard behind the house into the enclosure around the ricks.

"Some one at Salisbury, Muster Fenwick? Is it any one as I knows?"

"One that you did know well, Mr. Brattle. I've seen your sister Carry." Again there came upon the farmer's face that heavy look, which was almost a look of grief; but he did not at once utter a word. "Poor young thing!" continued the Vicar. "Poor, dear, unfortunate girl!"

"She brought it on herself, and on all of us," said the farmer.

"Yes, indeed, my friend. The light, unguarded folly of a moment has ruined her, and brought dreadful sorrow upon you all. But something should be done for her;—eh?"

Still the brother said nothing.

"You will help, I'm sure, to rescue her from the infamy into which she must fall if none help her?"

"If there's money wanted to get her into any of them places—," begun the farmer.

"It isn't that;—it isn't that, at any rate, as yet."

"What be it, then?"

"The personal countenance and friendship of some friend that loves her. You love your sister, Mr. Brattle?"

"I don't know as I does, Muster Fenwick."

"You used to, and you must still pity her."

"She's been and well-nigh broke the hearts of all on us. There wasn't one of us as wasn't respectable, till she come up;—and now there's Sam. But a boy as is bad ain't never so bad as a girl."

It must be understood that in the expression of this opinion Mr. Brattle was alluding, not to the personal wickedness of the wicked of the two sexes, but to the effect of their wickedness on those belonging to them.

"And therefore more should be done to help a girl."

"I'll stand the money, Muster Fenwick,—if it ain't much."

"What is wanted is a home in your own house."

"Here—at Startup?"

"Yes; here, at Startup. Your father will not take her."

"Neither won't I. But it ain't me in such a matter as this. You ask my missus, and see what she'll say. Besides, Muster Fenwick, it's clean out of all reason."

"Out of all reason to help a sister?"

"So it be. Sister, indeed! Why did she go and make—. I won't say what she's made of herself. Ain't she brought trouble and sorrow enough upon us? Have her here! Why, I'm that angry with her, I shouldn't be keeping my hands off her. Why didn't she keep herself to herself, and not disgrace the whole family?"

Nevertheless, in spite of these strong expressions of opinion, Mr. Fenwick, by the dint of the bitter words which he spoke in reference to the brother's duty as a Christian, did get leave from the farmer to make the proposition to Mrs. George Brattle,—such permission as would have bound the brother to accept Carry, providing that Mrs. George would also consent to accept her. But even this permission was accompanied by an assurance that it would not have been given had he not felt perfectly convinced that his wife would not listen for a moment to the scheme. He spoke of his wife almost with awe, when Mr. Fenwick left him to make this second attack. "She has never had nothing to say to none sich as that," said the farmer, shaking his head, as he alluded both to his wife and to his sister; "and I ain't sure as she'll be first-rate civil to any one as mentions sich in her hearing."

But Mr. Fenwick persevered, in spite even of this caution. When the Vicar re-entered the house, Mrs. George Brattle had retired to her parlour, and the kitchen was in the hands of the maid-servant. He followed the lady, however, and found that she had been at the trouble, since he had seen her last, of putting on a clean cap on his behalf. He began at once, jumping again into the middle of things by a reference to her husband.

"Mrs. Brattle," he said, "your husband and I have been talking about his poor sister Carry."

"The least said the soonest mended about that one, I'm afeared," said the dame.

"Indeed, I agree with you. Were she once placed in safe and kind hands, the less then said the better. She has left the life she was leading—"

"They never leaves it," said the dame.

"It is so seldom that an opportunity is given them. Poor Carry is at the present moment most anxious to be placed somewhere out of danger."

"Mr. Fenwick, if you ask me, I'd rather not talk about her;—I would indeed. She's been and brought a slur upon us all, the vile thing! If you ask me, Mr. Fenwick, there ain't nothing too bad for her."

Fenwick, who, on the other hand, thought that there could be hardly anything too good for his poor penitent, was beginning to be angry with the woman. Of course, he made in his own mind those comparisons which are common to us all on such occasions. What was the great virtue of this fat, well-fed, selfish, ignorant woman before him, that she should turn up her nose at a sister who had been unfortunate? Was it not an abominable case of the Pharisee thanking the Lord that he was not such a one as the Publican;—whereas the Publican was in a fair way to heaven?

"Surely you would have her saved, if it be possible to save her?" said the Vicar.

"I don't know about saving. If such as them is to be made all's one as others as have always been decent, I'm sure I don't know who it is as isn't to be saved."

"Have you never read of Mary Magdalen, Mrs. Brattle?"

"Yes, I have, Mr. Fenwick. Perhaps she hadn't got no father, nor brothers, and sisters, and sisters-in-law, as would be pretty well broken-hearted when her vileness would be cast up again' 'em. Perhaps she hadn't got no decent house over her head afore she begun. I don't know how that was."

"Our Saviour's tender mercy, then, would not have been wide enough for such sin as that." This the Vicar said with intended irony; but irony was thrown away on Mrs. George Brattle.

"Them days and ours isn't the same, Mr. Fenwick, and you can't make 'em the same. And Our Saviour isn't here now to say who is to be a Mary Magdalen and who isn't. As for Carry Brattle, she has made her bed and she must lie upon it. We shan't interfere."

Fenwick was determined, however, that he would make his proposition. It was almost certain now that he could do no good to Carry by making it; but he felt that it would be a pleasure to him to make this self-righteous woman know what he conceived to be her duty in the matter. "My idea was this—that you should take her in here, and endeavour to preserve her from future evil courses."

"Take her in here?" shrieked the woman.

"Yes; here. Who is nearer to her than a brother?"

"Not if I know it, Mr. Fenwick; and if that is what you have been saying to Brattle, I must tell you that you've come on a very bad errand. People, Mr. Fenwick, knows how to manage things such as that for themselves in their own houses. Strangers don't usually talk about such things, Mr. Fenwick. Perhaps, Mr. Fenwick, you didn't know as how we have got girls of our own coming up. Have her in here—at Startup? I think I see her here!"

"But, Mrs. Brattle—"

"Don't Mrs. Brattle me, Mr. Fenwick, for I won't be so treated. And I must tell you that I don't think it over decent of you,—a clergyman, and a young man, too, in a way,—to come talking of such a one in a house like this."

"Would you have her starve, or die in a ditch?"

"There ain't no question of starving. Such as her don't starve. As long as it lasts, they've the best of eating and drinking,—only too much of it. There's prisons; let 'em go there if they means repentance. But they never does,—never, till there ain't nobody to notice 'em any longer; and by that time they're mostly thieves and pickpockets."

"And you would do nothing to save your own husband's sister from such a fate?"

"What business had she to be sister to any honest man? Think of what she's been and done to my children, who wouldn't else have had nobody to be ashamed of. There never wasn't one of the Hugginses who didn't behave herself;—that is of the women," added Mrs. George, remembering the misdeeds of a certain drunken uncle of her own, who had come to great trouble in a matter of horseflesh. "And now, Mr. Fenwick, let me beg that there mayn't be another word about her. I don't know nothing of such women, nor what is their ways, and I don't want. I never didn't speak a word to such a one in my life, and I certainly won't begin under my own roof. People knows well enough what's good for them to do and what isn't without being dictated to by a clergyman. You'll excuse me, Mr. Fenwick; but I'll just make bold to say as much as that. Good morning, Mr. Fenwick."

In the yard, standing close by the gig, he met the farmer again.

"You didn't find she'd be of your way of thinking, Muster Fenwick?"

"Not exactly, Mr. Brattle."

"I know'd she wouldn't. The truth is, Muster Fenwick, that young women as goes astray after that fashion is just like any sick animal, as all the animals as ain't comes and sets upon immediately. It's just as well, too. They knows it beforehand, and it keeps 'em straight."

"It didn't keep poor Carry straight."

"And, by the same token, she must suffer, and so must we all. But, Muster Fenwick, as far as ten or fifteen pounds goes, if it can be of use—"

But the Vicar, in his indignation, repudiated the offer of money, and drove himself back to Salisbury with his heart full of sorrow at the hardness of the world. What this woman had been saying to him was only what the world had said to her,—the world that knows so much better how to treat an erring sinner than did Our Saviour when on earth.

He went with his sad news to Mrs. Stiggs's house, and then made terms for Carry's board and lodging, at any rate, for a fortnight. And he said much to the girl as to the disposition of her time. He would send her books, and she was to be diligent in needle-work on behalf of the Stiggs family. And then he begged her to go to the daily service in the cathedral,—not so much because he thought that the public worship was necessary for her, as that thus she would be provided with a salutary employment for a portion of her day. Carry, as she bade him farewell, said very little. Yes; she would stay with Mrs. Stiggs. That was all that she did say.

CHAPTER XLII.

MR. QUICKENHAM, Q.C.

On the Thursday in Passion week, which fell on the 6th of April, Mr. and Mrs. Quickenham came to Bullhampton Vicarage. The lawyer intended to take a long holiday,—four entire days,—and to return to London on the following Tuesday; and Mrs. Quickenham meant to be very happy with her sister.

"It is such a comfort to get him out of town, if it's only for two days," said Mrs. Quickenham; "and I do believe he has run away this time without any papers in his portmanteau."

Mrs. Fenwick, with something of apology in her tone, explained to her sister that she was especially desirous of getting a legal opinion on this occasion from her brother-in-law.

"That's mere holiday work," said the barrister's anxious wife. "There's nothing he likes so much as that; but it is the reading of those horrible long papers by gaslight. I wouldn't mind how much he had to talk, nor yet how much he had to write, if it wasn't for all that weary reading. Of course he does have juniors with him now, but I don't find that it makes much difference. He's at it every night, sheet after sheet; and though he always says he's coming up immediately, it's two or three before he's in bed."

Mrs. Quickenham was three or four years older than her sister, and Mr. Quickenham was twelve years older than his wife. The lawyer therefore was considerably senior to the clergyman. He was at the Chancery bar, and after the usual years of hard and almost profitless struggling, had worked himself up into a position in which his income was very large, and his labours never ending. Since the days in which he had begun to have before his eyes some idea of a future career for himself, he had always been struggling hard for a certain goal, struggling successfully, and yet never getting nearer to the thing he desired. A scholarship had been all in all to him when he left school; and, as he got it, a distant fellowship already loomed before his eyes. That attained was only a step towards his life in London. His first brief, anxiously as it had been desired, had given no real satisfaction. As soon as it came to him it was a rung of the ladder already out of sight. And so it had been all through his life, as he advanced upwards, making a business, taking a wife to himself, and becoming the father of many children. There was always something before him which was to make him happy when he reached it. His gown was of silk, and his income almost greater than his desires; but he would fain sit upon the Bench, and have at any rate his evenings for his own enjoyment. He firmly believed now, that that had been the object of his constant ambition; though could he retrace his thoughts as a young man, he would find that in the early days of his forensic toils, the silent, heavy, unillumined solemnity of the judge had appeared to him to be nothing in comparison with the glittering audacity of the successful advocate. He had tried the one, and might probably soon try the other. And when that time shall have come, and Mr. Quickenham shall sit upon his seat of honour in the new Law Courts, passing long, long hours in the tedious labours of conscientious painful listening; then he will look forward again to the happy ease of dignified retirement, to the coming time in which all his hours will be his own. And then, again, when those unfurnished hours are there, and with them shall have come the infirmities which years and toil shall have brought, his mind will run on once more to that eternal rest in which fees and salary, honours and dignity, wife and children, with all the joys of satisfied success, shall be brought together for him in one perfect amalgam which he will call by the name of Heaven. In the meantime, he has now come down to Bullhampton to enjoy himself for four days,—if he can find enjoyment without his law papers.

Mr. Quickenham was a tall, thin man, with eager gray eyes, and a long projecting nose, on which, his enemies in the courts of law were wont to say, his wife would hang a kettle, in order that the unnecessary heat coming from his mouth might not be wasted. His hair was already grizzled, and, in the matter of whiskers, his heavy impatient hand had nearly altogether cut away the only intended ornament to his face. He was a man who allowed himself time for nothing but his law work, eating all his meals as though the saving of a few minutes in that operation were matter of vital importance, dressing and undressing at railroad speed, moving ever with a quick, impetuous step, as though the whole world around him went too slowly. He was short-sighted, too, and would tumble about in his unnecessary hurry, barking his shins, bruising his knuckles, and breaking most things that were breakable,— but caring nothing for his sufferings either in body or in purse so that he was not reminded of his awkwardness by his wife. An untidy man he was, who spilt his soup on his waistcoat and slobbered with his tea, whose fingers were apt to be ink-stained, and who had a grievous habit of mislaying papers that were most material to him. He would bellow to the servants to have his things found for him, and would then scold them for looking. But when alone he would be ever scolding himself because of the faults which he thus committed. A conscientious, hard-working, friendly man he was, but one difficult to deal with; hot in his temper, impatient of all stupidities, impatient often of that which he wrongly thought to be stupidity, never owning himself to be wrong, anxious always for the truth, but often missing to see it, a man who would fret grievously for the merest trifle, and think nothing of the greatest success when it had once been gained. Such a one was Mr. Quickenham; and he was a man of whom all his enemies and most of his friends were a little afraid. Mrs. Fenwick would declare herself to be much in awe of him; and our Vicar, though he would not admit as much, was always a little on his guard when the great barrister was with him.

How it had come to pass that Mr. Chamberlaine had not been called upon to take a part in the Cathedral services during Passion week cannot here be explained; but it was the fact, that when Mr. Quickenham arrived at Bullhampton, the Canon was staying at The Privets. He had come over there early in the week,—as it was supposed by Mr. Fenwick with some hope of talking his nephew into a more reasonable state of mind respecting Miss Lowther; but, according to Mrs. Fenwick's uncharitable views, with the distinct object of escaping the long church services of the Holy week,—and was to return to Salisbury on the Saturday. He was, therefore, invited to meet Mr. Quickenham at dinner on the Thursday. In his own city and among his own neighbours he would have thought it indiscreet to dine out in Passion week; but, as he explained to Mr. Fenwick, these things were very different in a rural parish.

Mr. Quickenham arrived an hour or two before dinner, and was immediately taken out to see the obnoxious building; while Mrs. Fenwick, who never would go to see it, described all its horrors to her sister within the guarded precincts of her own drawing-room.

"It used to be a bit of common land, didn't it?" said Mr. Quickenham.

"I hardly know what is common land," replied the Vicar. "The children used to play here, and when there was a bit of grass on it some of the neighbours' cows would get it."

"It was never advertised—to be let on building lease?"

"Oh dear no! Lord Trowbridge never did anything of that sort."

"I dare say not," said the lawyer. "I dare say not." Then he walked round the plot of ground, pacing it, as though something might be learned in that way. Then he looked up at the building with his hands in his pockets, and his head on one side. "Has there been a deed of gift,—perhaps a peppercorn rent, or something of that kind?" The Vicar declared that he was altogether ignorant of what had been done between the agent for the Marquis and the trustees to whom had been committed the building of the chapel. "I dare say nothing," said Mr. Quickenham. "They've been in such a hurry to punish you, that they've gone on a mere verbal permission. What's the extent of the glebe?"

"They call it forty-two acres."

"Did you ever have it measured?"

"Never. It would make no difference to me whether it is forty-one or forty-three."

"That's as may be," said the lawyer. "It's as nasty a thing as I've looked at for many a day, but it wouldn't do to call it a nuisance."

"Of course not. Janet is very hot about it; but, as for me, I've made up my mind to swallow it. After all, what harm will it do me?"

"It's an insult,—that's all."

"But if I can show that I don't take it as an insult, the insult will be nothing. Of course the people know that their landlord is trying to spite me."

"That's just it."

"And for awhile they'll spite me too, because he does. Of course it's a bore. It cripples one's influence, and to a certain degree spreads dissent at the cost of the Church. Men and women will go to that place merely because Lord Trowbridge favours the building. I know all that, and it irks me; but still it will be better to swallow it."

"Who's the oldest man in the parish?" asked Mr. Quickenham; "the oldest with his senses still about him." The parson reflected for awhile, and then said that he thought Brattle, the miller, was as old a man as there was there, with the capability left to him of remembering and of stating what he remembered. "And what's his age,—about?" Fenwick said that the miller was between sixty and seventy, and had lived in Bullhampton all his life. "A church-going man?" asked the lawyer. To this the Vicar was obliged to reply that, to his very great regret, old Brattle never entered a church. "Then I'll step over and see him during morning service to-morrow," said the lawyer. The Vicar raised his eyebrows, but said nothing as to the propriety of Mr. Quickenham's personal attendance at a place of worship on Good Friday.

"Can anything be done, Richard?" said Mrs. Fenwick, appealing to her brother-in-law.

"Yes;—undoubtedly something can be done."

"Can there, indeed? I am so glad. What can be done?"

"You can make the best of it."

"That's just what I'm determined I won't do. It's mean-spirited, and so I tell Frank. I never would have hurt them as long as they treated us well; but now they are enemies, and as enemies I will regard them. I should think myself disgraced if I were to sit down in the presence of the Marquis of Trowbridge; I should, indeed."

"You can easily manage that by standing up when you meet him," said Mr. Quickenham. Mr. Quickenham could be very funny at times, but those who knew him would remark that whenever he was funny he had something to hide. His wife as she heard his wit was quite sure that he had some plan in his head about the chapel.

At half-past six there came Mr. Chamberlaine and his nephew. The conversation about the chapel was still continued, and the canon from Salisbury was very eloquent, and learned also, upon the subject. His eloquence was brightest while the ladies were still in the room, but his learning was brought forth most manifestly after they had retired. He was very clear in his opinion that the Marquis had the law on his side in giving the land for the purpose in question, even if it could be shown that he was simply the lord of the manor, and not so possessed of the spot as to do what he liked in it for his own purposes. Mr. Chamberlaine expressed his opinion that, although he himself might think otherwise, it would be held to be for the benefit of the community that the chapel should be built, and in no court could an injunction against the building be obtained.

"But he couldn't give leave to have it put on another man's ground," said the Queen's Counsel.

"There is no question of another man's ground here," said the member of the Chapter.

"I'm not so sure of that," continued Mr. Quickenham. "It may not be the ground of any one man, but if it's the ground of any ten or twenty it's the same thing."

"But then there would be a lawsuit," said the Vicar.

"It might come to that," said the Queen's Counsel.

"I'm sure you wouldn't have a leg to stand upon," said the member of the Chapter.

"I don't see that at all," said Gilmore. "If the land is common to the parish, the Marquis of Trowbridge cannot give it to a part of the parishioners because he is Lord of the Manor."

"For such a purpose I should think he can," said Mr. Chamberlaine.

"And I'm quite sure he can't," said Mr. Quickenham. "All the same, it may be very difficult to prove that he hasn't the right; and in the meantime there stands the chapel, a fact accomplished. If the ground had been bought and the purchasers had wanted a title, I think it probable the Marquis would never have got his money."

"There can be no doubt that it is very ungentlemanlike," said Mr. Chamberlaine.

"There I'm afraid I can't help you," said Mr. Quickenham. "Good law is not defined very clearly here in England; but good manners have never been defined at all."

"I don't want anyone to help me on such a matter as that," said Mr. Chamberlaine, who did not altogether like Mr. Quickenham.

"I dare say not," said Mr. Quickenham; "and yet the question may be open to argument. A man may do what he likes with his own, and can hardly be called ungentlemanlike because he gives it away to a person you don't happen to like."

"I dare say not," said Mr. Quickenham.

"I know what we all think about it in Salisbury," said Mr. Chamberlaine.

"It's just possible that you may be a little hypercritical in Salisbury," said Quickenham.

There was nothing else discussed and nothing else thought of in the Vicarage. The first of June had been the day now fixed for the opening of the new chapel, and here they were already in April. Mr. Fenwick was quite of opinion that if the services of Mr. Puddleham's congregation were once commenced in the building they must be continued there. As long as the thing was a thing not yet accomplished it might be practicable to stop it; but there could be no stopping it when the full tide of Methodist eloquence should have begun to pour itself from the new pulpit. It would then have been made the House of God,—even though not consecrated,—and as such it must remain. And now he was becoming sick of the grievance, and wished that it was over. As to going to law with the Marquis on a question of Common-right, it was a thing that he would not think of doing. The living had come to him from his college, and he had thought it right to let the Bursar of Saint John's know what was being done; but it was quite clear that the college could not interfere or spend their money on a matter which, though it was parochial, had no reference to their property in the parish. It was not for the college, as patron of the living, to inquire whether certain lands belonged to the Marquis of Trowbridge or to the parish at large, though the Vicar no doubt, as one of the inhabitants of the place, might raise the question at law if he chose to find the money and could find the ground on which to raise it. His old friend the Bursar wrote him back a joking letter, recommending him to put more fire into his sermons and thus to preach his enemy down.

"I have become so sick of this chapel," the Vicar said to his wife that night, "that I wish the subject might never be mentioned again in the house."

"You can't be more sick of it than I am," said his wife.

"What I mean is, that I'm sick of it as a subject of conversation. There it is, and let us make the best of it, as Quickenham says."

"You can't expect anything like sympathy from Richard, you know."

"I don't want any sympathy. I want simply silence. If you'll only make up your mind to take it for granted, and to put up with it—as you had to do with the frost when the shrubs were killed, or with anything that is disagreeable but unavoidable, the feeling of unhappiness about it would die away at once. One does not grieve at the inevitable."

"But one must be quite sure that it is inevitable."

"There it stands, and nothing that we can do can stop it."

"Charlotte says that she is sure Richard has got something in his head. Though he will not sympathise, he will think and contrive and fight."

"And half ruin us by his fighting," said the husband. "He fancies the land may be common land, and not private property."

"Then of course the chapel has no right to be there."

"But who is to have it removed? And if I could succeed in doing so, what would be said to me for putting down a place of worship after such a fashion as that?"

"Who could say anything against you, Frank?"

"The truth is, it is Lord Trowbridge who is my enemy here, and not the chapel or Mr. Puddleham. I'd have given the spot for the chapel, had they wanted it, and had I had the power to give it. I'm annoyed because Lord Trowbridge should know that he had got the better of me. If I can only bring myself to feel,—and you too,—that there is no better in it, and no worse, I shall be annoyed no longer. Lord Trowbridge cannot really touch me; and could he, I do not know that he would."

"I know he would."

"No, my dear. If he suddenly had the power to turn me out of the living I don't believe he'd do it,—any more than I would him out of his estate. Men indulge in little injuries who can't afford to be wicked enough for great injustice. My dear, you will do me a great favour,—the greatest possible kindness,—if you'll give up all outer, and, as far as possible, all inner hostility to the chapel."

"Oh, Frank!"

"I ask it as a great favour,—for my peace of mind."

"Of course I will."

"There's my darling! It shan't make me unhappy any longer. What!—a stupid lot of bricks and mortar, that, after all, are intended for a good purpose,—to think that I should become a miserable wretch just because this good purpose is carried on outside my own gate. Were it in my dining-room, I ought to bear it without misery."

"I will strive to forget it," said his wife. And on the next morning, which was Good Friday, she walked to church, round by the outside gate, in order that she might give proof of her intention to keep her promise to her husband. Her husband walked before her; and as she went she looked round at her sister and shuddered and turned up her nose. But this was involuntary.

In the mean time Mr. Quickenham was getting himself ready for his walk to the mill. Any such investigation as this which he had on hand was much more compatible with his idea of a holiday than attendance for two hours at the Church Service. On Easter Sunday he would make the sacrifice,—unless a headache, or pressing letters from London, or Apollo in some other beneficent shape, might interfere and save him from the necessity. Mr. Quickenham, when at home, would go to church as seldom as was possible, so that he might save himself from being put down as one who neglected public worship. Perhaps he was about equal to Mr. George Brattle in his religious zeal. Mr. George Brattle made a clear compromise with his own conscience. One good Sunday against a Sunday that was not good left him, as he thought, properly poised in his intended condition of human infirmity. It may be doubted whether Mr. Quickenham's mind was equally philosophic on the matter. He could hardly tell why he went to church, or why he stayed away. But he was aware when he went of the presence of some unsatisfactory feelings of imposture on his own part, and he was equally alive, when he did not go, to a sting of conscience in that he was neglecting a duty. But George Brattle had arranged it all in a manner that was perfectly satisfactory to himself.

Mr. Quickenham had inquired the way, and took the path to the mill along the river. He walked rapidly, with his nose in the air, as though it was a manifest duty, now that he found himself in the country, to get over as much ground as possible, and to refresh his lungs thoroughly. He did not look much as he went at the running river, or at the opening buds on the trees and hedges. When he met a rustic loitering on the path, he examined the man unconsciously, and could afterwards have described, with tolerable accuracy, how he was dressed; and he had smiled as he had observed the amatory pleasantness of a young couple, who had not thought it at all necessary to increase the distance between them because of his presence. These things he had seen, but the stream, and the hedges, and the twittering of the birds, were as nothing to him.

As he went he met old Mrs. Brattle making her weary way to church. He had not known Mrs. Brattle, and did not speak to her, but he had felt quite sure that she was the miller's wife. Standing with his hands in his pockets on the bridge which divided the house from the mill, with his pipe in his mouth, was old Brattle, engaged for the moment in saying some word to his daughter, Fanny, who was behind him. But she retreated as soon as she saw the stranger, and the miller stood his ground, waiting to be accosted, suspicion keeping his hands deep down in his pockets, as though resolved that he would not be tempted to put them forth for the purpose of any friendly greeting. The lawyer saluted him by name, and then the miller touched his hat, thrusting his hand back into his pocket as soon as the ceremony was accomplished. Mr. Quickenham explained that he had come from the Vicarage, that he was brother-in-law to Mr. Fenwick, and a lawyer,—at each of which statements old Brattle made a slight projecting motion with his chin, as being a mode of accepting the information slightly better than absolute discourtesy. At the present moment Mr. Fenwick was out of favour with him, and he was not disposed to open his heart to visitors from the Vicarage. Then Mr. Quickenham plunged at once into the affair of the day.

"You know that chapel they are building, Mr. Brattle, just opposite to the parson's gate?"

Mr. Brattle replied that he had heard of the chapel, but had never, as yet, been up to see it.

"Indeed; but you remember the bit of ground?"

Yes;—the miller remembered the ground very well. Man and boy he had known it for sixty years. As far as his mind went he thought it a very good thing that the piece of ground should be put to some useful purpose at last.

"I'm not sure but what you may be right there," said the lawyer.

"It's not been of use,—not to nobody,—for more than forty year," said the miller.

"And before that what did they do with it?"

"Parson, as we had then in Bull'umpton, kep' a few sheep."

"Ah!—just so. And he would get a bit of feeding off the ground?" The miller nodded his head. "Was that the Vicar just before Mr. Fenwick?" asked the lawyer.

"Not by no means. There was Muster Brandon, who never come here at all, but had a curate who lived away to Hinton. He come after Parson Smallbones."

"It was Parson Smallbones who kept the sheep?"

"And then there was Muster Threepaway, who was parson well nigh thirty years afore Muster Fenwick come. He died up at Parsonage House, did Muster Threepaway."

"He didn't keep sheep?"

"No; he kep' no sheep as ever I heard tell on. He didn't keep much barring hisself,—didn't Muster Threepaway. He had never no child, nor yet no wife, nor nothing at all, hadn't Muster Threepaway. But he was a good man as didn't go meddling with folk."

"But Parson Smallbones was a bit of a farmer?"

"Ay, ay. Parsons in them days warn't above a bit of farming. I warn't much more than a scrap of a boy, but I remember him. He wore a wig, and old black gaiters; and knew as well what was his'n and what wasn't as any parson in Wiltshire. Tithes was tithes then; and parson was cute enough in taking on 'em."

"But these sheep of his were his own, I suppose?"

"Whose else would they be, sir?"

"And did he fence them in on that bit of ground?"

"There'd be a boy with 'em, I'm thinking, sir. There wasn't so much fencing of sheep then as there be now. Boys was cheaper in them days."

"Just so; and the parson wouldn't allow other sheep there?"

"Muster Smallbones mostly took all he could get, sir."

"Exactly. The parsons generally did, I believe. It was the way in which they followed most accurately the excellent examples set them by the bishops. But, Mr. Brattle, it wasn't in the way of tithes that he had this grass for his sheep?"

"I can't say how he had it, nor yet how Muster Fenwick has the meadows t'other side of the river, which he lets to farmer Pierce; but he do have 'em, and farmer Pierce do pay him the rent."

"Glebe land, you know," said Mr. Quickenham.

"That's what they calls it," said the miller.

"And none of the vicars that came after old Smallbones have ever done anything with that bit of ground?"

"Ne'er a one on'em. Mr. Brandon, as I tell 'ee, never come nigh the place. I don't know as ever I see'd him. It was him as they made bishop afterwards, some'eres away in Ireland. He had a lord to his uncle. Then Muster Threepaway, he was here ever so long."

"But he didn't mind such things."

"He never owned no sheep; and the old 'oomen's cows was let to go on the land, as was best, and then the boys took to playing hopskotch there, with a horse or two over it at times, and now Mr. Puddleham has it for his preaching. Maybe, sir, the lawyers might have a turn at it yet;" and the miller laughed at his own wit.

"And get more out of it than any former occupant," said Mr. Quickenham, who would indeed have been very loth to allow his wife's brother-in-law to go into a law suit, but still felt that a very pretty piece of litigation was about to be thrown away in this matter of Mr. Puddleham's chapel.

Mr. Quickenham bade farewell to the miller, and thought that he saw a way to a case. But he was a man very strongly given to accuracy, and on his return to the Vicarage said no word of his conversation with the miller. It would have been natural that Fenwick should have interrogated him as to his morning's work; but the Vicar had determined to trouble himself no further about his grievance, to say nothing further respecting it to any man, not even to allow the remembrance of Mr. Puddleham and his chapel to dwell in his mind; and consequently held his peace. Mrs. Fenwick was curious enough on the subject, but she had made a promise to her husband, and would at least endeavour to keep it. If her sister should tell her anything unasked, that would not be her fault.

CHAPTER XLIII.

EASTER AT TURNOVER CASTLE.

It was not only at Bullhampton that this affair of the Methodist chapel demanded and received attention. At Turnover also a good deal was being said about it, and the mind of the Marquis was not easy. As has been already told, the bishop had written to him on the subject, remonstrating with him as to the injury he was doing to the present vicar, and to future vicars, of the parish which he, as landlord, was bound to treat with beneficent consideration. The Marquis had replied to the bishop with a tone of stern resolve. The Vicar of Bullhampton had treated him with scorn, nay, as he thought, with most unpardonable insolence, and he would not spare the Vicar. It was proper that the dissenters at Bullhampton should have a chapel, and he had a right to do what he liked with his own. So arguing with himself, he had written to the bishop very firmly; but his own mind had not been firm within him as he did so. There were misgivings at his heart. He was a Churchman himself, and he was pricked with remorse as he remembered that he was spiting the Church which was connected with the state, of which he was so eminent a supporter. His own chief agent, too, had hesitated, and had suggested that perhaps the matter might be postponed. His august daughters, though they had learned to hold the name of Fenwick in proper abhorrence, nevertheless were grieved about the chapel. Men and women were talking about it, and the words of the common people found their way to the august daughters of the house of Stowte.

"Papa," said Lady Carolina; "wouldn't it, perhaps, be better to build the Bullhampton chapel a little farther off from the Vicarage?"

"The next vicar might be a different sort of person," said the Lady Sophie.

"No; it wouldn't," said the Earl, who was apt to be very imperious with his own daughters, although he was of opinion that they should be held in great awe by all the world—excepting only himself and their eldest brother.

That eldest brother, Lord Saint George, was in truth regarded at Turnover as being, of all persons in the world, the most august. The Marquis himself was afraid of his son, and held him in extreme veneration. To the mind of the Marquis the heir expectant of all the dignities of the House of Stowte was almost a greater man than the owner of them; and this feeling came not only from a consciousness on the part of the father that his son was a bigger man than himself, cleverer, better versed in the affairs of the world, and more thought of by those around them, but also to a certain extent from an idea that he who would have all these grand things thirty or perhaps even fifty years hence, must be more powerful than one with whom their possession would come to an end probably after the lapse of eight or ten years. His heir was to him almost divine. When things at the castle were in any way uncomfortable, he could put up with the discomfort for himself and his daughters; but it was not to be endured that Saint George should be incommoded. Old carriage-horses must be changed if he were coming; the glazing of the new greenhouse must be got out of the way, lest he should smell the paint; the game must not be touched till he should come to shoot it. And yet Lord Saint George himself was a man who never gave himself any airs; and who in his personal intercourse with the world around him demanded much less acknowledgment of his magnificence than did his father.

And now, during this Easter week, Lord Saint George came down to the castle, intending to kill two birds with one stone, to take his parliamentary holiday, and to do a little business with his father. It not unfrequently came to pass that he found it necessary to repress the energy of his father's august magnificence. He would go so far as to remind his father that in these days marquises were not very different from other people, except in this, that they perhaps might have more money. The Marquis would fret in silence, not daring to commit himself to an argument with his son, and would in secret lament over the altered ideas of the age. It was his theory of politics that the old distances should be maintained, and that the head of a great family should be a patriarch, entitled to obedience from those around him. It was his son's idea that every man was entitled to as much obedience as his money would buy, and to no more. This was very lamentable to the Marquis; but nevertheless, his son was the coming man, and even this must be borne.

"I'm sorry about this chapel at Bullhampton," said the son to the father after dinner.

"Why sorry, Saint George? I thought you would have been of opinion that the dissenters should have a chapel."

"Certainly they should, if they're fools enough to want to build a place to pray in, when they have got one already built for them. There's no reason on earth why they shouldn't have a chapel, seeing that nothing that we can do will save them from schism."

"We can't prevent dissent, Saint George."

"We can't prevent it, because, in religion as in everything else, men like to manage themselves. This farmer or that tradesman becomes a dissenter because he can be somebody in the management of his chapel, and would be nobody in regard to the parish church."

"That is very dreadful."

"Not worse than our own people, who remain with us because it sounds the most respectable. Not one in fifty really believes that this or that form of worship is more likely to send him to heaven than any other."

"I certainly claim to myself to be one of the few," said the Marquis.

"No doubt; and so you ought, my lord, as every advantage has been given you. But, to come back to the Bullhampton chapel,—don't you think we could move it away from the parson's gate?"

"They have built it now, Saint George."

"They can't have finished it yet."

"You wouldn't have me ask them to pull it down? Packer was here yesterday, and said that the framework of the roof was up."

"What made them hurry it in that way? Spite against the Vicar, I suppose."

"He is a most objectionable man, Saint George; most insolent, overbearing, and unlike a clergyman. They say that he is little better than an infidel himself."

"We had better leave that to the bishop, my lord."

"We must feel about it, connected as we are with the parish," said the Marquis.

"But I don't think we shall do any good by going into a parochial quarrel."

"It was the very best bit of land for the purpose in all Bullhampton," said the Marquis. "I made particular inquiry, and there can be no doubt of that. Though I particularly dislike that Mr. Fenwick, it was not done to injure him."

"It does injure him damnably, my lord."

"That's only an accident."

"And I'm not at all sure that we shan't find that we have made a mistake."

"How a mistake?"

"That we have given away land that doesn't belong to us."

"Who says it doesn't belong to us?" said the Marquis, angrily. A suggestion so hostile, so unjust, so cruel as this, almost overcame the feeling of veneration which he entertained for his son. "That is really nonsense, Saint George."

"Have you looked at the title deeds?"

"The title deeds are of course with Mr. Boothby. But Packer knows every foot of the ground,—even if I didn't know it myself."

"I wouldn't give a straw for Packer's knowledge."

"I haven't heard that they have even raised the question themselves."

"I'm told that they will do so,—that they say it is common land. It's quite clear that it has never been either let or enclosed."

"You might say the same of the bit of green that lies outside the park gate,—where the great oak stands; but I don't suppose that that is common."

"I don't say that this is—but I do say that there may be difficulty of proof; and that to be driven to the proof in such a matter would be disagreeable."

"What would you do, then?"

"Take the bull by the horns, and move the chapel at our own expense to some site that shall be altogether unobjectionable."

"We should be owning ourselves wrong, Augustus."

"And why not? I cannot see what disgrace there is in coming forward handsomely and telling the truth. When the land was given we thought it was our own. There has come up a shadow of a doubt, and sooner than be in the wrong, we give another site and take all the expense. I think that would be the right sort of thing to do."

Lord Saint George returned to town two days afterwards, and the Marquis was left with the dilemma on his mind. Lord Saint George, though he would frequently interfere in matters connected with the property in the manner described, would never dictate and seldom insist. He had said what he had got to say, and the Marquis was left to act for himself. But the old lord had learned to feel that he was sure to fall into some pit whenever he declined to follow his son's advice. His son had a painful way of being right that was a great trouble to him. And this was a question which touched him very nearly. It was not only that he must yield to Mr. Fenwick before the eyes of Mr. Puddleham and all the people of Bullhampton; but that he must confess his own ignorance as to the borders of his own property, and must abandon a bit of land which he believed to belong to the Stowte estate. Now, if there was a point in his religion as to which Lord Trowbridge was more staunch than another, it was as to the removal of landmarks. He did not covet his neighbour's land; but he was most resolute that no stranger should, during his reign, ever possess a rood of his own.

CHAPTER XLIV.

THE MARRABLES OF DUNRIPPLE.

"If I were to go, there would be nobody left but you. You should remember that, Walter, when you talk of going to India." This was said to Walter Marrable at Dunripple, by his cousin Gregory, Sir Gregory's only son.

"And if I were to die in India, as I probably shall, who will come next?"

"There is nobody to come next for the title."

"But for the property?"

"As it stands at present, if you and I were to die before your father and uncle John, the survivor of them would be the last in the entail. If they, too, died, and the survivor of us all left no will, the property would go to Mary Lowther. But that is hardly probable. When my grandfather made the settlement, on my father's marriage, he had four sons living."

"Should my father have the handling of it I would not give much for anybody's chance after him," said Walter.

"If you were to marry there would, of course, be a new settlement as to your rights. Your father could do no harm except as your heir,—unless, indeed, he were heir to us all. My uncle John will outlive him, probably."

"My uncle John will live for ever, I should think," said Walter Marrable.

This conversation took place between the two cousins when Walter had been already two or three weeks at Dunripple. He had come there intending to stay over two or three days, and he had already accepted an invitation to make the house his home as long as he should remain in England. He had known but little of his uncle and nothing of his cousin, before this visit was made. He had conceived them to be unfriendly to him, having known them to be always unfriendly to his father. He was, of course, aware,—very well aware now, since he had himself suffered so grievously from his father's dishonesty,—that the enmity which had reached them from Dunripple had been well deserved. Colonel Marrable had, as a younger brother, never been content with what he was able to extract from the head of the family, who was, in his eyes, a milch cow that never ought to run dry. With Walter Marrable there had remained a feeling adverse to his uncle and cousin, even after he had been forced to admit to himself how many and how grievous were the sins of his own father. He had believed that the Dunripple people were stupid, and prejudiced, and selfish; and it had only been at the instance of his uncle, the parson, that he had consented to make the visit. He had gone there, and had been treated, at any rate, with affectionate consideration.

And he had found the house to be not unpleasant, though very quiet. Living at Dunripple there was a Mrs. Brownlow, a widowed sister of the late Lady Marrable, with her daughter, Edith Brownlow. Previous to this time Walter Marrable had never even heard of the Brownlows, so little had he known about Dunripple; and when he arrived there it had been necessary to explain to him who these people were.

He had found his uncle, Sir Gregory, to be much such a man as he had expected in outward appearance and mode of life. The baronet was old and disposed to regard himself as entitled to all the indulgences of infirmity. He rose late, took but little exercise, was very particular about what he ate, and got through his day with the assistance of his steward, his novel, and occasionally of his doctor. He slept a great deal, and was never tired of talking of himself. Occupation in life he had none, but he was a charitable, honourable man, who had high ideas of what was due to others. His son, however, had astonished Walter considerably. Gregory Marrable the younger was a man somewhat over forty, but he looked as though he were sixty. He was very tall and thin, narrow in the chest, and so round in the shoulders as to appear to be almost humpbacked. He was so short-sighted as to be nearly blind, and was quite bald. He carried his head so forward that it looked as though it were going to fall off. He shambled with his legs, which seemed never to be strong enough to carry him from one room to another; and he tried them by no other exercise, for he never went outside the house except when, on Sundays and some other very rare occasions, he would trust himself to be driven in a low pony-phaeton. But in one respect he was altogether unlike his father. His whole time was spent among his books, and he was at this moment engaged in revising and editing a very long and altogether unreadable old English chronicle in rhyme, for publication by one of those learned societies which are rife in London. Of Robert of Gloucester, and William Langland, of Andrew of Wyntown and the Lady Juliana Berners, he could discourse, if not with eloquence, at least with enthusiasm. Chaucer was his favourite poet, and he was supposed to have read the works of Gower in English, French, and Latin. But he was himself apparently as old as one of his own black-letter volumes, and as unfit for general use. Walter could hardly regard him as a cousin, declaring to himself that his uncle the parson, and his own father were, in effect, younger men than the younger Gregory Marrable. He was never without a cough, never well, never without various ailments and troubles of the flesh,—of which, however, he himself made but slight account, taking them quite as a matter of course. With such inmates the house no doubt would have been dull, had there not been women there to enliven it.

By degrees, too, and not by slow degrees, the new comer found that he was treated as one of the family,—found that, after a certain fashion, he was treated as the heir to the family. Between him and the title and the estate there were but the lives of four old men. Why had he not known that this was so before he had allowed himself to be separated from Mary Lowther? But he had known nothing of it,—had thought not at all about it. There had been another Marrable, of the same generation with himself, between him and the succession, who might marry and have children, and he had not regarded his heirship as being likely to have any effect, at any rate upon his early life. It had never occurred to him that he need not go to India, because he would probably outlive four old gentlemen and become Sir Walter Marrable and owner of Dunripple.

Nor would he have looked at the matter in that light now had not his cousin forced the matter upon him. Not a word was said to him at Dunripple about Mary Lowther, but very many words were said about his own condition. Gregory Marrable strongly advised him against going to India,—so strongly that Walter was surprised to find that such a man would have so much to say on such a subject. The young captain, in such circumstances, could not very well explain that he was driven to follow his profession in a fashion so disagreeable to him because, although he was heir to Dunripple, he was not near enough to it to be entitled to any allowance from its owner; but he felt that that would have been the only true answer when it was proposed to him to stay in England because he would some day become Sir Walter Marrable. But he did plead the great loss which he had encountered by means of his father's ill-treatment of him, and endeavoured to prove to his cousin that there was no alternative before him but to serve in some quarter of the globe in which his pay would be sufficient for his wants.

"Why should you not sell out, or go on half-pay, and remain here and marry Edith Brownlow?" said his cousin.

"I don't think I could do that," said Walter, slowly.

"Why not? There is nothing my father would like so much." Then he was silent for awhile, but, as his cousin made no further immediate reply, Gregory Marrable went on with his plan. "Ten years ago, when she was not much more than a little girl, and when it was first arranged that she should come here, my father proposed—that I should marry her."

"And why didn't you?"

The elder cousin smiled and shook his head, and coughed aloud as he smiled. "Why not, indeed? Well; I suppose you can see why not. I was an old man almost before she was a young woman. She is just twenty-four now, and I shall be dead, probably, in two years' time."

"Nonsense."

"Twice since that time I have been within an inch of dying. At any rate, even my father does not look to that any longer."

"Is he fond of Miss Brownlow?"

"There is no one in the world whom he loves so well. Of course an old man loves a young woman best. It is natural that he should do so. He never had a daughter; but Edith is the same to him as his own child. Nothing would please him so much as that she should be the mistress of Dunripple."

"I'm afraid that it cannot be so," said Walter.

"But why not? There need be no India for you then. If you would do that you would be to my father exactly as though you were his son. Your father might, of course, outlive my father, and no doubt will outlive me, and then for his life he will have the place, but some arrangement could be made so that you should continue here."

"I'm afraid it cannot be so," said Walter. Many thoughts were passing through his mind. Why had he not known that these good things were so near to him before he had allowed Mary Lowther to go off from him? And, had it chanced that he had visited Dunripple before he had gone to Loring, how might it have been between him and this other girl? Edith Brownlow was not beautiful, not grand in her beauty as was Mary Lowther; but she was pretty, soft, lady-like, with a sweet dash of quiet pleasant humour,—a girl who certainly need not be left begging about the world for a husband. And this life at Dunripple was pleasant enough. Though the two elder Marrables were old and infirm, Walter was allowed to do just as he pleased in the house. He was encouraged to hunt. There was shooting for him if he wished it. Even the servants about the place, the gamekeeper, the groom, and the old butler, seemed to have recognised him as the heir. There would have been so comfortable an escape from the dilemma into which his father had brought him,—had he not made his visit to Loring.

"Why not?" demanded Gregory Marrable.

"A man cannot become attached to a girl by order, and what right have I to suppose that she would accept me?"

"Of course she would accept you. Why not? Everybody around her would be in your favour. And as to not falling in love with her, I declare I do not know a sweeter human being in the world than Edith Brownlow."

Before the hunting season was over Captain Marrable had abandoned his intention of going to India, and had made arrangements for serving for awhile with his regiment in England. This he did after a discussion of some length with his uncle, Sir Gregory. During that discussion nothing was said about Edith Brownlow, and of course, not a word was said about Mary

Lowther. Captain Marrable did not even know whether his uncle or his cousin was aware that that engagement had ever existed. Between him and his uncle there had never been an allusion to his marriage, but the old man had spoken of his nearness to the property, and had expressed his regret that the last heir, the only heir likely to perpetuate the name and title, should take himself to India in the pride of his life. He made no offer as to money, but he told his nephew that there was a home for him if he would give up his profession, or a retreat whenever his professional duties might allow him to visit it. Horses should be kept for him, and he should be treated in every way as a son of the family.

"Take my father at his word," said Gregory Marrable. "He will never let you be short of money."

After much consideration Walter Marrable did take Sir Gregory at his word, and abandoned for ever all idea of a further career in India.

As soon as he had done this he wrote to Mary Lowther to inform her of his decision. "It does seem hard," he said in his letter, "that an arrangement which is in so many respects desirable, should not have been compatible with one which is so much more desirable." But he made no renewed offer. Indeed he felt that he could not do so at the present moment, in honesty either to his cousin or to his uncle, as he had accepted their hospitality and acceded to the arrangements which they had proposed without any word on his part of such intention. A home had been offered to him at Dunripple,— to him in his present condition, but certainly not a home to any wife whom he might bring there, nor a home to the family which might come afterwards. He thought that he was doing the best that he could with himself by remaining in England, and the best also towards a possible future renewal of his engagement with Mary Lowther. But of that he said nothing in his letter to her. He merely told her the fact as it regarded himself, and told that somewhat coldly. Of Edith Brownlow, and of the proposition in regard to her, of course he said nothing.

It was the intention both of Sir Gregory and his son that the new inmate of the house should marry Edith. The old man, who, up to a late date had with weak persistency urged the match upon his son, had taken up the idea from the very first arrival of his nephew at Dunripple. Such an arrangement would solve all the family difficulties, and would enable him to provide for Edith as though she were indeed his daughter. He loved Edith dearly, but he could not bear that she should leave Dunripple, and it had grieved him sorely when he reflected that in coming years Dunripple must belong to relatives of whom he knew nothing that was good, and that Edith Brownlow must be banished from the house. If his son would have married Edith, all might have been well, but even Sir Gregory was at last aware that no such marriage as that could take place. Then had come the quarrel between the Colonel and the Captain, and the latter had been taken into favour. Colonel Marrable would not have been allowed to put his foot inside Dunripple House, so great was the horror which he had created. And the son had been feared too as long as the father and son were one. But now the father, who had treated the whole family vilely, had treated his own son most vilely, and therefore the son had been received with open arms. If only he could be trusted with Edith,—and if Edith and he might be made to trust each other,—all might be well. Of the engagement between Walter and Mary Lowther no word had ever reached Dunripple. Twice or thrice in the year a letter would pass between Parson John and his nephew, Gregory Marrable, but such letters were very short, and the parson was the last man in the world to spread the tittle-tattle of a love-story. He had always known that that affair would lead to nothing, and that the less said about it the better.

Walter Marrable was to join his regiment at Windsor before the end of April. When he wrote to Mary Lowther to tell her of his plans he had only a fortnight longer for remaining in idleness at Dunripple. The hunting was over, and his life was simply idle. He perceived, or thought that he perceived, that all the inmates of the house, and especially his uncle, expected that he would soon return to them, and that they spoke of his work of soldiering as of a thing that was temporary. Mrs. Brownlow, who was a quiet woman, very reticent, and by no means inclined to interfere with things not belonging to her, had suggested that he would soon be with them again, and the housekeeper had given him to understand that his room was not to be touched. And then, too, he thought that he saw that Edith Brownlow was specially left in his way. If that were so it was necessary that the eyes of some one of the Dunripple party should be opened to the truth.

He was walking home with Miss Brownlow across the park from church one Sunday morning. Sir Gregory never went to church; his age was supposed to be too great, or his infirmities too many. Mrs. Brownlow was in the pony carriage driving her nephew, and Walter Marrable was alone with Edith. There had been some talk of cousinship,—of the various relationships of the family, and the like,—and of the way in which the Marrables were connected. They two, Walter and Edith, were not cousins. She was related to the family only by her aunt's marriage, and yet, as she said, she had always heard more of the Marrables than of the Brownlows.

Sunday Morning at Dunripple.

"You never saw Mary Lowther?" Walter asked.

"Never."

"But you have heard of her?"

"I just know her name,—hardly more. The last time your uncle was here,—Parson John, we were talking of her. He made her out to be wonderfully beautiful."

"That was as long ago as last summer," said the Captain, reflecting that his uncle's account had been given before he and Mary Lowther had seen each other.

"Oh, yes;—ever so long ago."

"She is wonderfully beautiful."

"You know her, then, Captain Marrable?"

"I know her very well. In the first place, she is my cousin."

"But ever so distant?"

"We are not first cousins. Her mother was a daughter of General Marrable, who was a brother of Sir Gregory's father."

"It is so hard to understand, is it not? She is wonderfully beautiful, is she?"

"Indeed, she is."

"And she is your cousin—in the first place. What is she in the second place?"

He was not quite sure whether he wished to tell the story or not. The engagement was broken, and it might be a question whether, as regarded Mary, he had a right to tell it; and, then, if he did tell it, would not his reason for doing so be apparent? Was it not palpable that he was expected to marry this girl, and that she would understand that he was explaining to her that he did not intend to carry out the general expectation of the family? And, then, was he sure that it might not be possible for him at some future time to do as he was desired?

"I meant to say that, as I was staying at Loring, of course I met her frequently. She is living with a certain old Miss Marrable, whom you will meet some day."

"I have heard of her, but I don't suppose I ever shall meet her. I never go anywhere. I don't suppose there are such stay-at-home people in the world as we are."

"Why don't you get Sir Gregory to ask them here?"

"Both he and my cousin are so afraid of having strange women in the house; you know, we never have anybody here; your coming has been quite an event. Old Mrs. Potter seems to think that an era of dissipation is to be commenced because she has been called upon to open so many pots of jam to make pies for you."

"I'm afraid I have been very troublesome."

"Awfully troublesome. You can't think of all that had to be said and done about the stables! Do you have your oats bruised? Even I was consulted about that. Most of the people in the parish are quite disappointed because you don't go about in your full armour."

"I'm afraid it's too late now."

"I own I was a little disappointed myself when you came down to dinner without a sword. You can have no idea in what a state of rural simplicity we live here. Would you believe it?—for ten years I have never seen the sea, and have never been into any town bigger than Worcester,—unless Hereford be bigger. We did go once to the festival at Hereford. We have not managed Gloucester yet."

"You've never seen London?"

"Not since I was twelve years old. Papa died when I was fourteen, and I came here almost immediately afterwards. Fancy, ten years at Dunripple! There is not a tree or a stone I don't know, and of course not a face in the parish."

She was very nice; but it was out of the question that she should ever become his wife. He had thought that he might explain this to herself by letting her know that he had within the last few months become engaged to, and had broken his engagement with, his cousin, Mary Lowther. But he found that he could not do it. In the first place, she would understand more than he meant her to understand if he made the attempt. She would know that he was putting her on her guard, and would take it as an insult. And then he could not bring himself to talk about Mary Lowther, and to tell their joint secrets. He was discontented with himself and with Dunripple, and he repented that he had yielded in respect to his Indian service. Everything had gone wrong with him. Had he refused to accede to Mary's proposition for a separation, and had he come to Dunripple as an engaged man, he might, he thought, have reconciled his uncle,—or at least his Cousin Gregory,—to his marriage with Mary. But he did not see his way back to that position now, having been entertained at his uncle's house as his uncle's heir for so long a time without having mentioned it.

At last he went off to Windsor, sad at heart, having received from Mary an answer to his letter, which he felt to be very cold, very discreet, and very unsatisfactory. She had merely expressed a fervent wish that whether he went to India or whether he remained in England, he might be prosperous and happy. The writer evidently intended that the correspondence should not be continued.

CHAPTER XLV.

WHAT SHALL I DO WITH MYSELF?

Parson John Marrable, though he said nothing in his letters to Dunripple about the doings of his nephew at Loring, was by no means equally reticent in his speech at Loring as to the doings at Dunripple. How he came by his news he did not say, but he had ever so much to tell. And Miss Marrable, who knew him well, was aware that his news was not simple gossip, but was told with an object. In his way, Parson John was a crafty man, who was always doing a turn of business. To his mind it was clearly inexpedient, and almost impracticable, that his nephew and Mary Lowther should ever become man and wife. He knew that they were separated; but he knew, also, that they had agreed to separate on terms which would easily admit of being reconsidered. He, too, had heard of Edith Brownlow, and had heard that if a marriage could be arranged between Walter and Edith, the family troubles would be in a fair way of settlement. No good could come to anybody from that other marriage. As for Mary Lowther, it was manifestly her duty to become Mrs. Gilmore. He therefore took some trouble to let the ladies at Uphill know that Captain Marrable had been received very graciously at Dunripple; that he was making himself very happy there, hunting, shooting, and forgetting his old troubles; that it was understood that he was to be recognised as the heir;—and that there was a young lady in the case, the favourite of Sir Gregory.

He understood the world too well to say a word to Mary Lowther herself about her rival. Mary would have perceived his drift. But he expressed his ideas about Edith confidentially to Miss Marrable, fully alive to the fact that Miss Marrable would know how to deal with her niece. "It is by far the best thing that could have happened to him," said the parson. "As for going out to India again, for a man with his prospects it was very bad."

"But his cousin isn't much older than he is," suggested Miss Marrable.

"Yes he is,—a great deal older. And Gregory's health is so bad that his life is not worth a year's purchase. Poor fellow! they tell me he only cares to live till he has got his book out. The truth is that if Walter could make a match of it with Edith Brownlow, they might arrange something about the property which would enable him to live there just as though the place were his own. The Colonel would be the only stumbling-block, and after what he has done, he could hardly refuse to agree to anything."

"They'd have to pay him," said Miss Marrable.

"Then he must be paid, that's all. My brother Gregory is wrapped up in that girl, and he would do anything for her welfare. I'm told that she and Walter have taken very kindly to each other already."

It would be better for Mary Lowther that Walter Marrable should marry Edith Brownlow. Such, at least, was Miss Marrable's belief. She could see that Mary, though she bore herself bravely, still did so as one who had received a wound for which there was no remedy;—as a man who has lost a leg and who nevertheless intends to enjoy life though he knows that he never can walk again. But in this case, the real bar to walking was the hope in Mary's breast,—a hope that was still present, though it was not nourished,—that the leg was not irremediably lost. If Captain Marrable would finish all that by marrying Edith, then,—so thought Miss Marrable,—in process of time the cure would be made good, and there might be another leg. She did not believe much in the Captain's constancy, and was quite ready to listen to the story about another love. And so from day to day words were dropped into Mary's ear which had their effect.

"I must say that I am glad that he is not to go to India," said Miss Marrable to her niece.

"So, indeed, am I," answered Mary.

"In the first place it is such an excellent thing that he should be on good terms at Dunripple. He must inherit the property some day, and the title too."

To this Mary made no reply. It seemed to her to have been hard that the real state of things should not have been explained to her before she gave up her lover. She had then regarded any hope of relief from Dunripple as being beyond measure distant. There had been a possibility, and that was all,—a chance to which no prudent man or woman would have looked in making their preparations for the life before them. That had been her idea as to the Dunripple prospects; and now it seemed that on a sudden Walter was to be regarded as almost the immediate heir. She did not blame him; but it did appear to be hard upon her.

"I don't see the slightest reason why he shouldn't live at Dunripple," continued Miss Marrable.

"Only that he would be dependent. I suppose he does not mean to sell out of the army altogether."

"At any rate, he may be backwards and forwards. You see, there is no chance of Sir Gregory's own son marrying."

"So they say."

"And his position would be really that of a younger brother in similar circumstances."

Mary paused a moment before she replied, and then she spoke out.

"Dear Aunt Sarah, what does all this mean? I know you are speaking at me, and yet I don't quite understand it. Everything between me and Captain Marrable is over. I have no possible means of influencing his life. If I were told to-morrow that he had given up the army and taken to living altogether at Dunripple, I should have no means of judging whether he had done well or ill. Indeed, I should have no right to judge."

"You must be glad that the family should be united."

"I am glad. Now, is that all?"

"I want you to bring yourself to think without regret of his probable marriage with this young lady."

"You don't suppose I shall blame him if he marries her."

"But I want you to see it in such a light that it shall not make you unhappy."

"I think, dear aunt, that we had better not talk of it. I can assure you of this, that if I could prevent him from marrying by holding up my little finger, I would not do it."

"It would be ten thousand pities," urged the old lady, "that either his life or yours should be a sacrifice to a little episode, which, after all, only took a week or two in the acting."

"I can only answer for myself," said Mary. "I don't mean to be a sacrifice."

There were many such conversations, and by degrees they did have an effect upon Mary Lowther. She learned to believe that it was probable that Captain Marrable should marry Miss Brownlow, and, of course, asked herself questions as to the effect such a marriage would have upon herself, which she answered more fully than she did those which were put to her by her aunt. Then there came to Parson John some papers, which required his signature, in reference to the disposal of a small sum of money, he having been one of the trustees to his brother's marriage settlement. This was needed in regard to some provision which the baronet was making for his niece, and which, if read aright, would rather have afforded evidence against than in favour of the chance of her immediate marriage; but it was taken at Loring to signify that the thing was to be done, and that the courtship was at any rate in progress. Mary did not believe all that she heard; but there was left upon her mind an idea that Walter Marrable was preparing himself for the sudden change of his affections. Then she determined that, should he do so, she would not judge him to have done wrong. If he could settle himself comfortably in this way, why should he not do so? She was told that Edith Brownlow was pretty, and gentle, and good, and would undoubtedly receive from Sir Gregory's hands all that Sir Gregory could give her. It was expedient, for the sake of the whole family, that such a marriage should be arranged. She would not stand in the way of it; and, indeed, how could she stand in the way of it? Had not her engagement with Captain Marrable been dissolved at her own instance in the most solemn manner possible? Let him marry whom he might, she could have no ground of complaint on that score.

She was in this state of mind when she received Captain Marrable's letter from Dunripple. When she opened it, for a moment she thought that it would convey to her tidings respecting Miss Brownlow. When she had read it, she told herself how impossible it was that he should have told her of his new matrimonial intentions, even if he entertained them. The letter gave no evidence either one way or the other; but it confirmed to her the news which had reached her through Parson John, that her former lover intended to abandon that special career, his choice of which had made it necessary that they two should abandon their engagement. When at Loring he had determined that he must go to India. He had found it to be impossible that he should live without going to India. He had now been staying a few weeks at Dunripple with his uncle, and with Edith Brownlow, and it turned out that he need not go to India at all. Then she sat down, and wrote to him that guarded, civil, but unenthusiastic letter, of which the reader has already heard. She had allowed herself to be wounded and made sore by what they had told her of Edith Brownlow.

It was still early in the spring, just in the middle of April, when Mary received another letter from her friend at Bullhampton, a letter which made her turn all these things in her mind very seriously. If Walter Marrable were to marry Edith Brownlow, what sort of future life should she, Mary Lowther, propose to herself? She was firmly resolved upon one thing, that it behoved her to look rather to what was right than to what might simply be pleasant. But would it be right that she should consider herself to be, as it were, widowed by the frustration of an unfortunate passion? Life would still be left to her,—such a life as that which her aunt lived,—such a life, with this exception, that whereas her aunt was a single lady with moderate means, she would be a single lady with very small means indeed. But that question of means did not go far with her; there was something so much more important that she could put that out of sight. She had told herself very plainly that it was a good thing for a woman to be married; that she would live and die unsuccessfully if she lived and died a single woman; that she had desired to do better with herself than that. Was it proper that she should now give up all such ambition because she had made a mistake? If it were proper, she would do so; and then the question resolved itself into this;—Could she be right if she married a man without loving him? To marry a man without esteeming him, without the possibility of loving him hereafter, she knew would be wrong.

Mrs. Fenwick's letter was as follows;—

Vicarage, Tuesday.

MY DEAR MARY,

My brother-in-law left us yesterday, and has put us all into a twitter. He said, just as he was going away, that he didn't believe that Lord Trowbridge had any right to give away the ground, because it had not been in his possession or his family's for a great many years, or something of that sort. We don't clearly understand all about it, nor does he; but he is to find out something which he says he can find out, and then let us know. But in the middle of all this, Frank declares that he won't stir in the matter, and that if he could put the abominable thing down by holding up his finger, he would not do it. And he has made me promise not to talk about it, and, therefore, all I can do is to be in a twitter. If that spiteful old man has really given away land that doesn't belong to him, simply to annoy us,—and it certainly has been done with no other object,—I think that he ought to be told of it. Frank, however, has got to be quite serious about it, and you know how very serious he can be when he is serious.

But I did not sit down to write specially about that horrid chapel. I want to know what you mean to do in the summer. It is always better to make these little arrangements beforehand; and when I speak of the summer, I mean the early summer. The long and the short of it is, will you come to us about the end of May?

Of course, I know which way your thoughts will go when you get this, and, of course, you will know what I am thinking of when I write it; but I will promise that not a word shall be said to you to urge you in any way. I do not suppose you will think it right that you should stay away from friends whom you love, and who love you dearly, for fear of a man who wants you to marry him. You are not afraid of Mr. Gilmore, and I don't suppose that you are going to shut yourself up all your life because Captain Marrable has not a fortune of his own. Come at any rate. If you find it unpleasant you shall go back just when you please, and I will pledge myself that you shall not be harassed by persuasions.

Yours most affectionately,

JANET FENWICK.

Frank has read this. He says that all I have said about his being serious is a tarradiddle; but that nothing can be more true than what I have said about your friends loving you, and wishing to have you here again. If you were here we might talk him over yet about the chapel.

To which, in the Vicar's handwriting, was added the word, "Never!"

It was two days before she showed this letter to her aunt—two days in which she had thought much upon the subject. She knew well that her aunt would counsel her to go to Bullhampton, and, therefore, she would not mention the letter till she had made up her own mind.

"What will you do?" said her aunt.

"I will go, if you do not object."

"I certainly shall not object," said Miss Marrable.

Then Mary wrote a very short letter to her friend, which may as well, also, be communicated to the reader:—

Loring, Thursday.

DEAR JANET,

I will go to you about the end of May; and yet, though I have made up my mind to do so, I almost doubt that I am not wise. If one could only ordain that things should be as though they had never been! That, however, is impossible, and one can only endeavour to live so as to come as nearly as possible to such a state. I know that I am confused; but I think you will understand what I mean.

I intend to be very full of energy about the chapel, and I do hope that your brother-in-law will be able to prove that Lord Trowbridge has been misbehaving himself. I never loved Mr. Puddleham, who always seemed to look upon me with wrath because I belonged to the Vicarage; and I certainly should take delight in seeing him banished from the Vicarage gate.

Always affectionately yours,

MARY LOWTHER.

CHAPTER XLVI.

MR. JAY OF WARMINSTER.

The Vicar had undertaken to maintain Carry Brattle at Mrs. Stiggs's house, in Trotter's Buildings, for a fortnight, but he found at the end of the fortnight that his responsibility on the poor girl's behalf was by no means over. The reader knows with what success he had made his visit to Startup, and how far he was from ridding himself of his burden by the aid of the charity and affections of the poor girl's relatives there. He had shaken the Startup dust, as it were, from his gig-wheels as he drove out of George Brattle's farmyard, and had declined even the offer of money which had been made. Ten or fifteen pounds! He would make up the amount of that offer out of his own pocket rather than let the brother think that he had bought off his duty to a sister at so cheap a rate. Then he convinced himself that in this way he owed Carry Brattle fifteen pounds, and comforted himself by reflecting that these fifteen pounds would carry the girl on a good deal beyond the fortnight; if only she would submit herself to the tedium of such a life as would be hers if she remained at Mrs. Stiggs's house. He named a fortnight both to Carry and to Mrs. Stiggs, saying that he himself would either come or send before the end of that time. Then he returned home, and told the whole story to his wife. All this took place before Mr. Quickenham's arrival at the vicarage.

"My dear Frank," said his wife to him, "you will get into trouble."

"What sort of trouble?"

"In the first place, the expense of maintaining this poor girl,—for life, as far as we can see,—will fall upon you."

"What if it does? But, as a matter of course, she will earn her bread sooner or later. How am I to throw her over? And what am I to do with her?"

"But that is not the worst of it, Frank."

"Then what is the worst of it? Let us have it at once."

"People will say that you, a clergyman and a married man, go to see a pretty young woman at Salisbury."

"You believe that people will say that?"

"I think you should guard against it, for the sake of the parish."

"What sort of people will say it?"

"Lord Trowbridge, and his set."

"On my honour, Janet, I think that you wrong Lord Trowbridge. He is a fool, and to a certain extent a vindictive fool; and I grant you that he has taken it into his silly old head to hate me unmercifully; but I believe him to be a gentleman, and I do not think that he would condescend to spread a damnably malicious report of which he did not believe a word himself."

"But, my dear, he will believe it."

"Why? How? On what evidence? He couldn't believe it. Let a man be ever such a fool, he can't believe a thing without some reason. I dislike Lord Trowbridge very much; and you might just as well say that because I dislike him I shall believe that he is a hard landlord. He is not a hard landlord; and were he to stick dissenting chapels all about the county, I should be a liar and a slanderer were I to say that he was."

"But then, you see, you are not a fool, Frank."

This brought the conversation to an end. The Vicar was willing enough to turn upon his heel and say nothing more on a matter as to which he was by no means sure that he was in the right; and his wife felt a certain amount of reluctance in urging any arguments upon such a subject. Whatever Lord Trowbridge might say or think, her Frank must not be led to suppose that any unworthy suspicion troubled her own mind. Nevertheless, she was sure that he was imprudent.

When the fortnight was near at an end, and nothing had been done, he went again over to Salisbury. It was quite true that he had business there, as a gentleman almost always does have business in the county town where his banker lives, whence tradesmen supply him, and in which he belongs to some club. And our Vicar, too, was a man fond of seeing his bishop, and one who loved to move about in the precincts of the cathedral, to shake hands with the dean, and to have a little subrisive fling at Mr. Chamberlaine, or such another as Mr. Chamberlaine, if the opportunity came in his way. He was by no means indisposed to go into Salisbury in the ordinary course of things; and on this occasion absolutely did see Mr. Chamberlaine, the dean, his saddler, and the clerk at the Fire Insurance Office,—as well as Mrs. Stiggs and Carry Brattle. If, therefore, anyone had said that on this day he had gone into Salisbury simply to see Carry Brattle, such person would have maligned him. He reduced the premium on his Fire Insurance by 5*s*. 6*d*. a year, and he engaged Mr. Chamberlaine to meet Mr. Quickenham, and he borrowed from the dean an old book about falconry; so that in fact the few minutes which he spent at Mrs. Stiggs's house were barely squeezed in among the various affairs of business which he had to transact at Salisbury.

All that he could say to Carry Brattle was this,—that hitherto he had settled nothing. She must stay in Trotter's Buildings for another week or so. He had been so busy, in consequence of the time of the year, preparing for Easter and the like, that he had not been able to look about him. He had a plan; but would say nothing about it till he had seen whether it could be carried out. When Carry murmured something about the cost of her living the Vicar boldly declared that she need not fret herself about that, as he had money of hers in hand. He would some day explain all about that, but not now. Then he interrogated Mrs. Stiggs as to Carry's life. Mrs. Stiggs expressed her belief that Carry wouldn't stand it much longer. The hours had been inexpressibly long, and she had declared more than once that the best thing she could do was to go out and kill herself. Nevertheless, Mrs. Stiggs's report as to her conduct was favourable. Of Sam Brattle, the Vicar, though he inquired, could learn nothing. Carry declared that she had not heard from him since he left her all bruised and bleeding after his fight at the Three Honest Men.

The Vicar had told Carry Brattle that he had a plan,—but, in truth, he had no plan. He had an idea that he might overcome the miller by taking his daughter straight into his house, and placing the two face to face together; but it was one in which he himself put so little trust, that he could form no plan out of it. In the first place, would he be justified in taking such a step? Mrs. George Brattle had told him that people knew what was good for them without being dictated to by clergymen; and the rebuke had come home to him. He was the last man in the world to adopt a system of sacerdotal interference. "I could do it so much better if I was not a clergyman," he would say to himself. And then, if old Brattle chose to turn his daughter out of the house, on such provocation as the daughter had given him, what was that to him, Fenwick, whether priest or layman? The old man knew what he was about, and had shown his determination very vigorously.

"I'll try the ironmonger at Warminster," he said, to his wife.

"I'm afraid it will be of no use."

"I don't think it will. Ironmongers are probably harder than millers or farmers,—and farmers are very hard. That fellow, Jay, would not even consent to be bail for Sam Brattle. But something must be done."

"She should be put into a reformatory."

"It would be too late now. That should have been done at once. At any rate, I'll go to Warminster. I want to call on old Dr. Dickleburg, and I can do that at the same time."

He did go to Warminster. He did call on the Doctor, who was not at home;—and he did call also upon Mr. Jay, who was at home.

With Mr. Jay himself his chance was naturally much less than it would be with George Brattle. The ironmonger was connected with the unfortunate young woman only by marriage; and what brother-in-law would take such a sister-in-law to his bosom? And of Mrs. Jay he thought that he knew that she was puritanical, stiff, and severe. Mr. Jay he found in his shop along with an apprentice, but he had no difficulty in leading the master ironmonger along with him through a vista of pots, grates and frying pans, into a small recess at the back of the establishment, in which requests for prolonged credit were usually made, and urgent appeals for speedy payment as often put forth.

"Know the story of Caroline Brattle? Oh yes! I know it, sir," said Mr. Jay. "We had to know it." And as he spoke he shook his head, and rubbed his hands together, and looked down upon the ground. There was, however, a humility about the man, a confession on his part, that in talking to an undoubted gentleman he was talking to a superior being, which gave to Fenwick an authority which he had felt himself to want in his intercourse with the farmer.

"I am sure, Mr. Jay, you will agree with me in that she should be saved if possible."

"As to her soul, sir?" asked the ironmonger.

"Of course, as to her soul. But we must get at that by saving her in this world first."

Mr. Jay was a slight man, of middle height, with very respectable iron-grey hair that stood almost upright upon his head, but with a poor, inexpressive, thin face below it. He was given to bowing a good deal, rubbing his hands together, smiling courteously, and to the making of many civil little speeches; but his strength as a leading man in Warminster lay in his hair, and in the suit of orderly well-brushed black clothes which he wore on all occasions. He was, too, a man fairly prosperous, who went always to church, paid his way, attended sedulously to his business, and hung his bells, and sold his pots in such a manner as not actually to drive his old customers away by default of work. "Jay is respectable, and I don't like to leave him," men would say, when their wives declared that the backs of his grates fell out, and that his nails never would stand hammering. So he prospered; but, perhaps, he owed his prosperity mainly to his hair. He rubbed his hands, and smiled, and bowed his head about, as he thought what answer he might best make. He was quite willing that poor Carry's soul should be saved. That would naturally be Mr. Fenwick's affair. But as to saving her body, with any co-operation from himself or Mrs. Jay,—he did not see his way at all through such a job as that.

"I'm afraid she is a bad 'un, Mr. Fenwick; I'm afraid she is," said Mr. Jay.

"The thing is, whether we can't put our heads together and make her less bad," said the Vicar. "She must live somewhere, Mr. Jay."

"I don't know whether almost the best thing for 'em isn't to die,—of course after they have repented, Mr. Fenwick. You see, sir, it is so very low, and so shameful, and they do bring such disgrace on their poor families. There isn't anything a young man can do that is nearly so bad,—is there, Mr. Fenwick?"

"I'm not at all sure of that, Mr. Jay."

"Ain't you now?"

"I'm not going to defend Carry Brattle;—but if you will think how very small an amount of sin may bring a woman to this wretched condition, your heart will be softened. Poor Carry;—she was so bright, and so good and so clever!"

"Clever she was, Mr. Fenwick;—and bright, too, as you call it. But—"

"Of course we know all that. The question now is, what can we do to help her? She is living now at this present moment, an orderly, sober life; but without occupation, or means, or friends. Will your wife let her come to her,—for a month or so, just to try her?"

"Come and live here!" exclaimed the ironmonger.

"That is what I would suggest. Who is to give her the shelter of a roof, if a sister will not?"

"I don't think that Mrs. Jay would undertake that," said the ironmonger, who had ceased to rub his hands and to bow, and whose face had now become singularly long and lugubrious.

"May I ask her?"

"It wouldn't do any good, Mr. Fenwick;—it wouldn't indeed."

"It ought to do good. May I try?"

"If you ask me, Mr. Fenwick, I should say no; indeed I should. Mrs. Jay isn't any way strong, and the bare mention of that disreputable connexion produces a sickness internally;—it does, indeed, Mr. Fenwick."

"You will do nothing, then, to save from perdition the sister of your own wife;—and will let your wife do nothing?"

"Now, Mr. Fenwick, don't be hard on me;—pray don't be hard on me. I have been respectable, and have always had respectable people about me. If my wife's family are turning wrong, isn't that bad enough on me without your coming to say such things as this to me? Really, Mr. Fenwick, if you'd think of it, you wouldn't be so hard."

"She may die in a ditch, then, for you?" said the Vicar, whose feeling against the ironmonger was much stronger than it had been against the farmer. He could say nothing further, so he turned upon his heel and marched down the length of the shop, while the obsequious tradesman followed him,—again bowing and rubbing his hands, and attending him to his carriage. The Vicar didn't speak another word, or make any parting salutation to Mr. Jay. "Their hearts are like the nether millstone," he said to himself, as he drove away, flogging his horse. "Of what use are all the sermons? Nothing touches them. Do unto others as you think they would do unto you. That's their doctrine." As he went home he made up his mind that he would, as a last effort, carry out that scheme of taking Carry with him to the mill;—he would do so, that is, if he could induce Carry to accompany him. In the meantime, there was nothing left to him but to leave her with Mrs. Stiggs, and to pay ten shillings a week for her board and lodging. There was one point on which he could not quite make up his mind;—whether he would or would not first acquaint old Mrs. Brattle with his intention.

He had left home early, and when he returned his wife had received Mary Lowther's reply to her letter.

"She will come?" asked Frank.

"She just says that and nothing more."

"Then she'll be Mrs. Gilmore."

"I hope so, with all my heart," said Mrs. Fenwick.

"I look upon it as tantamount to accepting him. She wouldn't come unless she had made up her mind to take him. You mark my words. They'll be married before the chapel is finished."

"You say it as if you thought she oughtn't to come."

"No;—I don't mean that. I was only thinking how quickly a woman may recover from such a hurt."

"Frank, don't be ill-natured. She will be doing what all her friends advise."

"If I were to die, your friends would advise you not to grieve; but they would think you very unfeeling if you did not."

"Are you going to turn against her?"

"No."

"Then why do you say such things? Is it not better that she should make the effort than lie there helpless and motionless, throwing her whole life away? Will it not be much better for Harry Gilmore?"

"Very much better for him, because he'll go crazy if she don't."

"And for her too. We can't tell what is going on inside her breast. I believe that she is making a great effort because she thinks it is right. You will be kind to her when she comes?"

"Certainly I will,—for Harry's sake—and her own."

But in truth the Vicar at this moment was not in a good humour. He was becoming almost tired of his efforts to set other people straight, so great were the difficulties that came in his way. As he had driven into his own gate he had met Mr. Puddleham, standing in the road just in front of the new chapel. He had made up his mind to accept the chapel, and now he said a pleasant word to the minister. Mr. Puddleham turned up his eyes and his nose, bowed very stiffly, and then twisted himself round, without answering a word. How was it possible for a man to live among such people in good humour and Christian charity?

In the evening he was sitting with his wife in the drawing-room discussing all these troubles, when the maid came in to say that Constable Toffy was at the door.

Constable Toffy was shown into his study, and then the Vicar followed him. He had not spoken to the constable now for some months,—not since the time at which Sam had been liberated; but he had not a moment's doubt when he was thus summoned, that something was to be said as to the murder of Mr. Trumbull. The constable put his hand up to his head, and sat down at the Vicar's invitation, before he began to speak.

"What is it, Toffy?" said the Vicar.

"We've got 'em at last, I think," said Mr. Toffy, in a very low, soft voice.

"Got whom;—the murderers?"

"Just so, Mr. Fenwick; all except Sam Brattle,—whom we want."

"And who are the men?"

"Them as we supposed all along,—Jack Burrows, as they call the Grinder, and Lawrence Acorn as was along with him. He's a Birmingham chap, is Acorn. He's know'd very well at Birmingham. And then, Mr. Fenwick, there's Sam. That's all as seems to have been in it. We shall want Sam, Mr. Fenwick."

"You don't mean to tell me that he was one of the murderers?"

"We shall want him, Mr. Fenwick."

"Where did you find the other men?"

"They did get as far as San Francisco,—did the others. They haven't had a bad game of it,—have they, Mr. Fenwick? They've had more than seven months of a run. It was the 31st of August as Mr. Trumbull was murdered, and here's the 15th of April, Mr. Fenwick. There ain't a many runs as long as that. You'll have Sam Brattle for us all right, no doubt, Mr. Fenwick?" The Vicar told the constable that he would see to it, and get Sam Brattle to come forward as soon as he could. "I told you all through, Mr. Fenwick, as Sam was one of them as was in it, but you wouldn't believe me."

"I don't believe it now," said the Vicar.

CHAPTER XLVII.

SAM BRATTLE IS WANTED.

The next week was one of considerable perturbation, trouble, and excitement at Bullhampton, and in the neighbourhood of Warminster and Heytesbury. It soon became known generally that Jack the Grinder and Lawrence Acorn were in Salisbury gaol, and that Sam Brattle—was wanted. The perturbation and excitement at Bullhampton were, of course, greater than elsewhere. It was necessary that the old miller should be told,—necessary also that the people at the mill should be asked as to Sam's present whereabouts. If they did not know it, they might assist the Vicar in discovering it. Fenwick went to the mill, taking the Squire with him; but they could obtain no information. The miller was very silent, and betrayed hardly any emotion when he was told that the police again wanted his son.

"They can come and search," he said. "They can come and search." And then he walked slowly away into the mill. There was a scene, of course, with Mrs. Brattle and Fanny, and the two women were in a sad way.

"Poor boy,—wretched boy!" said the unfortunate mother, who sat sobbing with her apron over her face.

"We know nothing of him, Mr. Gilmore, or we would tell at once," said Fanny.

"I'm sure you would," said the Vicar. "And you may remember this, Mrs. Brattle; I do not for one moment believe that Sam had any more to do with the murder than you or I. You may tell his father that I say so, if you please."

For saying this the Squire rebuked him as soon as they had left the mill. "I think you go too far in giving such assurance as that," he said.

"Surely you would have me say what I think?"

"Not on such a matter as this, in which any false encouragement may produce so much increased suffering. You, yourself, are so prone to take your own views in opposition to those of others that you should be specially on your guard when you may do so much harm."

"I feel quite sure that he had nothing to do with it."

"You see that you have the police against you after a most minute and prolonged investigation."

"The police are asses," insisted the Vicar.

"Just so. That is, you prefer your own opinion to theirs in regard to a murder. I should prefer yours to theirs on a question of scriptural evidence, but not in such an affair as this. I don't want to talk you over, but I wish to make you careful with other people who are so closely concerned. In dealing with others you have no right to throw over the ordinary rules of evidence."

The Vicar accepted the rebuke and promised to be more careful,—repeating, however, his own opinion about Sam, to which he declared his intention of adhering in regard to his own conduct, let the police and magistrates say what they might. He almost went so far as to declare that he should do so even in opposition to the verdict of a jury; but Gilmore understood that this was simply the natural obstinacy of the man, showing itself in its natural form.

At this moment, which was certainly one of gloom to the parish at large, and of great sorrow at the Vicarage, the Squire moved about with a new life which was evident to all who saw him. He went about his farm, and talked about his trees, and looked at his horses and had come to life again. No doubt many guesses as to the cause of this were made throughout his establishment, and some of them, probably, very near the truth. But, for the Fenwicks there was no need of guessing. Gilmore had been told that Mary Lowther was coming to Bullhampton in the early summer, and had at once thrown off the cloak of his sadness. He had asked no further questions; Mrs. Fenwick had found herself unable to express a caution; but the extent of her friend's elation almost frightened her.

"I don't look at it," she said to her husband, "quite as he does."

"She'll have him now," he answered, and then Mrs. Fenwick said nothing further.

To Fenwick himself, this change was one of infinite comfort. The Squire was his old friend and almost his only near neighbour. In all his troubles, whether inside or outside of the parish, he naturally went to Gilmore; and, although he was a man not very prone to walk by the advice of friends, still it had been a great thing to him to have a friend who would give an opinion, and perhaps the more so, as the friend was one who did not insist on having his opinion taken. During the past winter Gilmore had been of no use whatever to his friend. His opinions on all matters had gone so vitally astray, that they had not been worth having. And he had become so morose, that the Vicar had found it to be almost absolutely necessary to leave him alone as far as ordinary life was concerned. But now the Squire was himself again, and on this exciting topic of Trumbull's murder, the prisoners in Salisbury gaol, and the necessity for Sam's reappearance, could talk sensibly and usefully.

It was certainly very expedient that Sam should be made to reappear as soon as possible. The idea was general in the parish that the Vicar knew all about him. George Brattle, who had become bail for his brother's reappearance, had given his name on the clear understanding that the Vicar would be responsible. Some half-sustained tidings of Carry's presence in Salisbury and of the Vicar's various visits to the city were current in Bullhampton, and with these were mingled an idea that Carry and Sam were in league together. That Fenwick was chivalrous, perhaps Quixotic, in his friendships for those whom he regarded, had long been felt, and this feeling was now stronger than ever. He certainly could bring up Sam Brattle if he pleased;—or, if he pleased, as might, some said, not improbably be the case, he could keep him away. There would be £400 to pay for the bail-bond, but the Vicar was known to be rich as well as Quixotic, and,—so said the Puddlehamites,—would care very little about that, if he might thus secure for himself his own way.

He was constrained to go over again to Salisbury in order that he might, if possible, learn from Carry how to find some trace to her brother, and of this visit the Puddlehamites also informed themselves. There were men and women in Bullhampton who knew exactly how often the Vicar had visited the young woman at Salisbury, how long he had been with her on each occasion, and how much he paid Mrs. Stiggs for the accommodation. Gentlemen who are Quixotic in their kindness to young women are liable to have their goings and comings chronicled with much exactitude, if not always with accuracy.

His interview with Carry on this occasion was very sad. He could not save himself from telling her in part the cause of his inquiries. "They haven't taken the two men, have they?" she asked, with an eagerness that seemed to imply that she possessed knowledge on the matter which could hardly not be guilty.

"What two men?" he asked, looking full into her face. Then she was silent and he was unwilling to catch her in a trap, to cross-examine her as a lawyer would do, or to press out of her any communication which she would not make willingly and of her own free action. "I am told," he said, "that two men have been taken for the murder."

"Where did they find 'em, sir?"

"They had escaped to America, and the police have brought them back. Did you know them, Carry?" She was again silent. The men had not been named, and it was not for her to betray them. Hitherto, in their interviews, she had hardly ever looked him in the face, but now she turned her blue eyes full upon him. "You told me before at the old woman's cottage," he said, "that you knew them both,—had known one too well."

"If you please, sir, I won't say nothing about 'em."

"I will not ask you, Carry. But you would tell me about your brother, if you knew?"

"Indeed I would, sir;—anything. He hadn't no more to do with Farmer Trumbull's murder nor you had. They can't touch a hair of his head along of that."

"Such is my belief;—but who can prove it?" Again she was silent. "Can you prove it? If speaking could save your brother, surely you would speak out. Would you hesitate, Carry, in doing anything for your brother's sake? Whatever may be his faults, he has not been hard to you like the others."

"Oh, sir, I wish I was dead."

"You must not wish that, Carry. And if you know ought of this you will be bound to speak. If you could bring yourself to tell me what you know, I think it might be good for both of you."

"It was they who had the money. Sam never seed a shilling of it."

"Who is 'they'?"

"Jack Burrows and Larry Acorn. And it wasn't Larry Acorn neither, sir. I know very well who did it. It was Jack Burrows who did it."

"That is he they call the Grinder?"

"But Larry was with him then," said the girl, sobbing.

"You are sure of that?"

"I ain't sure of nothing, Mr. Fenwick, only that Sam wasn't there at all. Of that I am quite, quite, quite sure. But when you asks me, what am I to say?"

Then he left her without speaking to her on this occasion a word about herself. He had nothing to say that would give her any comfort. He had almost made up his mind that he would take her over with him to the mill, and try what might be done by the meeting between the father, mother, and daughter, but all this new matter about the police and the arrest, and Sam's absence, made it almost impossible for him to take such a step at present. As he went, he again interrogated Mrs. Stiggs, and was warned by her that words fell daily from her lodger which made her think that the young woman would not remain much longer with her. In the meantime there was nothing of which she could complain. Carry insisted on her liberty to go out and about the city alone; but the woman was of opinion that she did this simply with the object of asserting her independence. After that the necessary payment was made, and the Vicar returned to the Railway Station. Of Sam he had learned nothing, and now he did not know where to go for tidings. He still believed that the young man would come of his own accord, if the demand for his appearance were made so public as to reach his ear.

On that same day there was a meeting of the magistrates at Heytesbury, and the two men who had been so cruelly fetched back from San Francisco were brought before it. Mr. Gilmore was on the bench, along with Sir Thomas Charleys, who was the chairman, and three other gentlemen. Lord Trowbridge was in the court house, and sat upon the bench, but gave it out that he was not sitting there as a magistrate. Samuel Brattle was called upon to answer to his bail, and Jones, the attorney appearing for him, explained that he had gone from home to seek work elsewhere, alluded to the length of time that had elapsed, and to the injustice of presuming that a man against whom no evidence had been adduced, should be bound to remain always in one parish,—and expressed himself without any doubt that Mr. Fenwick and Mr. George Brattle, who were his bailsmen, would cause him to be found and brought forward. As neither the clergyman nor the farmer were in court, nothing further could be done at once; and the magistrates were quite ready to admit that time must be allowed. Nor was the case at all ready against the two men who were in custody. Indeed, against them the evidence was so little substantial that a lawyer from Devizes, who attended on their behalf, expressed his amazement that the American authorities should have given them up, and suggested that it must have been done with some view to a settlement of the Alabama claims. Evidence, however, was brought up to show that the two men had been convicted before, the one for burglary, and the other for horse-stealing; that the former, John Burrows, known as the Grinder, was a man from Devizes with whom the police about that town, and at Chippenham, Bath, and Wells, were well acquainted; that the other, Acorn, was a young man who had been respectable, as a partner in a livery stable at Birmingham, but who had taken to betting, and had for a year past been living by evil courses, having previously undergone two years of imprisonment with hard labour. It was proved that they had been seen in the neighbourhood both before and after the murder; that boots found in the cottage at Pycroft Common fitted certain footmarks in the mud of the farmer's yard; that Burrows had been supplied with a certain poison at a county chemist's at Lavington, and that the dog Bone'm had been poisoned with the like. Many other matters were proved, all of which were declared by the lawyer from Devizes to amount to nothing, and by the police authorities, who were prosecutors, to be very much. The magistrates of course ordered a remand, and ordered also that on the day named Sam Brattle should appear. It was understood that that day week was only named pro formâ, the constables having explained that at least a fortnight would be required for the collection of further evidence. This took place on Tuesday, the 25th of April, and it was understood that time up to the 8th of May would be given to the police to complete their case.

So far all went on quietly at Heytesbury; but before the magistrates left the little town there was a row. Sir Thomas Charleys, in speaking to his brother magistrate, Mr. Gilmore, about the whole affair and about the Brattles in particular, had alluded to "Mr. Fenwick's unfortunate connexion with Carry Brattle" at Salisbury. Gilmore fired up at once, and demanded to know the meaning of this. Sir Thomas, who was not the wisest man in the world, but who had ideas of justice, and as to whom, in giving him his due, it must be owned that he was afraid of no one, after some hesitation, acknowledged that what he had heard respecting Mr. Fenwick had fallen from Lord Trowbridge. He had heard from Lord Trowbridge that the Vicar of Bullhampton was * * *. Gilmore on the occasion became full of energy, and pressed the baronet very hard. Sir Thomas hoped that Mr. Gilmore was not going to make mischief. Mr. Gilmore declared that he would not submit to the injury done to his friend, and that he would question Lord Trowbridge on the subject. He did question Lord Trowbridge, whom he found waiting for his carriage, in the parlour of the Bull Inn, Sir Thomas having accompanied him in the search. The Marquis was quite outspoken. He had heard, he said, from what he did not doubt to be good authority, that Mr. Fenwick was in the habit of visiting alone a young woman who had lived in his parish, but whom he now maintained in lodgings in a low alley in the suburbs of Salisbury. He had said so much as that. In so saying, had he spoken truth or falsehood? If he had said anything untrue, he would be the first to acknowledge his own error.

Then there had come to be very hot words. "My lord," said Mr. Gilmore, "your insinuation is untrue. Whatever your words may have been, in the impression which they have made, they are slanderous."

"Who are you, sir," said the Marquis, looking at him from head to foot, "to talk to me of the impression of my words?"

But Mr. Gilmore's blood was up. "You intended to convey to Sir Thomas Charleys, my lord, that Mr. Fenwick's visits were of a disgraceful nature. If your words did not convey that, they conveyed nothing."

"Who are you, sir, that you should interpret my words? I did no more than my duty in conveying to Sir Thomas Charleys my conviction,—my well-grounded conviction,—as to the gentleman's conduct. What I said to him I will say aloud to the whole county. It is notorious that the Vicar of Bullhampton is in the habit of visiting a profligate young woman in a low part of the city. That I say is disgraceful to him, to his cloth, and to the parish, and I shall give my opinion to the bishop to that effect. Who are you, sir, that you should question my words?" And again the Marquis eyed the Squire from head to foot, leaving the room with a majestic strut as Gilmore went on to assert that the allegation made, with the sense implied by it, contained a wicked and a malicious slander. Then there were some words, much quieter than those preceding them, between Mr. Gilmore and Sir Thomas, in which the Squire pledged himself to,—he hardly knew what, and Sir Thomas promised to hold his tongue,—for the present. But, as a matter of course, the quarrel flew all over the little town. It was out of the question that such a man as the Marquis of Trowbridge should keep his wrath confined. Before he had left the inn-yard he had expressed his opinion very plainly to half-a-dozen persons, both as to the immorality of the Vicar and the impudence of the Squire; and as he was taken home his hand was itching for pen and paper in order that he might write to the bishop. Sir Thomas shrugged his shoulders, and did not tell the story to more than three or four confidential friends, to all of whom he remarked that on the matter of the visits made to the girl, there never was smoke without fire. Gilmore's voice, too, had been loud, and all the servants about the inn had heard him. He knew that the quarrel was already public, and felt that he had no alternative but to tell his friend what had passed.

"Who are you, sir, that you should interpret my words?"

On that same evening he saw the Vicar. Fenwick had returned from Salisbury, tired, dispirited, and ill at ease, and was just going in to dress for dinner, when Gilmore met him at his own stable-door, and told him what had occurred.

"Then, after all, my wife was right and I was wrong," said Fenwick.

"Right about what?" Gilmore asked.

"She said that Lord Trowbridge would spread these very lies. I confess that I made the mistake of believing him to be a gentleman. Of course I may use your information?"

"Use it just as you please," said Gilmore. Then they parted, and Gilmore, who was on horseback, rode home.

CHAPTER XLVIII.

MARY LOWTHER RETURNS TO BULLHAMPTON.

A month went by after the scenes described in the last chapter, and summer had come at Bullhampton. It was now the end of May, and, with the summer, Mary Lowther had arrived. During the month very little progress had been made with the case at Heytesbury. There had been two or three remands, and now there was yet another. The police declared that this was rendered necessary by the absence of Sam Brattle,—that the magistrates were anxious to give all reasonable time for the production of the man who was out upon bail,—and that, as he was undoubtedly concerned in the murder, they were determined to have him. But they who professed to understand the case, among whom were the lawyer from Devizes and Mr. Jones of Heytesbury, declared that no real search had been made for Brattle because the evidence in regard to the other men was hitherto inefficient. The remand now stood again till Tuesday, June the 5th, and it was understood that if Brattle did not then appear the bail would be declared to have been forfeited.

Fenwick had written a very angry letter to Lord Trowbridge, to which he had got no answer, and Lord Trowbridge had written a very silly letter to the bishop, in replying to which the bishop had snubbed him. "I am informed by my friend, Mr. Gilmore," said the Vicar to the Marquis, "that your lordship has stated openly that I have made visits to a young woman in Salisbury which are disgraceful to me, to my cloth, and to the parish of which I am the incumbent. I do not believe that your lordship will deny that you have done so, and I, therefore, call upon you at once to apologise to me for the calumny, which, in its nature, is as injurious and wicked as calumny can be, and to promise that you will not repeat the offence." The Marquis, when he received this, had not as yet written that letter to the bishop on which he had resolved after his interview with Gilmore,—feeling, perhaps, some qualms of conscience, thinking that it might be well that he should consult his son,—though with a full conviction that, if he did so, his son would not allow him to write to the bishop at all,—possibly with some feeling that he had been too hard upon his enemy, the Vicar. But, when the letter from Bullhampton reached him, all feelings of doubt, caution, and mercy, were thrown to the winds. The tone of the letter was essentially aggressive and impudent. It was the word calumny that offended him most, that, and the idea that he, the Marquis of Trowbridge, should be called upon to promise not to commit an offence! The pestilent infidel at Bullhampton, as he called our friend, had not attempted to deny the visits to the young woman at Salisbury. And the Marquis had made fresh inquiry which had completely corroborated his previous information. He had learned Mrs. Stiggs's address, and the name of Trotter's Buildings, which details were to his mind circumstantial, corroborative, and damnatory. Some dim account of the battle at the Three Honest Men had reached him, and the undoubted fact that Carry Brattle was maintained by the Vicar. Then he remembered all Fenwick's old anxiety on behalf of the brother, whom the Marquis had taught himself to regard as the very man who had murdered his tenant. He reminded himself, too, of the murderer's present escape from justice by aid of this pestilent clergyman; and thus became convinced that in dealing with Mr. Fenwick, as it was his undoubted duty to do, he had to deal with one of the very worst of the human race. His lordship's mind was one utterly incapable of sifting evidence,—unable even to understand evidence when it came to him. He was not a bad man. He desired nothing that was not his own, and remitted much that was. He feared God, honoured the Queen, and loved his country. He was not self-indulgent. He did his duties as he knew them. But he was an arrogant old fool, who could not keep himself from mischief,— who could only be kept from mischief by the aid of some such master as his son. As soon as he received the Vicar's letter he at once sat down and wrote to the bishop. He was so sure that he was right, that he sent Fenwick's letter to the bishop, acknowledging what he himself had said at Heytesbury, and justifying it altogether by an elaborate account of the Vicar's wickedness. "And now, my lord, let me ask you," said he, in conclusion, "whether you deem this a proper man to have the care of souls in the large and important parish of Bullhampton."

The bishop felt himself to be very much bullied. He had no doubt whatsoever about his parson. He knew that Fenwick was too strong a man to be acted upon beneficially by such advice as to his private conduct as a bishop might give, and too good a man to need any caution as to his conduct. "My Lord Marquis," he said, in reply, "in returning the endorsed letter from Mr. Fenwick to your lordship, I can only say that nothing has been brought before me by your lordship which seems to me to require my interference. I should be wrong if I did not add to this the expression of my opinion that Mr. Fenwick is a moral man, doing his duty in his parish well, and an example in my diocese to be followed, rather than a stumbling block."

When this letter reached the Castle Lord St. George was there. The poor old Marquis was cut to the quick. He immediately perceived,—so he told himself,—that the bishop was an old woman, who understood nothing; but he was sure that St. George would not look at the matter in the same light. And yet it was impossible not to tell St. George. Much as he dreaded his son, he did honestly tell everything to his Mentor. He had already told St. George of Fenwick's letter to him and of his letter to the bishop, and St. George had whistled. Now he showed the bishop's letter to his son. St. George read the letter, refolded it slowly, shrugged his shoulders, and said, as he returned it to his father,—

"Well, my lord, I suppose you like a hornet's nest."

This was the uncomfortable position of things at Bullhampton about the beginning of June, at which time Mary Lowther was again staying with her friend Mrs. Fenwick. Carry Brattle was still at Salisbury, but had not been seen by the Vicar for more than a fortnight. The Marquis's letter, backed as it was in part by his wife's counsel, had, much to his own disgust, deterred him from seeing the girl. His wife, however, had herself visited Trotter's Buildings, and had seen Carry, taking to her a little present from her mother, who did not dare to go over to Salisbury to see her child, because of words that had passed between her and her husband.

Mrs. Fenwick, on her return home, had reported that Carry was silent, sullen, and idle; that her only speech was an expression of a wish that she was dead, and that Mrs. Stiggs had said that she could get no good of her. In the meantime Sam Brattle had not yet turned up, and the 5th of June was at hand.

Mary Lowther was again at the vicarage, and of course it was necessary that she and Mr. Gilmore should meet each other. A promise had been made to her that no advice should be pressed upon her,—the meaning of which, of course, was that nothing should be said to her urging her to marry Mr. Gilmore. But it was of course understood by all the parties concerned that Mr. Gilmore was to be allowed to come to the house; and, indeed, this was understood by the Fenwicks to mean almost as plainly that she would at least endeavour to bring herself to accept him when he did come. To Mary herself, as she made the journey, the same meaning seemed to be almost inevitable; and as she perceived this, she told herself that she had been wrong to leave home. She knew,—she thought she knew,—that she must refuse him, and in doing so would simply be making fresh trouble. Would it not have been better for her to have remained at Loring,—to have put herself at once on a par with her aunt, and have commenced her life of solitary spinsterhood and dull routine? But, then, why should she refuse him? She endeavoured to argue it out with herself in the railway carriage. She had been told that Walter Marrable would certainly marry Edith Brownlow, and she believed it. No doubt it was much better that he should do so. At any rate, she and Walter were separated for ever. When he wrote to her, declaring his purpose of remaining in England, he had said not a word of renewing his engagement with her. No doubt she loved him. About that she did not for a moment endeavour to deceive herself. No doubt, if that fate in life which she most desired might be hers, she would become the wife of Walter Marrable. But that fate would not be hers, and then there arose the question whether, on that account, she was unfit to be the wife of any other man. Of this she was quite certain, that should it ever seem to her to be her duty to accept the other man, she would first explain to him clearly the position in which she found herself. At last the whole matter resolved itself to this;—was it possible for her to divest her idea of life of all romance, and to look for contentment and satisfaction in the performance of duties to others? The prospect of an old maid's life at Loring was not pleasant to her eyes; but she would bear that, and worse than that, rather than do wrong. It was, however, so hard for her to know what was right and what was wrong! Supposing that she were to consent to marry Mr. Gilmore, would she be forsworn when at the altar she promised to love him? All her care would be henceforth for him, all her heart, as far as she could command her heart, and certainly all her truth. There should not be a secret of her mind hidden from him. She would force herself to love him, and to forget that other man. He should be the object of all her idolatry. She would, in that case, do her very utmost to reward him for the constancy of the affection with which he had regarded her; and yet, as she was driven in at the vicarage gate, she told herself that it would have been better for her to remain at Loring.

During the first evening Mr. Gilmore's name was not mentioned. There were subjects enough for conversation, as the period was one of great excitement in Bullhampton.

"What did you think of our chapel?" asked Mrs. Fenwick.

"I had no idea it was so big."

"Why, they are not going to leave us a single soul to go to church. Mr. Puddleham means to make a clean sweep of the parish."

"You don't mean to say that any have left you?"

"Well; none as yet," replied Mrs. Fenwick. "But then the chapel isn't finished; and the Marquis has not yet sent his order to his tenants to become dissenters. We expect that he will do so, unless he can persuade the bishop to turn Frank out of the living."

"But the bishop couldn't turn him out."

"Of course, he couldn't,—and wouldn't if he could. The bishop and Frank are the best friends in the world. But that has nothing to do with it. You mustn't abuse the chapel to Frank; just at this moment the subject is tabooed. My belief is that the whole edifice will have to come down, and that the confusion of Mr. Puddleham and the Marquis will be something more complete than ever was yet seen. In the meantime, I put my finger to my lip, and just look at Frank whenever the chapel is mentioned."

And then there was the matter of the murder, and the somewhat sad consideration of Sam's protracted absence.

"And will you have to pay four hundred pounds, Mr. Fenwick?" Mary asked.

"I shall be liable to pay it if he does not appear to-morrow, and no doubt must absolutely pay it if he does not turn up soon."

"But you don't think that he was one of them?"

"I am quite sure he was not. But he has had trouble in his family, and he got into a quarrel, and I fancy he has left the country. The police say that he has been traced to Liverpool."

"And will the other men be convicted?" Mrs. Fenwick asked.

"I believe they will, and most fervently hope so. They have some evidence about the wheels of a small cart in which Burrows certainly, and, I believe, no doubt Acorn also, were seen to drive across Pycroft Common early on the Sunday morning. A part of the tire had come off, and another bit, somewhat broader, and an inch or so too short, had been substituted. The impress made by this wheel in the mud, just round the corner by the farm gate, was measured and copied at the time, and they say that this will go far to identify the men. That the man's cart was there is certain,—also that he was in the same cart at Pycroft Common an hour or two after the murder."

"That does seem clear," said Mary.

"But somebody suggests that Sam had borrowed the cart. I believe, however, that it will all come out;—only, if I have to pay four hundred pounds I shall think that Farmer Trumbull has cost me very dear."

On the next morning Gilmore came to the vicarage. It had been arranged that he would drive Fenwick over to Heytesbury, and that he would call for him after breakfast. A somewhat late hour,—two in the afternoon,—had been fixed for going on with the murder case, as it was necessary that a certain constable should come down from London on that morning; and, therefore, there would be no need for the two men to start very early from Bullhampton. This was explained to Mary by Mrs. Fenwick. "He dines here to-day," she had said when they met in the morning before prayers, "and you may as well get over the first awkwardness at once." Mary had assented to this, and, after breakfast, Gilmore made his appearance among them in the garden. He was just one moment alone with the girl he loved.

"Miss Lowther," he said, "I cannot be with you for an instant without telling you that I am unchanged."

Mary made no reply, and he said nothing further. Mrs. Fenwick was with them so quickly that there was no need for a reply,—and then he was gone.

During the whole day the two friends talked of the murder, and of the Brattles, and the chapel,—which was thoroughly inspected from the roof to the floor,—but not a word was said about the loves of Harry Gilmore or Walter Marrable. Gilmore's name was often mentioned as the whole story was told of Lord Trowbridge's new quarrel, and of the correspondence with the bishop,—of which Fenwick had learned the particulars from the bishop's chaplain. And in the telling of this story Mrs. Fenwick did not scruple to express her opinion that Harry Gilmore had behaved well, with good spirit, and like a true friend. "If the Marquis had been anywhere near his own age I believe he would have horsewhipped him," said the Vicar's wife, with that partiality for the corporal chastisement of an enemy which is certainly not uncommon to the feminine mind. This was all very well, and called for no special remark from Mary, and possibly might have an effect.

The gentlemen returned late in the evening, and the Squire dressed at the vicarage. But the great event of the day had to be told before anyone was allowed to dress. Between four and five o'clock, just as the magistrates were going to leave the bench, Sam Brattle had walked into Court.

"And your money is safe?" said his wife.

"Yes, my money is safe; but, I declare, I think more of Sam's truth. He was there, as it seemed, all of a sudden. The police had learned nothing of him. He just walked into the court, and we heard his voice. 'They tell me I'm wanted,' he said; and so he gave himself up."

"And what was done?" asked his wife.

"It was too late to do anything; so they allowed a remand for another week, and Sam was walked off to prison."

At dinner time the conversation was still about the murder. It had been committed after Mary Lowther had left Bullhampton; but she had heard all the details, and was now as able to be interested about it as were the others. It was Gilmore's opinion that, instead of proceeding against Sam, they would put him into the witness-box and make him tell what he knew about the presence of the other two men. Fenwick declared that, if they did so, such was Sam's obstinacy that he would tell nothing. It was his own idea,—as he had explained both to his wife and to Gilmore,—that Carry Brattle could give more evidence respecting the murder than her brother. Of this he said nothing at present, but he had informed Constable Toffy that if Caroline Brattle were wanted for the examination she would be found at the house of Mrs. Stiggs.

Thus for an hour or two the peculiar awkwardness of the meeting between Harry Gilmore and Mary was removed. He was enabled to talk with energy on a matter of interest, and she could join the conversation. But when they were round the tea-table it seemed to be arranged by common consent that Trumbull's murder and the Brattles should, for a while, be laid aside. Then Mary became silent and Gilmore became awkward. When inquiries were made as to Miss Marrable, he did not know whether to seem to claim, or not to claim, that lady's acquaintance. He could not, of course, allude to his visit to Loring, and yet he could hardly save himself from having to acknowledge that he had been there. However, the hour wore itself away, and he was allowed to take his departure.

During the next two days he did not see Mary Lowther. On the Friday he met her with Mrs. Fenwick as the two were returning from the mill. They had gone to visit Mrs. Brattle and Fanny, and to administer such comfort as was possible in the present circumstances. The poor woman told them that the father was now as silent about his son as about his daughter, but that he had himself gone over to Heytesbury to secure legal advice for the lad, and to learn from Mr. Jones, the attorney, what might be the true aspect of the case. Of what he had learned he had told nothing to the women at the mill, but the two ladies had expressed their strong opinion of Sam's innocence. All this was narrated by Mrs. Fenwick to Gilmore, and Mary Lowther was enabled to take her part in the narrative. The Squire was walking between the two, and it seemed to him as he walked that Mary at least had no desire to avoid him. He became high in hope, and began to wish that even now, at this moment, he might be left alone with her and might learn his fate. He parted from them when they were near the village, and as he went he held Mary's hand within his own for a few moments. There was no return of his pressure, but it seemed to him that her hand was left with him almost willingly.

"What do you think of him?" her friend said to her, as soon as he had parted from them.

"What do I think of him? I have always thought well of him."

"I know you have; to think otherwise of one who is positively so good would be impossible. But do you feel more kindly to him than you used?"

"Janet," said Mary, after pausing awhile, "you had better leave me alone. Don't be angry with me; but really it will be better that you should leave me alone."

"I won't be angry with you, and I will leave you alone," said Mrs. Fenwick. And, as she considered this request afterwards, it seemed to her that the very making of such a request implied a determination on the girl's part to bring herself to accept the man's offer,—if it might be possible.

CHAPTER XLIX.

MARY LOWTHER'S DOOM.

The police were so very tedious in managing their business, and the whole affair of the second magisterial investigation was so protracted, that people in the neighbourhood became almost tired of it, in spite of that appetite for excitement which the ordinary quiet life of a rural district produces. On the first Tuesday in June Sam had surrendered himself at Heytesbury, and on the second Tuesday it was understood that the production of the prisoners was only formal. The final examination, and committal, if the evidence should be sufficient, was to take place on the third Tuesday in the month. Against this Mr. Jones had remonstrated very loudly on Sam's behalf, protesting that the magistrates were going beyond their power in locking up a man against whom there was no more evidence now than there had been when before they had found themselves compelled to release him on bail. But this was of no avail. Sam had been released before because the men who were supposed to have been his accomplices were not in custody; and now that they were in custody the police declared it to be out of the question that he should be left at large. The magistrates of course agreed with the police, in spite of the indignation of Mr. Jones. In the meantime a subpœna was served upon Carry Brattle to appear on that final Tuesday,—Tuesday the nineteenth of June. The policeman, when he served her with the paper, told her that on the morning in question he would come and fetch her. The poor girl said not a word as she took into her hand the dreadful document. Mrs. Stiggs asked a question or two of the man, but got from him no information. But it was well known in Trotter's Buildings, and round about the Three Honest Men, that Sam Brattle was to be tried for the murder of Mr. Trumbull, and public opinion in that part of Salisbury was adverse to Sam. Public opinion was averse, also, to poor Carry; and Mrs. Stiggs was becoming almost tired of her lodger, although the payment made for her was not ungenerous and was as punctual as the sun. In truth, the tongue of the landlady of the Three Honest Men was potential in those parts, and was very bitter against Sam and his sister.

In the meantime there was a matter of interest which, to our friends at Bullhampton, exceeded even that of the Heytesbury examinations. Mr. Gilmore was now daily at the vicarage on some new or old lover's pretence. It might be that he stood but for a minute or two on the terrace outside the drawing-room windows, or that he would sit with the ladies during half the afternoon, or that he would come down to dinner,—some excuse having arisen for an invitation to that effect during the morning. Very little was said on the subject between Mrs. Fenwick and Mary Lowther, and not a word between the Vicar and his guest; but between Mr. and Mrs. Fenwick many words were spoken, and before the first week was over they were sure that she would yield.

"I think she will," said Mrs. Fenwick;—"but she will do it in agony."

"Then if I were Harry I would leave her alone," said the Vicar.

"But you are not Harry; and if you were, you would be wrong. She will not be happy when she accepts him; but by the time the day fixed for the wedding comes round, she will have reconciled herself to it, and then she will be as loving a wife as ever a man had." But the Vicar shook his head and said that, so far as he was concerned, love of that sort would not have sufficed for him.

"Of course," said his wife, "it is very pleasant for a man to be told that the woman he loves is dying for him; but men can't always have everything that they want."

Mary Lowther at this time became subject to a feeling of shame which almost overwhelmed her. There grew upon her a consciousness that she had allowed herself to come to Bullhampton on purpose that she might receive a renewed offer of marriage from her old lover, and that she had done so because her new and favoured lover had left her. Of course she must accept Mr. Gilmore. Of that she had now become quite sure. She had come to Bullhampton,—so she now told herself,—because she had been taught to believe that it would not be right for her to abandon herself to a mode of life which was not to her taste. All the friends in whose judgment she could confide expressed to her in every possible way their desire that she should marry this man; and now she had made this journey with the view of following their counsel. So she thought of herself and her doings; but such was not in truth the case. When she first determined to visit Bullhampton, she was very far from thinking that she would accept the man. Mrs. Fenwick's argument that she should not be kept away from Bullhampton by fear of Mr. Gilmore, had prevailed with her,—and she had come. And now that she was there, and that this man was daily with her, it was no longer possible that she should refuse him. And, after all, what did it matter? She was becoming sick of the importance which she imputed to herself in thinking of herself. If she could make the man happy why should she not do so? The romance of her life had become to her a rhodomontade of which she was ashamed. What was her love, that she should think so much about it? What did it mean? Could she not do her duty in the position in life in which her friends wished to place her, without hankering after a something which was not to be bestowed on her? After all, what did it all matter? She would tell the man the exact truth as well as she knew how to tell it, and then let him take her or leave her as he listed.

And she did tell him the truth, after the following fashion. It came to pass at last that a day and an hour was fixed in which Mr. Gilmore might come to the vicarage and find Mary alone. There were no absolute words arranging this to which she was a party, but it was understood. She did not even pretend an unwillingness to receive him, and had assented by silence when Mrs. Fenwick had said that the man should be put out of his suspense. Mary, when she was silent, knew well that it was no longer within her power to refuse him.

He came and found her alone. He knew, too, or fancied that he knew, what would be the result of the interview. She would accept him, without protestations of violent love for himself, acknowledging what had passed between her and her cousin, and proffering to him the offer of future affection. He had pictured it all to himself, and knew that he intended to accept what would be tendered. There were drawbacks in the happiness which was in store for him, but still he would take what he could get. As each so nearly understood the purpose of the other it was almost a pity that the arrangement could not be made without any words between them,—words which could hardly be pleasant either in the speaking or in the hearing.

He had determined that he would disembarrass himself of all preliminary flourishes in addressing her, and had his speech ready as he took her by the hand. "Mary," he said, "you know why I am here." Of course she made no reply. "I told you when I first saw you again that I was unchanged." Then he paused, as though he expected that she would answer him, but still she said nothing. "Indeed I am unchanged. When you were here before I told you that I could look forward to no happiness unless you would consent to be my wife. That was nearly a year ago, and I have come again now to tell you the same thing. I do not think but what you will believe me to be in earnest."

"I know that you are in earnest," she said.

"No man was ever more so. My constancy has been tried during the time that you have been away. I do not say so as a reproach to you. Of course there can be no reproach. I have nothing to complain of in your conduct to me. But I think I may say that if my regard for you has outlived the pain of those months there is some evidence that it is sincere."

"I have never doubted your sincerity."

"Nor can you doubt my constancy."

"Except in this, that it is so often that we want that which we have not, and find it so little worthy of having when we get it."

"You do not say that from your heart, Mary. If you mean to refuse me again, it is not because you doubt the reality of my love."

"I do not mean to refuse you again, Mr. Gilmore." Then he attempted to put his arm round her waist, but she recoiled from him, not in anger, but very quietly, and with a womanly grace that was perfect. "But you must hear me first, before I can allow you to take me in the only way in which I can bestow myself. I have been steeling myself to this, and I must tell you all that has occurred since we were last together."

"I know it all," said he, anxious that she should be spared;—anxious also that he himself should be spared the pain of hearing that which she was about to say to him.

But it was necessary for her that she should say it. She would not go to him as his accepted mistress upon other terms than those she had already proposed to herself. "Though you know it, I must speak of it," she said. "I should not, otherwise, be dealing honestly either with you or with myself. Since I saw you last, I have met my cousin, Captain Marrable. I became attached to him with a quickness which I cannot even myself understand. I loved him dearly, and we were engaged to be married."

"You wrote to me, Mary, and told me all that." This he said, striving to hide the impatience which he felt; but striving in vain.

"I did so, and now I have to tell you that that engagement is at an end. Circumstances occurred,—a sad loss of income that he had expected,—which made it imperative on him, and also on me in his behalf, that we should abandon our hopes. He would have been ruined by such a marriage,—and it is all over." Then she paused, and he thought that she had done; but there was more to be said, words heavier to be borne than any which she had yet uttered. "And I love him still. I should lie if I said that it was not so. If he were free to marry me this moment I should go to him." As she said this, there came a black cloud across his brow; but he stood silent to hear it all to the last. "My respect and esteem for you are boundless," she continued,—"but he has my heart. It is only because I know that I cannot be his wife that I have allowed myself to think whether it is my duty to become the wife of another man. After what I now say to you, I do not expect that you will persevere. Should you do so, you must give me time." Then she paused, as though it were now his turn to speak; but there was something further that she felt herself bound to say, and, as he was still silent, she continued. "My friends,—those whom I most trust in the world, my aunt and Janet Fenwick, all tell me that it will be best for me to accept your offer. I have made no promise to either of them. I would tell my mind to no one till I told it to you. I believe I owe as much to you,—almost as much as a woman can owe to a man; but still, were my cousin so placed that he could afford to marry a poor wife, I should leave you and go to him at once. I have told you everything now; and if, after this, you can think me worth having, I can only promise that I will endeavour, at some future time, to do my duty to you as your wife." Then she had finished, and she stood before him—waiting her doom.

His brow had become black and still blacker as she continued her speech. He had kept his eyes upon her without quailing for a moment, and had hoped for some moment of tenderness, some sparkle of feeling, at seeing which he might have taken her in his arms and have stopped the sternness of her speech. But she had been at least as strong as he was, and had not allowed herself to show the slightest sign of weakness.

"You do not love me, then?" he said.

"I esteem you as we esteem our dearest friends."

"And you will never love me?"

"How shall I answer you? I do love you,—but not as I love him. I shall never again have that feeling."

"Except for him?"

"Except for him. If it is to be conquered, I will conquer it. I know, Mr. Gilmore, that what I have told you will drive you from me. It ought to do so."

"It is for me to judge of that," he said, turning upon her quickly.

"In judging for myself I have thought it right to tell you the exact truth, and to let you know what it is that you would possess if you should choose to take me." Then again she was silent, and waited for her doom.

There was a pause of, perhaps, a couple of minutes, during which he made no reply. He walked the length of the room twice, slowly, before he uttered a word, and during that time he did not look at her. Had he chosen to take an hour, she would not have interrupted him again. She had told him everything, and it was for him now to decide. After what she had said he could not but recall his offer. How was it possible that he should desire to make a woman his wife after such a declaration as that which she had made to him?

"And now," he said, "it is for me to decide."

"Yes, Mr. Gilmore, it is for you to decide."

"Then," said he, coming up to her and putting out his hand, "you are my betrothed. May God in his mercy soften your heart to me, and enable you to give me some return for all the love that I bear you." She took his hand and raised it to her lips and kissed it, and then had left the room before he was able to stop her.

CHAPTER L.

MARY LOWTHER INSPECTS HER FUTURE HOME.

Of course it was soon known in the vicarage that Mary Lowther had accepted the Squire's hand. She had left him standing in the drawing-room;—had left him very abruptly, though she had condescended to kiss his hand. Perhaps in no way could she have made a kinder reply to his petition for mercy. In ordinary cases it is probably common for a lady, when she has yielded to a gentleman's entreaties for the gift of herself, to yield also something further for his immediate gratification, and to submit herself to his embrace. In this instance it was impossible that the lady should do so. After the very definite manner in which she had explained to him her feelings, it was out of the question that she should stay and toy with him;—that she should bear the pressure of his arm, or return his caresses. But there had come upon her a sharp desire to show her gratitude before she left him,—to show her gratitude, and to prove, by some personal action towards him, that though she had been forced to tell him that she did not love him,—that she did not love him after the fashion in which his love was given to her,—that yet he was dear to her, as our dearest friends are dear. And therefore, when he had stretched out his hand to her in sign of the offer which he was making her, she had raised it to her lips and kissed it.

Very shortly after she had left the room Mrs. Fenwick came to him. "Well, Harry," she said, coming up close to him, and looking into his eyes to see how it had fared with him, "tell me that I may wish you joy."

"She has promised that she will be my wife," he said.

"And is not that what you have so long wished?"

"Yes, indeed."

"Then why are you not elated?"

"I have no doubt she will tell you all. But do not suppose, Mrs. Fenwick, that I am not thankful. She has behaved very well,—and she has accepted me. She has explained to me in what way her acceptance has been given, and I have submitted to it."

"Now, Harry, you are going to make yourself wretched about some romantic trifle."

"I am not going to make myself miserable at all. I am much less miserable than I could have believed to be possible six months ago. She has told me that she will be my wife, and I do not for a moment think that she will go back from her word."

"Then what is it?"

"I have not won her as other men do. Never mind;—I do not mean to complain. Mrs. Fenwick, I shall trust you to let me know when she will be glad to see me here."

"Of course you will come when you like and how you like. You must be quite at home here."

"As far as you and Frank are concerned, that would be a matter-of-course to me. But it cannot be so—yet—in regard to Mary. At any rate, I will not intrude upon her till I know that my coming will not be a trouble to her." After this it was not necessary that Mrs. Fenwick should be told much more of the manner in which these new betrothals had been made.

Mary was, of course, congratulated both by the Vicar and his wife, and she received their congratulations with a dignity of deportment which, even from her, almost surprised them. She said scarcely a word, but smiled as she was kissed by each of them and did whisper something as to her hope that she might be able to make Mr. Gilmore happy. There was certainly no triumph; and there was no visible sign of regret. When she was asked whether she would not wish that he should come to the vicarage, she declared that she would have him come just as he pleased. If she only knew of his coming beforehand she would take care that she would be within to receive him. Whatever might be his wishes, she would obey them. Mrs. Fenwick suggested that Gilmore would like her to go up to the Privets, and look at the house which was to be her future home. She promised that she would go with him at any hour that he might appoint. Then there was something said as to fixing the day of the wedding. "It is not to be immediately," she replied; "he promised me that he would give me time." "She speaks of it as though she was going to be hung," the Vicar said afterwards to his wife.

On the day after her engagement she saw Gilmore, and then she wrote to her aunt to tell her the tidings. Her letter was very short, and had not Miss Marrable thoroughly understood the character of her niece, and the agony of the struggle to which Mary was now subjected, it would have seemed to be cold and ungrateful. "My dear Aunt," said the letter, "Yesterday I accepted Mr. Gilmore's offer. I know you will be glad to hear this, as you have always thought that I ought to do so. No time has been fixed for the wedding, but it will not be very soon. I hope I may do my duty to him and make him happy; but I do not know whether I should not have been more useful in remaining with my affectionate aunt." That was the whole letter, and there was no other friend to whom she herself communicated the tidings. It occurred to her for a moment that she would write to Walter Marrable;— but Walter Marrable had told her nothing of Edith Brownlow. Walter

Marrable would learn the news fast enough. And then, the writing of such a letter would not have been very easy to her.

On the Sunday afternoon, after church, she walked up to the Privets with her lover. The engagement had been made on the previous Thursday, and this was the first occasion on which she had been alone with him for more than a minute or two at a time since she had then parted from him. They started immediately from the churchyard, passing out through the gate which led into Mr. Trumbull's field, and it was understood that they were to return for an early dinner at the vicarage. Mary had made many resolutions as to this walk. She would talk much, so that it might not be tedious and melancholy to him; she would praise everything, and show the interest which she took in the house and grounds; she would ask questions, and display no hesitation as to claiming her own future share of possession in all that belonged to him. She went off at once as soon as she was through the wicket gate, asking questions as to the division of the property of the parish between the two owners, as to this field and that field, and the little wood which they passed, till her sharp intelligence told her that she was over-acting her part. He was no actor, but unconsciously he perceived her effort; and he resented it, unconsciously also, by short answers and an uninterested tone. She was aware of it all, and felt that there had been a mistake. It would be better for her to leave the play in his hands, and to adapt herself to his moods.

"We had better go straight up to the house," he said, as soon as the pathway had led them off Lord Trowbridge's land into his own domain.

"I think we had," said she.

"If we go round by the stables it will make us late for Fenwick's dinner."

"We ought to be back by half-past two," she said. They had left the church exactly at half-past twelve, and were therefore to be together for two hours.

He took her over the house. The showing of a house in such circumstances is very trying, both to the man and to the woman. He is weighted by a mixed load of pride in his possession and of assumed humility. She, to whom every detail of the future nest is so vitally important, is almost bound to praise, though every encomium she pronounces will be a difficulty in the way of those changes which she contemplates. But on the present occasion Mary contemplated no change. Marrying this man, as she was about to do, professedly without loving him, she was bound to take everything else as she found it. The dwelling rooms of the house she had known before; the dining-room, the drawing-room, and the library. She was now taken into his private chamber, where he sat as a magistrate, and paid his men, and kept his guns and fishing-rods. Here she sat down for a moment, and when he had told her this and that,—how he was always here for so long in the morning, and how he hoped that she would come to him sometimes when he was thus busy, he came and stood over her, putting his hand upon her shoulder. "Mary," he said, "will you not kiss me?"

"Certainly I will," she said, jumping up, and offering her face to his salute. A month or two ago he would have given the world for permission to kiss her; and now it seemed as though the thing itself were a matter but of little joy. A kiss to be joyful should be stolen, with a conviction on the part of the offender that she who has suffered the loss will never prosecute the thief. She had meant to be good to him, but the favour would have gone further with him had she made more of it.

Then they went up stairs. Who does not know the questions that were asked and that were answered? On this occasion they were asked and answered with matter-of-fact useful earnestness. The papers on the walls were perhaps old and ugly; but she did not mind it if they were so. If he liked to have the rooms new papered, of course it would be nice. Would she like new furniture? Did she object to the old-fashioned four-post bedsteads? Had she any special taste about hangings and colours? Of course she had, but she could not bring herself to indulge them by giving orders as to this or that. She praised everything; was satisfied with everything; was interested in everything; but would propose no changes. What right had she, seeing that she was to give him so little, to ask him to do this or that for her? She meant on this occasion to do all that she could for his happiness, but had she ordered new furniture for the whole house, begged that every room might be fresh papered, and pointed out that the panelling was old and must be altered, and the entire edifice re-painted inside and out, he would have been a happier man. "I hope you will find it comfortable," he said, in a tone of voice that was beyond measure lugubrious.

"I am sure that I shall," she replied. "What more can any woman want than there is here? And then there are so many comforts to which I have never been used."

This passed between them as they stood on the steps of the house, looking down upon green paddocks in front of the house; "I think we will come and see the gardens another day," he said.

"Whenever you like," she answered. "Perhaps if we stay now we shall be keeping them waiting." Then, as they returned by the road, she remembered an account that Janet Fenwick had given her of a certain visit which Janet had made to the vicarage as Miss Balfour, and of all the joys of that inspection. But what right had she, Mary Lowther, to suppose that she could have any of the same pleasure? Janet Balfour, in her first visit to the vicarage, had been to see the home in which she was to live with the man to whom her whole heart had been given without reserve.

CHAPTER LI.

THE GRINDER AND HIS COMRADE.

As the day drew near for the final examination at Heytesbury of the suspected murderers,—the day on which it was expected that either all the three prisoners, or at least two of them, would be committed to take their trial at the summer assizes, the Vicar became anxious as to the appearance of Carry Brattle in the Court. At first he entertained an idea that he would go over to Salisbury and fetch her; but his wife declared that this was imprudent and Quixotic,—and that he shouldn't do it. Fenwick's argument in support of his own idea amounted to little more than this,—that he would go for the girl because the Marquis of Trowbridge would be sure to condemn him for taking such a step. "It is intolerable to me," he said, "that I should be impeded in my free action by the interference and accusations of such an ass as that." But the question was one on which his wife felt herself to be so strong that she would not yield, either to his logic or to his anger. "It can't be fit for you to go about and fetch witnesses; and it won't make it more fit because she is a pretty young woman who has lost her character." "Honi soit qui mal y pense," said the Vicar. But his wife was resolute, and he gave up the plan. He wrote, however, to the constable at Salisbury, begging the man to look to the young woman's comfort, and offering to pay for any special privilege or accommodation that might be accorded to her. This occurred on the Saturday before the day on which Mary Lowther was taken up to look at her new home.

The Sunday passed by, with more or less of conversation respecting the murder; and so also the Monday morning. The Vicar had himself been summoned to give his evidence as to having found Sam Brattle in his own garden, in company with another man with whom he had wrestled, and whom he was able to substantiate as the Grinder; and, indeed, the terrible bruise made by the Vicar's life-preserver on the Grinder's back, would be proved by evidence from Lavington. On the Monday evening he was sitting, after dinner, with Gilmore, who had dined at the vicarage, when he was told that a constable from Salisbury wished to see him. The constable was called into the room, and soon told his story. He had gone up to Trotter's Buildings that day after dinner, and was told that the bird had flown. She had gone out that morning, and Mrs. Stiggs knew nothing of her departure. When they examined the room in which she slept, they found that she had taken what little money she possessed and her best clothes. She had changed her frock and put on a pair of strong boots, and taken her cloak with her. Mrs. Stiggs acknowledged that had she seen the girl going forth thus provided, her suspicions would have been aroused; but Carry had managed to leave the house without being observed. Then the constable went on to say that Mrs. Stiggs had told him that she had been sure that Carry would go. "I've been a waiting for it all along," she had said; "but when there came the law rumpus atop of the other, I knew as how she'd hop the twig." And now Carry Brattle had hopped the twig, and no one knew whither she had gone. There was much sorrow at the vicarage; for Mrs. Fenwick, though she had been obliged to restrain her husband's impetuosity in the matter, had nevertheless wished well for the poor girl;—and who could not believe aught of her now but that she would return to misery and degradation? When the constable was interrogated as to the need for her attendance on the morrow, he declared that nothing could now be done towards finding her and bringing her to Heytesbury in time for the magistrates' session. He supposed there would be another remand, and that then she, too, would be—wanted.

But there had been so many remands that on the Tuesday the magistrates were determined to commit the men, and did commit two of them. Against Sam there was no tittle of evidence, except as to that fact that he had been seen with these men in Mr. Fenwick's garden; and it was at once proposed to put him into the witness-box, instead of proceeding against him as one of the murderers. As a witness he was adjudged to have behaved badly; but the assumed independence of his demeanour was probably the worst of his misbehaviour. He would tell them nothing of the circumstances of the murder, except that having previously become acquainted with the two men, Burrows and Acorn, and having, as he thought, a spite against the Vicar at the time, he had determined to make free with some of the vicarage fruit. He had, he said, met the men in the village that afternoon, and had no knowledge of their business there. He had known Acorn more intimately than the other man, and confessed at last that his acquaintance with that man had arisen from a belief that Acorn was about to marry his sister. He acknowledged that he knew that Burrows had been a convicted thief, and that Acorn had been punished for horse stealing. When he was asked how it had come to pass that he was desirous of seeing his sister married to a horse-stealer, he declined to answer, and, looking round the Court, said that he hoped there was no man there who would be coward enough to say anything against his sister. They who heard him declared that there was more of a threat than a request expressed in his words and manner.

A question was put to him as to his knowledge of Farmer Trumbull's money. "There was them as knew; but I knew nothing," he said. He was pressed on this point by the magistrates, but would say not a word further. As to this, however, the police were indifferent, as they believed that they would be able to prove at the trial, from other sources, that the mother of the man called the Grinder had certainly received tidings of the farmer's wealth. There were many small matters of evidence to which the magistrates trusted. One of the men had bought poison, and the dog had been poisoned. The presence of the cart at the farmer's gate was proved, and the subsequent presence of the two men in the same cart at Pycroft Common. The size of the footprints, the characters and subsequent flight of the men, and certain damaging denials and admissions which they themselves had made, all went to make up the case against them, and they were committed to be tried for the murder. Sam, however, was allowed to go free, being served, however, with a subpœna to attend at the trial as a witness. "I will," said he, "if you send me down money enough to bring me up from South Shields, and take me back again. I ain't a coming on my own hook as I did this time;—and wouldn't now, only for Muster Fenwick." Our friends left the police to settle this question with Sam, and then drove home to Bullhampton.

The Vicar was triumphant, though his triumph was somewhat quelled by the disappearance of Carry Brattle. There could, however, be no longer any doubt that Sam Brattle's innocence as to the murder was established. Head-Constable Toffy had himself acknowledged to him that Sam could have had no hand in it. "I told you so from the beginning," said the Vicar. "We 'as got the right uns, at any rate," said the constable; "and it wasn't none of our fault that we hadn't 'em before." But though Constable Toffy was thus honest, there were one or two in Heytesbury on that day who still persisted in declaring that Sam was one of the murderers. Sir Thomas Charleys stuck to that opinion to the last; and Lord Trowbridge, who had again sat upon the bench, was quite convinced that justice was being shamefully robbed of her due.

When the Vicar reached Bullhampton, instead of turning into his own place at once, he drove himself on to the mill. He dropped Gilmore at the gate, but he could not bear that the father and mother should not know immediately, from a source which they would trust, that Sam had been declared innocent of that great offence. Driving round by the road, Fenwick met the miller about a quarter of a mile from his own house. "Mr. Brattle," he said, "they have committed the two men."

"Have they, sir?" said the miller, not condescending to ask a question about his own son.

"As I have said all along, Sam had no more to do with it than you or I."

"You have been very good, Muster Fenwick."

"Come, Mr. Brattle, do not pretend that this is not a comfort to you."

"A comfort as my son ain't proved a murderer! If they'd a hanged 'im, Muster Fenwick, that'd a been bad, for certain. It ain't much of comfort we has; but there may be a better and a worser in everything, no doubt. I'm obleeged to you, all as one, Muster Fenwick—very much obleeged; and it will take a heavy load off his mother's heart." Then the Vicar turned his gig round, and drove himself home.

CHAPTER LII.

CARRY BRATTLE'S JOURNEY.

Mrs. Stiggs had been right in her surmise about Carry Brattle. The confinement in Trotter's Buildings and want of interest in her life was more than the girl could bear, and she had been thinking of escape almost from the first day that she had been there. Had it not been for the mingled fear and love with which she regarded Mr. Fenwick, had she not dreaded that he should think her ungrateful, she would have flown even before the summons came to her which told her that she must appear before the magistrates and lawyers, and among a crowd of people, in the neighbourhood of her old home. That she could not endure, and therefore she had flown. When it had been suggested to her that she should go and live with her brother's wife as her servant, that idea had been hard to bear. But there had been uncertainty, and an opinion of her own which proved to be right, that her sister-in-law would not receive her. Now about this paper that the policeman had handed to her, and the threatened journey to Heytesbury, there was no uncertainty,—unless she might possibly escape the evil by running away. Therefore she ran away.

The straight-going people of the world, in dealing with those who go crooked, are almost always unreasonable. "Because you have been bad," say they who are not bad to those who are bad, "because you have hitherto indulged yourself with all pleasures within your reach, because you have never worked steadily or submitted yourself to restraint, because you have been a drunkard, and a gambler, and have lived in foul company, therefore now,—now that I have got a hold of you and can manipulate you in reference to your repentance and future conduct,—I will require from you a mode of life that, in its general attractions, shall be about equal to that of a hermit in the desert. If you flinch you are not only a monster of ingratitude towards me, who am taking all this trouble to save you, but you are also a poor wretch for whom no possible hope of grace can remain." When it is found that a young man is neglecting his duties, doing nothing, spending his nights in billiard rooms and worse places, and getting up at two o'clock in the day, the usual prescription of his friends is that he should lock himself up in his own dingy room, drink tea, and spend his hours in reading good books. It is hardly recognised that a sudden change from billiards to good books requires a strength of character which, if possessed, would probably have kept the young man altogether from falling into bad habits. If we left the doors of our prisons open, and then expressed disgust because the prisoners walked out, we should hardly be less rational. The hours at Mrs. Stiggs's house had been frightfully heavy to poor Carry Brattle, and at last she escaped.

It was half-past ten on the Monday morning when she went out. It was her custom to go out at that hour. Mr. Fenwick had desired her to attend the morning services at the Cathedral. She had done so for a day or two, and had then neglected them. But she had still left the house always at that time; and once, when Mrs. Stiggs had asked some question on the subject, she had replied almost in anger that she was not a prisoner. On this occasion she made changes in her dress which were not usual, and therefore she was careful to avoid being seen as she went; but had she been interrogated she would have persevered. Who had a right to stop her?

But where should she go? The reader may perhaps remember that once when Mr. Fenwick first found this poor girl, after her flight from home and her great disgrace, she had expressed a desire to go to the mill and just look at it,—even if she might do no more than that. The same idea was now in her mind, but as she left the city she had no concerted plan. There were two things between which she must choose at once,—either to go to London, or not to go to London. She had money enough for her fare, and perhaps a few shillings over. In a dim way she did understand that the choice was between going to the devil at once,—and not going quite at once; and then, weakly, wistfully, with uncertain step, almost without an operation of her mind, she did not take the turn which, from the end of Trotter's Buildings, would have brought her to the Railway Station, but did take that which led her by the Three Honest Men out on to the Devizes road,—the road which passes across Salisbury Plain, and leads from the city to many Wiltshire villages,— of which Bullhampton is one.

She walked slowly, but she walked nearly the whole day. Nothing could be more truly tragical than the utterly purposeless tenour of her day,—and of her whole life. She had no plan,—nothing before her; no object even for the evening and night of that very day in which she was wasting her strength on the Devizes road. It is the lack of object, of all aim, in the lives of the houseless wanderers that gives to them the most terrible element of their misery. Think of it! To walk forth with, say, ten shillings in your pocket,— so that there need be no instant suffering from want of bread or shelter,— and have no work to do, no friend to see, no place to expect you, no duty to accomplish, no hope to follow, no bourn to which you can draw nigher,— except that bourn which, in such circumstances, the traveller must surely regard as simply the end of his weariness! But there is nothing to which humanity cannot attune itself. Men can live upon poison, can learn to endure absolute solitude, can bear contumely, scorn, and shame, and never show it. Carry Brattle had already become accustomed to misery, and as she walked she thought more of the wretchedness of the present hour, of her weary feet, of her hunger, and of the nature of the rest which she might purchase for herself at some poor wayside inn, than she did of her future life.

Carry Brattle.

She got a lump of bread and a glass of beer in the middle of the day, and then she walked on and on till the evening came. She went very slowly, stopping often and sitting down when the road side would afford her some spot of green shade. At eight o'clock she had walked fifteen miles, straight along the road, and, as she knew well, had passed the turn which would have taken her by the nearest way from Salisbury to Bullhampton. She had formed no plan, but entertained a hope that if she continued to walk they would not catch her so as to take her to Heytesbury on the morrow. She knew that if she went on she might get to Pycroft Common by this road; and though there was no one in the whole world whom she hated worse than Mrs.

Burrows, still at Pycroft Common she might probably be taken in and sheltered. At eight she reached a small village which she remembered to have seen before, of which she saw the name written up on a board, and which she knew to be six miles from Bullhampton. She was so tired and weary that she could go no further, and here she asked for a bed. She told them that she was walking from Salisbury to the house of a friend who lived near Devizes, and that she had thought she could do it in one day and save her railway fare. She was simply asked to pay for her bed and supper beforehand, and then she was taken in and fed and sheltered. On the next morning she got up very late and was unwilling to leave the house. She paid for her breakfast, and, as she was not told to go her way, she sat on the chair in which she had been placed, without speaking, almost without moving, till late in the afternoon. At three o'clock she roused herself, asked for some bread and cheese which she put in her pocket, and started again upon her journey. She thought that she would be safe, at any rate for that day, from the magistrates and the policemen, from the sight of her brother, and from the presence of that other man at Heytesbury. But whither she would go when she left the house,— whether on to the hated cottage at Pycroft Common, or to her father's house, she had not made up her mind when she tied on her hat. She went on along the road towards Devizes, and about two miles from the village she came to a lane turning to the left, with a finger-post. On this was written a direction,—To Bullhampton and Imber; and here she turned short off towards the parish in which she had been born. It was then four o'clock, and when she had travelled a mile further she found a nook under the wall of a little bridge, and there she seated herself, and ate her dinner of bread and cheese. While she was there a policeman on foot passed along the road. The man did not see her, and had he seen her would have taken no more than a policeman's ordinary notice of her; but she saw him, and in consequence did not leave her hiding-place for hours.

About nine o'clock she crept on again, but even then her mind was not made up. She did not even yet know where she would bestow herself for that night. It seemed to her that there would be an inexpressible pleasure to her, even in her misery, in walking round the precincts of the mill, in gazing at the windows of the house, in standing on the bridge where she had so often loitered, and in looking once more on the scene of her childhood. But, as she thought of this, she remembered the darkness of the stream, and the softly-gurgling but rapid flow with which it hurried itself on beneath the black abyss of the building. She had often shuddered as she watched it, indulging herself in the luxury of causeless trepidation. But now, were she there, she would surely take that plunge into the blackness, which would bring her to the end of all her misery!

And yet, as she went on towards her old home, through the twilight, she had no more definite idea than that of looking once more on the place which had been cherished in her memory through all her sufferings. As to her rest for the night she had no plan,—unless, indeed, she might find her rest in the hidden mill-pool of that dark, softly-gurgling stream.

On that same day, between six and seven in the evening, the miller was told by Mr. Fenwick that his son was no longer accused of the murder. He had not received the information in the most gracious manner; but not the less quick was he in making it known at the mill. "Them dunderheads over at He'tsbry has found out at last as our Sam had now't to do with it." This he said, addressing no one in particular, but in the hearing of his wife and Fanny Brattle. Then there came upon him a torrent of questions and a torrent also of tears. Mrs. Brattle and Fanny had both made up their minds that Sam was innocent; but the mother had still feared that he would be made to suffer in spite of his innocence. Fanny, however, had always persisted that the goodness of the Lord would save him and them from such injustice. To the old man himself they had hardly dared to talk about it, but now they strove to win him to some softness. Might not a struggle be made to bring Sam back to the mill? But it was very hard to soften the miller. "After what's come and gone, the lad is better away," he said, at last. "I didn't think as he'd ever raised his hand again an old man," he said, shortly afterwards; "but he's kep' company with them as did. It's a'most as bad." Beyond this the miller would not go; but, when they separated for the night, the mother took herself for awhile into the daughter's chamber in order that they might weep and rejoice together. It was now all but midsummer, and the evenings were long and sultry. The window of Fanny's bedroom looked out on to the garden of the mill, and was but a foot or two above the ground. This ground had once been pleasant to them all, and profitable withal. Of late, since the miller had become old, and Sam had grown to be too restive and self-willed to act as desired for the general welfare of the family, but little of pleasure, or profit either, had been forthcoming from the patch of ground. There were a few cabbages there, and rows of untended gooseberry and currant bushes, and down towards the orchard there was a patch of potatoes; but no one took pride now in the garden. As for Fanny, if she could provide that there should always be a sufficient meal on the table for her father and mother, it was as much as she could do. The days were clean gone by in which she had had time and spirits to tend her roses, pinks, and pansies. Now she sat at the open window with her mother, and with bated breath they spoke of the daughter and sister that was lost to them.

"He wouldn't take it amiss, mother, if I was to go over to Salisbury?"

"If you was to ask him, Fan, he'd bid you not," said the mother.

"But I wouldn't ask him. I wouldn't tell him till I was back. She was to be before the magistrates to-day. Mr. Fenwick told me so on Sunday."

"It will about be the death of her."

"I don't know, mother. She's bolder now, mother, I fear, than what she was in old days. And she was always sprightly,—speaking up to the quality, with no fear like. Maybe it was what she said that got them to let Sam go. She was never a coward, such as me."

"Oh, Fan, if she'd only a taken after thee!"

"The Lord, mother, makes us different for purposes of his own. Of all the lasses I ever see, to my eyes she was the comeliest." The old woman couldn't speak now, but rubbed her moist cheeks with her raised apron. "I'll ask Mr. Toffy to-morrow, mother," continued Fanny, "and if she be still at that place in Salisbury where Mr. Fenwick put her, I'll just go to her. Father won't turn me out of the house along of it."

"Turn thee out, Fan! He'll never turn thee out. What 'd a do, or what 'd I do if thee was to go away from us? If thou dost go, Fan, take her a few bits of things that are lying there in the big press, and 'll never be used other gait. I warrant the poor child 'll be but badly off for under-clothing."

And then they planned how the journey on the morrow should be made,—after the constable should have been questioned, and the Vicar should have been consulted. Fanny would leave home immediately after breakfast, and when the miller should ask after her at dinner his wife should tell him that his daughter had gone to Salisbury. If further question should be asked,—and it was thought possible that no further question would be asked, as the father would then guess the errand on which his daughter would have gone,—but if the subject were further mooted, Mrs. Brattle, with such courage as she might be able to assume, should acknowledge the business that had taken Fanny to Salisbury. Then there arose questions about money. Mr. Fenwick had owned, thinking that he might thereby ease the mother's heart, that for the present Carry was maintained by him. To take this task upon themselves the mother and daughter were unable. The money which they had in hand, very small in amount, was, they knew, the property of the head of the family. That they could do no permanent good to Carry was a great grief. But it might be something if they could comfort her for awhile.

"I don't think but what her heart 'll still be soft to thee, Fan; and who knows but what it may bring her round to see thy face, and hear thy voice."

At that moment Fanny heard a sound in the garden, and stretched her head and shoulders quickly out of the window. They had been late at the mill that evening, and it was now eleven o'clock. It had been still daylight when the miller had left them at tea; but the night had crept on them as they had sat there. There was no moon, but there was still something left of the reflection of the last colours of the setting sun, and the night was by no means dark. Fanny saw at once the figure of a woman, though she did not at once recognise the person of her sister. "Oh, mother! oh, mother! oh, mother!" said a voice from the night; and in a moment Carry Brattle had stretched herself so far within the window that she had grasped her mother by the arm.

CHAPTER LIII.

THE FATTED CALF.

Mrs. Brattle, when she heard her daughter's voice, was so confounded, dismayed, and frightened, that for awhile she could give no direction as to what should be done. She had screamed at first, having some dim idea in her mind that the form she saw was not of living flesh and blood. And Carry herself had been hardly more composed or mistress of herself than her mother. She had strayed thither, never having quite made up her mind to any settled purpose. From the spot in which she had hidden herself under the bridge when the policeman passed her she had started when the evening sun was setting, and had wandered on slowly till the old familiar landmarks of the parish were reached. And then she came to the river, and looking across could just see the eaves of the mill through the willows by the last gloaming of the sunlight. Then she stood and paused, and every now and again had crept on a few feet as her courage came to her, and at last, by the well known little path, she had crept down behind the mill, crossing the stream by the board which had once been so accustomed to her feet, and had made her way into the garden and had heard her mother and sister as they talked together at the open window. Any idea which she had hitherto entertained of not making herself known to them at the mill,—of not making herself known at any rate to her mother and sister,—left her at once at that moment. There had been upon her a waking dream, a horrid dream, that the waters of the mill-stream might flow over her head, and hide her wickedness and her misery from the eyes of men; and she had stood and shuddered as she saw the river; but she had never really thought that her own strength would suffice for that termination to her sorrows. It was more probable that she would be doomed to lie during the night beneath a hedge, and then perish of the morning cold! But now, as she heard the voices at the window, there could be no choice for her but that she should make herself known,—not though her father should kill her.

Even Fanny was driven beyond the strength of her composure by the strangeness of this advent. "Carry! Carry!" she exclaimed over and over again, not aloud,—and indeed her voice was never loud,—but with bated wonder. The two sisters held each other by the hand, and Carry's other hand still grasped her mother's arm. "Oh, mother, I am so tired," said the girl. "Oh, mother, I think that I shall die."

"My child;—my poor child. What shall we do, Fan?"

"Bring her in, of course," said Fanny.

"But your father—"

"We couldn't turn her away from the very window, and she like that, mother."

"Don't turn me away, Fanny. Dear Fanny, do not turn me away," said Carry, striving to take her sister by the other hand.

"No, Carry, we will not," said Fanny, trying to settle her mind to some plan of action. Any idea of keeping the thing long secret from her father she knew that she could not entertain; but for this night she resolved at last that shelter should be given to the discarded daughter without the father's knowledge. But even in doing this there would be difficulty. Carry must be brought in through the window, as any disturbance at the front of the house would arouse the miller. And then Mrs. Brattle must be made to go to her own room, or her absence would create suspicion and confusion. Fanny, too, had terrible doubts as to her mother's powers of going to her bed and lying there without revealing to her husband that some cause of great excitement had arisen. And then it might be that the miller would come to his daughter's room, and insist that the outcast should be made an outcast again, even in the middle of the night. He was a man so stern, so obstinate, so unforgiving, so masterful, that Fanny, though she would face any danger as regarded herself, knew that terrible things might happen. It seemed to her that Carry was very weak. If their father came to them in his wrath, might she not die in her despair? Nevertheless it was necessary that something should be done. "We must let her get in at the window, mother," she said. "It won't do, nohow, to unbar the door."

"But what if he was to kill her outright! Oh, Carry; oh, my child. I dunna know as she can get in along of her weakness." But Carry was not so tired as that. She had been in and out of that window scores of times; and now, when she heard that the permission was accorded to her, she was not long before she was in her mother's arms. "My own Carry, my own bairn;—my girl, my darling." And the poor mother satisfied the longings of her heart with infinite caresses.

Fanny in the meantime had crept out to the kitchen, and now returned with food in a plate and cold tea. "My girl," she said, "you must eat a bit, and then we will have you to bed. When the morn comes, we must think about it."

"Fanny, you was always the best that there ever was," said Carry, speaking from her mother's bosom.

"And now, mother," continued Fanny, "you must creep off. Indeed you must, or of course father'll wake up. And mother, don't say a word to-morrow when he rises. I'll go to him in the mill myself. That'll be best." Then, with longings that could hardly be repressed, with warm, thick, clinging kisses, with a hot, rapid, repeated assurance that everything,—everything had been forgiven, that her own Carry was once more her own, own Carry, the poor mother allowed herself to be banished. There seemed to her to be such a world of cruelty in the fact that Fanny might remain for the whole of that night with the dear one who had returned to them, while she must be sent away,—perhaps not to see her again if the storm in the morning should rise too loudly! Fanny, with great craft, accompanied her mother to her room, so that if the old man should speak she might be there to answer;—but the miller slept soundly after his day of labour, and never stirred.

"What will he do to me, Fan?" the wanderer asked as soon as her sister returned.

"Don't think of it now, my pet," said Fanny, softened almost as her mother was softened by the sight of her sister.

"Will he kill me, Fan?"

"No, dear; he will not lay a hand upon you. It is his words that are so rough! Carry, Carry, will you be good?"

"I will, dear; indeed I will. I have not been bad since Mr. Fenwick came."

"My sister,—if you will be good, I will never leave you. My heart's darling, my beauty, my pretty one! Carry, you shall be the same to me as always, if you'll be good. I'll never cast it up again you, if you'll be good." Then she, too, filled herself full, and satisfied the hungry craving of her love with the warmth of her caresses. "But thee'll be famished, lass. I'll see thee eat a bit, and then I'll put thee comfortable to bed."

Poor Carry Brattle was famished, and ate the bread and bacon which were set before her, and drank the cold tea, with an appetite which was perhaps unbecoming the romance of her position. Her sister stood over her, cutting a slice now and then from the loaf, telling her that she had taken nothing, smoothing her hair, and wishing for her sake that the fire were better. "I'm afeard of father, Fan,—awfully; but for all that, it's the sweetest meal as I've had since I left the mill." Then Fanny was on her knees beside the returned profligate, covering even the dear one's garments with her kisses.

It was late before Fanny laid herself down by her sister's side that night. "Carry," she whispered when her sister was undressed, "will you kneel here and say your prayers as you used to?" Carry, without a word, did as she was bidden, and hid her face upon her hands in her sister's lap. No word was spoken out loud, but Fanny was satisfied that her sister had been in earnest. "Now sleep, my darling;—and when I've just tidied your things for the morning, I will be with you." The wanderer again obeyed, and in a few moments the work of the past two days befriended her, and she was asleep. Then the sister went to her task with the soiled frock and the soiled shoes, and looked up things clean and decent for the morrow. It would be at any rate well that Carry should appear before her father without the stain of the road upon her.

As the lost one lay asleep there, with her soft ringlets all loose upon the pillow, still beautiful, still soft, lovely though an outcast from the dearest rights of womanhood, with so much of innocence on her brow, with so much left of the grace of childhood though the glory of the flower had been destroyed by the unworthy hand that had ravished its sweetness, Fanny, sitting in the corner of the room over her work, with her eye from moment to moment turned upon the sleeper, could not keep her mind from wandering away in thoughts on the strange destiny of woman. She knew that there had been moments in her life in which her great love for her sister had been tinged with envy. No young lad had ever waited in the dusk to hear the sound of her footfall; no half-impudent but half-bashful glances had ever been thrown after her as she went through the village on her business. To be a homely, household thing, useful indeed in this world, and with high hopes for the future,—but still to be a drudge; that had been her destiny. There was never a woman to whom the idea of being loved was not the sweetest thought that her mind could produce. Fate had made her plain, and no man had loved her. The same chance had made Carry pretty,—the belle of the village, the acknowledged beauty of Bullhampton. And there she lay, a thing said to be so foul that even a father could not endure to have her name mentioned in his ears! And yet, how small had been her fault compared with other crimes for which men and women are forgiven speedily, even if it has been held that pardon has ever been required.

She came over, and knelt down and kissed her sister on her brow; and as she did so she swore to herself that by her, even in the inmost recesses of her bosom, Carry should never be held to be evil, to be a castaway, to be one of whom, as her sister, it would behove her to be ashamed. She had told Carry that she would "never cast it up against her." She now resolved that there should be no such casting up even in her own judgment. Had she, too, been fair, might not she also have fallen?

At five o'clock on the following morning the miller went out from the house to his mill, according to his daily practice. Fanny heard his heavy step, heard the bar withdrawn, heard the shutters removed from the kitchen window, and knew that her father was as yet in ignorance of the inmate who had been harboured. Fanny at once arose from her bed, careful not to disturb her companion. She had thought it all out, whether she would have Carry ready dressed for an escape, should it be that her father would demand imperiously that she should be sent adrift from the mill, or whether it might not be better that she should be able to plead at the first moment that her sister was in bed, tired, asleep,—at any rate undressed,—and that some little time must be allowed. Might it not be that even in that hour her father's heart might be softened? But she must lose no time in going to him. The hired man who now tended the mill with her father came always at six, and that which she had to say to him must be said with no ear to hear her but his own. It would have been impossible even for her to remind him of his daughter before a stranger. She slipped her clothes on, therefore, and within ten minutes of her father's departure followed him into the mill.

The old man had gone aloft, and she heard his slow, heavy feet as he was moving the sacks which were above her head. She considered for a moment, and thinking it better that she should not herself ascend the little ladder,—knowing that it might be well that she should have the power of instant retreat to the house,—she called to him from below. "What's wanted now?" demanded the old man as soon as he heard her. "Father, I must speak to you," she said. "Father, you must come down to me." Then he came down slowly, without a word, and stood before her waiting to hear her tidings.

"Father," she said, "there is some one in the house, and I have come to tell you."

"Sam has come, then?" said he; and she could see that there was a sparkle of joy in his eye as he spoke. Oh, if she could only make the return of that other child as grateful to him as would have been the return of his son!

"No, father; it isn't Sam."

"Who be it, then?" The tone of his voice, and the colour and bearing of his face were changed as he asked the question. She saw at once that he had guessed the truth. "It isn't—it isn't—?"

"Yes, father; it is Carry." As she spoke she came close to him, and strove to take his hand; but he thrust both his hands into his pockets and turned himself half away from her. "Father, she is our flesh and blood; you will not turn against her now that she has come back to us, and is sorry for her faults."

"She is a—" But his other daughter had stopped his mouth with her hand before the word had been uttered.

"Father, who among us has not done wrong at times?"

"She has disgraced my gray hairs, and made me a reproach and a shame. I will not see her. Bid her begone. I will not speak to her or look at her. How came she there? When did she come?"

Then Fanny told her father the whole story,—everything as it occurred, and did not forget to add her own conviction that Carry's life had been decent in all respects since the Vicar had found a home for her in Salisbury. "You would not have it go on like that, father. She is naught to our parson."

"I will pay. As long as there is a shilling left, I will pay for her. She shall not live on the charity of any man, whether parson or no parson. But I will not see her. While she be here you may just send me my vittels to the mill. If she be not gone afore night, I will sleep here among the sacks."

She stayed with him till the labourer came, and then she returned to the house, having failed as yet to touch his heart. She went back and told her story to her mother, and then a part of it to Carry who was still in bed. Indeed, she had found her mother by Carry's bedside, and had to wait till she could separate them before she could tell any story to either. "What does he say of me, Fan?" asked the poor sinner. "Does he say that I must go? Will he never speak to me again? I will just throw myself into the mill-race and have done with it." Her sister bade her to rise and dress herself, but to remain where she was. It could not be expected, she said, but that their father would be hard to persuade. "I know that he will kill me when he sees me," said Carry.

At eight o'clock Fanny took the old man his breakfast to the mill, while Mrs. Brattle waited on Carry, as though she had deserved all the good things which a mother could do for a child. The miller sat upon a sack at the back of the building, while the hired man took his meal of bread and cheese in the front, and Fanny remained close at his elbow. While the old man was eating she said nothing to him. He was very slow, and sat with his eyes fixed upon the morsel of sky which was visible through the small aperture, thinking evidently of anything but the food that he was swallowing. Presently he returned the empty bowl and plate to his daughter, as though he were about at once to resume his work. Hitherto he had not uttered a single word since she had come to him.

"Father," she said, "think of it. Is it not good to have mercy and to forgive? Would you drive your girl out again upon the streets?"

The miller still did not speak, but turned his face round upon his daughter with a gaze of such agony that she threw herself on the sack beside him, and clung to him with her arms round his neck.

"If she were such as thee, Fan," he said. "Oh, if she were such as thee!" Then again he turned away his face that she might not see the tear that was forcing itself into the corner of his eye.

She remained with him an hour before he moved. His companion in the mill did not come near them, knowing, as the poor do know on such occasions, there was something going on which would lead them to prefer that he should be absent. The words that were said between them were not very many; but at the end of the hour Fanny returned to the house.

"Carry," she said, "father is coming in."

"If he looks at me, it will kill me," said Carry.

Mrs. Brattle was so lost in her hopes and fears that she knew not what to do, or how to bestow herself. A minute had hardly passed when the miller's step was heard, and Carry knew that she was in the presence of her father. She had been sitting, but now she rose, and went to him and knelt at his feet.

"Father," she said, "if I may bide with you,—if I may bide with you—." But her voice was lost in sobbing, and she could make no promise as to her future conduct.

"If I may bide with you,—if I may bide with you—."

"She may stay with us," the father said, turning to his eldest daughter; "but I shall never be able to show my face again about the parish."

He had uttered no words of forgiveness to his daughter, nor had he bestowed upon her any kiss. Fanny had raised her when she was on the ground at his feet, and had made her seat herself apart.

"In all the whole warld," he said, looking round upon his wife and his elder child, raising his hand as he uttered the words, and speaking with an emphasis that was terrible to the hearers, "there is no thing so vile as a harlot." All the dreaded fierceness of his manner had then come back to him, and neither of them had dared to answer him. After that he at once went back to the mill, and to Fanny who followed him he vouchsafed to repeat the permission that his daughter should be allowed to remain beneath his roof.

Between twelve and one she again went to fetch him to his dinner. At first he declared that he would not come, that he was busy, and that he would eat a morsel, where he was, in the mill. But Fanny argued the matter with him.

"Is it always to be so, father?"

"I do not know. What matters it, so as I have strength to do a turn of work?"

"It must not be that her presence should drive you from the house. Think of mother, and what she will suffer. Father, you must come."

Then he allowed himself to be led into the house, and he sat in his accustomed chair, and ate his dinner in gloomy silence. But after dinner he would not smoke.

"I tell 'ee, lass, I do not want the pipe to-day. Now't has got itself done. D'ye think as grist 'll grind itself without hands?"

When Carry said that it would be better than this that she should go again, Fanny told her to remember that evil things could not be cured in a day. With the mother that afternoon was, on the whole, a happy time, for she sat with her lost child's hand within her own. Late in the evening, when the miller returned to his rest, Carry moved about the house softly, resuming some old task to which in former days she had been accustomed; and as she did so the miller's eyes would wander round the room after her; but he did not speak to her on that day, nor did he pronounce her name.

Two other circumstances which bear upon our story occurred at the mill that afternoon. After their tea, at which the miller did not make his appearance, Fanny Brattle put on her bonnet and ran across the fields to the vicarage. After all the trouble that Mr. Fenwick had taken, it was, she thought, necessary that he should be told what had happened.

"That is the best news," said he, "that I have heard this many a day."

"I knew that you would be glad to hear that the poor child has found her home again." Then Fanny told the whole story,—how Carry had escaped from Salisbury, being driven to do so by fear of the law proceedings at which she had been summoned to attend, how her father had sworn that he would not yield, and how at length he had yielded. When Fanny told the Vicar and Mrs. Fenwick that the old man had as yet not spoken to his daughter, they both desired her to be of good cheer.

"That will come, Fanny," said Mrs. Fenwick, "if she once be allowed to sit at table with him."

"Of course it will come," said the Vicar. "In a week or two you will find that she is his favourite."

"She was the favourite with us all, sir, once," said Fanny, "and may God send that it shall be so again. A winsome thing like her is made to be loved. You'll come and see her, Mr. Fenwick, some day?" Mr. Fenwick promised that he would, and Fanny returned to the mill.

The other circumstance was the arrival of Constable Toffy at the mill during Fanny's absence. In the course of the day news had travelled into the village that Carry Brattle was again at the mill;—and Constable Toffy, who in regard to the Brattle family, was somewhat discomfited by the transactions of the previous day at Heytesbury, heard the news. He was aware,—being in that respect more capable than Lord Trowbridge of receiving enlightenment,— that the result of all the inquiries made, in regard to the murder, did, in truth, contain no tittle of evidence against Sam. As constables go, Constable Toffy was a good man, and he would be wronged if it were to be said of him that he regretted Sam's escape; but his nature was as is the nature of constables, and he could not rid himself of that feeling of disappointment which always attends baffled efforts. And though he saw that there was no evidence against Sam, he did not, therefore, necessarily think that the young man was innocent. It may be doubted whether, to the normal policeman's mind, any man is ever altogether absolved of any crime with which that man's name has been once connected. He felt, therefore, somewhat sore against the Brattles;—and then there was the fact that Carry Brattle, who had been regularly "subpœnaed," had kept herself out of the way,—most flagitiously, illegally and damnably. She had run off from Salisbury, just as though she were a free person to do as she pleased with herself, and not subject to police orders! When, therefore, he heard that Carry was at the mill,—she having made herself liable to some terribly heavy fine by her contumacy,—it was manifestly his duty to see after her and let her know that she was wanted.

At the mill he saw only the miller himself, and his visit was not altogether satisfactory. Old Brattle, who understood very little of the case, but who did understand that his own son had been made clear in reference to that accusation, had no idea that his daughter had any concern with that matter, other than what had fallen to her lot in reference to her brother. When, therefore, Toffy inquired after Caroline Brattle, and desired to know whether she was at the mill, and also was anxious to be informed why she had not attended at Heytesbury in accordance with the requirements of the law, the miller turned upon him and declared that if anybody said a word against Sam Brattle in reference to the murder,—the magistrates having settled that matter,—he, Jacob Brattle, old as he was, would "see it out" with that malignant slanderer. Constable Toffy did his best to make the matter clear to the miller, but failed utterly. Had he a warrant to search for anybody?

Toffy had no warrant. Toffy only desired to know whether Caroline Brattle was or was not beneath her father's roof. The old miller, declaring to himself that, though his child had shamed him, he would not deny her now that she was again one of the family, acknowledged so much, but refused the constable admittance to the house.

"But, Mr. Brattle," said the constable, "she was subpœnaed."

"I know now't o' that," answered the miller, not deigning to turn his face round to his antagonist.

"But you know, Mr. Brattle, the law must have its course."

"No, I don't. And it ain't law as you should come here a hindering o' me; and it ain't law as you should walk that unfortunate young woman off with you to prison."

"But she's wanted, Mr. Brattle;—not in the way of going to prison, but before the magistrates."

"There's a deal of things is wanted as ain't to be had. Anyways, you ain't no call to my house now, and as them as is there is in trouble, I'll ax you to be so kind as—as just to leave us alone."

Toffy, pretending that he was satisfied with the information received, and merely adding that Caroline Brattle must certainly, at some future time, be made to appear before the magistrates at Heytesbury, took his departure with more good-humour than the miller deserved from him, and returned to the village.

CHAPTER LIV.

MR. GILMORE'S RUBIES.

Mary Lowther struggled hard for a week to reconcile herself to her new fate, and at the end of the week had very nearly given way. The gloom which had fallen upon her acted upon her lover and then reacted upon herself. Could he have been light in hand, could he have talked to her about ordinary subjects, could he have behaved towards her with any even of the light courtesies of the every-day lover, she would have been better able to fight her battle. But when he was with her there was a something in his manner which always seemed to accuse her in that she, to whom he was giving so much, would give him nothing in return. He did not complain in words. He did not wilfully resent her coldness to him. But he looked, and walked, and spoke, and seemed to imply by every deed that he was conscious of being an injured man. At the end of the week he made her a handsome present, and in receiving it she had to assume some pleasure. But the failure was complete, and each of the two knew how great was the failure. Of course, there would be other presents. And he had already,—already, though no allusion to the day for the marriage had yet been made,—begun to press on for those changes in his house for which she would not ask, but which he was determined to effect for her comfort. There had been another visit to the house and gardens, and he had told her that this should be done,—unless she objected; and that that other change should be made, if it were not opposed to her wishes. She made an attempt to be enthusiastic,—enthusiastic on the wrong side, to be zealous to save him money, and the whole morning was beyond measure sad and gloomy. Then she asked herself whether she meant to go through with it. If not, the sooner that she retreated and hid herself and her disgrace for the rest of her life the better. She had accepted him at last, because she had been made to believe that by doing so she would benefit him, and because she had taught herself to think that it was her duty to disregard herself. She had thought of herself till she was sick of the subject. What did it matter,—about herself,—as long as she could be of some service to some one? And so thinking, she had accepted him. But now she had begun to fear that were she to marry this man she could not be of service to him. And when the thing should be done,—if ever it were done,—there would be no undoing it. Would not her life be a life of sin if she were to live as the wife of a man whom she did not love,—while, perhaps, she would be unable not to love another man?

Nothing of all this was told to the Vicar, but Mrs. Fenwick knew what was going on in her friend's mind, and spoke her own very freely. "Hitherto," she said, "I have given you credit all through for good conduct and good feeling;

but I shall be driven to condemn you if you now allow a foolish, morbid, sickly idea to interfere with his happiness and your own."

"But what if I can do nothing for his happiness?"

"That is nonsense. He is not a man whom you despise or dislike. If you will only meet him half-way you will soon find that your sympathies will grow."

"There never will be a spark of sympathy between us."

"Mary, that is most horribly wicked. What you mean is this, that he is not light and gay as a lover. Of course he remembers the occurrences of the last six months. Of course he cannot be so happy as he might have been had Walter Marrable never been at Loring. There must be something to be conquered, something to be got over, after such an episode. But you may set your face against doing that, or you may strive to do it. For his sake, if not for your own, the struggle should be made."

"A man may struggle to draw a loaded wagon, but he won't move it."

"The load in this case is of your own laying on. One hour of frank kindness on your part would dispel his gloom. He is not gloomy by nature."

Then Mary Lowther tried to achieve that hour of frank kindness and again failed. She failed and was conscious of her failure, and there came a time,—and that within three weeks of her engagement,—in which she had all but made up her mind to return the ring which he had given her, and to leave Bullhampton for ever. Could it be right that she should marry a man that she did not love?

That was her argument with herself, and yet she was deterred from doing as she contemplated by a circumstance which could have had no effect on that argument. She received from her Aunt Marrable the following letter, in which was certainly no word capable of making her think that now, at last, she could love the man whom she had promised to marry. And yet this letter so affected her, that she told herself that she would go on and become the wife of Harry Gilmore. She would struggle yet again, and force herself to succeed. The wagon, no doubt, was heavily laden, but still, with sufficient labour, it might perhaps be moved.

Miss Marrable had been asked to go over to Dunripple, when Mary Lowther went to Bullhampton. It had been long since she had been there, and she had not thought ever to make such a visit. But there came letters, and there were rejoinders,—which were going on before Mary's departure,—and at last it was determined that Miss Marrable should go to Dunripple, and pay a visit to her cousin. But she did not do this till long after Walter Marrable had left the place. She had written to Mary soon after her arrival, and in this first letter there had been no word about Walter; but in her second letter she spoke very freely of Walter Marrable,—as the reader shall see.

Dunripple, 2nd July, 1868.

DEAR MARY,

I got your letter on Saturday, and cannot help wishing that it had been written in better spirits. However, I do not doubt but that it will all come right soon. I am quite sure that the best thing you can do is to let Mr. Gilmore name an early day. Of course you never intended that there should be a long engagement. Such a thing, where there is no possible reason for it, must be out of the question. And it will be much better to take advantage of the fine weather than to put it off till the winter has nearly come. Fix some day in August or early in September. I am sure you will be much happier married than you are single; and he will be gratified, which is, I suppose, to count for something.

I am very happy here, but yet I long to get home. At my time of life, one must always be strange among strangers. Nothing can be kinder than Sir Gregory, in his sort of fashion. Gregory Marrable, the son, is, I fear, in a bad way. He is unlike his father, and laughs at his own ailments, but everybody in the house,—except perhaps Sir Gregory,—knows that he is very ill. He never comes down at all now, but lives in two rooms, which he has together up-stairs. We go and see him every day, but he is hardly able to talk to any one. Sir Gregory never mentions the subject to me, but Mrs. Brownlow is quite confident that if anything were to happen to Gregory Marrable, Walter would be asked to come to Dunripple as the heir, and to give up the army altogether.

I get on very well with Mrs. Brownlow, but of course we cannot be like old friends. Edith is a very nice girl, but rather shy. She never talks about herself, and is too silent to be questioned. I do not, however, doubt for a moment but that she will be Walter Marrable's wife. I think it likely that they are not engaged as yet, as in that case I think Mrs. Brownlow would tell me; but many things have been said which leave on my mind a conviction that it will be so. He is to be here again in August, and from the way in which Mrs. Brownlow speaks of his coming, there is no doubt that she expects it. That he paid great attention to Edith when he was here before, I am quite sure; and I take it he is only waiting till—

In writing so far, Miss Marrable had intended to signify that Captain Marrable had been slow to ask Edith Brownlow to be his wife while he was at Dunripple, because he could not bring himself so soon to show himself indifferent to his former love; but that now he would not hesitate, knowing as he would know, that his former love had bestowed herself elsewhere; but in this there would have been a grievous accusation against Mary, and she was therefore compelled to fill up her sentence in some other form;—

> till things should have arranged themselves a little.
>
> And it will be all for the best. She is a very nice, quiet, lady-like girl, and so great a favourite with her uncle, that should his son die before him, his great object in life will be her welfare. Walter Marrable, as her husband, would live at Dunripple, just as though the place were his own. And indeed there would be no one between him and the property except his own father. Some arrangement could be made as to buying out his life interest,—for which indeed he has taken the money beforehand with a vengeance,—and then Walter would be settled for life. Would not this be all for the best?
>
> I shall go home about the 14th. They want me to stay, but I shall have been away quite long enough. I don't know whether people ought to go from home at all after a certain age. I get cross because I can't have the sort of chair I like to sit on; and then they don't put any green tea into the pot, and I don't like to ask to have any made, as I doubt whether they have any green tea in the house. And I find it bad to be among invalids with whom, indeed, I can sympathise, but for whom I cannot pretend that I feel any great affection. As we grow old we become incapable of new tenderness, and rather resent the calls that are made upon us for pity. The luxury of devotion to misery is as much the privilege of the young as is that of devotion to love.
>
> Write soon, dearest; and remember that the best news I can have, will be tidings as to the day fixed for your marriage. And remember, too, that I won't have any question about your being married at Bullhampton. It would be quite improper. He must come to Loring; and I needn't say how

glad I shall be to see the Fenwicks. Parson John will expect to marry you, but Mr. Fenwick might come and assist.

Your most affectionate aunt,

SARAH MARRABLE.

It was not the entreaty made by her aunt that an early day should be fixed for the marriage which made Mary Lowther determine that she would yet once more attempt to drag the wagon. She could have withstood such entreaty as that, and, had the letter gone no further, would probably have replied to it by saying that no day could be fixed at all. But, with the letter there came an assurance that Walter Marrable had forgotten her, was about to marry Edith Brownlow, and that therefore all ideas of love and truth and sympathy and joint beating of mutual hearts, with the rest of it, might be thrown to the winds. She would marry Harry Gilmore, and take care that he had good dinners, and would give her mind to flannel petticoats and coal for the poor of Bullhampton, and would altogether come down from the pedestal which she had once striven to erect for herself. From that high but tottering pedestal, propped up on shafts of romance and poetry, she would come down; but there would remain for her the lower, firmer standing block, of which duty was the sole support. It was no doubt most unreasonable that any such change should come upon her in consequence of her aunt's letter. She had never for a moment told herself that Walter Marrable could ever be anything to her, since that day on which she had by her own deed liberated him from his troth; and, indeed, had done more than that, had forced him to accept that liberation. Why then should his engagement with another woman have any effect with her either in one direction or in the other? She herself had submitted to a new engagement,—had done so before he had shown any sign of being fickle. She could not therefore be angry with him. And yet, because he could be fickle, because he could do that very thing which she had openly declared her purpose of doing, she persuaded herself,—for a week or two,—that any sacrifice made to him would be a sacrifice to folly, and a neglect of duty.

At this time, during this week or two, there came to her direct from the jewellers in London, a magnificent set of rubies,—ear-rings, brooch, bracelets, and necklace. The rubies she had seen before, and knew that they had belonged to Mr. Gilmore's mother. Mrs. Fenwick had told him that the setting was so old that no lady could wear them now, and there had been a presentiment that they would be forthcoming in a new form. Mary had said that, of course, such ornaments as these would come into her hands only when she became Mrs. Gilmore. Mrs. Fenwick had laughed and told her that she did not understand the romantic generosity of her lover. And now the jewellery had come to her at the parsonage without a word from Gilmore, and was spread out in its pretty cases on the vicarage drawing-room table. Now, if ever, must she say that she could not do as she had promised.

"Mary," said Mrs. Fenwick, "you must go up to him to-morrow, and tell him how noble he is."

Mary waited, perhaps, for a whole minute before she answered. She would willingly have given the jewels away for ever and ever, so that they might not have been there now to trouble her. But she did answer at last, knowing, as she did so, that her last chance was gone.

"He is noble," she said, slowly; "and I will go and tell him so. I'll go now, if it is not too late."

"Do, do. You'll be sure to find him." And Mrs. Fenwick, in her enthusiasm, embraced her friend and kissed her.

Mary put on her hat and walked off at once through the garden and across the fields, and into the Privets; and close to the house she met her lover. He did not see her till he heard her step, and then turned short round, almost as though fearing something.

"Harry," she said, "those jewels have come. Oh, dear. They are not mine yet. Why did you have them sent to me?"

There was something in the word yet, or in her tone as she spoke it, which made his heart leap as it had never leaped before.

"If they're not yours, I don't know whom they belong to," he said. And his eye was bright, and his voice almost shook with emotion.

"Are you doing anything?" she asked.

"Nothing on earth."

"Then come and see them."

So they walked off, and he, at any rate, on that occasion was a happy lover. For a few minutes,—perhaps for an hour,—he did allow himself to believe that he was destined to enjoy that rapture of requited affection, in longing for which his very soul had become sick. As she walked back with him to the vicarage her hand rested heavily on his arm, and when she asked him some question about his land, she was able so to modulate her voice as to make him believe that she was learning to regard his interests as her own. He stopped her at the gate leading into the vicarage garden, and once more made to her an assurance of his regard.

"Mary," he said, "if love will beget love, I think that you must love me at last."

"I will love you," she said, pressing his arm still more closely. But even then she could not bring herself to tell him that she did love him.

CHAPTER LV.

GLEBE LAND.

The fifteenth of July was a Sunday, and it had been settled for some time past that on this day Mr. Puddleham would preach for the first time in his new chapel. The building had been hurried on through the early summer in order that this might be achieved; and although the fittings were not completed, and the outward signs of the masons and labourers had not been removed,—although the heaps of mortar were still there, and time had not yet sufficed to have the chips cleared away,—on Sunday the fifteenth of July the chapel was opened. Great efforts were made to have it filled on the occasion. The builder from Salisbury came over with all his family, not deterred by the consideration that whereas the Puddlehamites of Bullhampton were Primitive Methodists, he was a regular Wesleyan. And many in the parish were got to visit the chapel on this the day of its glory, who had less business there than even the builder from Salisbury. In most parishes there are some who think it well to let the parson know that they are independent and do not care for him, though they profess to be of his flock; and then, too, the novelty of the thing had its attraction, and the well-known fact that the site chosen for the building had been as gall and wormwood to the parson and his family. These causes together brought a crowd to the vicarage-gate on that Sunday morning, and it was quite clear that the new chapel would be full, and that Mr. Puddleham's first Sunday would be a success. And the chapel, of course, had a bell,—a bell which was declared by Mrs. Fenwick to be the hoarsest, loudest, most unmusical, and ill-founded miscreant of a bell that was ever suspended over a building for the torture of delicate ears. It certainly was a loud and brazen bell; but Mr. Fenwick expressed his opinion that there was nothing amiss with it. When his wife declared that it sounded as though it came from the midst of the shrubs at their own front gate, he reminded her that their own church bells sounded as though they came from the lower garden. That one sound should be held by them to be musical and the other abominable, he declared to be a prejudice. Then there was a great argument about the bells, in which Mrs. Fenwick, and Mary Lowther, and Harry Gilmore were all against the Vicar. And, throughout the discussion, it was known to them all that there were no ears in the parish to which the bells were so really odious as they were to the ears of the Vicar himself. In his heart of hearts he hated the chapel, and, in spite of all his endeavours to the contrary, his feelings towards Mr. Puddleham were not those which the Christian religion requires one neighbour to bear to another. But he made the struggle, and for some weeks past had not said a word against Mr. Puddleham. In regard to the Marquis the thing was different. The Marquis should have known better, and against the Marquis he did say a great many words.

They began to ring the bell on that Sunday morning before ten o'clock. Mrs. Fenwick was still sitting at the breakfast-table, with the windows open, when the sound was first heard,—first heard, that is, on that morning. She looked at Mary, groaned, and put her hands to her ears. The Vicar laughed, and walked about the room.

"At what time do they begin?" said Mary.

"Not till eleven," said Mrs. Fenwick. "There, it wants a quarter to ten now, and they mean to go on with that music for an hour and a quarter."

"We shall be keeping them company by-and-by," said the Vicar.

"The poor old church bells won't be heard through it," said Mrs. Fenwick.

Mrs. Fenwick was in the habit of going to the village school for half an hour before the service on Sunday mornings, and on this morning she started from the house according to her custom at a little after ten. Mary Lowther went with her, and as the school was in the village and could be reached much more shortly by the front gate than by the path round by the church, the two ladies walked out boldly before the new chapel. The reader may perhaps remember that Mrs. Fenwick had promised her husband to withdraw that outward animosity to the chapel which she had evinced by not using the vicarage entrance. As they went there was a crowd collected, and they found that after the manner of the Primitive Methodists in their more enthusiastic days, a procession of worshippers had been formed in the village, which at this very moment was making its way to the chapel. Mrs. Fenwick, as she stood aside to make way for them, declared that the bell sounded as though it were within her bonnet. When they reached the school they found that many a child was absent who should have been there, and Mrs. Fenwick knew that the truant urchins were amusing themselves at the new building. And with those who were not truant the clang of the new bell distracted terribly that attention which was due to the collect. Mrs. Fenwick herself confessed afterwards that she hardly knew what she was teaching.

Mr. Fenwick, according to his habit, went into his own study when the ladies went to the school, and there, according to custom also on Sunday mornings, his letters were brought to him, some few minutes before he started on his walk through the garden to the church. On this morning there were a couple of letters for himself, and he opened them both. One was from a tradesman in Salisbury, and the other was from his wife's brother-in-law, Mr. Quickenham. Before he started he read Mr. Quickenham's letter, and then did his best to forget it and put it out of his mind till the morning service should be over. The letter was as follows:—

Pump Court, June 30, 1868.

DEAR FENWICK,

I have found, as I thought I should, that Lord Trowbridge has no property in, or right whatever to, the bit of ground on which your enemies have been building their new Ebenezer. The spot is a part of the glebe, and as such seems to have been first abandoned by a certain parson named Brandon, who was your predecessor's predecessor. There can, however, be no doubt that the ground is glebe, and that you are bound to protect it as such, on behalf of your successors, and of the patrons of the living.

I found some difficulty in getting at the terrier of the parish,—which you, who consider yourself to be a model parson, I dare say, have never seen. I have, however, found it in duplicate. The clerk of the Board of Guardians, who should, I believe, have a copy of it, knew nothing about it; and had never heard of such a document. Your bishop's registrar was not much more learned,—but I did find it in the bishop's chancery; and there is a copy of it also at Saint John's, which seems to imply that great attention has been paid by the college as patron to the interests of the parish priest. This is more than has been done by the incumbent, who seems to be an ignorant fellow in such matters. I wonder how many parsons there are in the Church who would let a Marquis and a Methodist minister between them build a chapel on the parish glebe?

Yours ever,

RICHARD QUICKENHAM.

If I were to charge you through an attorney for my trouble you'd have to mortgage your life interest in the bit of land to pay me. I enclose a draft from the terrier as far as the plot of ground and the vicarage-gate are concerned.

Here was information! This detestable combination of dissenting and tyrannically territorial influences had been used to build a Methodist Chapel upon land of which he, during his incumbency in the parish, was the freehold possessor! What an ass he must have been not to know his own possessions! How ridiculous would he appear when he should come forward to claim as a part of the glebe a morsel of land to which he had paid no special attention whatever since he had been in the parish! And then, what would it be his duty to do? Mr. Quickenham had clearly stated that on behalf of the college, which was the patron of the living, and on behalf of his successors, it was his duty to claim the land. And was it possible that he should not do so after such usage as he had received from Lord Trowbridge? So meditating,—but grieving that he should be driven at such a moment to have his mind forcibly filled with such matters,—still hearing the chapel bell, which in his ears drowned the sound from his own modest belfry, and altogether doubtful as to what step he would take, he entered his own church. It was manifest to him that of the poorer part of his usual audience, and of the smaller farmers, one half were in attendance upon Mr. Puddleham's triumph.

During the whole of that afternoon he said not a word of the barrister's letter to any one. He struggled to banish the subject from his thoughts. Failing to do that, he did banish it from his tongue. The letter was in the pocket of his coat; but he showed it to no one. Gilmore dined at the vicarage; but even to him he was silent. Of course the conversation at dinner turned upon the chapel. It was impossible that on such a day they should speak of anything else. Even as they sat at their early dinner Mr. Puddleham's bell was ringing, and no doubt there was a vigour in the pulling of it which would not be maintained when the pulling of it should have become a thing of every week. There had been a compact made, in accordance with which the Vicar's wife was to be debarred from saying anything against the chapel, and, no doubt, when the compact was made, the understanding was that she should give over hating the chapel. This had, of course, been found to be impossible, but in a certain way she had complied with the compact. The noise of the bell however, was considered to be beyond the compact, and on this occasion she was almost violent in the expression of her wrath. Her husband listened to her, and sat without rebuking her, silent, with the lawyer's letter in his pocket. This bell had been put up on his own land, and he could pull it down to-morrow. It had been put up by the express agency of Lord Trowbridge, and with the direct view of annoying him; and Lord Trowbridge had behaved to him in a manner which set all Christian charity at defiance. He told himself plainly that he had no desire to forgive Lord Trowbridge,—that life in this world, as it is constituted, would not be compatible with such forgiveness,— that he would not, indeed, desire to injure Lord Trowbridge otherwise than by exacting such penalty as would force him and such as he to restrain their tyranny; but that to forgive him, till he should have been so forced, would be weak and injurious to the community. As to that, he had quite made up his mind, in spite of all doctrine to the contrary. Men in this world would have to go naked if they gave their coats to the robbers who took their cloaks; and going naked is manifestly inexpedient. His office of parish priest would be lowered in the world if he forgave, out of hand, such offences as these which had been committed against him by Lord Trowbridge. This he understood clearly. And now he might put down, not only the bell, but with the bell the ill-conditioned peer who had caused it to be put up—on glebe land. All this went through his mind again and again, as he determined that on that day, being Sunday, he would think no more about it.

When the Monday came it was necessary that he should show the letter to his wife,—to his wife, and to the Squire, and to Mary Lowther. He had no idea of keeping the matter secret from his near friends and advisers; but he had an idea that it would be well that he should make up his mind as to what he would do before he asked their advice. He started, therefore, for a turn through the parish before breakfast on Monday morning,—and resolved as to his course of action. On no consideration whatever would he have the chapel pulled down. It was necessary for his purpose that he should have his triumph over the Marquis,—and he would have it. But the chapel had been built for a good purpose which it would adequately serve, and let what might be said to him by his wife or others, he would not have a brick of it disturbed. No doubt he had no more power to give the land for its present or any other purpose than had the Marquis. It might very probably be his duty to take care that the land was not appropriated to wrong purposes. It might be that he had already neglected his duty, in not knowing, or in not having taken care to learn the precise limits of the glebe which had been given over to him for his use during his incumbency. Nevertheless, there was the chapel, and there it should stand, as far as he was concerned. If the churchwardens, or the archdeacon, or the college, or the bishop had power to interfere, as to which he was altogether ignorant, and chose to exercise that power, he could not help it. He was nearly sure that his own churchwardens would be guided altogether by himself,—and as far as he was concerned the chapel should remain unmolested. Having thus resolved he came back to breakfast and read Mr. Quickenham's letter aloud to his wife and Mary Lowther.

"Glebe!" said the Vicar's wife.

"Do you mean that it is part of your own land?" asked Mary.

"Exactly that," said the Vicar.

"And that old thief of a Marquis has given away what belongs to us?" said Mrs. Fenwick.

"He has given away what did not belong to himself," said the Vicar. "But I can't admit that he's a thief."

"Surely he ought to have known," said Mary.

"As for that, so ought I to have known, I suppose. The whole thing is one of the most ridiculous mistakes that ever was made. It has absolutely come to pass that here, in the middle of Wiltshire, with all our maps, and surveys, and parish records, no one concerned has known to whom belonged a quarter of an acre of land in the centre of the village. It is just a thing to write an article about in a newspaper; but I can't say that one party is more to blame than the other; that is, in regard to the ignorance displayed."

"And what will you do, Frank?"

"Nothing."

"You will do nothing, Frank?"

"I will do nothing; but I will take care to let the Marquis know the nature of his generosity. I fancy that I am bound to take on myself that labour, and I must say that it won't trouble me much to have to write the letter."

"You won't pull it down, Frank?"

"No, my dear."

"I would, before a week was over."

"So would I," said Mary. "I don't think it ought to be there."

"Of course it ought not to be there," said Mrs. Fenwick.

"They might as well have it here in the garden," said Mary.

"Just the same," said Mrs. Fenwick.

"It is not in the garden; and, as it has been built, it shall remain,—as far as I am concerned. I shall rather like it, now that I know I am the landlord. I think I shall claim a sitting." This was the Vicar's decision on the Monday morning, and from that decision the two ladies were quite unable to move him.

This occurred a day or two after the affair of the rubies, and at a time when Mary was being very hard pressed to name a day for her wedding. Of course such pressure had been the result of Mr. Gilmore's success on that occasion. She had then resolutely gone to work to overcome her own, and his, melancholy gloom, and, having in a great degree succeeded, it was only natural that he should bring up that question of his marriage day. She, when she had accepted him, had done so with a stipulation that she should not be hurried; but we all know what such stipulations are worth. Who is to define what is and what is not hurry? They had now been engaged a month, and the Squire was clearly of opinion that there had been no hurry. "September was the nicest month in the year," he said, "for getting married and going abroad. September in Switzerland, October among the Italian lakes, November in Florence and Rome. So that they might get home before Christmas after a short visit to Naples." That was the Squire's programme, and his whole manner was altered as he made it. He thought he knew the nature of the girl well enough to be sure that, though she would profess no passionate love for him before starting on such a journey, she would change her tone before she returned. It should be no fault of his if she did not change it. Mary had at first declined to fix any day, had talked of next year, had declared that she would not be hurried. She had carried on the fight even after the affair of the rubies, but she had fought in opposition to strong and well-disciplined forces on the other side, and she had begun to admit to herself that it might be expedient that she should yield. The thing was to be done, and why not have it done at once? She had not as yet yielded, but she had begun to think that she would yield.

At such a period it was of course natural that the Squire should be daily at the vicarage, and on this Monday morning he came down while the minds of all his friends there were intent on the strange information received from Mr. Quickenham. The Vicar was not by when Mr. Gilmore was told, and he was thus easily induced to join in the opinion that the chapel should be made to disappear. He had a landlord's idea about land, and was thoroughly well-disposed to stop any encroachment on the part of the Marquis.

"Lord Trowbridge must pull it down himself, and put it up again elsewhere," said the Squire.

"But Frank says that he won't let the Marquis pull it down," said Mrs. Fenwick, almost moved to tears by the tragedy of the occasion.

Mr. Quickenham's letter discussed.

Then the Vicar joined them, and the matter was earnestly debated;—so earnestly that, on that occasion, not a word was said as to the day of the wedding.

CHAPTER LVI.

THE VICAR'S VENGEANCE.

No eloquence on the part of the two ladies at the vicarage, or of the Squire, could turn Mr. Fenwick from his purpose, but he did consent at last to go over with the Squire to Salisbury, and to consult Mr. Chamberlaine. A proposition was made to him as to consulting the bishop, for whom personally he always expressed a liking, and whose office he declared that he held in the highest veneration; but he explained that this was not a matter in which the bishop should be invited to exercise authority.

"The bishop has nothing to do with my freehold," he said.

"But if you want an opinion," said the Squire, "why not go to a man whose opinion will be worth having?"

Then the Vicar explained again. His respect for the bishop was so great, that any opinion coming from his lordship would, to him, be more than advice; it would be law. So great was his mingled admiration of the man and respect for the office!

"What he means," said Mrs. Fenwick, "is, that he won't go to the bishop, because he has made up his mind already. You are, both of you, throwing away your time and money in going to Salisbury at all."

"I'm not sure but what she's right there," said the Vicar. Nevertheless they went to Salisbury.

The Rev. Henry Fitzackerly Chamberlaine was very eloquent, clear, and argumentative on the subject, and perhaps a little overbearing. He insisted that the chapel should be removed without a moment's delay; and that notice as to its removal should be served upon all the persons concerned,—upon Mr. Puddleham, upon the builder, upon the chapel trustees, the elders of the congregation,—"if there be any elders," said Mr. Chamberlaine, with a delightful touch of irony,—and upon the Marquis and the Marquis's agent. He was eloquent, authoritative and loud. When the Vicar remarked that after all the chapel had been built for a good purpose, Mr. Chamberlaine became quite excited in his eloquence.

"The glebe of Bullhampton, Mr. Fenwick," said he, "has not been confided to your care for the propagation of dissent."

"Nor has the vicarage house been confided to me for the reading of novels; but that is what goes on there."

"The house is for your private comfort," said the prebendary.

"And so is the glebe," said the Vicar; "and I shall not be comfortable if I make these people put down a house of prayer."

And there was another argument against the Vicar's views, very strong. This glebe was only given to him in trust. He was bound so to use it, that it should fall into the hands of his successor unimpaired and with full capability for fruition. "You have no right to leave to another the demolition of a building, the erection of which you should have prevented." This argument was more difficult of answer than the other, but Mr. Fenwick did answer it.

"I feel all that," said he; "and I think it likely that my estate may be liable for the expense of removal. The chapel may be brought in as a dilapidation. But that which I can answer with my purse, need not lie upon my conscience. I could let the bit of land, I have no doubt,—though not on a building lease."

"But they have built on it," said Mr. Chamberlaine.

"No doubt, they have; and I can see that my estate may be called upon to restore the bit of ground to its former position. What I can't see is, that I am bound to enforce the removal now."

Mr. Chamberlaine took up the matter with great spirit, and gave a couple of hours to the discussion, but the Vicar was not shaken.

The Vicar was not shaken, but his manner as he went out from the prebendary's presence, left some doubt as to his firmness in the mind both of that dignitary and of the Squire. He thanked Mr. Chamberlaine very courteously, and acknowledged that there was a great deal in the arguments which had been used.

"I am sure you will find it best to clear your ground of the nuisance at once," said Mr. Chamberlaine, with that high tone which he knew so well how to assume; and these were the last words spoken.

"Well?" said the Squire, as soon as they were out in the Close, asking his friend as to his decision.

"It's a very knotty point," said Fenwick.

"I don't much like my uncle's tone," said the Squire; "I never do. But I think he is right."

"I won't say but what he may be."

"It'll have to come down, Frank," said the Squire.

"No doubt, some day. But I am quite sure as to this, Harry; that when you have a doubt as to your duty, you can't be wrong in delaying that, the doing of which would gratify your own ill will. Don't you go and tell this to the women; but to my eyes that conventicle at Bullhampton is the most hideous, abominable, and disagreeable object that ever was placed upon the earth!"

"So it is to mine," said the Squire.

"And therefore I won't touch a brick of it. It shall be my hair shirt, my fast day, my sacrifice of a broken heart, my little pet good work. It will enable me to take all the good things of the world that come in my way, and flatter myself that I am not self-indulgent. There is not a dissenter in Bullhampton will get so much out of the chapel as I will."

"I fancy they can make you have it pulled down."

"Then their making me shall be my hair shirt, and I shall be fitted just as well." Upon that they went back to Bullhampton, and the Squire told the two ladies what had passed; as to the hair shirt and all.

Mr. Fenwick in making for himself his hair shirt did not think it necessary to abstain from writing to the Marquis of Trowbridge. This he did on that same day after his return from Salisbury. In the middle of the winter he had written a letter to the Marquis, remonstrating against the building of the chapel opposite to his own gate. He now took out his copy of that letter, and the answer to it, in which the agent of the Marquis had told him that the Marquis considered that the spot in question was the most eligible site which his lordship could bestow for the purpose in question. Our Vicar was very anxious not to disturb the chapel now that it was built; but he was quite as anxious to disturb the Marquis. In the formation of that hair shirt which he was minded to wear, he did not intend to weave in any mercy towards the Marquis. It behoved him to punish the Marquis,—for the good of society in general. As a trespasser he forgave the Marquis, in a Christian point of view; but as a pestilent wasp on the earth, stinging folks right and left with an arrogance, the ignorance of which was the only excuse to be made for his cruelty, he thought it to be his duty to set his heel upon the Marquis; which he did by writing the following letter.

Bullhampton Vicarage, July 18, 186—.

MY LORD MARQUIS,

On the 3rd of January last I ventured to write to your lordship with the object of saving myself and my family from a great annoyance, and of saving you also from the disgrace of subjecting me to it. I then submitted to you the expediency of giving in the parish some other site for the erection of a dissenting chapel than the small patch of ground immediately opposite to the vicarage gate, which, as I explained to you, I had always regarded as belonging to the vicarage. I did not for a moment question your lordship's right to give the land in question, but appealed simply to your good-feeling. I confess that I took it for granted that even your lordship, in so very high-handed a proceeding, would take care to have right on your side. In answer to this I received a letter from your man of business, of which, as coming from him, I do not complain, but which, as a reply to my letter to your lordship, was an insult. The chapel has been built, and on last Sunday was opened for worship.

I have now learned that the land which you have given away did not belong to your lordship, and never formed a portion of the Stowte estate in this parish. It was, and is, glebe land; and formed, at the time of your bestowal, a portion of my freehold as Vicar. I acknowledge that I was remiss in presuming that you as a landlord knew the limits of your own rights, and that you would not trespass beyond them. I should have made my inquiry more urgently. I have made it now, and your lordship may satisfy yourself by referring to the maps of the parish lands, which are to be found in the bishop's chancery, and also at St. John's, Oxford, if you cannot do so by any survey of the estate in your own possession. I enclose a sketch showing the exact limits of the glebe in respect to the vicarage entrance and the patch of ground in question. The fact is, that the chapel in question has been built on the glebe land by authority—illegally and unjustly given by your lordship.

The chapel is there, and though it is a pity that it should have been built, it would be a greater pity that it should be pulled down. It is my purpose to offer to the persons concerned a lease of the ground for the term of my incumbency at a nominal rent. I presume that a lease may be so framed as to protect the rights of my successor.

I will not conclude this letter without expressing my opinion that gross as has been your lordship's ignorance in giving away land which did not belong to you, your fault in that respect has been very trifling in comparison with the malice you have shown to a clergyman of your own church, settled in a parish partly belonging to yourself, in having caused the erection of this chapel on the special spot selected with no other object than that of destroying my personal comfort and that of my wife.

I have the honour to be
Your lordship's most obedient servant,

FRANCIS FENWICK.

When he had finished his epistle he read it over more than once, and was satisfied that it would be vexatious to the Marquis. It was his direct object to vex the Marquis, and he had set about it with all his vigour. "I would skin him if I knew how," he had said to Gilmore. "He has done that to me which no man should forgive. He has spoken ill of me, and calumniated me, not because he has thought ill of me, but because he has had a spite against me. They may keep their chapel as far as I am concerned. But as for his lordship, I should think ill of myself if I spared him." He had his lordship on the hip, and he did not spare him. He showed the letter to his wife.

"Isn't malice a very strong word?" she said.

"I hope so," answered the Vicar.

"What I mean is, might you not soften it without hurting your cause?"

"I think not. I conscientiously believe the accusation to be true. I endeavour so to live among my neighbours that I may not disgrace them, or you, or myself. This man has dared to accuse me openly of the grossest immorality and hypocrisy, when I am only doing my duty as I best know how to do it; and I do now believe in my heart that in making these charges he did not himself credit them. At any rate, no man can be justified in making such charges without evidence."

"But all that had nothing to do with the bit of ground, Frank."

"It is part and parcel of the same thing. He has chosen to treat me as an enemy, and has used all the influence of his wealth and rank to injure me. Now he must look to himself. I will not say a word of him, or to him, that is untrue; but as he has said evil of me behind my back which he did not believe, so will I say the evil of him, which I do believe, to his face." The letter was sent, and before the day was over the Vicar had recovered his good humour.

And before the day was over the news was all through the parish. There was a certain ancient shoemaker in the village who had carried on business in Devizes, and had now retired to spend the evening of his life in his native place. Mr. Bolt was a quiet, inoffensive old man, but he was a dissenter, and was one of the elders and trustees who had been concerned in raising money for the chapel. To him the Vicar had told the whole story, declaring at the same time that, as far as he was concerned, Mr. Puddleham and his congregation should, at any rate for the present, be made welcome to their chapel. This he had done immediately on his return from Salisbury, and before the letter to the Marquis was written. Mr. Bolt, not unnaturally, saw his minister the same evening, and the thing was discussed in full conclave by the Puddlehamites. At the end of that discussion, Mr. Puddleham expressed his conviction that the story was a mare's nest from beginning to end. He didn't believe a word of it. The Marquis was not the man to give away anything that did not belong to him. Somebody had hoaxed the Vicar, or the Vicar had hoaxed Mr. Bolt; or else,—which Mr. Puddleham thought to be most likely,—the Vicar had gone mad with vexation at the glory and the triumph of the new chapel.

"He was uncommon civil," said Mr. Bolt, who at this moment was somewhat inclined to favour the Vicar.

"No doubt, Mr. Bolt; no doubt," said Mr. Puddleham, who had quite recovered from his first dismay, and had worked himself up to a state of eloquent enthusiasm. "I dare say he was civil. Why not? In old days when we hardly dared to talk of having a decent house of prayer of our own in which to worship our God, he was always civil. No one has ever heard me accuse Mr. Fenwick of incivility. But will any one tell me that he is a friend to our mode of worship? Gentlemen, we must look to ourselves, and I for one tell you that that chapel is ours. You won't find that his ban will keep me out of my pulpit. Glebe, indeed! why should the Vicar have glebe on the other side of the road from his house? Or, for the matter of that, why should he have glebe at all?" This was so decisive that no one at the meeting had a word to say after Mr. Puddleham had finished his speech.

When the Marquis received his letter he was up in London. Lord Trowbridge was not much given to London life, but was usually compelled by circumstances,—the circumstances being the custom of society as pleaded by his two daughters,—to spend the months of May, June, and July at the family mansion in Grosvenor Square. Moreover, though the Marquis never opened his mouth in the House of Lords, it was, as he thought, imperative on him to give to the leader of his party the occasional support of his personal presence. Our Vicar, knowing this, had addressed his letter to Grosvenor Square, and it had thus reached its destination without loss of time. Lord Trowbridge by this time knew the handwriting of his enemy; and, as he broke the envelope, there came upon him an idea that it might be wise to refuse the letter, and to let it go back to its writer unopened. It was beneath his dignity to correspond with a man, or to receive letters from a man who would probably insult him. But before he could make up his mind, the envelope had been opened, and the letter had been read. His wrath, when he had read it, no writer of a simple prose narration should attempt to describe. "Disgrace," "insult," "ignorance," and "malice,"—these were the words with which the Marquis found himself pelted by this pestilent, abominable, and most improper clergyman. As to the gist of the letter itself, it was some time before he understood it. And when he did begin to understand it, he did not as yet begin to believe it. His intelligence worked slowly, whereas his wrath worked quickly. But at last he began to ask himself whether the accusation made against him could possibly be based on truth. When the question of giving the land had been under consideration, it had never occurred to any one concerned that it could belong to the glebe. There had been some momentary suspicion that the spot might possibly have been so long used as common land as to give room for a question on that side; but no one had dreamed that any other claimant could arise. That the whole village of Bullhampton belonged to the Marquis was notorious. Of course there was the glebe. But who could think that the morsel of neglected land lying on the other side of the road belonged to the vicarage? The Marquis did not believe it now. This was some piece of wickedness concocted by the venomous brain of the iniquitous Vicar, more abominable than all his other wickednesses. The Marquis did not believe it; but he walked up and down his room all the morning thinking of it. The Marquis was sure that it was not true, and yet he could not for a moment get the idea out of his mind. Of course he must tell St. George. The language of the letter which had been sent to him was so wicked, that St. George must at least agree with him now in his anger against this man. And could nothing be done to punish the man? Prosecutions in regard to anonymous letters, threatening letters, begging letters, passed through his mind. He knew that punishment had been inflicted on the writers of insolent letters to royalty. And letters had been proved to be criminal as being libellous,—only then they must be published; and letters were sometimes held to form a conspiracy;—but he could not quite see his way to that. He knew that he was not royal; and he knew that the Vicar neither threatened him or begged aught from him. What if St. George should tell him again that this Vicar had right on his side! He cast the matter about in his mind all the day; and then, late in the afternoon, he got into his carriage, and had himself driven to the chambers of Messrs. Boothby, the family lawyers.

CHAPTER LVII.

OIL IS TO BE THROWN UPON THE WATERS.

Messrs. Boothby in Lincoln's Inn had for very many years been the lawyers of the Stowte family, and probably knew as much about the property as any of the Stowtes themselves. They had not been consulted about the giving away of the bit of land for the chapel purposes, nor had they been instructed to draw up any deed of gift. The whole thing had been done irregularly. The land had been only promised, and not in truth as yet given, and the Puddlehamites, in their hurry, had gone to work and had built upon a promise. The Marquis, when, after the receipt of Mr. Fenwick's letter, his first rage was over, went at once to the chambers of Messrs. Boothby, and was forced to explain all the circumstances of the case to the senior partner before he could show the clergyman's wicked epistle. Old Mr. Boothby was a man of the same age as the Marquis, and, in his way, quite as great. Only the lawyer was a clever old man, whereas the Marquis was a stupid old man. Mr. Boothby sat, bowing his head, as the Marquis told his story. The story was rather confused, and for awhile Mr. Boothby could only understand that a dissenting chapel had been built upon his client's land.

"We shall have to set it right by some scrap of a conveyance," said the lawyer.

"But the Vicar of the parish claims it," said the Marquis.

"Claims the chapel, my lord!"

"He is a most pestilent, abominable man, Mr. Boothby. I have brought his letter here." Mr. Boothby held out his hand to receive the letter. From almost any client he would prefer a document to an oral explanation, but he would do so especially from his lordship. "But you must understand," continued the Marquis, "that he is quite unlike any ordinary clergyman. I have the greatest respect for the church, and am always happy to see clergymen at my own house. But this is a litigious, quarrelsome fellow. They tell me he's an infidel, and he keeps—! Altogether, Mr. Boothby, nothing can be worse."

"Indeed!" said the lawyer, still holding out his hand for the letter.

"He has taken the trouble to insult me continually. You heard how a tenant of mine was murdered? He was murdered by a young man whom this clergyman screens, because,—because,—he is the brother of,—of,—of the young woman."

"That would be very bad, my lord."

"It is very bad. He knows all about the murder;—I am convinced he does. He went bail for the young man. He used to associate with him on most intimate terms. As to the sister;—there's no doubt about that. They live on the land of a person who owns a small estate in the parish."

"Mr. Gilmore, my lord?"

"Exactly so. This Mr. Fenwick has got Mr. Gilmore in his pocket. You can have no idea of such a state of things as this. And now he writes me this letter! I know his handwriting now, and any further communication I shall return." The Marquis ceased to speak, and the lawyer at once buried himself in the letter.

"It is meant to be offensive," said the lawyer.

"Most insolent, most offensive, most improper! And yet the bishop upholds him!"

"But if he is right about the bit of land, my lord, it will be rather awkward." And as he spoke, the lawyer examined the sketch of the vicarage entrance. "He gives this as copied from the terrier of the parish, my lord."

"I don't believe a word of it," said the Marquis.

"You didn't look at the plan of the estate, my lord?"

"I don't think we did; but Packer had no doubt. No one knows the property in Bullhampton so well as Packer, and Packer said—"

But while the Marquis was still speaking the lawyer rose, and begging his client's pardon, went to the clerk in the outer room. Nor did he return till the clerk had descended to an iron chamber in the basement, and returned from thence with a certain large tin box. Into this a search was made, and presently Mr. Boothby came back with a weighty lump of dusty vellum documents, and a manuscript map, or sketch of a survey of the Bullhampton estate, which he had had opened. While the search was being made he had retired to another room, and had had a little conversation with his partner about the weather. "I am afraid the parson is right, my lord," said Mr. Boothby, as he closed the door.

"Right!"

"Right in his facts, my lord. It is glebe, and is marked so here very plainly. There should have been a reference to us,—there should, indeed, my lord. Packer, and men like him, really know nothing. The truth is, in such matters nobody knows anything. You should always have documentary evidence."

"And it is glebe?"

"Not a doubt of it, my lord."

Then the Marquis knew that his enemy had him on the hip, and he laid his old head down upon his folded arms and wept. In his weeping it is probable that no tears rolled down his cheeks, but he wept inward tears,—tears of hatred, remorse, and self-commiseration. His enemy had struck him with scourges, and, as far as he could see at present, he could not return a blow. And he must submit himself,—must restore the bit of land, and build those nasty dissenters a chapel elsewhere on his own property. He had not a doubt as to that for a moment. Could he have escaped the shame of it,—as far as the expense was concerned he would have been willing to build them ten chapels. And in doing this he would give a triumph, an unalloyed triumph, to a man whom he believed to be thoroughly bad. The Vicar had accused the Marquis of spreading reports which he, the Marquis, did not himself believe; but the Marquis believed them all. At this moment there was no evil that he could not have believed of Mr. Fenwick. While sitting there an idea, almost amounting to a conviction, had come upon him, that Mr. Fenwick had himself been privy to the murder of old Trumbull. What would not a parson do who would take delight in insulting and humiliating the nobleman who owned the parish in which he lived? To Lord Trowbridge the very fact that the parson of the parish which he regarded as his own was opposed to him, proved sufficiently that that parson was,—scum, dregs, riff-raff, a low radical, and everything that a parson ought not to be. The Vicar had been wrong there. The Marquis did believe it all religiously.

"What must I do?" said the Marquis.

"As to the chapel itself, my lord, the Vicar, bad as he is, does not want to move it."

"It must come down," said the Marquis, getting up from his chair. "It shall come down. Do you think that I would allow it to stand when it has been erected on his ground,—through my error? Not for a day!—not for an hour! I'll tell you what, Mr. Boothby,—that man has known it all through;—has known it as well as you do now; but he has waited till the building was complete before he would tell me. I see it all as plain as the nose on your face, Mr. Boothby."

The lawyer was meditating how best he might explain to his angry client that he had no power whatsoever to pull down the building,—that if the Vicar and the dissenting minister chose to agree about it the new building must stand, in spite of the Marquis,—must stand, unless the churchwardens, patron, or ecclesiastical authorities generally should force the Vicar to have it removed,—when a clerk came in and whispered a word to the attorney. "My lord," said Mr. Boothby, "Lord St. George is here. Shall he come in?"

The Marquis did not wish to see his son exactly at this minute; but Lord St. George was, of course, admitted. This meeting at the lawyer's chambers was altogether fortuitous, and father and son were equally surprised. But so great was the anger and dismay and general perturbation of the Marquis at the time, that he could not stop to ask any question. St. George must, of course, know what had happened, and it was quite as well that he should be told at once.

"That bit of ground they've built the chapel on at Bullhampton, turns out to be—glebe," said the Marquis. Lord St. George whistled. "Of course, Mr. Fenwick knew it all along," said the Marquis.

"I should hardly think that," said his son.

"You read his letter. Mr. Boothby, will you be so good as to show Lord St. George the letter? You never read such a production. Impudent scoundrel! Of course he knew it all the time."

Lord St. George read the letter. "He is very impudent, whether he be a scoundrel or not."

"Impudent is no word for it."

"Perhaps he has had some provocation, my lord."

"Not from me, St. George;—not from me. I have done nothing to him. Of course the chapel must be—removed."

"Don't you think the question might stand over for a while?" suggested Mr. Boothby. "Matters would become smoother in a month or two."

"Not for an hour," said the Marquis.

Lord St. George walked about the room with the letter in his hand, meditating. "The truth is," he said, at last, "we have made a mistake, and we must get out of it as best we can. I think my father is a little wrong about this clergyman's character."

"St. George! Have you read his letter? Is that a proper letter to come from a clergyman of the Church of England to—to—to—" the Marquis longed to say to the Marquis of Trowbridge; but he did not dare so to express himself before his son,—"to the landlord of his parish?"

"A red-brick chapel, just close to your lodge, isn't nice, you know."

"He has got no lodge," said the Marquis.

"And so we thought we'd build him one. Let me manage this. I'll see him, and I'll see the minister, and I'll endeavour to throw some oil upon the waters."

"I don't want to throw oil upon the waters."

"Lord St. George is in the right, my lord," said the attorney; "he really is. It is a case in which we must throw a little oil upon the waters. We've made a mistake, and when we've done that we should always throw oil upon the waters. I've no doubt Lord St. George will find a way out of it." Then the father and the son went away together, and before they had reached the Houses of Parliament Lord St. George had persuaded his father to place the matter of the Bullhampton chapel in his hands. "And as for the letter," said St. George, "do not you notice it."

"I have not the slightest intention of noticing it," said the Marquis, haughtily.

CHAPTER LVIII.

EDITH BROWNLOW'S DREAM.

"My dear, sit down; I want to speak to you. Do you know I should like to see you—married." This speech was made at Dunripple to Edith Brownlow by her uncle, Sir Gregory, one morning in July, as she was attending him with his breakfast. His breakfast consisted always of a cup of chocolate, made after a peculiar fashion, and Edith was in the habit of standing by the old man's bedside while he took it. She would never sit down, because she knew that were she to do so she would be pretty nearly hidden out of sight in the old arm-chair that stood at the bed-head; but now she was specially invited to do so, and that in a manner which almost made her think that it would be well that she should hide herself for a space. But she did not sit down. There was the empty cup to be taken from Sir Gregory's hands, and, after the first moment of surprise, Edith was not quite sure that it would be good that she should hide herself. She took the cup and put it on the table, and then returned, without making any reply. "I should like very much to see you married, my dear," said Sir Gregory, in the mildest of voices.

"Do you want to get rid of me, uncle?"

"No, my dear; that is just what I don't want. Of course you'll marry somebody."

"I don't see any of course, Uncle Gregory."

"But why shouldn't you? I suppose you have thought about it."

"Only in a general way, Uncle Gregory."

Sir Gregory Marrable was not a wise man. His folly was of an order very different from that of Lord Trowbridge,—very much less likely to do harm to himself or others, much more innocent, and, folly though it was, a great deal more compatible with certain intellectual gifts. Lord Trowbridge, not to put too fine a point upon it, was a fool all round. He was much too great a fool to have an idea of his own folly. Now Sir Gregory distrusted himself in everything, conceived himself to be a poor creature, would submit himself to a child on any question of literature, and had no opinion of his own on any matter outside his own property,—and even as to that his opinion was no more than lukewarm. Yet he read a great deal, had much information stored away somewhere in his memory, and had learned at any rate to know how small a fly he was himself on the wheel of the world. But, alas, when he did meddle with anything he was apt to make a mess of it. There had been some conversation between him and his sister-in-law, Edith's mother, about Walter Marrable; some also between him and his son, and between him and

Miss Marrable, his cousin. But as yet no one had spoken to Edith, and as Captain Marrable himself had not spoken, it would have been as well, perhaps, if Sir Gregory had held his tongue. After Edith's last answer the old man was silent for awhile, and then he returned to the subject with a downright question,—

"How did you like Walter when he was here?"

"Captain Marrable?"

"Yes,—Captain Marrable."

"I liked him well enough,—in a way, Uncle Gregory."

"Nothing would please me so much, Edith, as that you should become his wife. You know that Dunripple will belong to him some day."

"If Gregory does not marry." Edith had hardly known whether to say this or to leave it unsaid. She was well aware that her cousin Gregory would never marry,—that he was a confirmed invalid, a man already worn out, old before his time, and with one foot in the grave. But had she not said it, she would have seemed to herself to have put him aside as a person altogether out of the way.

"Gregory will never marry. Of course while he lives Dunripple will be his; but if Walter were to marry he would make arrangements. I dare say you can't understand all about that, my dear; but it would be a very good thing. I should be so happy if I thought that you were to live at Dunripple always."

Edith kissed him and escaped without giving any other answer. Ten days after that Walter Marrable was to be again at Dunripple,—only for a few days; but still in a few days the thing might be settled. Edith had heard something of Mary Lowther, but not much. There had been some idea of a match between Walter and his cousin Mary, but the idea had been blown away. So much Edith had heard. To herself Walter Marrable had been very friendly, and, in truth, she had liked him much. They two were not cousins, but they were so connected, and had for some weeks been so thrown together, as to be almost as good as cousins. His presence at Dunripple had been very pleasant to her, but she had never thought of him as a lover. And she had an idea of her own, that girls ought not to think of men as lovers without a good deal of provocation.

Sir Gregory spoke to Mrs. Brownlow on the same subject, and as he told her what had taken place between him and Edith, she felt herself compelled to speak to her daughter.

"If it should take place, my dear, it would be very well; but I would rather your uncle had not mentioned it."

"It won't do any harm, mamma. I mean, that I shan't break my heart."

"I believe him to be a very excellent young man,—not at all like his father, who has been as bad as he can be."

"Wasn't he in love with Mary Lowther last winter?"

"I don't know, my dear. I never believe stories of this kind. When I hear that a young man is going to be married to a young lady, then I believe that they are in love with each other."

"It is to be hoped so then, mamma?"

"But I never believe any thing before. And I think you may take it for granted that there is nothing in that."

"It would be nothing to me, mamma."

"It might be something. But I will say nothing more about it. You've so much good sense that I am quite sure you won't get into trouble. I wish Sir Gregory had not spoken to you; but as he has, it may be as well that you should know that the family arrangement would be very agreeable to your uncle and to cousin Gregory. The title and the property must go to Captain Marrable at last, and Sir Gregory would make immediate sacrifices for you, which perhaps he would not make for him."

Edith understood all about it very clearly, and would have understood all about it with half the words. She would have little or no fortune of her own, and in money her uncle would have very little to give to her. Indeed, there was no reason why he should give her anything. She was not connected with any of the Marrables by blood, though chance had caused her to live at Dunripple almost all her life. She had become half a Marrable already, and it might be very well that she should become a Marrable altogether. Walter was a remarkably handsome man, would be a baronet, and would have an estate, and might, perhaps, have the enjoyment of the estate by marrying her earlier than he would were he to marry any one else. Edith Brownlow understood it all with sufficient clearness. But then she understood also that young women shouldn't give away their hearts before they are asked for them; and she was quite sure that Walter Marrable had made no sign of asking for hers. Nevertheless, within her own bosom she did become a little anxious about Mary Lowther, and she wished that she knew that story.

On the fourth of August Walter Marrable reached Dunripple, and found the house given up almost entirely to the doctor. Both his uncle and his cousin were very ill. When he was able to obtain from the doctor information on which he could rely, he learned that Mr. Marrable was in real danger, but that Sir Gregory's ailment was no more than his usual infirmity heightened by anxiety on behalf of his son. "Your uncle may live for the next ten years," said the doctor; "but I do not know what to say about Mr. Marrable." All this time the care and time of the two ladies were divided between the invalids. Mrs. Brownlow tended her nephew, and Edith, as usual, waited upon Sir Gregory. In such circumstances it was not extraordinary that Edith Brownlow and Walter Marrable should be thrown much together,—especially as it was the desire of all concerned with them that they should become man and wife. Poor Edith was subject to a feeling that everybody knew that she was expected to fall in love with the man. She thought it probable, too, that the man himself had been instructed to fall in love with her. This no doubt created a great difficulty for her, a difficulty which she felt to be heavy and inconvenient;—but it was lessened by the present condition of the household. When there is illness in a house, the feminine genius and spirit predominates the male. If the illness be so severe as to cause a sense of danger, this is so strongly the case that the natural position of the two is changed. Edith, quite unconscious of the reason, was much less afraid of her proposed lover than she would have been had there been no going about on tiptoe, no questions asked with bated breath, no great need for womanly aid.

Walter had been there four days, and was sitting with Edith one evening out on the lawn among the rhododendrons. When he had found what was the condition of the household, he had offered to go back at once to his regiment at Birmingham. But Sir Gregory would not hear of it. Sir Gregory hated the regiment, and had got an idea in his head that his nephew ought not to be there at all. He was too weak and diffident to do it himself; but if any one would have arranged it for him, he would have been glad to fix an income for Walter Marrable on condition that Walter should live at home, and look after the property, and be unto him as a son. But nothing had been fixed, nothing had been said, and on the day but one following, the captain was to return to Birmingham. Mrs. Brownlow was with her nephew, and Walter was sitting with Edith among the rhododendrons, the two having come out of the house together after such a dinner as is served in a house of invalids. They had become very intimate, but Edith Brownlow had almost determined that Walter Marrable did not intend to fall in love with her. She had quite determined that she would not fall in love with him till he did. What she might do in that case she had not told herself. She was not quite sure. He was very nice,—but she was not quite sure. One ought to be very fond of a young man, she said to herself, before one falls in love with him. Nevertheless her mind was by no means set against him. If one can oblige one's friends one ought, she said, again to herself.

She had brought him out a cup of coffee, and he was sitting in a garden chair with a cigar in his mouth. They were Walter and Edith to each other, just as though they were cousins. Indeed, it was necessary that they should be cousins to each other, for the rest of their lives, if no more.

She had brought him out a cup of coffee.

"Let us drop the Captain and the Miss," he had said himself; "the mischief is in it if you and I can't suppose ourselves to be related." She had assented cordially, and had called him Walter without a moment's hesitation. "Edith," he said to her now, after he had sat for a minute or two with the coffee in his hand; "did you ever hear of a certain cousin of ours, called Mary Lowther?"

"Oh, dear, yes; she lives with Aunt Sarah at Loring; only Aunt Sarah isn't my aunt, and Miss Lowther isn't my cousin."

"Just so. She lives at Loring. Edith, I love you so much that I wonder whether I may tell you the great secret of my life?"

"Of course you may. I love secrets; and I specially love the secrets of those who love me." She said this with a voice perfectly clear, and a face without a sign of disappointment; but her little dream had already been dissipated. She knew the secret as well as though it had been told.

"I was engaged to marry her."

"And you will marry her?"

"It was broken off,—when I thought that I should be forced to go to India. The story is very long, and very sad. It is my own father who has ruined me. But I will tell it you some day." Then he told it all, as he was sitting there with his cigar in his hand. Stories may seem to be very long, and yet be told very quickly.

"But you will go back to her now?" said Edith.

"She has not waited for me."

"What do you mean?"

"They tell me that she is to be married to a—to a—certain Mr. Gilmore."

"Already!"

"He had offered to her twenty times before I ever saw her. She never loved him, and does not now."

"Who has told you this, Captain Marrable?" She had not intended to alter her form of speech, and when she had done so would have given anything to have called him then by his Christian name.

"My Uncle John."

"I would ask herself."

"I mean to do so. But somehow, treated as I am here, I am bound to tell my uncle of it first. And I cannot do that while Gregory is so ill."

"I must go up to my uncle now, Walter. And I do so hope she may be true to you. And I do so hope I may like her. Don't believe anything till she has told you herself." Saying this, Edith Brownlow returned to the house, and at once put her dream quietly out of her sight. She said nothing to her mother about it then. It was not necessary that she should tell her mother as yet.

CHAPTER LIX.

NEWS FROM DUNRIPPLE.

At the end of the first week in August news reached the vicarage at Bullhampton that was not indeed very important to the family of Mr. Fenwick, but which still seemed to have an immediate effect on their lives and comfort. The Vicar for some days past had been, as regarded himself, in a high good humour, in consequence of a communication which he had received from Lord St. George. Further mention of this communication must be made, but it may be deferred to the next chapter, as other matters, more momentous, require our immediate attention. Mr. Gilmore had pleaded very hard that a day might be fixed, and had almost succeeded. Mary Lowther, driven into a corner, had been able to give no reason why she should not fix a day, other than this,—that Mr. Gilmore had promised her that she should not be hurried. "What do you mean?" Mrs. Fenwick had said, angrily. "You speak of the man who is to be your husband as though your greatest happiness in life were to keep away from him." Mary Lowther had not dared to answer that such would be her greatest happiness. Then news had reached the vicarage of the illness of Gregory Marrable, and of Walter Marrable's presence at Dunripple. This had come of course from Aunt Sarah, at Loring; but it had come in such a manner as to seem to justify, for a time, Mary's silence in reference to that question of naming the day. The Marrables of Dunripple were not nearly related to her. She had no personal remembrance of either Sir Gregory or his son. But there was an importance attached to the tidings, which, if analysed, would have been found to attach itself to Captain Marrable, rather than to the two men who were ill; and this was tacitly allowed to have an influence. Aunt Sarah had expressed her belief that Gregory Marrable was dying; and had gone on to say,—trusting to the known fact that Mary had engaged herself to Mr. Gilmore, and to the fact, as believed to be a fact, that Walter was engaged to Edith Brownlow,—had gone on to say that Captain Marrable would probably remain at Dunripple, and would take immediate charge of the estate. "I think there is no doubt," said Aunt Sarah, "that Captain Marrable and Edith Brownlow will be married." Mary was engaged to Mr. Gilmore, and why should not Aunt Sarah tell her news?

The Squire, who had become elated and happy at the period of the rubies, had, in three days, again fallen away into a state of angry gloom, rather than of melancholy. He said very little just now either to Fenwick or to Mrs. Fenwick about his marriage; and, indeed, he did not say very much to Mary herself. Men were already at work about the gardens at the Privets, and he would report to her what was done, and would tell her that the masons and painters would begin in a few days. Now and again he would ask for her company up to the place; and she had been there twice at his instance since the day on which she had gone after him of her own accord, and had fetched him down to look at the jewels. But there was little or no sympathy between them. Mary could not bring herself to care about the house or the gardens, though she told herself again and again that there was she to live for the remainder of her life.

Two letters she received from her aunt at Loring within an interval of three days, and these letters were both filled with details as to the illness of Sir Gregory and his son, at Dunripple. Walter Marrable sent accounts to his uncle, the parson, and Mrs. Brownlow sent accounts to Miss Marrable herself. And then, on the day following the receipt of the last of these two letters, there came one from Walter Marrable himself, addressed to Mary Lowther. Gregory Marrable was dead, and the letter announcing the death of the baronet's only son was as follows:—

Dunripple, August 12, 1868.

MY DEAR MARY,

I hardly know whether you will have expected that the news which I have to tell you should reach you direct from me; but I think, upon the whole, that it is better that I should write. My cousin, Gregory Marrable, Sir Gregory's only son, died this morning. I do not doubt but that you know that he has been long ill. He has come to the end of all his troubles, and the old baronet is now childless. He also has been, and is still, unwell, though I do not know that he is much worse than usual. He has been an invalid for years and years. Of course he feels his son's death acutely; for he is a father who has ever been good to his son. But it always seems to me that old people become so used to death, that they do not think of it as do we who are younger. I have seen him twice to-day since the news was told to him, and though he spoke of his son with infinite sorrow, he was able to talk of other things.

I write to you myself, especially, instead of getting one of the ladies here to do so, because I think it proper to tell you how things stand with myself. Everything is changed with me since you and I parted because it was necessary that I should seek my fortune in India. You already know that I have abandoned that idea; and I now find that I shall leave the army altogether. My uncle has wished it since I first came here, and he now proposes that I shall live here permanently. Of course the meaning is that I should assume the position of his heir. My father, with whom I personally will have no dealing in the matter, stands between us. But I do suppose that the family affairs will be so arranged that I may feel secure that I shall not be turned altogether adrift upon the world.

Dear Mary,—I do not know how to tell you, that as regards my future everything now depends on you. They have told me that you have accepted an offer from Mr. Gilmore. I know no more than this,—that they have told me so. If you will tell me also that you mean to be his wife, I will say no more. But until you tell me so, I will not believe it. I do not think that you can ever love him as you certainly once loved me;—and when I think of it, how short a time ago that was! I know that I have no right to complain. Our separation was my doing as much as yours. But I will settle nothing as to my future life till I hear from yourself whether or no you will come back to me.

I shall remain here till after the funeral, which will take place on Friday. On Monday I shall go back to Birmingham. This is Sunday, and I shall expect to hear from you before the week is over. If you bid me, I will be with you early next week. If you tell me that my coming will be useless,—why, then, I shall care very little what happens.

Yours, with all the love of my heart,

WALTER MARRABLE.

Luckily for Mary she was alone when she read the letter. Her first idea on reading it was to think of the words which she had used when she had most ungraciously consented to become the wife of Harry Gilmore. "Were he so placed that he could afford to marry a poor wife, I should leave you and go to him." She remembered them accurately. She had made up her mind at the time that she would say them, thinking that thus he would be driven from her, and that she would be at rest from his solicitation, from those of her friends, and from the qualms of her own conscience. He had chosen to claim her in spite of those words,—and now the thing had happened to the possibility of which she had referred. Poor as she was, Walter Marrable was able to make her his wife. She held in her hand his letter telling her that it was so. All her heart was his,—as much now as it had ever been; and it was impossible that she should not go to him. She had told Mr. Gilmore herself that she could never love again as she loved Walter Marrable. She had been driven to believe that she could never be his wife, and she had separated herself from him. She had separated herself from him, and persuaded herself that it would be expedient for her to become the wife of this other man. But up to this very moment she had never been able to overcome her horror at the prospect. From day to day she had thought that she must give it up, even when they were dinning into her ears the tidings that Walter Marrable was to marry that girl at Dunripple. But that had been a falsehood,—an absolute falsehood. There had been no such thought in his bosom. He had never been untrue to her. Ah! how much the nobler of the two had he been!

And yet she had struggled hard to do right,—to think of others more than of herself;—so to dispose of herself that she might be of some use in the world. And it had come to this! It was quite impossible now that she should marry Harry Gilmore. There had hitherto been at any rate an attempt on her part to reconcile herself to that marriage; but now the attempt was impossible. What right could she have to refuse the man she loved when he told her that all his happiness depended on her love! She could see it now. With all her desire to do right, she had done foul wrong in accepting Mr. Gilmore. She had done foul wrong, though she had complied with the advice of all her friends. It could not but have been wrong, as it had brought her to this,—her and him. But for the future, she might yet be right,—if she only knew how. That it would be wrong to marry Harry Gilmore,—to think of marrying him when her heart was so stirred by the letter which she held in her hand,—of that she was quite sure. She had done the man an injury for which she could never atone. Of that she was well aware. But the injury was done and could not now be undone. And had she not told him when he came to her, that she would even yet return to Walter Marrable if Walter Marrable were able to take her?

She went down stairs, slowly, just before the hour for the children's dinner, and found her friend, with one or two of the bairns, in the garden. "Janet," she said, "I have had a letter from Dunripple."

Mrs. Fenwick looked into her face, and saw that it was sad and sorrowful. "What news, Mary?"

"My cousin, Gregory Marrable, is—no more; he died on Sunday morning." This was on the Tuesday.

"You expected it, I suppose, from your aunt's letter?"

"Oh, yes;—it has been sudden at last, it seems."

"And Sir Gregory?"

"He is pretty well. He is getting better."

"I pity him the loss of his son;—poor old man!" Mrs. Fenwick was far too clever not to see that the serious, solemn aspect of Mary's face was not due altogether to the death of a distant cousin, whom she herself did not even remember;—but she was too wise, also, to refer to what she presumed to be Mary's special grief at the moment. Mary was doubtless thinking of the altered circumstances of her cousin Walter; but it was as well now that she should speak as little as possible about that cousin. Mrs. Fenwick could not turn altogether to another subject, but she would, if possible, divert her friend from her present thoughts. "Shall you go into mourning?" she asked; "he was only your second cousin; but people have ideas so different about those things."

"I do not know," said Mary, listlessly.

"If I were you, I would consult Mr. Gilmore. He has a right to be consulted. If you do, it should be very slight."

"I shall go into mourning," said Mary, suddenly,—remembering at the moment what was Walter's position in the household at Dunripple. Then the tears came up into her eyes, she knew not why; and she walked off by herself amidst the garden shrubs. Mrs. Fenwick watched her as she went, but could not quite understand it. Those tears had not been for a second cousin who had never been known. And then, during the last few weeks, Mary, in regard to herself, had been prone to do anything that Mr. Gilmore would advise, as though she could make up by obedience for the want of that affection which she owed to him. Now, when she was told that she ought to consult Mr. Gilmore, she flatly refused to do so.

Mary came up the garden a few minutes afterwards, and as she passed towards the house, she begged to be excused from going into lunch that day. Lord St. George was coming up to lunch at the vicarage, as will be explained in the next chapter.

CHAPTER LX.

LORD ST. GEORGE IS VERY CUNNING.

Lord St. George began to throw his oil upon the waters in reference to that unfortunate chapel at Bullhampton a day or two after his interview with his father in the lawyer's chambers. His father had found himself compelled to yield; had been driven, as it were, by the Fates, to accord to his son permission to do as his son should think best. There came to be so serious a trouble in consequence of that terrible mistake of Packer's, that the poor old Marquis was unable to defend himself from the necessity of yielding. On that day, before he left his son at Westminster, when their roads lay into the different council-chambers of the state, he had prayed hard that the oil might not be very oily. But his son would not bate him an inch of his surrender.

"He is so utterly worthless," the Marquis had said, pleading hard as he spoke of his enemy.

"I'm not quite sure, my lord, that you understand the man," St. George had said. "You hate him, and no doubt he hates you."

"Horribly!" ejaculated the Marquis.

"You intend to be as good as you know how to be to all those people at Bullhampton?"

"Indeed I do, St. George," said the Marquis, almost with tears in his eyes.

"And I shouldn't wonder if he did, too."

"But look at his life," said the Marquis.

"It isn't always easy to look at a man's life. We are always looking at men's lives, and always making mistakes. The bishop thinks he is a good sort of fellow, and the bishop isn't the man to like a debauched, unbelieving, reckless parson, who, according to your ideas, must be leading a life of open shame and profligacy. I'm inclined to think there must be a mistake."

The unfortunate Marquis groaned deeply as he walked away to the august chamber of the Lords.

These and such like are the troubles that sit heavy on a man's heart. If search for bread, and meat, and raiment, be set aside, then, beyond that, our happiness or misery here depends chiefly on success or failure in small things. Though a man when he turns into bed may be sure that he has unlimited thousands at his command, though all society be open to him, though he know himself to be esteemed handsome, clever, and fashionable, even though his digestion be good, and he have no doctor to deny him tobacco, champagne, or made dishes, still, if he be conscious of failure there where he has striven to succeed, even though it be in the humbling of an already humble adversary, he will stretch, and roll, and pine,—a wretched being. How happy is he who can get his fretting done for him by deputy!

Lord St. George wrote to the parson a few days after his interview with his father. He and Lord Trowbridge occupied the same house in London, and always met at breakfast; but nothing further was said between them during the remaining days in town upon the subject. Lord St. George wrote to the parson, and his father had left London for Turnover before Mr. Fenwick's answer was received.

> MY DEAR SIR,—(Lord St. George had said,)—My father has put into my hands your letter about the dissenting chapel at Bullhampton. It seems to me, that he has made a mistake, and that you are very angry. Couldn't we arrange this little matter without fighting? There is not a landlord in England more desirous of doing good to his tenants than my father; and I am quite willing to believe that there is not an incumbent in England more desirous of doing good to his parishioners than you. I leave London for Wiltshire on Saturday the 11th. If you will meet me I will drive over to Bullhampton on Monday the 13th.
>
> Yours truly,
>
> ST. GEORGE.
>
> No doubt you'll agree with me in thinking that internecine fighting in a parish between the landlord and the clergyman cannot be for the good of the people.

Thus it was that Lord St. George began to throw his oil upon the waters.

It may be a doubt whether it should be ascribed to Mr. Fenwick as a weakness or a strength that, though he was very susceptible of anger, and though he could maintain his anger at glowing heat as long as fighting continued, it would all evaporate and leave him harmless as a dove at the first glimpse of an olive-branch. He knew this so well of himself, that it would sometimes be a regret to him in the culmination of his wrath that he would not be able to maintain it till the hour of his revenge should come. On receiving Lord St. George's letter, he at once sat down and wrote to that nobleman, telling him that he would be happy to see him at lunch on the Monday at two o'clock. Then there came a rejoinder from Lord St. George, saying that he would be at the vicarage at the hour named.

Mrs. Fenwick was of course there to entertain the nobleman, whom she had never seen before, and during the lunch very little was said about the chapel, and not a word was said about other causes of complaint.

"That is a terrible building, Mrs. Fenwick," Lord St. George had remarked.

"We're getting used to it now," Mrs. Fenwick had replied; "and Mr. Fenwick thinks it good for purposes of mortification."

"We must see and move the sackcloth and ashes a little further off," said his lordship.

Then they ate their lunch, and talked about the parish, and expressed a joint hope that the Grinder would be hung at Salisbury.

"Now let us go and see the corpus delicti," said the Vicar as soon as they had drawn their chairs from the table.

The two men went out and walked round the chapel, and, finding it open, walked into it. Of course there were remarks made by both of them. It was acknowledged that it was ugly, misplaced, uncomfortable, detestable to the eye, and ear, and general feeling,—except in so far as it might suit the wants of people who were not sufficiently educated to enjoy the higher tone, and more elaborate language of the Church of England services. It was thus that they spoke to each other, quite in an æsthetic manner.

Lord St. George had said as he entered the chapel, that it must come down as a matter of course; and the Vicar had suggested that there need be no hurry.

"They tell me that it must be removed some day," said the Vicar, "but as I am not likely to leave the parish, nobody need start the matter for a year or two." Lord St. George was declaring that advantage could not be taken of such a concession on Mr. Fenwick's part, when a third person entered the building, and walked towards them with a quick step.

"Here is Mr. Puddleham, the minister," said Mr. Fenwick; and the future lord of Bullhampton was introduced to the present owner of the pulpit under which they were standing.

"My lord," said the minister, "I am proud, indeed, to have the honour of meeting your lordship in our new chapel, and of expressing to your lordship the high sense entertained by me and my congregation of your noble father's munificent liberality to us in the matter of the land."

In saying this Mr. Puddleham never once turned his face upon the Vicar. He presumed himself at the present moment to be at feud with the Vicar in most deadly degree. Though the Vicar would occasionally accost him in the village, he always answered the Vicar as though they two were enemies. He had bowed when he came up the chapel, but he had bowed to the stranger. If the Vicar took any of that courtesy to himself, that was not his fault.

"I'm afraid we were a little too quick there," said Lord St. George.

"I hope not, my lord; I hope not. I have heard a rumour; but I have inquired. I have inquired, and—"

"The truth is, Mr. Puddleham, that we are standing on Mr. Fenwick's private ground this moment."

"You are quite welcome to the use of it, Mr. Puddleham," said the Vicar. Mr. Puddleham assumed a look of dignity, and frowned. He could not even yet believe that his friend the Marquis had made so fatal a mistake.

"We must build you another chapel,—that will be about the long and short of it, Mr. Puddleham."

"My lord, I should think there must be some—mistake. Some error must have crept in somewhere, my lord. I have made inquiry—"

"It has been a very big error," said Lord St. George, "and it has crept into Mr. Fenwick's glebe in a very palpable form. There is no use in discussing it, Mr. Puddleham."

"And why didn't the reverend gentleman claim the ground when the works were commenced?" demanded the indignant minister, turning now for the first time to the Vicar, and doing so with a visage full of wrath, and a graceful uplifting of his right hand.

"The reverend gentleman was very ignorant of matters with which he ought to have been better acquainted," said Mr. Fenwick himself.

"Very ignorant, indeed," said Mr. Puddleham. "My lord, I am inclined to think that we can assert our right to this chapel and maintain it. My lord, I am of opinion that the whole hierarchy of the Episcopal Established Church in England cannot expel us. My lord, who will be the man to move the first brick from this sacred edifice?" And Mr. Puddleham pointed up to the pulpit as though he knew well where that brick was ever to be found when duty required its presence. "My lord, I would propose that nothing should be done; and then let us see who will attempt to close this chapel door against the lambs of the Lord who come here for pasture in their need."

"The lambs shall have pasture and shall have their pastor," said St. George, laughing. "We'll move this chapel to ground that is our own, and make everything as right as a trivet for you. You don't want to intrude, I'm sure."

Mr. Puddleham's eloquence was by no means exhausted; but at last, when they had left the chapel, and the ground immediately around the chapel which Mr. Puddleham would insist upon regarding as his own, they did manage to shake him off.

"And now, Mr. Fenwick," said Lord St. George, in his determined purpose to throw oil upon the waters, "what is this unfortunate quarrel between you and my father?"

"You had better ask him that, my lord."

"I have asked him, of course,—and of course he has no answer to make. No doubt you intended to enrage him when you wrote him that letter which he showed me."

"Certainly I did."

"I hardly see how good is to be done by angering an old man who stands high in the world's esteem."

"Had he not stood high, my lord, I should probably have passed him by."

"I can understand all that,—that one man should be a mark for another's scorn because he is a Marquis, and wealthy. But what I can't understand is, that such a one as you should think that good can come from it."

"Do you know what your father has said of me?"

"I've no doubt you both say very hard things of each other."

"I never said an evil thing of him behind his back that I have not said as strongly to his face," said Mr. Fenwick, with much of indignation in his tone.

"Do you really think that that mitigates the injury done to my father?" said Lord St. George.

"Do you know that he has complained of me to the bishop?"

"Yes,—and the bishop took your part."

"No thanks to your father, Lord St. George. Do you know that he has accused me publicly of the grossest vices; that he has,—that he has,—that he has—. There is nothing so bad that he hasn't said it of me."

"Upon my word, I think you are even with him, Mr. Fenwick, I do indeed."

"What I have said, I have said to his face. I have made no accusation against him. Come, my lord, I am willing enough to let bygones be bygones. If Lord Trowbridge will condescend to say that he will drop all animosity to me, I will forgive him the injuries he has done me. But I cannot admit myself to have been wrong."

"I never knew any man who would," said Lord St. George.

"If the Marquis will put out his hand to me, I will accept it," said the Vicar.

"Allow me to do so on his behalf," said the son.

And thus the quarrel was presumed to be healed. Lord St. George went to the inn for his horse, and the Vicar, as he walked across to the vicarage, felt that he had been—done. This young lord had been very clever,—and had treated the quarrel as though on even terms, as if the offences on each side had been equal. And yet the Vicar knew very well that he had been right,—right without a single slip,—right from the beginning to the end. "He has been clever," he said to himself, "and he shall have the advantage of his cleverness." Then he resolved that as far as he was concerned the quarrel should in truth be over.

CHAPTER LXI.

MARY LOWTHER'S TREACHERY.

While the Vicar was listening to the eloquence of Mr. Puddleham in the chapel, and was being cozened out of his just indignation by Lord St. George, a terrible scene was going on in the drawing-room of the vicarage. Mary Lowther, as the reader knows, had declared that she would wear mourning for her distant cousin, and had declined to appear at lunch before Lord St. George. Mrs. Fenwick, putting these things together, knew that much was the matter, but she did not know how much. She did not as yet anticipate the terrible state of things which was to be made known to her that afternoon.

Mary was quite aware that the thing must be settled. In the first place she must answer Captain Marrable's letter. And then it was her bounden duty to let Mr. Gilmore know her mind as soon as she knew it herself. It might be easy enough for her to write to Walter Marrable. That which she had to say to him would be pleasant enough in the saying. But that could not be said till the other thing should be unsaid. And how was that unsaying to be accomplished? Nothing could be done without the aid of Mrs. Fenwick; and now she was afraid of Mrs. Fenwick,—as the guilty are always afraid of those who will have to judge their guilt. While the children were at dinner, and while the lord was sitting at lunch, she remained up in her own room. From her window she could see the two men walking across the vicarage grounds towards the chapel, and she knew that her friend would be alone. Her story must be told to Mrs. Fenwick, and to Mrs. Fenwick only. It would be impossible for her to speak of her determination before the Vicar till he should have received a first notice of it from his wife. And there certainly must be no delay. The men were hardly out of sight before she had resolved to go down at once. She looked at herself in the glass, and spunged the mark of tears from her eyes, and smoothed her hair, and then descended. She never before had felt so much in fear of her friend; and yet it was her friend who was mainly the cause of this mischief which surrounded her, and who had persuaded her to evil. At Janet Fenwick's instance she had undertaken to marry a man whom she did not love; and yet she feared to go to Janet Fenwick with the story of her repentance. Why not indignantly demand of her friend assistance in extricating herself from the injury which that friend had brought upon her?

She found Mrs. Fenwick with the children in the little breakfast parlour to which they had been banished by the coming of Lord St. George. "Janet," she said, "come and take a turn with me in the garden." It was now the middle of August, and life at the vicarage was spent almost as much out of doors as within. The ladies went about with parasols, and would carry their hats hanging in their hands. There was no delay therefore, and the two were on the gravel-path almost as soon as Mary's request was made. "I did not show you my letter from Dunripple," she said, putting her hand into her pocket; "but I might as well do so now. You will have to read it."

She took out the document, but did not at once hand it to her companion. "Is there anything wrong, Mary?" said Mrs. Fenwick.

"Wrong. Yes;—very, very wrong. Janet, it is no use your talking to me. I have quite made up my mind. I cannot and I will not marry Mr. Gilmore."

"Mary, this is insanity."

"You may say what you please, but I am determined. I cannot and I will not. Will you help me out of my difficulty?"

"Certainly not in the way you mean;—certainly not. It cannot be either for your good or for his. After what has passed, how on earth could you bring yourself to make such a proposition to him?"

"I do not know; that is what I feel the most. I do not know how I shall tell him. But he must be told. I thought that perhaps Mr. Fenwick would do it."

"I am quite sure he will do nothing of the kind. Think of it, Mary. How can you bring yourself to be so false to a man?"

"I have not been false to him. I have been false to myself, but never to him. I told him how it was. When you drove me on—"

"Drove you on, Mary?"

"I do not mean to be ungrateful, or to say hard things; but when you made me feel that if he were satisfied I also might put up with it, I told him that I could never love him. I told him that I did love, and ever should love, Walter Marrable. I told him that I had nothing—nothing—nothing to give him. But he would take no answer but the one; and I did—I did give it him. I know I did; and I have never had a moment of happiness since. And now has come this letter. Janet, do not be cruel to me. Do not speak to me as though everything must be stern and hard and cruel." Then she handed up the letter, and Mrs. Fenwick read it as they walked.

"And is he to be made a tool, because the other man has changed his mind?" said Mrs. Fenwick.

"Walter has never changed his mind."

"His plans, then. It comes to the same thing. Do you know that you will have to answer for his life, or for his reason? Have you not learned yet to understand the constancy of his nature?"

"Is it my fault that he should be constant? I told him when he offered to me that if Walter were to come back to me and ask me again, I should go to him in spite of any promise that I had made. I said so as plain as I am saying this to you."

"I am quite sure that he did not understand it so."

"Janet, indeed he did."

"No man would have submitted himself to an engagement with such a condition. It is quite impossible. What! Mr. Gilmore knew when you took him that if this gentleman should choose to change his mind at any moment before you were actually married, you would walk off and go back to him!"

"I told him so, Janet. He will not deny that I told him so. When I told him so, I was sure that he would have declined such an engagement. But he did not, and I had no way of escape. Janet, if you could know what I have been suffering, you would not be cruel to me. Think what it would have been to you to have to marry a man you did not love, and to break the heart of one you did love. Of course Mr. Gilmore is your friend."

"He is our friend!"

"And, of course, you do not care for Captain Marrable?"

"I never even saw him."

"But you might put yourself in my place, and judge fairly between us. There has not been a thought or a feeling in my heart concealed from you since first all this began. You have known that I have never loved your friend."

"I know that, after full consideration, you have accepted him; and I know also, that he is a man who will devote his whole life to make you happy."

"It can never be. You may as well believe me. If you will not help me, nor Mr. Fenwick, I must tell him myself;—or I must write to him and leave the place suddenly. I know that I have behaved badly. I have tried to do right, but I have done wrong. When I came here I was very unhappy. How could I help being unhappy when I had lost all that I cared for in the world? Then you told me that I might at any rate be of some use to some one, by marrying your friend. You do not know how I strove to make myself fond of him! And then, at last, when the time came that I had to answer him, I thought that I would tell him everything. I thought that if I told him the truth he would see that we had better be apart. But when I told him, leaving him, as I imagined, no choice but to reject me,—he chose to take me. Well, Janet; at any rate, then, as I was taught to believe, there was no one to be ruined by this,—no one to be broken on the wheel,—but myself: and I thought that if I struggled, I might so do my duty that he might be satisfied. I see that I was wrong, but you should not rebuke me for it. I had tried to do as you bade me. But I did tell him that if ever this thing happened I should leave him. It has happened, and I must leave him." Mrs. Fenwick had let her speak on without interrupting her, intending when she had finished, to say definitely, that they at the vicarage could not make themselves parties to any treason towards Mr. Gilmore; but when Mary had come to the end of her story her friend's heart was softened towards her. She walked silently along the path, refraining at any rate from those bitter arguments with which she had at first thought to confound Mary in her treachery. "I do think you love me," said Mary.

"Indeed I love you."

"Then help me; do help me. I will go on my knees to him to beg his pardon."

"I do not know what to say to it. Begging his pardon will be of no avail. As for myself, I should not dare to tell him. We used to think, when he was hopeless before, that dwelling on it all would drive him to some absolute madness. And it will be worse now. Of course it will be worse."

"What am I to do?" Mary paused a moment, and then added, sharply,— "There is one thing I will not do; I will not go to the altar and become his wife."

"I suppose I had better tell Frank," said Mrs. Fenwick, after another pause.

This was, of course, what Mary Lowther desired, but she begged for and obtained permission not to see the Vicar herself that evening. She would keep her own room that night, and meet him the next morning before prayers as best she might.

When the Vicar came back to the house, his mind was so full of the chapel, and Lord St. George, and the admirable manner in which he had been cajoled out of his wrath without the slightest admission on the part of the lord that his father had ever been wrong,—his thoughts were so occupied with all this, and with Mr. Puddleham's oratory, that he did not at first give his wife an opportunity of telling Mary Lowther's story.

"We shall all of us have to go over to Turnover next week," he said.

"You may go. I won't."

"And I shouldn't wonder if the Marquis were to offer me a better living, so that I might be close to him. We are to be the lamb and the wolf sitting down together."

"And which is to be the lamb?"

"That does not matter. But the worst of it is, Puddleham won't come and be a lamb too. Here am I, who have suffered pretty nearly as much as St. Paul, have forgiven all my enemies all round, and shaken hands with the Marquis by proxy, while Puddleham has been man enough to maintain the dignity of his indignation. The truth is, that the possession of a grievance is the one state of human blessedness. As long as the chapel was there, malgré moi, I could revel in my wrong. It turns out now that I can send poor Puddleham adrift to-morrow, and he immediately becomes the hero of the hour. I wish your brother-in-law had not been so officious in finding it all out."

Mrs. Fenwick postponed her story till the evening.

"Where is Mary?" Fenwick asked, when dinner was announced.

"She is not quite well, and will not come down. Wait awhile, and you shall be told." He did wait; but the moment that they were alone again he asked his question. Then Mrs. Fenwick told the whole story, hardly expressing an opinion herself as she told it. "I don't think she is to be shaken," she said at last.

"She is behaving very badly,—very badly,—very badly."

"I am not quite sure, Frank, whether we have behaved wisely," said his wife.

"If it must be told him, it will drive him mad," said Fenwick.

"I think it must be told."

"And I am to tell it?"

"That is what she asks."

"I can't say that I have made up my mind; but, as far as I can see at present, I will do nothing of the kind. She has no right to expect it."

Before they went to bed, however, he also had been somewhat softened. When his wife declared, with tears in her eyes, that she would never interfere at match-making again, he began to perceive that he also had endeavoured to be a match-maker and had failed.

CHAPTER LXII.

UP AT THE PRIVETS.

The whole of the next day was passed in wretchedness by the party at the vicarage. The Vicar, as he greeted Miss Lowther in the morning, had not meant to be severe, having been specially cautioned against severity by his wife; but he had been unable not to be silent and stern. Not a word was spoken about Mr. Gilmore till after breakfast, and then it was no more than a word.

"I would think better of this, Mary," said the Vicar.

"I cannot think better of it," she replied.

He refused, however, to go to Mr. Gilmore that day, demanding that she should have another day in which to revolve the matter in her mind. It was understood, however, that if she persisted he would break the matter to her lover. Then this trouble was aggravated by the coming of Mr. Gilmore to the vicarage, though it may be that the visit was of use by preparing him in some degree for the blow. When he came Mary was not to be seen. Fancying that he might call, she remained up-stairs all day, and Mrs. Fenwick was obliged to say that she was unwell. "Is she really ill?" the poor man had asked. Mrs. Fenwick, driven hard by the difficulty of her position, had said that she did not believe Mary to be very ill, but that she was so discomposed by news from Dunripple that she could not come down. "I should have thought that I might have seen her," said Mr. Gilmore, with that black frown upon his brow which now they all knew so well. Mrs. Fenwick made no reply, and then the unhappy man went away. He wanted no further informant to tell him that the woman to whom he was pledged regarded her engagement to him with aversion.

"I must see her again before I go," Fenwick said to his wife the next morning. And he did see her. But Mary was absolutely firm. When he remarked that she was pale and worn and ill, she acknowledged that she had not closed her eyes during those two nights.

"And it must be so?" he asked, holding her hand tenderly.

"I am so grieved that you should have such a mission," she replied.

Then he explained to her that he was not thinking of himself, sad as the occasion would be to him. But if this great sorrow could have been spared to his friend! It could not, however, be spared. Mary was quite firm, at any rate as to that. No consideration should induce her now to marry Mr. Gilmore. Mr. Fenwick, on her behalf, might express his regret for the grief she had caused in any terms that he might think fit to use,—might humiliate her to the ground if he thought it proper. And yet, had not Mr. Gilmore sinned more against her than had she against him? Had not the manner in which he had grasped at her hand been unmanly and unworthy? But of this, though she thought much of it, she said nothing now to Mr. Fenwick. This commission to the Vicar was that he should make her free; and in doing this he might use what language, and make what confessions he pleased. He must, however, make her free.

After breakfast he started upon his errand with a very heavy heart. He loved his friend dearly. Between these two there had grown up now during a period of many years, that undemonstrative, unexpressed, almost unconscious affection which, with men, will often make the greatest charm of their lives, but which is held by women to be quite unsatisfactory and almost nugatory. It may be doubted whether either of them had ever told the other of his regard. "Yours always," in writing, was the warmest term that was ever used. Neither ever dreamed of suggesting that the absence of the other would be a cause of grief or even of discomfort. They would bicker with each other, and not unfrequently abuse each other. Chance threw them much together, but they never did anything to assist chance. Women, who love each other as well, will always be expressing their love, always making plans to be together, always doing little things each for the gratification of the other, constantly making presents backwards and forwards. These two men had never given any thing, one to the other, beyond a worn-out walking-stick, or a cigar. They were rough to each other, caustic, and almost ill-mannered. But they thoroughly trusted each other; and the happiness, prosperity, and, above all, the honour of the one were, to the other, matters of keenest moment. The bigger man of the two, the one who felt rather than knew himself to be the bigger, had to say that which would go nigh to break his friend's heart, and the task which he had in hand made him sick at his own heart. He walked slowly across the fields, turning over in his own mind the words he would use. His misery for his friend was infinitely greater than any that he had suffered on his own account, either in regard to Mr. Puddleham's chapel or the calumny of the Marquis.

He found Gilmore sauntering about the stable yard. "Old fellow," he said, "come along, I have got something to say to you."

"It is about Mary, I suppose?"

"Well, yes; it is about Mary. You mustn't be a woman, Harry, or let a woman make you seriously wretched."

"I know it all. That will do. You need not say anything more." Then he put his hands into the pockets of his shooting coat, and walked off as though all had been said that was necessary. Fenwick had told his message and might now go away. As for himself, in the sharpness of his agony he had as yet made no scheme for a future purpose. Only this he had determined. He would see that false woman once again, and tell her what he thought of her conduct.

But Fenwick knew that his task was not yet done. Gilmore might walk off, but he was bound to follow the unhappy man.

"Harry," he said, "you had better let me come with you for awhile. You had better hear what I have to say."

"I want to hear nothing more. What good can it be? Like a fool, I had set my fortune on one cast of the die, and I have lost it. Why she should have added on the misery and disgrace of the last few weeks to the rest, I cannot imagine. I suppose it has been her way of punishing me for my persistency."

"It has not been that, Harry."

"God knows what it has been. I do not understand it." He had turned from the stables towards the house, and had now come to a part of the grounds in which workmen were converting a little paddock in front of the house into a garden. The gardener was there with four or five labourers, and planks, and barrows, and mattocks, and heaps of undistributed earth and gravel were spread about. "Give over with this," he said to the gardener, angrily. The man touched his hat, and stood amazed. "Leave it, I say, and send these men away. Pay them for the work, and let them go."

"You don't mean as we are to leave it all like this, sir?"

"I do mean that you are to leave it just as it is." There was a man standing with a shovel in his hand levelling some loose earth, and the Squire, going up to him, took the shovel from him and threw it upon the ground. "When I say a thing, I mean it. Ambrose, take these men away. I will not have another stroke of work done here." The Vicar came up to him and whispered into his ear a prayer that he would not expose himself before the men; but the Squire cared nothing for his friend's whisper. He shook off the Vicar's hand from his arm and stalked away into the house.

Two rooms, the two drawing-rooms as they were called, on the ground floor had been stripped of the old paper, and were now in that state of apparent ruin which always comes upon such rooms when workmen enter them with their tools. There were tressels with a board across them, on which a man was standing at this moment, whose business it was to decorate the ceiling.

"That will do," said the Squire. "You may get down, and leave the place." The man stood still on his board with his eyes open and his brush in his hand. "I have changed my mind, and you may come down," said Mr. Gilmore. "Tell Mr. Cross to send me his bill for what he has done, and it shall be paid. Come down, when I tell you. I will have nothing further touched in the house." He went from room to room and gave the same orders, and, after a while, succeeded in turning the paper-hangers and painters out of the house. Fenwick had followed him from room to room, making every now and then an attempt at remonstrance; but the Squire had paid no attention either to his words or to his presence.

At last they were alone together in Gilmore's own study or office, and then the Vicar spoke. "Harry," he said, "I am, indeed, surprised that such a one as you should not have more manhood at his command."

"Were you ever tried as I am?"

"What matters that? You are responsible for your own conduct, and I tell you that your conduct is unmanly."

"Why should I have the rooms done up? I shall never live here. What is it to me how they are left? The sooner I stop a useless expenditure the better. It was being done for her, not for me."

"Of course you will live here."

"You know nothing about it. You cannot know anything about it. Why has she treated me in this way? To send up to a man and simply tell him that she has changed her mind! God in heaven!—that you should bring me such a message!"

"You have not allowed me to give my message yet."

"Give it me, then, and have done with it. Has she not sent you to tell me that she has changed her mind?"

Now that opportunity was given to him, the Vicar did not know how to tell his message. "Perhaps it would have been better that Janet should have come to you."

"It don't make much difference who comes. She'll never come again. I don't suppose, Frank, you can understand the sort of love I have had for her. You have never been driven by failure to such longing as mine has been. And then I thought it had come at last!"

"Will you be patient while I speak to you, Harry?" said the Vicar, again taking him by the arm. They had now left the house, and were out alone among the shrubs.

"Patient! yes; I think I am patient. Nothing further can hurt me now;—that's one comfort."

"Mary bids me remind you,"—Gilmore shuddered and shook himself when Mary Lowther's name was mentioned, but he did not attempt to stop the

Vicar,—"she bids me remind you that when the other day she consented to be your wife, she did so——." He tried to tell it all, but he could not. How could he tell the man the story which Mary had told to him?

"I understand," said Gilmore. "It's all of no use, and you are troubling yourself for nothing. She told me that she did not care a straw for me;—but she accepted me."

"If that was the case, you were both wrong."

"It was the case. I don't say who was wrong, but the punishment has come upon me only. Look here, Frank; I will not take this message from you. I will not even give her up yet. I have a right, at least, to see her, and see her I will. I don't suppose you will try to prevent me?"

"She must do as she pleases, Harry, as long as she is in my house."

"She shall see me. She is self-willed enough, but she shall not refuse me that. Be so good as to tell her with my compliments, that I expect her to see me. A man is not going to be treated like this, and then not speak his own mind. Be good enough to tell her that from me. I demand an interview." So saying he turned upon his heel, and walked quickly away through the shrubbery.

The Vicar stood for awhile to think, and then slowly returned to the vicarage by himself. What Gilmore had said to him was true enough. He had, indeed, never been tried after that fashion. It did seem to him that his friend was in fact broken-hearted. Harry Gilmore might live on,—as is the way with men and women who are broken-hearted;—but life for the present, life for some years to come, could be to him only a burden.

CHAPTER LXIII.

THE MILLER TELLS HIS TROUBLES.

When the Vicar went on his unhappy mission to the Squire's house Carry Brattle had been nearly two months at the mill. During that time both Mr. and Mrs. Fenwick had seen her more than once, and at last she had been persuaded to go to church with her sister. On the previous Sunday she had crept through the village at Fanny's side, and had taken a place provided for her in the dark corner of a dark pew under the protection of a thick veil. Fanny walked with her boldly across the village street, as though she were not in any slightest degree ashamed of her companion, and sat by her side, and then conveyed her home. On the next Sunday the sacrament would be given, and this was done in preparation for that day.

Things had not gone very pleasantly at the mill. Up to this moment old Brattle had expressed no forgiveness towards his daughter, had uttered no word of affection to her, had made no sign that he had again taken her to his bosom as his own child. He had spoken to her, because in the narrow confines of their home it was almost impossible that he should live in the house with her without doing so. Carry had gradually fallen into the way of doing her share of the daily work. She cooked, and baked, and strove hard that her presence in the house should be found to be a comfort. She was useful, and the very fact of her utility brought her father into a certain state of communion with her; but he never addressed her specially, never called her by her name, and had not yet even acknowledged to his wife or to Fanny that he recognised her as one of the family. They had chosen to bring her in against his will, and he would not turn their guest from the door. It was thus that he seemed to regard his daughter's presence in the mill-house.

Under this treatment Carry was becoming restive and impatient. On such an occasion as that of going to church and exposing herself to the eyes of those who had known her as an innocent, laughing, saucy girl, she could not but be humble, quiet, and awestruck; but at home she was beginning again gradually to assert her own character. "If father won't speak to me, I'd better go," she said to Fanny.

"And where will you go to, Carry?"

"I dun' know;—into the mill-pond would be best for them as belongs to me. I suppose there ain't anybody as 'd have me?"

"Nobody can have you as will love you as we do, Carry."

"Why won't father come round and speak to me? You can't tell what it is to have him looking at one that way. I sometimes feels like getting up and telling him to turn me out if he won't speak a word to me." But Fanny had softened her, and encouraged her, bidding her wait still again, explaining the sorrow that weighed upon their father's heart as well as she could without saying a single cruel word as to Carry's past life. Fanny's task was not easy, and it was made the harder by their mother's special tenderness towards Carry. "The less she says and the more she does, the better for her," said Fanny to her mother. "You shouldn't let her talk about father." Mrs. Brattle did not attempt to argue the matter with her elder daughter, but she found it to be quite out of her power to restrain Carry's talking.

During these two months old Brattle had not even seen either his landlord or the Vicar. They had both been at the mill, but the miller had kept himself up among his grist, and had not condescended to come down to them. Nor had he even, since Carry's return, been seen in Bullhampton, or even up on the high road leading to it. He held no communion with men other than was absolutely necessary for his business, feeling himself to be degraded, not so much by his daughter's fall as by his concession to his fallen daughter. He would sit out in the porch of an evening, and smoke his pipe; but if he heard a footstep on the lane he would retreat, and cross the plank and get among the wheels of his mill, or out into the orchard. Of Sam nothing had been heard. He was away, it was believed in Durham, working at some colliery engine. He gave no sign of himself to his mother or sister; but it was understood that he would appear at the assizes, towards the end of the present month, as he had been summoned there as a witness at the trial of the two men for the murder of Mr. Trumbull.

And Carry, also, was to be a witness at the assizes; and, as it was believed, a witness much more material than her brother. Indeed, it was beginning to be thought that after all Sam would have no evidence to give. If, indeed, he had had nothing to do with the murder, it was not probable that any of the circumstances of the murder would have been confided to him. He had, it seemed, been on intimate terms with the man Acorn,—and, through Acorn, had known Burrows and the old woman who lived at Pycroft Common, the mother of Burrows. He had been in their company when they first visited Bullhampton, and had, as we know, invited them into the Vicar's garden,— much to the damage of Mr. Burrows' shoulder-blade; but it was believed that beyond this he could say nothing as to the murder. But Carry Brattle was presumed to have a closer knowledge of at least one of the men. She had now confessed to her sister that, after leaving Bullhampton, she had consented to become Acorn's wife. She had known then but little of his mode of life or past history; but he was young, good-looking, fairly well-dressed, and had promised to marry her. By him she was taken to the cottage on Pycroft Common, and by him she had certainly been visited on the morning after the murder. He had visited her and given her money;—and since that, according to her own story, she had neither seen him nor heard from him. She had never cared for him, she told her sister; but what was that to one such as her as long as he would make her an honest woman? All this was repeated by Fanny Brattle to Mrs. Fenwick;—and now the assizes were at hand, and how was Carry to demean herself there? Who would take her? Who would stand near her and support her, and save her from falling into that abyss of self-abasement and almost of self-annihilation which would be her doom, unless there were some one there to give her strength and aid?

"I would not go to Salisbury at all during the assizes, if I were you," Mrs. Fenwick had said to her husband. The Vicar understood thoroughly what was meant. Because of the evil things which had been said of him by that stupid old Marquis whom he had been cheated into forgiving, he was not to be allowed to give a helping hand to his parishioner! Nevertheless, he acknowledged his wife's wisdom,—tacitly, as is fitting when such acknowledgments have to be made; and he contented himself with endeavouring to find for her some other escort. It had been hoped from day to day that the miller would yield, that he would embrace poor Carry, and promise her that she should again be to him as a daughter. If this could be brought about, then,—so thought the Vicar and Fanny too,—the old man would steel himself to bear the eyes of the whole county, and would accompany the girl himself. But now the day was coming on, and Brattle seemed to be as far from yielding as ever. Fanny had dropped a word or two in his hearing about the assizes, but he had only glowered at her, taking no other notice whatever of her hints.

When the Vicar left his friend Gilmore, as has been told in the last chapter, he did not return to the vicarage across the fields, but took the carriage road down to the lodge, and from thence crossed the stile that led into the path down to the mill. This was on the 15th of August, a Wednesday, and Carry was summoned to be at Salisbury on that day week. As the day drew near she became very nervous. At the Vicar's instance Fanny had written to her brother George, asking him whether he would be good to his poor sister, and take her under his charge. He had written back,—or rather his wife had written for him,—sending Carry a note for £20 as a present, but declining, on the score of his own children, to be seen with her in Salisbury on the occasion. "I shall go with her myself, Mr. Fenwick," Fanny had said to the Vicar; "it'll just be better than nobody at all to be along with her." The Vicar was now going down to the mill to give his assent to this. He could see nothing better. Fanny at any rate would be firm; would not be prevented by false shame from being a very sister to her sister; and would perhaps be admitted where a brother's attendance might be refused. He had promised to see the women at the mill as early in the week as he could, and now he went thither intent on giving them advice as to their proceedings at Salisbury.

It would doubtless be necessary that they should sleep there, and he hoped that they might be accommodated by Mrs. Stiggs.

As he stepped out from the field path on to the lane, almost immediately in front of the mill, he came directly upon the miller. It was between twelve and one o'clock, and old Brattle was wandering about for a minute or two waiting for his dinner. The two men met so that it was impossible that they should not speak; and on this occasion the miller did not seem to avoid his visitor. "Muster Fenwick," said he, as he took the Vicar's hand, "I am bound to say as I'm much obliged to ye for all y' have done for that poor lass in there."

"Don't say a word about that, Mr. Brattle."

"But I must say a word. There's money owing as I knows. There was ten shilling a week for her keep all that time she was at Salsbry yonder."

"I will not hear a word as to any money."

"Her brother George has sent her a gift, Muster Fenwick,—twenty pound."

"I am very glad to hear it."

"George is a well-to-do man, they tell me," continued the father, "and can afford to part with his money. But he won't come forward to help the girl any other gait. I'll thank you just to take what's due, Muster Fenwick, and you can give her sister the change. Our Fanny has got the note as George sent."

Then there was a dispute about the money, as a matter of course. Fenwick swore that nothing was due, and the miller protested that as the money was there all his daughter's expenses at Salisbury should be repaid. And the miller at last got the best of it. Fenwick promised that he would look to his book, see how much he had paid, and mention the sum to Fanny at some future time. He positively refused to take the note at present, protesting that he had no change, and that he would not burden himself with the responsibility of carrying so much money about with him in his pocket. Then he asked whether, if he went into the house, he would be able to say a word or two to the women before dinner. He had made up his mind that he would make no further attempt at reconciling the father to his daughter. He had often declared to his wife that there could be nothing so hateful to a man as the constant interference of a self-constituted adviser. "I so often feel that I am making myself odious when I am telling them to do this or that; and then I ask myself what I should say if anybody were to come and advise me how to manage you and the bairns." And he had told his wife more than once how very natural and reasonable had been the expression of the lady's wrath at Startup, when he had taken upon himself to give her advice. "People know what is good for them to do, well enough, without being dictated to by a clergyman!" He had repeated the words to himself and to his wife a dozen times, and talked of having them put up in big red letters over the fire-place in his own study. He had therefore quite determined to say never another word to old Brattle in reference to his daughter Carry. But now the miller himself began upon the subject.

"You can see 'em, Muster Fenwick, in course. It don't make no odds about dinner. But I was wanting just to say a word to you about that poor young ooman there." This he said in a slow, half-hesitating voice, as though he could hardly bring himself to speak of the unfortunate one to whom he alluded. The Vicar muttered some word of assent, and then the miller went on. "You knows, of course, as how she be back here at the mill?"

"Certainly I do. I've seen her more than once."

"Muster Fenwick, I don't suppose as any one as asn't tried it knows what it is. I hopes you mayn't never know it; nor it ain't likely. Muster Fenwick, I'd sooner see her dead body stretched afore me,—and I loved her a'most as well as any father ever loved his da'ter,—I'd sooner a see'd her brought home to the door stiff and stark than know her to be the thing she is." His hesitation had now given way to emphasis, and he raised his hand as he spoke. The Vicar caught it and held it in his own, and strove to find some word to say as the old man paused in his speech. But to Jacob Brattle it was hard for a clergyman to find any word to say on such an occasion. Of what use could it be to preach of repentance to one who believed nothing; or to tell of the opportunity which forgiveness by an earthly parent might afford to the sinner of obtaining lasting forgiveness elsewhere? But let him have said what he might, the miller would not have listened. He was full of that which lay upon his own heart. "If they only know'd what them as cares for 'em 'd has to bear, maybe they'd think a little. But it ain't natural they should know, Muster Fenwick, and one's a'most tempted to say that a man 'd better have no child at all."

"Think of your son George, Mr. Brattle, and of Mrs. Jay."

"What's them to me? He sends the girl a twenty-pun'-note, and I wish he'd a kep' it. As for t'other, she wouldn't let the girl inside her door! It's here she has to come."

"What comfort would you have, Mr. Brattle, without Fanny?"

"Fanny! I'm not saying nothing against Fanny. Not but what she hadn't no business to let the girl into the house in the middle of the night without saying a word to me."

"Would you have had her leave her sister outside in the cold and damp all night?"

"Why didn't she come and ax? All the same, I ain't a saying nowt again Fanny. But, Muster Fenwick, if you ever come to have one foot bad o' the gout, it won't make you right to know that the other ain't got it. Y'll have the pain a gnawing of you from the bad foot till you clean forget all the rest o' your body. It's so with me, I knows."

"What can I say to you, Mr. Brattle? I do feel for you. I do,—I do."

"Not a doubt on it, Muster Fenwick. They all on 'em feels for me. They all on 'em knows as how I'm bruised and mangled a'most as though I'd fallen through into that water-wheel. There ain't one in all Bull'ompton as don't know as Jacob Brattle is a broken man along of his da'ter that is a—"

"Silence, Mr. Brattle. You shall not say it. She is not that;—at any rate not now. Have you no knowledge that sin may be left behind and deserted as well as virtue?"

"It ain't easy to leave disgrace behind, any ways. For ought I knows a girl may be made right arter a while; but as for her father, nothing 'll ever make him right again. It's in here, Muster Fenwick,—in here. There's things as is hard on us; but when they comes one can't send 'em away just because they is hardest of all to bear. I'd a put up with aught, only this, and defied all Bull'ompton to say as it broke me;—but I'm about broke now. If I hadn't more nor a crust at home, nor a decent coat to my back, I'd a looked 'em all square in the face as ever I did. But I can't look no man square in the face now;—and as for other folk's girls, I can't bear 'em near me,—no how. They makes me think of my own." Fenwick had now turned his back to the miller, in order that he might wipe away his tears without showing them. "I'm thinking of her always, Muster Fenwick;—day and night. When the mill's agoing, it's all the same. It's just as though there warn't nothing else in the whole world as I minded to think on. I've been a man all my life, Muster Fenwick; and now I ain't a man no more."

"It's in here, Muster Fenwick,—in here."

Our friend the Vicar never before felt himself so utterly unable to administer comfort in affliction. There was nothing on which he could take hold. He could tell the man, no doubt, that beyond all this there might be everlasting joy, not only for him, but for him and the girl together;—joy which would be sullied by no touch of disgrace. But there was a stubborn strength in the infidelity of this old Pagan which was utterly impervious to any adjuration on that side. That which he saw and knew and felt, he would believe; but he would believe nothing else. He knew now that he was wounded and sore and wretched, and he understood the cause. He knew that he must bear his misery to the last, and he struggled to make his back broad for the load. But even the desire for ease, which is natural to all men, would not make him flinch in his infidelity. As he would not believe when things went well with him, and when the comfort of hope for the future was not imperatively needed for his daily solace,—so would he not believe now, when his need for such comfort was so pressing.

The upshot of it all was, that the miller thought that he would take his own daughter into Salisbury, and was desirous of breaking the matter in this way to the friend of his family. The Vicar, of course, applauded him much. Indeed, he applauded too much;—for the miller turned on him and declared that he was by no means certain that he was doing right. And when the Vicar asked him to be gentle with the girl, he turned upon him again.

"Why ain't she been gentle along of me? I hates such gentility, Muster Fenwick. I'll be honest with her, any way." But he thought better of it before he let the Vicar go. "I shan't do her no hurt, Muster Fenwick. Bad as she's been, she's my own flesh and blood still."

After what he had heard, Mr. Fenwick declined going into the mill-house, and returned home without seeing Mrs. Brattle and her daughters. The miller's determination should be told by himself; and the Vicar felt that he could hardly keep the secret were he now to see the women.

CHAPTER LXIV.

IF I WERE YOUR SISTER!

Mr. Gilmore in his last words to his friend Fenwick, declared that he would not accept the message which the Vicar delivered to him as the sufficient expression of Mary's decision. He would see Mary Lowther herself, and force her to confess her own treachery face to face with him,—to confess it or else to deny it. So much she could not refuse to grant him. Fenwick had indeed said that as long as the young lady was his guest she must be allowed to please herself as to whom she would see or not see. Gilmore should not be encouraged to force himself upon her at the vicarage. But the Squire was quite sure that so much as that must be granted to him. It was impossible that even Mary Lowther should refuse to see him after what had passed between them. And then, as he walked about his own fields, thinking of it all, he allowed himself to feel a certain amount of hope that after all she might be made to marry him. His love for her had not dwindled,—or rather his desire to call her his own, and to make her his wife; but it had taken an altered form out of which all its native tenderness had been pressed by the usage to which he had been subjected. It was his honour rather than his love that he now desired to satisfy. All those who knew him best were aware that he had set his heart upon this marriage, and it was necessary to him that he should show them that he was not to be disappointed. Mary's conduct to him from the day on which she had first engaged herself to him had been of such a kind as naturally to mar his tenderness and to banish from him all those prettinesses of courtship in which he would have indulged as pleasantly as any other man. She had told him in so many words that she intended to marry him without loving him, and on these terms he had accepted her. But in doing so he had unconsciously flattered himself that she would be better than her words,—that as she submitted herself to him as his affianced bride she would gradually become soft and loving in his hands. She had, if possible, been harder to him even than her words. She had made him understand thoroughly that his presence was not a joy to her, and that her engagement to him was a burden on her which she had taken on her shoulders simply because the romance of her life had been nipped in the bud in reference to the man whom she did love. Still he had persevered. He had set his heart sturdily on marrying this girl, and marry her he would, if, after any fashion, such marriage should come within his power. Mrs. Fenwick, by whose judgment and affection he had been swayed through all this matter, had told him again and again, that such a girl as Mary Lowther must love her husband,—if her husband loved her and treated her with tenderness. "I think I can answer for myself," Gilmore had once replied, and his friend had thoroughly believed in him. Trusting to the assurance he had persevered; he had persevered even when his trust in that assurance had been weakened by the girl's hardness. Anything would be better than breaking from an engagement on which he had so long rested all his hopes of happiness. She was pledged to be his wife; and, that being so, he could reform his gardens and decorate his house, and employ himself about his place with some amount of satisfaction. He had at least a purpose in his life. Then by degrees there grew upon him a fear that she still meant to escape from him, and he swore to himself,—without any tenderness,—that this should not be so. Let her once be his wife and she should be treated with all consideration,—with all affection, if she would accept it; but she should not make a fool of him now. Then the Vicar had come with his message, and he had been simply told that the engagement between them was over!

Of course he would see her,—and that at once. As soon as Fenwick had left him, he went with rapid steps over his whole place, and set the men again upon their work. This took place on a Wednesday, and the men should be continued at their work, at any rate, till Saturday. He explained this clearly to Ambrose, his gardener, and to the foreman in the house.

"It may be," said he to Ambrose, "that I shall change my mind altogether about the place;—but as I am still in doubt, let everything go on till Saturday."

Of course they all knew why it was that the conduct of the Squire was so like the conduct of a madman.

He sent down a note to Mary Lowther that evening.

> DEAR MARY,
>
> I have seen Fenwick, and of course I must see you. Will you name an hour for to-morrow morning?
>
> Yours, H. G.

When Mary read this, which she did as they were sitting on the lawn after dinner, she did not hesitate for a moment. Hardly a word had been said to her by Fenwick, or his wife, since his return from the Privets. They did not wish to show themselves to be angry with her, but they found conversation to be almost impossible. "You have told him?" Mary had asked. "Yes, I have told him," the Vicar had replied; and that had been nearly all. In the course of the afternoon she had hinted to Janet Fenwick that she thought she had better leave Bullhampton. "Not quite yet, dear," Mrs. Fenwick had said, and Mary had been afraid to urge her request.

"Shall I name eleven to-morrow?" she said, as she handed the Squire's note to Mrs. Fenwick. Mrs. Fenwick and the Vicar both assented, and then she went in and wrote her answer.

> I will be at home at the vicarage at eleven.—M. L.

She would have given much to escape what was coming, but she had not expected to escape it.

The next morning after breakfast Fenwick himself went away. "I've had more than enough of it," he said, to his wife, "and I won't be near them."

Mrs. Fenwick was with her friend up to the moment at which the bell was heard at the front door. There was no coming up across the lawn now.

"Dear Janet," Mary said, when they were alone, "how I wish that I had never come to trouble you here at the vicarage!"

Mrs. Fenwick was not without a feeling that much of all this unhappiness had come from her own persistency on behalf of her husband's friend, and thought that some expression was due from her to Mary to that effect. "You are not to suppose that we are angry with you," she said, putting her arm round Mary's waist.

"Pray,—pray do not be angry with me."

"The fault has been too much ours for that. We should have left this alone, and not have pressed it. We have meant it for the best, dear."

"And I have meant to do right;—but, Janet, it is so hard to do right."

When the ring at the door was heard, Mrs. Fenwick met Harry Gilmore in the hall, and told him that he would find Mary in the drawing-room. She pressed his hand warmly as she looked into his face, but he spoke no word as he passed on to the room which she had just left. Mary was standing in the middle of the floor, half-way between the window and the door, to receive him. When she heard the door-bell she put her hand to her heart, and there she held it till he was approaching; but then she dropped it and stood without support, with her face upraised to meet him. He came up to her very quickly and took her by the hand. "Mary," he said, "I am not to believe this message that has been sent to me. I do not believe it. I will not believe it. I will not accept it. It is out of the question;—quite out of the question. It shall be withdrawn, and nothing more shall be said about it."

"That cannot be, Mr. Gilmore."

"What cannot be? I say that it must be. You cannot deny, Mary, that you are betrothed to me as my wife. Are such betrothals to be nothing? Are promises to go for nothing because there has been no ceremony? You might as well come and tell me that you would leave me even though you were my wife."

"But I am not your wife."

"What does it mean? Have I not been patient with you? Have I been hard to you, or cruel? Have you heard anything of me that is to my discredit?" She shook her head, eagerly. "Then what does it mean? Are you aware that you are proposing to yourself to make an utter wreck of me—to send me adrift upon the world without a purpose or a hope? What have I done to deserve such treatment?"

He pleaded his cause very well,—better than she had ever heard him plead a cause before. He held her still by the hand, not with a grasp of love, but with a retention which implied his will that she should not pass away from out of his power. He looked her full in the face, and she did not quail before his eyes. Nevertheless she would have given the world to have been elsewhere, and to have been free from the necessity of answering him. She had been fortifying herself throughout the morning with self-expressed protests that on no account would she yield, whether she had been right before or wrong;—of this she was convinced, that she must be right now to save herself from a marriage that was so distasteful to her.

"You have deserved nothing but good at my hands," she said.

"And is this good that you are doing to me?"

"Yes,—certainly. It is the best that I know how to do now."

"Why is it to be done now? What is it that has changed you?"

She withdrew her hand from him, and waited a while before she answered. It was necessary that she should tell him all the tidings that had been conveyed to her in the letter which she had received from her cousin Walter; but in order that he should perfectly understand them and be made to know their force upon herself she must remind him of the stipulation which she had made when she consented to her engagement. But how could she speak words which would seem to him to be spoken only to remind him of the abjectness of his submission to her?

"I was broken-hearted when I came here," she said.

"And therefore you would leave me broken-hearted now."

"You should spare me, Mr. Gilmore. You remember what I told you. I loved my cousin Walter entirely. I did not hide it from you. I begged you to leave me because it was so. I told you that my heart would not change. When I said so, I thought that you would—desist."

"I am to be punished, then, for having been too true to you?"

"I will not defend myself for accepting you at last. But you must remember that when I did so I said that I should go—back—to him, if he could take me."

"And you are going back to him?"

"If he will have me."

"You can stand there and look me in the face and tell me that you are false as that! You can confess to me that you will change like a weathercock;—be his one day, and then mine, and his again the next! You can own that you give yourself about first to one man, and then to another, just as may suit you at the moment! I would not have believed it of any woman. When you tell it me of yourself, I begin to think that I have been wrong all through in my ideas of a woman's character."

The time had now come in which she must indeed speak up. And speech seemed to be easier with her now that he had allowed himself to express his anger. He had expressed more than his anger. He had dared to shower his scorn upon her, and the pelting of the storm gave her courage. "You are unjust upon me, Mr. Gilmore,—unjust and cruel. You know in your heart that I have not changed."

"Were you not betrothed to me?"

"I was;—but in what way? Have I told you any untruth? Have I concealed anything? When I accepted you, did I not explain to you how and why it was so,—against my own wish, against my own judgment,—because then I had ceased to care what became of me. I do care now. I care very much."

"And you think that is justice to me?"

"If you will bandy accusations with me, why did you accept me when I told you that I could not love you? But, indeed, indeed, I would not say a word to displease you, if you would only spare me. We were both wrong; but the wrong must now be put right. You would not wish to take me for your wife when I tell you that my heart is full of affection for another man. Then, when I yielded, I was struggling to cure that as a great evil. Now I welcome it as the sweetest blessing of my life. If I were your sister, what would you have me do?"

He stood silent for a moment, and then the colour rose to his forehead as he answered her. "If you were my sister, my ears would tingle with shame when your name was mentioned in my presence."

The blood rushed also over her face, suffusing her whole countenance, forehead and all, and fire flashed from her eyes, and her lips were parted, and even her nostrils seemed to swell with anger. She looked full into his face for a second, and then she turned and walked speechless away from him. When the handle of the door was in her hand, she turned again to address him. "Mr. Gilmore," she said, "I will never willingly speak to you again." Then the door was opened and closed behind her before a word had escaped from his lips.

He knew that he had insulted her. He knew that he had uttered words so hard, that it might be doubted whether, under any circumstances, they could be justified from a gentleman to a lady. And certainly he had not intended to insult her as he was coming down to the vicarage. As far as any settled purpose had been formed in his mind, he had meant to force her back to her engagement with himself, by showing to her how manifest would be her injustice, and how great her treachery, if she persisted in leaving him. But he knew her character well enough to be aware that any word of insult addressed to her as a woman, would create offence which she herself would be unable to quell. But his anger had got the better of his judgment, and when the suggestion was made to him of a sister of his own, he took the opportunity which was offered to him of hitting her with all his force. She had felt the blow, and had determined that she would never encounter another.

He was left alone, and he must retreat. He waited a while, thinking that perhaps Mrs. Fenwick or the Vicar would come to him; but nobody came. The window of the room was open, and it was easy for him to leave the house by the garden. But as he prepared to do so, his eye caught the writing materials on a side table, and he sat down and addressed a note to Mrs. Fenwick. "Tell Mary," he said, "that in a matter which to me is of life and death, I was forced to speak plainly. Tell her, also, that if she will be my wife, I know well that I shall never have to blush for a deed of hers,—or for a word,—or for a thought.—H. G." Then he went out on to the lawn, and returned home by the path at the back of the church farm.

He had left the vicarage, making another offer for the girl's hand, as it were, with his last gasp. But as he went, he told himself that it was impossible that it should be accepted. Every chance had now gone from him, and he must look his condition in the face as best he could. It had been bad enough with him before, when no hope had ever been held out to him; when the answers of the girl he loved had always been adverse to him; when no one had been told that she was to be his bride. Even then the gnawing sense of disappointment and of failure,—just there, when only he cared for success,—had been more than he could endure without derangement of the outer tranquillity of his life. Even then he had been unable so to live that men should not know that his sorrow had disturbed him. When he had gone to Loring, travelling with a forlorn hope into the neighbourhood of the girl he loved, he had himself been aware that he had lacked strength to control himself in his misfortune. But if his state then had been grievous, what must it be now? It had been told to all the world around him that he had at last won his bride, and he had proceeded, as do jolly thriving bridegrooms, to make his house ready for her reception. Doubting nothing he had mingled her wishes, her tastes, his thoughts of her, with every action of his life. He had prepared jewels for her, and decorated chambers, and laid out pleasure gardens. He was a man, simple in his own habits, and not given to squandering his means; but now, at this one moment of his life, when everything was to be done for the delectation of her who was to be his life's companion, he could afford to let prudence go by the board. True that his pleasure in doing this had been sorely marred by her coldness, by her indifference, even by her self-abnegation; but he had continued to buoy himself up with the idea that all would come right when she should be his wife. Now she had told him that she would never willingly speak to him again,—and he believed her.

He went up to his house, and into his bedroom, and then he sat thinking of it all. And as he thought he heard the voices and the tools of the men at their work; and knew that things were being done which, for him, would never be of avail. He remained there for a couple of hours without moving. Then he got up and gave the housekeeper instructions to pack up his portmanteau, and the groom orders to bring his gig to the door. "He was going away," he said, and his letters were to be addressed to his club in London. That afternoon he drove himself into Salisbury that he might catch the evening express train up, and that night he slept at a hotel in London.

CHAPTER LXV.

MARY LOWTHER LEAVES BULLHAMPTON.

It was considerably past one o'clock, and the children's dinner was upon the table in the dining parlour before anyone in the vicarage had seen Mary Lowther since the departure of the Squire. When she left Mr. Gilmore, she had gone to her own room, and no one had disturbed her. As the children were being seated, Fenwick returned, and his wife put into his hand the note which Gilmore had left for her.

"What passed between them?" he asked in a whisper.

His wife shook her head. "I have not seen her," she said, "but he talks of speaking plainly, and I suppose it was bitter enough."

"He can be very bitter if he's driven hard," said the Vicar; "and he has been driven very hard," he added, after a while.

As soon as the children had eaten their dinner, Mrs. Fenwick went up to Mary's room with the Squire's note in her hand. She knocked, and was at once admitted, and she found Mary sitting at her writing-desk.

"Will you not come to lunch, Mary?"

"Yes,—if I ought. I suppose I might not have a cup of tea brought up here?"

"You shall have whatever you like,—here or anywhere else, as far as the vicarage goes. What did he say to you this morning?"

"It is of no use that I should tell you, Janet."

"You did not yield to him, then?"

"Certainly, I did not. Certainly I never shall yield to him. Dear Janet, pray take that as a certainty. Let me make you sure at any rate of that. He must be sure of it himself."

"Here is his note to me, written, I suppose, after you left him." Mary took the scrap of paper from her hand and read it. "He is not sure, you see," continued Mrs. Fenwick. "He has written to me, and I suppose that I must answer him."

"He shall certainly never have to blush for me as his wife," said Mary. But she would not tell her friend of the hard words that had been said to her. She understood well the allusion in Mr. Gilmore's note, but she would not explain it. She had determined, as she thought about it in her solitude, that it would be better that she should never repeat to anyone the cruel words which her lover had spoken to her. Doubtless he had received provocation. All his anger, as well as all his suffering, had come from a constancy in his love for her, which was unsurpassed, if not unequalled, in all that she had read of among men. He had been willing to accept her on conditions most humiliating to himself; and had then been told, that, even with those conditions, he was not to have her. She was bound to forgive him almost any offence that he could bestow upon her. He had spoken to her in his wrath words which she thought to be not only cruel but unmanly. She had told him that she would never speak willingly to him again; and she would keep her word. But she would forgive him. She was bound to forgive him any injury, let it be what it might. She would forgive him;—and as a sign to herself of her pardon she would say no word of his offence to her friends, the Fenwicks. "He shall certainly never have to blush for me as his wife," she said, as she returned the note to Mrs. Fenwick.

"You mean, that you never will be his wife?"

"Certainly I mean that."

"Have you quarrelled with him, Mary?"

"Quarrelled? How am I to answer that? It will be better that we should not meet again. Of course, our interview could not be pleasant for either of us. I do not wish him to think that there has been a quarrel."

"No man ever did a woman more honour than he has done to you."

"Dearest Janet, let it be dropped;—pray let it be dropped. I am sure you believe me now when I say that it can do no good. I am writing to my aunt this moment to tell her that I will return. What day shall I name?"

"Have you written to your cousin?"

"No I have not written to my cousin. I have not been able to get through it all, Janet, quite so easily as that."

"I suppose you had better go now."

"Yes;—I must go now. I should be a thorn in his side if I were to remain here."

"He will not remain, Mary."

"He shall have the choice as far as I am concerned. You must let him know at once that I am going. I think I will say Saturday,—the day after to-morrow. I could hardly get away to-morrow."

"Certainly not. Why should you?"

"Yet I am bound to hurry myself,—to release him. And, Janet, will you give him these? They are all here,—the rubies and all. Ah, me! he touched me that day."

"How like a gentleman he has behaved always."

"It was not that I cared for the stupid stones. You know that I care nothing for anything of the kind. But there was a sort of trust in it,—a desire to show me that everything should be mine,—which would have made me love him,—if it had been possible."

"I would give one hand that you had never seen your cousin."

"And I will give one hand because I have," said Mary, stretching out her right arm. "Nay, I will give both; I will give all, because, having seen him, he is what he is to me. But, Janet, when you return to him these things say a gentle word from me. I have cost him money, I fear."

"He will think but little of that. He would have given you willingly the last acre of his land, had you wanted it."

"But I did not want it. That was the thing. And all these have been altered, as they would not have been altered, but for me. I do repent that I have brought all this trouble upon him. I cannot do more now than ask you to say so when you restore to him his property."

"He will probably pitch them into the cart-ruts. Indeed, I will not give them to him. I will simply tell him that they are in my hands, and Frank shall have them locked up at the banker's. Well;—I suppose I had better go down and write him a line."

"And I will name Saturday to my aunt," said Mary.

Mrs. Fenwick immediately went to her desk, and wrote to her friend.

> DEAR HARRY,
>
> I am sure it is of no use. Knowing how persistent is your constancy, I would not say so were I not quite, quite certain. She goes to Loring on Saturday. Will it not be better that you should come to us for awhile after she has left us. You will be less desolate with Frank than you would be alone.
>
> Ever yours,
>
> JANET FENWICK.
>
> She has left your jewels with me. I merely tell you this for your information;—not to trouble you with the things now.

And then she added a second postscript.

> She regrets deeply what you have suffered on her account, and bids me beg you to forgive her.

Thus it was settled that Mary Lowther should leave Bullhampton, again returning to Loring, as she had done before, in order that she might escape from her suitor. In writing to her aunt she had thought it best to say nothing of Walter Marrable. She had not as yet written to her cousin, postponing that work for the following day. She would have postponed it longer had it been possible; but she felt herself to be bound to let him have her reply before he left Dunripple. She would have much preferred to return to Loring, to have put miles between herself and Bullhampton, before she wrote a letter which must contain words of happy joy. It would have gratified her to have postponed for awhile all her future happiness, knowing that it was there before her, and that it would come to her at last. But it could not be postponed. Her cousin's letter was burning her pocket. She already felt that she was treating him badly in keeping it by her without sending him the reply that would make him happy. She could not bring herself to write the letter till the other matter was absolutely settled; and yet, all delay was treachery to him; for,—as she repeated to herself again and again,—there could be no answer but one. She had, however, settled it all now. On the Saturday morning she would start for Loring, and she would write her letter on the Friday in time for that day's post. Walter would still be at Dunripple on the Sunday, and on the Sunday morning her letter would reach him. She had studied the course of post between Bullhampton and her lover's future residence, and knew to an hour when her letter would be in his hands.

On that afternoon she could hardly maintain the tranquillity of her usual demeanour when she met the Vicar before dinner. Not a word, however, was said about Gilmore. Fenwick partly understood that he and his wife were in some degree responsible for the shipwreck that had come, and had determined that Mary was to be forgiven,—at any rate by him. He and his wife had taken counsel together, and had resolved that, unless circumstances should demand it, they would never again mention the Squire's name in Mary Lowther's hearing. The attempt had been made and had utterly failed, and now there must be an end of it. On the next morning he heard that Gilmore had gone up to London, and he went up to the Privets to learn what he could from the servants there. No one knew more than that the Squire's letters were to be directed to him at his Club. The men were still at work about the place; but Ambrose told him that they were all at sea as to what they should do, and appealed to him for orders. "If we shut off on Saturday, sir, the whole place'll be a muck of mud and nothin' else all winter," said the gardener. The Vicar suggested that after all a muck of mud outside the house wouldn't do much harm. "But master ain't the man to put up with that all'ays, and it'll cost twice as much to have 'em about the place again arter a bit." This, however, was the least trouble. If Ambrose was disconsolate out of doors, the man who was looking after the work indoors was twice more so. "If we be to work on up to Saturday night," he said, "and then do never a stroke more, we be a doing nothing but mischief. Better leave it at once nor that, sir." Then Fenwick was obliged to take upon himself to give certain orders. The papering of the rooms should be finished where the walls had been already disturbed, and the cornices completed, and the wood-work painted. But as for the furniture, hangings, and such like, they should be left till further orders should be received from the owner. As for the mud and muck in the garden, his only care was that the place should not be so left as to justify the neighbours in saying that Mr. Gilmore was demented. But he would be able to get instructions from his friend, or perhaps to see him, in time to save danger in that respect.

In the meantime Mary Lowther had gone up to her room, and seated herself with her blotting-book and pens and ink. She had now before her the pleasure,—or was it a task?—of answering her cousin's letter. She had that letter in her hand, and had already read it twice this morning. She had thought that she would so well know how to answer it; but, now that the pen was in her hand, she found that the thing to be done was not so easy. How much must she tell him, and how should she tell it? It was not that there was anything which she desired to keep back from him. She was willing,—nay, desirous,—that he should know all that she had said, and done, and thought; but it would have been a blessing if all could have been told to him by other agency than her own. He would not condemn her. Nor, as she thought of her own conduct back from one scene to another, did she condemn herself. Yet there was that of which she could not write without a feeling of shame. And then, how could she be happy, when she had caused so much misery? And how could she write her letter without expressing her happiness? She wished that her own identity might be divided, so that she might rejoice over Walter's love with the one moiety, and grieve with the other at all the trouble she had brought upon the man whose love to her had been so constant. She sat with the open letter in her hand, thinking over all this, till she told herself at last that no further thinking could avail her. She must bend herself over the table, and take the pen in her hand, and write the words, let them come as they would.

Her letter, she thought, must be longer than his. He had a knack of writing short letters; and then there had been so little for him to say. He had merely a single question to ask; and, although he had asked it more than once,—as is the manner of people in asking such questions,—still, a sheet of note-paper loosely filled had sufficed. Then she read it again. "If you bid me, I will be with you early next week." What if she told him nothing, but only bade him come to her? After all, would it not be best to write no more than that? Then she took her pen, and in three minutes her letter was completed.

The Vicarage, Friday.

DEAREST, DEAREST WALTER,

Do come to me,—as soon as you can, and I will never send you away again. I go to Loring to-morrow, and, of course, you must come there. I cannot write it all; but I will tell you everything when we meet. I am very sorry for your cousin Gregory, because he was so good.

Always your own,

MARY.

> But do not think that I want to hurry you. I have said come at once; but I do not mean that so as to interfere with you. You must have so many things to do; and if I get one line from you to say that you will come, I can be ever so patient. I have not been happy once since we parted. It is easy for people to say that they will conquer their feelings, but it has seemed to me to be quite impossible to do it. I shall never try again.

As soon as the body of her letter was written, she could have continued her postscript for ever. It seemed to her then as though nothing would be more delightful than to let the words flow on with full expressions of all her love and happiness. To write to him was pleasant enough, as long as there came on her no need to mention Mr. Gilmore's name.

That was to be her last evening at Bullhampton; and though no allusion was made to the subject, they were all thinking that she could never return to Bullhampton again. She had been almost as much at home with them as with her aunt at Loring; and now she must leave the place for ever. But they said not a word; and the evening passed by almost as had passed all other evenings. The remembrance of what had taken place since she had been at Bullhampton made it almost impossible to speak of her departure.

In the morning she was to be again driven to the railway-station at Westbury. Mr. Fenwick had work in his parish which would keep him at home, and she was to be trusted to the driving of the groom. "If I were to be away to-morrow," he said, as he parted from her that evening, "the churchwardens would have me up to the archdeacon, and the archdeacon might tell the Marquis, and where should I be then?" Of course she begged him not to give it a second thought. "Dear Mary," he said, "I should of all things have liked to have seen the last of you,—that you might know that I love you as well as ever." Then she burst into tears, and kissed him, and told him that she would always look to him as to a brother.

She called Mrs. Fenwick into her own room before she undressed. "Janet," she said, "dearest Janet, we are not to part for ever?"

"For ever! No, certainly. Why for ever?"

"I shall never see you, unless you will come to me. Promise me that if ever I have a house you will come to me."

"Of course you will have a house, Mary."

"And you will come and see me,—will you not? Promise that you will come to me. I can never come back to dear, dear Bullhampton."

"No doubt we shall meet, Mary."

"And you must bring the children—my darling Flos! How else ever shall I see her? And you must write to me, Janet."

"I will write,—as often as you do, I don't doubt."

"You must tell me how he is, Janet. You must not suppose that I do not care for his welfare because I have not loved him. I know that my coming here has been a curse to him. But I could not help it. Could I have helped it, Janet?"

"Poor fellow! I wish it had not been so."

"But you do not blame me;—not much? Oh, Janet, say that you do not condemn me."

"I can say that with most perfect truth. I do not blame you. It has been most unfortunate; but I do not blame you. I am sure that you have struggled to do the best that you could."

"God bless you, my dearest, dearest friend! If you could only know how anxious I have been not to be wrong. But things have been wrong, and I could not put them right."

On the next morning they packed her into the little four-wheeled phaeton, and so she left Bullhampton. "I believe her to be as good a girl as ever lived," said the Vicar; "but all the same, I wish with all my heart that she had never come to Bullhampton."

CHAPTER LXVI.

AT THE MILL.

The presence of Carry Brattle was required in Salisbury for the trial of John Burrows and Lawrence Acorn on Wednesday the 22nd of August. Our Vicar, who had learned that the judges would come into the city only late on the previous evening, and that the day following their entrance would doubtless be so fully occupied with other matters as to render it very improbable that the affair of the murder would then come up, had endeavoured to get permission to postpone Carry's journey; but the little men in authority are always stern on such points, and witnesses are usually treated as persons who are not entitled to have any views as to their own personal comfort or welfare. Lawyers, who are paid for their presence, may plead other engagements, and their pleas will be considered; and if a witness be a lord, it may perhaps be thought very hard that he should be dragged away from his amusements. But the ordinary commonplace witness must simply listen and obey—at his peril. It was thus decided that Carry must be in Salisbury on the Wednesday, and remain there, hanging about the Court, till her services should be wanted. Fenwick, who had been in Salisbury, had seen that accommodation should be provided for her and for the miller at the house of Mrs. Stiggs.

The miller had decided upon going with his daughter. The Vicar did not go down to the mill again; but Mrs. Fenwick had seen Brattle, and had learned that such was to be the case. The old man said nothing to his own people about it till the Monday afternoon, up to which time Fanny was prepared to accompany her sister. He was then told, when he came in from the mill for his tea, that word had come down from the vicarage that there would be two bed-rooms for them at Mrs. Stiggs' house. "I don't know why there should be the cost of a second room," said Fanny; "Carry and I won't want two beds."

Up to this time there had been no reconciliation between the miller and his younger daughter. Carry would ask her father whether she should do this or that, and the miller would answer her as a surly master will answer a servant whom he does not like; but the father, as a father, had never spoken to the child; nor, up to this moment, had he said a word even to his wife of his intended journey to Salisbury. But now he was driven to speak. He had placed himself in the arm chair, and was sitting with his hands on his knees gazing into the empty fire-grate. Carry was standing at the open window, pulling the dead leaves off three or four geraniums which her mother kept there in pots. Fanny was passing in and out from the back kitchen, in which the water for their tea was being boiled, and Mrs. Brattle was in her usual place with her spectacles on, and a darning needle in her hand. A minute was allowed to pass by before the miller answered his eldest daughter.

"There'll be two beds wanted," he said; "I told Muster Fenwick as I'd go with the girl myself;—and so I wull."

Carry started so that she broke the flower which she was touching. Mrs. Brattle immediately stopped her needle, and withdrew her spectacles from her nose. Fanny, who was that instant bringing the tea-pot out of the back kitchen, put it down among the tea cups, and stood still to consider what she had heard.

"Dear, dear, dear!" said the mother.

"Father," said Fanny, coming up to him, and just touching him with her hand; "'twill be best for you to go, much best. I am heartily glad on it, and so will Carry be."

"I knows nowt about that," said the miller; "but I mean to go, and that's all about it. I ain't a been to Salsbry these fifteen year and more, and I shan't be there never again."

"There's no saying that, father," said Fanny.

"And it ain't for no pleasure as I'm agoing now. Nobody 'll s'pect that of me. I'd liever let the millstone come on my foot."

There was nothing more said about it that evening, nothing more at least in the miller's hearing. Carry and her sister were discussing it nearly the whole night. It was very soon plain to Fanny that Carry had heard the tidings with dismay. To be alone with her father for two, three, or perhaps four days, seemed to her to be so terrible, that she hardly knew how to face the misery and gloom of his company,—in addition to the fears she had as to what they would say and do to her in the Court. Since she had been home, she had learned almost to tremble at the sound of her father's foot; and yet she had known that he would not harm her, would hardly notice her, would not do more than look at her. But now, for three long frightful days to come, she would be subject to his wrath during every moment of her life.

"Will he speak to me, Fanny, d'ye think?" she asked.

"Of course he'll speak to you, child."

"But he hasn't, you know,—not since I've been home; not once; not as he does to you and mother. I know he hates me, and wishes I was dead. And, Fanny, I wishes it myself every day of my life."

"He wishes nothing of the kind, Carry."

"Why don't he say one kind word to me, then? I know I've been bad. But I ain't a done a single thing since I've been home as 'd a' made him angry if he seed it, or said a word as he mightn't a' heard."

"I don't think you have, dear."

"Then why can't he come round, if it was ever so little? I'd sooner he'd beat me; that I would."

"He'll never do that, Carry. I don't know as he ever laid a hand upon one of us since we was little things."

"It 'd be better than never speaking to a girl. Only for you and mother, Fan, I'd be off again."

"You would not. You know you would not. How dare you say that?"

"But why shouldn't he say a word to one, so that one shouldn't go about like a dead body in the house?"

"Carry dear, listen to this. If you'll manage well; if you'll be good to him, and patient while you are with him; if you'll bear with him, and yet be gentle when he—"

"I am gentle,—always,—now."

"You are, dear; but when he speaks, as he'll have to speak when you're all alone like, be very gentle. Maybe, Carry, when you've come back, he will be gentle with you."

They had ever so much more to discuss. Would Sam be at the trial? And, if so, would he and his father speak to each other? They had both been told that Sam had been summoned, and that the police would enforce his attendance; but they were neither of them sure whether he would be there in custody or as a free man. At last they went to sleep, but Carry's slumbers were not very sound. As has been told before, it was the miller's custom to be up every morning at five. The two girls would afterwards rise at six, and then, an hour after that, Mrs. Brattle would be instructed that her time had come. On the Tuesday morning, however, the miller was not the first of the family to leave his bed. Carry crept out of hers by the earliest dawn of daylight, without waking her sister, and put on her clothes stealthily. Then she made her way silently to the front door, which she opened, and stood there outside waiting till her father should come. The morning, though it was in August, was chill, and the time seemed to be very long. She had managed to look at the old clock as she passed, and had seen that it wanted a quarter to five. She knew that her father was never later than five. What, if on this special morning he should not come, just because she had resolved, after many inward struggles, to make one great effort to obtain his pardon.

At last he was coming. She heard his step in the passage, and then she was aware that he had stopped when he found the fastenings of the door unloosed. She perceived too that he delayed to examine the lock,—as it was natural that he should do; and she had forgotten that he would be arrested by the open door. Thinking of this in the moment of time that was allowed to her, she hurried forward and encountered him.

"Father," she said; "it is I."

He was angry that she should have dared to unbolt the door, or to withdraw the bars. What was she, that she should be trusted to open or to close the house? And there came upon him some idea of wanton and improper conduct. Why was she there at that hour? Must it be that he should put her again from the shelter of his roof?

Carry was clever enough to perceive in a moment what was passing in the old man's mind. "Father," she said, "it was to see you. And I thought,—perhaps,—I might say it out here." He believed her at once. In whatever spirit he might accept her present effort, that other idea had already vanished. She was there that they two might be alone together in the fresh morning air, and he knew that it was so. "Father," she said, looking up into his face. Then she fell on the ground at his feet, and embraced his knees, and lay there sobbing. She had intended to ask him for forgiveness, but she was not able to say a word. Nor did he speak for awhile; but he stooped and raised her up tenderly; and then, when she was again standing by him, he stepped on as though he were going to the mill without a word. But he had not rebuked her, and his touch had been very gentle. "Father," she said, following him, "if you could forgive me! I know I have been bad, but if you could forgive me!"

He went to the very door of the mill before he turned; and she, when she saw that he did not come back to her, paused upon the bridge. She had used all her eloquence. She knew no other words with which to move him. She felt that she had failed, but she could do no more. But he stopped again without entering the mill.

"Child," he said at last, "come here, then." She ran at once to meet him. "I will forgive thee. There. I will forgive thee, and trust thou may'st be a better girl than thou hast been."

She flew to him and threw her arms round his neck and kissed his face and breast. "Oh, father," she said, "I will be good. I will try to be good. Only you will speak to me."

"Oh, father," she said, "I will be good."

"Get thee into the house now. I have forgiven thee." So saying he passed on to his morning's work.

Carry, running into the house, at once roused her sister. "Fanny," she exclaimed, "he has forgiven me at last; he has said that he will forgive me."

But to the miller's mind, and to his sense of justice, the forgiveness thus spoken did not suffice. When he returned to breakfast, Mrs. Brattle had, of course, been told of the morning's work, and had rejoiced greatly. It was to her as though the greatest burden of her life had now been taken from her weary back. Her girl, to her loving motherly heart, now that he who had in all things been the lord of her life had vouchsafed his pardon to the poor sinner, would be as pure as when she had played about the mill in all her girlish innocence. The mother had known that her child was still under a cloud, but the cloud to her had consisted in the father's wrath rather than in the feeling of any public shame. To her a sin repented was a sin no more, and her love for her child made her sure of the sincerity of that repentance. But there could be no joy over the sinner in this world till the head of the house should again have taken her to his heart. When the miller came in to his breakfast the three women were standing together, not without some outward marks of contentment. Mrs. Brattle's cap was clean, and even Fanny, who was ever tidy and never smart, had managed in some way to add something bright to her appearance. Where is the woman who, when she has been pleased, will not show her pleasure by some sign in her outward garniture? But still there was anxiety. "Will he call me Carry?" the girl had asked. He had not done so when he pronounced her pardon at the mill door. Though they were standing together they had not decided on any line of action. The pardon had been spoken and they were sure that it would not be revoked; but how it would operate at first none of them had even guessed.

The miller, when he had entered the room and come among them, stood with his two hands resting on the round table, and thus he addressed them: "It was a bad time with us when the girl, whom we had all loved a'most too well, forgot herself and us, and brought us to shame,—we who had never known shame afore,—and became a thing so vile as I won't name it. It was well nigh the death o' me, I know."

"Oh, father!" exclaimed Fanny.

"Hold your peace, Fanny, and let me say my say out. It was very bad then; and when she come back to us, and was took in, so that she might have her bit to eat under an honest roof, it was bad still;—for she was a shame to us as had never been shamed afore. For myself I felt so, that though she was allays near me, my heart was away from her, and she was not one with me, not as her sister is one, and her mother, who never know'd a thought in her heart as wasn't fit for a woman to have there." By this time Carry was sobbing on her mother's bosom, and it would be difficult to say whose affliction was the sharpest. "But them as falls may right themselves, unless they be chance killed as they falls. If my child be sorry for her sin—"

"Oh, father, I am sorry."

"I will bring myself to forgive her. That it won't stick here," and the miller struck his heart violently with his open palm, "I won't be such a liar as to say. For there ain't no good in a lie. But there shall be never a word about it more out o' my mouth,—and she may come to me again as my child."

There was a solemnity about the old man's speech which struck them all with so much awe that none of them for a while knew how to move or to speak. Fanny was the first to stir, and she came to him and put her arm through his and leaned her head upon his shoulder.

"Get me my breakfast, girl," he said to her. But before he had moved Carry had thrown herself weeping on his bosom. "That will do," he said. "That will do. Sit down and eat thy victuals." Then there was not another word said, and the breakfast passed off in silence.

Though the women talked of what had occurred throughout the day, not a word more dropped from the miller's mouth upon the subject. When he came in to dinner he took his food from Carry's hand and thanked her,—as he would have thanked his elder daughter,—but he did not call her by her name. Much had to be done in preparing for the morrow's journey, and for the days through which they two might be detained at the assizes. The miller had borrowed a cart in which he was to drive himself and his daughter to the Bullhampton road station, and, when he went to bed, he expressed his determination of starting at nine, so as to catch a certain train into Salisbury. They had been told that it would be sufficient if they were in the city that day at one o'clock.

On the next morning the miller was in his mill as usual in the morning. He said nothing about the work, but the women knew that it must in the main stand still. Everything could not be trusted to one man, and that man a hireling. But nothing was said of this. He went into his mill, and the women prepared his breakfast, and the clean shirt and the tidy Sunday coat in which he was to travel. And Carry was ready dressed for the journey;—so pretty, with her bright curls and sweet dimpled cheeks, but still with that look of fear and sorrow which the coming ordeal could not but produce. The miller returned, dressed himself as he was desired, and took his place at the table in the kitchen; when the front door was again opened,—and Sam Brattle stood among them!

"Father," said he, "I've turned up just in time."

Of course the consternation among them was great; but no reference was made to the quarrel which had divided the father and son when last they had parted. Sam explained that he had come across the country from the north, travelling chiefly by railway, but that he had walked from the Swindon station to Marlborough on the preceding evening, and from thence to Bullhampton that morning. He had come by Birmingham and Gloucester, and thence to Swindon.

"And now, mother, if you'll give me a mouthful of some'at to eat, you won't find that I'm above eating of it."

He had been summoned to Salisbury, he said, for that day, but nothing should induce him to go there till the Friday. He surmised that he knew a thing or two, and as the trial wouldn't come off before Friday at the earliest, he wouldn't show his face in Salisbury before that day. He strongly urged Carry to be equally sagacious, and used some energetic arguments to the same effect on his father, when he found that his father was also to be at the assizes; but the miller did not like to be taught by his son, and declared that as the legal document said Wednesday, on the Wednesday his daughter should be there.

"And what about the mill?" asked Sam. The miller only shook his head. "Then there's only so much more call for me to stay them two days," said Sam. "I'll be at it hammer and tongs, father, till it's time for me to start o' Friday. You tell 'em as how I'm coming. I'll be there afore they want me. And when they've got me they won't get much out of me, I guess."

To all this the miller made no reply, not forbidding his son to work the mill, nor thanking him for the offer. But Mrs. Brattle and Fanny, who could read every line in his face, knew that he was well-pleased.

And then there was the confusion of the start. Fanny, in her solicitude for her father, brought out a little cushion for his seat. "I don't want no cushion to sit on," said he; "give it here to Carry." It was the first time that he had called her by her name, and it was not lost on the poor girl.

CHAPTER LXVII.

SIR GREGORY MARRABLE HAS A HEADACHE.

Mary Lowther, in her letter to her aunt, had in one line told the story of her rupture with Mr. Gilmore. This line had formed a postscript, and the writer had hesitated much before she added it. She had not intended to write to her aunt on this subject; but she had remembered at the last moment how much easier it would be to tell the remainder of her story on her arrival at Loring, if so much had already been told beforehand. Therefore it was that she had added these words. "Everything has been broken off between me and Mr. Gilmore—for ever."

This was a terrible blow upon poor Miss Marrable, who, up to the moment of her receiving that letter, thought that her niece was disposed of in the manner that had seemed most desirable to all her friends. Aunt Sarah loved her niece dearly, and by no means looked forward to improved happiness in her own old age when she should be left alone in the house at Uphill; but she entertained the view about young women which is usual with old women who have young women under their charge, and she thought it much best that this special young woman should get herself married. The old women are right in their views on this matter; and the young women, who on this point are not often refractory, are right also. Miss Marrable, who entertained a very strong opinion on the subject above-mentioned, was very unhappy when she was thus abruptly told by her own peculiar young woman that this second engagement had been broken off and sent to the winds. It had become a theory on the part of Mary's friends that the Gilmore match was the proper thing for her. At last, after many difficulties, the Gilmore match had been arranged. The anxiety as to Mary's future life was at an end, and the theory of the elders concerned with her welfare was to be carried out. Then there came a short note, proclaiming her return home, and simply telling as a fact almost indifferent,—in a single line,—that all the trouble hitherto taken as to her own disposition had entirely been thrown away. "Everything has been broken off between me and Mr. Gilmore." It was a cruel and a heartrending postscript!

Poor Miss Marrable knew very well that she was armed with no parental authority. She could hold her theory, and could advise; but she could do no more. She could not even scold. And there had been some qualm of conscience on her part as to Walter Marrable, now that Walter Marrable had been taken in hand and made much of by the baronet,—and now, also, that poor Gregory had been removed from the path. No doubt she, Aunt Sarah, had done all in her power to aid the difficulties which had separated the two cousins;—and while she thought that the Gilmore match had been the consequence of such aiding on her part, she was happy enough in reflecting upon what she had done. Old Sir Gregory would not have taken Walter by the hand unless Walter had been free to marry Edith Brownlow; and though she could not quite resolve that the death of the younger Gregory had been part of the family arrangement due to the happy policy of the elder Marrables generally, still she was quite sure that Walter's present position at Dunripple had come entirely from the favour with which he had regarded the baronet's wishes as to Edith. Mary was provided for with the Squire, who was in immediate possession; and Walter with his bride would become as it were the eldest son of Dunripple. It was all as comfortable as could be till there came this unfortunate postscript.

The letter reached her on Friday, and on Saturday Mary arrived. Miss Marrable determined that she would not complain. As regarded her own comfort it was doubtless all for the best. But old women are never selfish in regard to the marriage of young women. That the young women belonging to them should be settled,—and thus got rid of,—is no doubt the great desire; but, whether the old woman be herself married or a spinster, the desire is founded on an adamantine confidence that marriage is the most proper and the happiest thing for the young woman. The belief is so thorough that the woman would cease to be a woman, would already have become a brute, who would desire to keep any girl belonging to her out of matrimony for the sake of companionship to herself. But no woman does so desire in regard to those who are dear and near to her. A dependant, distant in blood, or a paid assistant, may find here and there a want of the true feminine sympathy; but in regard to a daughter, or one held as a daughter, it is never wanting. "As the pelican loveth her young do I love thee; and therefore will I give thee away in marriage to some one strong enough to hold thee, even though my heartstrings be torn asunder by the parting." Such is always the heart's declaration of the mother respecting her daughter. The match-making of mothers is the natural result of mother's love; for the ambition of one woman for another is never other than this,—that the one loved by her shall be given to a man to be loved more worthily. Poor Aunt Sarah, considering of these things during those two lonely days, came to the conclusion that if ever Mary were to be so loved again that she might be given away, a long time might first elapse; and then she was aware that such gifts given late lose much of their value, and have to be given cheaply.

Mary herself, as she was driven slowly up the hill to her aunt's door, did not share her aunt's melancholy. To be returned as a bad shilling, which has been presented over the counter and found to be bad, must be very disagreeable to a young woman's feelings. That was not the case with Mary Lowther. She had, no doubt, a great sorrow at heart. She had created a shipwreck which she did regret most bitterly. But the sorrow and the regret were not humiliating, as they would have been had they been caused by failure on her own part. And then she had behind her the strong comfort of her own rock, of which nothing should now rob her,—which should be a rock for rest and safety, and not a rock for shipwreck, and as to the disposition of which Aunt Sarah's present ideas were so very erroneous!

It was impossible that the first evening should pass without a word or two about poor Gilmore. Mary knew well enough that she had told her aunt nothing of her renewed engagement with her cousin; but she could not bring herself at once to utter a song of triumph, as she would have done had she blurted out all her story. Not a word was said about either lover till they were seated together in the evening. "What you tell me about Mr. Gilmore has made me so unhappy," said Miss Marrable, sadly.

"It could not be helped, Aunt Sarah. I tried my best, but it could not be helped. Of course I have been very, very unhappy myself."

"I don't pretend to understand it."

"And yet it is so easily understood!" said Mary, pleading hard for herself. "I did not love him, and—"

"But you had accepted him, Mary."

"I know I had. It is so natural that you should think that I have behaved badly."

"I have not said so, my dear."

"I know that, Aunt Sarah; but if you think so,—and of course you do,—write and ask Janet Fenwick. She will tell you everything. You know how devoted she is to Mr. Gilmore. She would have done anything for him. But even she will tell you that at last I could not help it. When I was so very wretched I thought that I would do my best to comply with other people's wishes. I got a feeling that nothing signified for myself. If they had told me to go into a convent or to be a nurse in a hospital I would have gone. I had nothing to care for, and if I could do what I was told perhaps it might be best."

"But why did you not go on with it, my dear?"

"It was impossible—after Walter had written to me."

"But Walter is to marry Edith Brownlow."

"No, dear aunt; no. Walter is to marry me. Don't look like that, Aunt Sarah. It is true;—it is, indeed." She had now dragged her chair close to her aunt's seat upon the sofa, so that she could put her hands upon her aunt's knees. "All that about Miss Brownlow has been a fable."

"Parson John told me that it was fixed."

"It is not fixed. The other thing is fixed. Parson John tells many fables. He is to come here."

"Who is to come here?"

"Walter,—of course. He is to be here,—I don't know how soon; but I shall hear from him. Dear aunt, you must be good to him;—indeed you must. He is your cousin just as much as mine."

"I'm not in love with him, Mary."

"But I am, Aunt Sarah. Oh dear, how much I am in love with him! It never changed in the least, though I struggled, and struggled not to think of him. I broke his picture and burned it;—and I would not have a scrap of his handwriting;—I would not have near me anything that he had even spoken of. But it was no good. I could not get away from him for an hour. Now I shall never want to get away from him again. As for Mr. Gilmore, it would have come to the same thing at last, had I never heard another word from Walter Marrable. I could not have done it."

"I suppose we must submit to it," said Aunt Sarah, after a pause. This certainly was not the most exhilarating view which might have been taken of the matter as far as Mary was concerned; but as it did not suggest any open opposition to her scheme, and as there was no refusal to see Walter when he should again appear at Uphill as her lover, she made no complaint. Miss Marrable went on to inquire how Sir Gregory would like these plans, which were so diametrically opposed to his own. As to that, Mary could say nothing. No doubt Walter would make a clean breast of it to Sir Gregory before he left Dunripple, and would be able to tell them what had passed when he came to Loring. Mary, however, did not forget to argue that the ground on which Walter Marrable stood was his own ground. After the death of two men, the youngest of whom was over seventy, the property would be his property, and could not be taken from him. If Sir Gregory chose to quarrel with him,—as to the probability of which, Mary and her aunt professed very different opinions,—they must wait. Waiting now would be very different from what it had been when their prospects in life had not seemed to depend in any degree upon the succession to the family property. "And I know myself better now than I did then," said Mary. "Though it were to be for all my life, I would wait."

On the Monday she got a letter from her cousin. It was very short, and there was not a word in it about Sir Gregory or Edith Brownlow. It only said that he was the happiest man in the world, and that he would be at Loring on the following Saturday. He must return at once to Birmingham, but would certainly be at Loring on Saturday. He had written to his uncle to ask for hospitality. He did not suppose that Parson John would refuse; but should this be the case, he would put up at The Dragon. Mary might be quite sure that she would see him on Saturday.

And on the Saturday he came. The parson had consented to receive him; but, not thinking highly of the wisdom of the proposed visit, had worded his letter rather coldly. But of that Walter in his present circumstances thought but little. He was hardly within the house before he had told his story. "You haven't heard, I suppose," he said, "that Mary and I have made it up?"

"How made it up?"

"Well,—I mean that you shall make us man and wife some day."

"But I thought you were to marry Edith Brownlow."

"Who told you that, sir? I am sure Edith did not, nor yet her mother. But I believe these sort of things are often settled without consulting the principals."

"And what does my brother say?"

"Sir Gregory, you mean?"

"Of course I mean Sir Gregory. I don't suppose you'd ask your father."

"I never had the slightest intention, sir, of asking either one or the other. I don't suppose that I am to ask his leave to be married, like a young girl; and it isn't likely that any objection on family grounds could be made to such a woman as Mary Lowther."

"You needn't ask leave of any one, most noble Hector. That is a matter of course. You can marry the cook-maid to-morrow, if you please. But I thought you meant to live at Dunripple?"

"So I shall,—part of the year; if Sir Gregory likes it."

"And that you were to have an allowance and all that sort of thing. Now, if you do marry the cook-maid—"

"I am not going to marry the cook-maid,—as you know very well."

"Or if you marry any one else in opposition to my brother's wishes, I don't suppose it likely that he'll bestow that which he intended to give as a reward to you for following his wishes."

"He can do as he pleases. The moment that it was settled I told him."

"And what did he say?"

"He complained of headache. Sir Gregory very often does complain of headache. When I took leave of him, he said I should hear from him."

"Then it's all up with Dunripple for you,—as long as he lives. I've no doubt that since poor Gregory's death your father's interest in the property has been disposed of among the Jews to the last farthing."

"I shouldn't wonder."

"And you are,—just where you were, my boy."

"That depends entirely upon Sir Gregory. You may be sure of this, sir,—that I shall ask him for nothing. If the worst comes to the worst, I can go to the Jews as well as my father. I won't, unless I am driven."

He was with Mary, of course, that evening, walking again along the banks of the Lurwell, as they had first done now nearly twelve months since. Then the autumn had begun, and now the last of the summer months was near its close. How very much had happened to her, or had seemed to happen, during the interval. At that time she had thrice declined Harry Gilmore's suit; but she had done so without any weight on her own conscience. Her friends had wished her to marry the man, and therefore she had been troubled; but the trouble had lain light upon her, and as she looked back at it all, she felt that at that time there had been something of triumph at her heart. A girl when she is courted knows at any rate that she is thought worthy of courtship, and in this instance she had been at least courted worthily. Since then a whole world of trouble had come upon her from that source. She had been driven hither and thither, first by love, and then by a false idea of duty, till she had come almost to shipwreck. And in her tossing she had gone against another barque which, for aught she knew, might even yet go down from the effects of the collision. She could not be all happy, even though she were again leaning on Walter Marrable's arm, or again sitting with it round her waist, beneath the shade of the trees on the banks of the Lurwell.

"Then we must wait, and this time we must be patient," she said, when he told her of poor Sir Gregory's headache.

"I cannot ask him for anything," said Walter.

"Of course not. Do not ask anybody for anything,—but just wait. I have quite made up my mind that forty-five for the gentleman, and thirty-five for the lady, is quite time enough for marrying."

"The grapes are sour," said Walter.

"They are not sour at all, sir," said Mary.

"I was speaking of my own grapes, as I look at them when I use that argument for my own comfort. The worst of it is that when we know that the grapes are not sour,—that they are the sweetest grapes in the world,—

the argument is of no use. I won't tell any lies about it, to myself or anybody else. I want my grapes at once."

"And so do I," said Mary, eagerly; "of course I do. I am not going to make any pretence with you. Of course I want them at once. But I have learned to know that they are precious enough to be worth the waiting for. I made a fool of myself once; but I shall not do it again, let Sir Gregory make himself ever so disagreeable."

This was all very pleasant for Captain Marrable. Ah, yes! what other moment in a man's life is at all equal to that in which he is being flattered to the top of his bent by the love of the woman he loves. To be flattered by the love of a woman whom he does not love is almost equally unpleasant,—if the man be anything of a man. But at the present moment our Captain was supremely happy. His Thais was telling him that he was indeed her king, and should he not take the goods with which the gods provided him? To have been robbed of his all by a father, and to have an uncle who would have a headache instead of making settlements,—these indeed were drawbacks; but the pleasure was so sweet that even such drawbacks as these could hardly sully his bliss. "If you knew what your letter was to me!" she said, as she leaned against his shoulder. His father and his uncle and all the Marrables on the earth might do their worst, they could not rob the present hour of its joy.

CHAPTER LXVIII.

THE SQUIRE IS VERY OBSTINATE.

Mr. Gilmore left his own home on a Thursday afternoon, and on the Monday when the Vicar again visited the Privets nothing had been heard of him. Money had been left with the bailiff for the Saturday wages of the men working about the place, but no provision for anything had been made beyond that. The Sunday had been wet from morning to night, and nothing could possibly be more disconsolate than the aspect of things round the house, or more disreputable if they were to be left in their present condition. The barrows, and the planks, and the pickaxes had been taken away, which things, though they are not in themselves beautiful, are safeguards against the ill-effects of ugliness, as they inform the eyes why it is that such disorder lies around. There was the disorder at the Privets now without any such instruction to the eye. Pits were full of muddy water, and half-formed paths had become the beds of stagnant pools. The Vicar then went into the house, and though there was still a workman and a boy who were listlessly pulling about some rolls of paper, there were ample signs that misfortune had come and that neglect was the consequence. "And all this," said Fenwick to himself, "because the man cannot get the idea of a certain woman out of his head!" Then he thought of himself and his own character, and asked himself whether, in any position of life, he could have been thus overruled to misery by circumstances altogether outside himself. Misfortunes might come which would be very heavy; his wife or children might die; or he might become a pauper; or subject to some crushing disease. But Gilmore's trouble had not fallen upon him from the hands of Providence. He had set his heart upon the gaining of a thing, and was now absolutely broken-hearted because he could not have it. And the thing was a woman. Fenwick admitted to himself that the thing itself was the most worthy for which a man can struggle; but would not admit that even in his search for that a man should allow his heart to give way, or his strength to be broken down.

He went up to the house again on the Wednesday, and again on the Thursday,—but nothing had been heard from the Squire. The bailiff was very unhappy. Even though there might come a cheque on the Saturday morning, which both Fenwick and the bailiff thought to be probable, still there would be grave difficulties.

"Here'll be the first of September on us afore we know where we are," said the bailiff, "and is we to go on with the horses?"

For the Squire was of all men the most regular, and began to get his horses into condition on the first of September as regularly as he began to shoot partridges. The Vicar went home and then made up his mind that he would go up to London after his friend. He must provide for his next Sunday's duty, but he could do that out of a neighbouring parish, and he would start on the morrow. He arranged the matter with his wife and with his friend's curate, and on the Friday he started.

He drove himself into Salisbury instead of to the Bullhampton Road station in order that he might travel by the express train. That at least was the reason which he gave to himself and to his wife. But there was present to his mind the idea that he might look into the court and see how the trial was going on. Poor Carry Brattle would have a bad time of it beneath a lawyer's claws. Such a one as Carry, of the evil of whose past life there was no doubt, and who would appear as a witness against a man whom she had once been engaged to marry, would certainly meet with no mercy from a cross-examining barrister. The broad landmarks between the respectable and the disreputable may guide the tone of a lawyer somewhat, when he has a witness in his power; but the finer lines which separate that which is at the moment good and true from that which is false and bad cannot be discerned amidst the turmoil of a trial, unless the eyes, and the ears, and the inner touch of him who has the handling of the victim be of a quality more than ordinarily high.

The Vicar drove himself over to Salisbury and had an hour there for strolling into the court. He had heard on the previous day that the case would be brought on the first thing on the Friday, and it was half-past eleven when he made his way in through the crowd. The train by which he was to be taken on to London did not start till half-past twelve. At that moment the court was occupied in deciding whether a certain tradesman, living at Devizes, should or should not be on the jury. The man himself objected that, being a butcher, he was, by reason of the second nature acquired in his business, too cruel, and bloody-minded to be entrusted with an affair of life and death. To a proposition in itself so reasonable no direct answer was made; but it was argued with great power on behalf of the crown, which seemed to think at the time that the whole case depended on getting this one particular man into the jury box, that the recalcitrant juryman was not in truth a butcher, that he was only a dealer in meat, and that though the stain of the blood descended the cruelty did not. Fenwick remained there till he heard the case given against the pseudo-butcher, and then retired from the court. He had, however, just seen Carry Brattle and her father seated side by side on a bench in a little outside room appropriated to the witnesses, and there had been a constable there seeming to stand on guard over them. The miller was sitting, leaning on his stick, with his eyes fixed upon the ground, and Carry was pale, wretched, and draggled. Sam had not yet made his appearance.

"I'm afeard, sir, he'll be in trouble," said Carry to the Vicar.

"Let 'un alone," said the miller; "when they wants 'im he'll be here. He know'd more about it nor I did."

That afternoon Fenwick went to the club of which he and Gilmore were both members, and found that his friend was in London. He had been so, at least, that morning at nine o'clock. According to the porter at the club door, Mr. Gilmore called there every morning for his letters as soon as the club was open. He did not eat his breakfast in the house, nor, as far as the porter's memory went, did he even enter the club. Fenwick had lodged himself at an hotel in the immediate neighbourhood of Pall-Mall, and he made up his mind that his only chance of catching his friend was to be at the steps of the club door when it was opened at nine o'clock. So he eat his dinner,—very much in solitude, for on the 28th of August it is not often that the coffee rooms of clubs are full,—and in the evening took himself to one of the theatres which was still open. His club had been deserted, and it had seemed to him that the streets also were empty. One old gentleman, who, together with himself, had employed the forces of the establishment that evening, had told him that there wasn't a single soul left in London. He had gone to his tailor's and had found that both the tailor and the foreman were out of town. His publisher,—for our Vicar did a little in the way of light literature on social subjects, and had brought out a pretty volume in green and gold on the half-profit system, intending to give his share to a certain county hospital,—his publisher had been in the north since the 12th, and would not be back for three weeks. He found, however, a confidential young man who was able to tell him that the hospital need not increase the number of its wards on this occasion. He had dropped down to Dean's Yard to see a clerical friend,—but the house was shut up and he could not even get an answer. He sauntered into the Abbey, and found them mending the organ. He got into a cab and was driven hither and thither because all the streets were pulled up. He called at the War-Office to see a young clerk, and found one old messenger fast asleep in his arm-chair. "Gone for his holiday, sir," said the man in the arm-chair, speaking amidst his dreams, without waiting to hear the particular name of the young clerk who was wanted. And yet, when he got to the theatre, it was so full that he could hardly find a seat on which to sit. In all the world around us there is nothing more singular than the emptiness and the fullness of London.

He was up early the next morning and breakfasted before he went out, thinking that even should he succeed in catching the Squire, he would not be able to persuade the unhappy man to come and breakfast with him. At a little before nine he was in Pall-Mall, walking up and down before the club, and as the clocks struck the hour he began to be impatient. The porter had said that Gilmore always came exactly at nine, and within two minutes after that hour the Vicar began to feel that his friend was breaking an engagement and behaving badly to him. By ten minutes past, the idea had got into his head that all the people in Pall-Mall were watching him, and at the quarter he was angry and unhappy. He had just counted the seconds up to twenty minutes, and had begun to consider that it would be absurd for him to walk there all the day, when he saw the Squire coming slowly along the street. He had been afraid to make himself comfortable within the club, and there to wait for his friend's coming, lest Gilmore should have escaped him, not choosing to be thus caught by any one;—and even now he had his fear lest his quarry should slip through his fingers. He waited till the Squire had gone up to the porter and returned to the street, and then he crossed over and seized him by the arm. "Harry," he said, "you didn't expect to see me in London;—did you?"

"Certainly not," said the other, implying very plainly by his looks that the meeting had given him no special pleasure.

"I came up yesterday afternoon, and I was at Cutcote's the tailor's, and at Messrs. Bringémout and Neversell's. Bringémout has retired, but it's Neversell that does the business. And then I went down to see old Drybird, and I called on young Dozey at his office. But everybody is out of town. I never saw anything like it. I vote that we take to having holidays in the country, and all come to London, and live in the empty houses."

"I suppose you came up to look after me?" said Gilmore, with a brow as black as a thunder-cloud.

Fenwick perceived that he need not carry on any further his lame pretences. "Well, I did. Come, old fellow, this won't do, you know. Everything is not to be thrown overboard because a girl doesn't know her own mind. Aren't your anchors better than that?"

"I haven't an anchor left," said Gilmore.

"How can you be so weak and so wicked as to say so? Come, Harry, take a turn with me in the park. You may be quite sure I shan't let you go now I've got you."

"You'll have to let me go," said the other.

"Not till I've told you my mind. Everybody is out of town, so I suppose even a parson may light a cigar down here. Harry, you must come back with me."

"No;—I cannot."

"Do you mean to say that you will yield up all your strength, all your duty, all your life, and throw over every purpose of your existence because you have been ill-used by a wench? Is that your idea of manhood,—of that manhood you have so often preached?"

"After what I have suffered there I cannot bear the place."

"You must force yourself to bear it. Do you mean to say that because you are unhappy you will not pay your debts?"

"I owe no man a shilling;—or, if I do, I will pay it to-morrow."

"There are debts you can only settle by daily payments. To every man living on your land you owe such a debt. To every friend connected with you by name, or blood, or love, you owe such a debt. Do you suppose that you can cast yourself adrift, and make yourself a by-word, and hurt no one but yourself? Why is it that we hate a suicide?"

"Because he sins."

"Because he is a coward, and runs away from the burden which he ought to bear gallantly. He throws his load down on the roadside, and does not care who may bear it, or who may suffer because he is too poor a creature to struggle on! Have you no feeling that, though it may be hard with you here,"—and the Vicar, as he spoke, struck his breast,—"you should so carry your outer self, that the eyes of those around you should see nothing of the sorrow within? That is my idea of manliness, and I have ever taken you to be a man."

"We work for the esteem of others while we desire it. I desire nothing now. She has so knocked me about that I should be a liar if I were to say that there is enough manhood left in me to bear it. I shan't kill myself."

"No, Harry, you won't do that."

"But I shall give up the place, and go abroad."

"Whom will you serve by that?"

"It is all very well to preach, Frank. Bad as I am I could preach to you if there were a matter to preach about. I don't know that there is anything much easier than preaching. But as for practising, you can't do it if you have not got the strength. A man can't walk if you take away his legs. If you break a bird's wing he can't fly, let the bird be ever so full of pluck. All that there was in me she has taken out of me. I could fight him, and would willingly, if I thought there was a chance of his meeting me."

"He would not be such a fool."

"But I could not stand up and look at her."

"She has left Bullhampton, you know."

"It does not matter, Frank. There is the place that I was getting ready for her. And if I were there, you and your wife would always be thinking about it. And every fellow about the estate knows the whole story. It seems to me to be almost inconceivable that a woman should have done such a thing."

"She has not meant to act badly, Harry."

"To tell the truth, when I look back at it all, I blame myself more than her. A man should never be ass enough to ask any woman a second time. But I had got it into my head that it was a disgraceful thing to ask and not to have. It is that which kills me now. I do not think that I will ever again attempt anything, because failure is so hard to me to bear. At any rate, I won't go back to the Privets." This he added after a pause, during which the Vicar had been thinking what new arguments he could bring up to urge his friend's return.

Fenwick learned that Gilmore had sent a cheque to his bailiff by the post of the preceding night. He acknowledged that in sending the cheque he had said no more than to bid the man pay what wages were due. He had not as yet made up his mind as to any further steps. As they walked round the enclosure of St. James's Park together, and as the warmth of their old friendship produced freedom of intercourse, Gilmore acknowledged a dozen wild schemes that had passed through his brain. That to which he was most wedded was a plan for meeting Walter Marrable and cudgelling him pretty well to death. Fenwick pointed out three or four objections to this. In the first place, Marrable had committed no offence whatever against Gilmore. And then, in all probability, Marrable might be as good at cudgelling as the Squire himself. And thirdly, when the cudgelling was over, the man who began the row would certainly be put into prison, and in atonement for that would receive no public sympathy. "You can't throw yourself on the public pity as a woman might," said the Vicar.

"D—— the public pity," said the Squire, who was not often driven to make his language forcible after that fashion.

Another scheme was that he would publish the whole transaction. And here again his friend was obliged to remind him, that a man in his position should be reticent rather than outspoken. "You have already declared," said the Vicar, "that you can't endure failure, and yet you want to make your failure known to all the world." His third proposition was more absurd still. He would write such a letter to Mary Lowther as would cover her head with red hot coals. He would tell her that she had made the world utterly unbearable to him, and that she might have the Privets for herself and go and live there. "I do not doubt but that such a letter would annoy her," said the Vicar.

"Why should I care how much she is annoyed?"

"Just so;—but everyone who saw the letter would know that it was pretence and bombast. Of course you will do nothing of the kind."

They were together pretty nearly the whole day. Gilmore, no doubt, would have avoided the Vicar in the morning had it been possible; but now that he had been caught, and had been made to undergo his friend's lectures, he was rather grateful than otherwise for something in the shape of society. It was Fenwick's desire to induce him to return to Bullhampton. If this could not be done, it would no doubt be well that some authority should be obtained from him as to the management of the place. But this subject had not been mooted as yet, because Fenwick felt that if he once acknowledged that the runaway might continue to be a runaway, his chance of bringing the man back to his own home would be much lessened. As yet, however, he had made no impression in that direction. At last they parted on an understanding that they were to breakfast together the next morning at Fenwick's hotel, and then go to the eleven o'clock Sunday service at a certain noted metropolitan church. At breakfast, and during the walk to church, Fenwick said not a word to his friend about Bullhampton. He talked of church services, of ritual, of the quietness of a Sunday in London, and of the Sunday occupations of three millions of people not a fourth of whom attend divine service. He chose any subject other than that of which Gilmore was thinking. But as soon as they were out of church he made another attack upon him. "After that, Harry, don't you feel like trying to do your duty?"

"I feel that I can't fly because my wing is broken," said the Squire.

They spent the whole of the afternoon and evening together, but no good was done. Gilmore, as far as he had a plan, intended to go abroad, travel to the East, or to the West,—or to the South, if so it came about. The Privets might be let if any would choose to take the place. As far as he was concerned his income from his tenants would be more than he wanted. "As for doing them any good, I never did them any good," he said, as he parted from the Vicar for the night. "If they can't live on the land without my being at home, I am sure they won't if I stay there."

CHAPTER LXIX.

THE TRIAL.

The miller, as he was starting from his house door, had called his daughter by her own name for the first time since her return home,—and Carry had been comforted. But no further comfort came to her during her journey to Salisbury from her father's speech. He hardly spoke the whole morning, and when he did say a word as to any matter on the work they had in hand, his voice was low and melancholy. Carry knew well, as did every one at Bullhampton, that her father was a man not much given to conversation, and she had not expected him to talk to her; but the silence, together with the load at her heart as to the ordeal of her examination, was very heavy on her. If she could have asked questions, and received encouragement, she could have borne her position comparatively with ease.

The instructions with which the miller was furnished required that Carry Brattle should present herself at a certain office in Salisbury at a certain hour on that Wednesday. Exactly at that hour she and her father were at the place indicated, already having visited their lodgings at Mrs. Stiggs'. They were then told that they would not be again wanted on that day, but that they must infallibly be in the Court the next morning at half-past nine. The attorney's clerk whom they saw, when he learned that Sam Brattle was not yet in Salisbury, expressed an opinion as to that young man's iniquity which led Carry to think that he was certainly in more danger than either of the prisoners. As they left the office, she suggested to her father that a message should be immediately sent to Bullhampton after Sam. "Let 'un be," said the miller; and it was all that he did say. On that evening they retired to the interior of one of the bedrooms at Trotter's Buildings, at four o'clock in the afternoon, and did not leave the house again. Anything more dreary than those hours could not be imagined. The miller, who was accustomed to work hard all day and then to rest, did not know what to do with his limbs. Carry, seeing his misery, and thinking rather of that than her own, suggested to him that they should go out and walk round the town. "Bide as thee be," said the miller; "it ain't no time now for showing theeself." Carry took the rebuke without a word, but turned her head to hide her tears.

And the next day was worse, because it was longer. Exactly at half-past nine they were down at the court; and there they hung about till half-past ten. Then they were told that their affair would not be brought on till the Friday, but that at half-past nine on that day, it would undoubtedly be commenced; and that if Sam was not there then, it would go very hard with Sam. The miller, who was beginning to lose his respect for the young man from whom he received these communications, muttered something about Sam being all right. "You'll find he won't be all right if he isn't here at half-past nine tomorrow," said the young man. "There is them as their bark is worse than their bite," said the miller. Then they went back to Trotter's Buildings, and did not stir outside of Mrs. Stiggs' house throughout the whole day.

On the Friday, which was in truth to be the day of the trial, they were again in court at half-past nine; and there, as we have seen, they were found, two hours later, by Mr. Fenwick, waiting patiently while the great preliminary affair of the dealer in meat was being settled. At that hour Sam had not made his appearance; but between twelve and one he sauntered into the comfortless room in which Carry was still sitting with her father. The sight of him was a joy to poor Carry, as he would speak to her, and tell her something of what was going on. "I'm about in time for the play, father," he said, coming up to them. The miller picked up his hat, and scratched his head, and muttered something. But there had been a sparkle in his eye when he saw Sam. In truth, the sight in all the world most agreeable to the old man's eyes was the figure of his youngest son. To the miller no Apollo could have been more perfect in beauty, and no Hercules more useful in strength. Carry's sweet woman's brightness had once been as dear to him,—but all that had now passed away.

"Is it a'going all through?" asked the miller, referring to the mill.

"Running as pretty as a coach-and-four when I left at seven this morning," said Sam.

"And how did thee come?"

"By the marrow-bone stage, as don't pay no tolls; how else?" The miller did not express a single word of approbation, but he looked up and down at his son's legs and limbs, delighted to think that the young man was at work in the mill this morning, had since that walked seventeen miles, and now stood before them showing no sign of fatigue.

"What are they a'doing on now, Sam?" asked Carry, in a whisper. Sam had already been into the court, and was able to inform them that the "big swell of all was making a speech, in which he was telling everybody every 'varsal thing about it. And what do you think, father?"

"I don't think nothing," said the miller.

"They've been and found Trumbull's money-box buried in old mother Burrows's garden at Pycroft." Carry uttered the slightest possible scream as she heard this, thinking of the place which she had known so well. "Dash my buttons if they ain't," continued Sam. "It's about up with 'em now."

"They'll be hung—of course," said the miller.

"What asses men is," said Sam; "—to go to bury the box there! Why didn't they smash it into atoms?"

"Them as goes crooked in big things is like to go crooked in little," said the miller.

At about two Sam and Carry were told to go into Court, and way was made for the old man to accompany them. At that moment the cross-examination was being continued of the man who, early on the Sunday morning, had seen the Grinder with his companion in the cart on the road leading towards Pycroft Common. A big burly barrister, with a broad forehead and grey eyes, was questioning this witness as to the identity of the men in the cart; and at every answer that he received he turned round to the jury as though he would say "There, then, what do you think of the case now, when such a man as that is brought before you to give evidence?" "You will swear, then, that these two men who are here in the dock were the two men you saw that morning in that cart?" The witness said that he would so swear. "You knew them both before, of course?" The witness declared that he had never seen either of them before in his life. "And you expect the jury to believe, now that the lives of these men depend on their believing it, that after the lapse of a year you can identify these two men, whom you had never seen before, and who were at that time being carried along the road at the rate of eight or ten miles an hour?" The witness, who had already encountered a good many of these questions, and who was inclined to be rough rather than timid, said that he didn't care twopence what the jury believed. It was simply his business to tell what he knew. Then the judge looked at that wicked witness,—who had talked in this wretched, jeering way about twopence!—looked at him over his spectacles, and shaking his head as though with pity at that witness's wickedness, cautioned him as to the peril of his body, making, too, a marked reference to the peril of his soul by that melancholy wagging of the head. Then the burly barrister with the broad forehead looked up beseechingly to the jury. Was it right that any man should be hung for any offence against whom such a witness as this was brought up to give testimony? It was the manifest feeling of the crowd in the court that the witness himself ought to be hung immediately. "You may go down, sir," said the burly barrister, giving an impression to those who looked on, but did not understand, that the case was over as far as it depended on that man's evidence. The burly barrister himself was not so sanguine. He knew very well that the judge who had wagged his head in so melancholy a way at the iniquity of a witness who had dared to say that he didn't care twopence, would, when he was summing up, refer to the presence of the two prisoners in the cart as a thing fairly supported by evidence. The amount of the burly barrister's achievement was simply this,—that for the moment a sort of sympathy was excited on behalf of the prisoners by the disapprobation which was aroused against the wicked man who hadn't cared twopence. Sympathy, like electricity, will run so quick that no man may stop it. If sympathy might be made to run through the jury-box there might perchance be a man or two there weak enough to entertain it to the prejudice of his duty on that day. The hopes of the burly barrister in this matter did not go further than that.

Then there was another man put forward who had seen neither of the prisoners, but had seen the cart and pony at Pycroft Common, and had known that the cart and pony were for the time in the possession of the Grinder. He was questioned by the burly barrister about himself rather than about his evidence; and when he had been made to own that he had been five times in prison, the burly barrister was almost justified in the look he gave to the jury, and he shook his head as though in sorrow that his learned friend on the other side should have dared to bring such a man as that before them as a witness.

Various others were brought up and examined before poor Carry's turn had come; and on each occasion, as one after another was dismissed from the hands of the burly barrister, here one crushed and confounded, there another loud and triumphant, her heart was almost in her throat. And yet though she so dreaded the moment when it should come, there was a sense of wretched disappointment in that she was kept waiting. It was now between four and five, and whispers began to be rife that the Crown would not finish their case that day. There was much trouble and more amusement with the old woman who had been Trumbull's housekeeper. She was very deaf; but it had been discovered that there was an old friendship between her and the Grinder's mother, and that she had at one time whispered the fact of the farmer's money into the ears of Mrs. Burrows of Pycroft Common. Deaf as she was, she was made to admit this. Mrs. Burrows was also examined, but she would admit nothing. She had never heard of the money, or of Farmer Trumbull, or of the murder,—not till the world heard of it, and she knew nothing about her son's doings or comings or goings. No doubt she had given shelter to a young woman at the request of a friend of her son, the young woman paying her ten shillings a week for her board and lodging. That young woman was Carry Brattle. Her son and that young man had certainly been at her house together; but she could not at all say whether they had been there on that Sunday morning. Perhaps, of all who had been examined Mrs. Burrows was the most capable witness, for the lawyer who examined her on behalf of the Crown was able to extract absolutely nothing from her. When she turned herself round with an air of satisfaction, to face the questions of the burly barrister, she was told that he had no question to ask her. "It's all as one to me, sir," said Mrs. Burrows, as she smoothed her apron and went down.

And then it was poor Carry's turn. When the name of Caroline Brattle was called she turned her eyes beseechingly to her father, as though hoping that he would accompany her in this the dreaded moment of her punishment. She caught him convulsively by the sleeve of the coat, as she was partly dragged and partly shoved on towards the little box in which she was to take her stand. He accompanied her to the foot of the two or three steps which she was called on to ascend, but of course he could go no further with her.

"I'll bide nigh thee, Carry," he said; and it was the only word which he had spoken to comfort her that day. It did, however, serve to lessen her present misery, and added something to her poor stock of courage. "Your name is Caroline Brattle?" "And you were living on the thirty-first of last August with Mrs. Burrows at Pycroft Common?" "Do you remember Sunday the thirty-first of August?" These, and two or three other questions like them were asked by a young barrister in the mildest tone he could assume. "Speak out, Miss Brattle," he said, "and then there will be nothing to trouble you." "Yes, sir," she said, in answer to each of the questions, still almost in a whisper.

Nothing to trouble her, and all the eyes of that cruel world around fixed upon her! Nothing to trouble her, and every ear on the alert to hear her,—young and pretty as she was,—confess her own shame in that public court! Nothing to trouble her, when she would so willingly have died to escape the agony that was coming on her! For she knew that it would come. Though she had never been in a court of law before, and had had no one tell her what would happen, she knew that the question would be asked. She was sure that she would be made to say what she had been before all that crowd of men.

The evidence which she could give, though it was material, was very short. John Burrows and Lawrence Acorn had come to the cottage on Pycroft Common on that Sunday morning, and there she had seen both of them. It was daylight when they came, but still it was very early. She had not observed the clock, but she thought that it may have been about five. The men were in and out of the house, but they had some breakfast. She had risen from bed to help to get them their breakfast. If anything had been buried by them in the garden, she had known nothing of it. She had then received three sovereigns from Acorn, whom she was engaged to marry. From that day to the present she had never seen either of the men. As soon as she heard of the suspicion against Acorn, and that he had fled, she conceived her engagement to be at an end. All this she testified, with infinite difficulty, in so low a voice that a man was sworn to stand by her and repeat her answers aloud to the jury;—and then she was handed over to the burly barrister.

She had been long enough in the court to perceive, and had been clever enough to learn, that this man would be her enemy. Though she had been unable to speak aloud in answering the counsel for the prosecution, she had quite understood that the man was her friend,—that he was only putting to her those questions which must be asked,—and questions which she could answer without much difficulty. But when she was told to attend to what the other gentleman would say to her, then, indeed, her poor heart failed her.

It came at once. "My dear, I believe you have been indiscreet?" The words, perhaps, had been chosen with some idea of mercy, but certainly there was no mercy in the tone. The man's voice was loud, and there was something in it almost of a jeer,—something which seemed to leave an impression on the hearer that there had been pleasure in the asking it. She struggled to make an answer, and the monosyllable, yes, was formed by her lips. The man who was acting as her mouthpiece stooped down his ears to her lips, and then shook his head. Assuredly no sound had come from them that could have reached his sense, had he been ever so close. The burly barrister waited in patience, looking now at her, and now round at the court. "I must have an answer. I say that I believe you have been indiscreet. You know, I dare say, what I mean. Yes or no will do; but I must have an answer." She glanced round for an instant, trying to catch her father's eye; but she could see nothing; everything seemed to swim before her except the broad face of that burly barrister. "Has she given any answer?" he asked of the mouthpiece; and the mouthpiece again shook his head. The heart of the mouthpiece was tender, and he was beginning to hate the burly barrister. "My dear," said the burly barrister, "the jury must have the information from you."

Then gradually there was heard through the court the gurgling sounds of irrepressible sobs,—and with them there came a moan from the old man, who was only divided from his daughter by the few steps,—which was understood by the whole crowd. The story of the poor girl, in reference to the trial, had been so noised about that it was known to all the listeners. That spark of sympathy, of which we have said that its course cannot be arrested when it once finds its way into a crowd, had been created, and there was hardly present then one, either man or woman, who would not have prayed that Carry Brattle might be spared if it were possible. There was a juryman there, a father with many daughters, who thought that it might not misbecome him to put forward such a prayer himself.

"Perhaps it mayn't be necessary," said the soft-hearted juryman.

But the burly barrister was not a man who liked to be taught his duty by any one in court,—not even by a juryman,—and his quick intellect immediately told him that he must seize the spark of sympathy in its flight. It could not be stopped, but it might be turned to his own purpose. It would not suffice for him now that he should simply defend the question he had asked. The court was showing its aptitude for pathos, and he also must be pathetic on his own side. He knew well enough that he could not arrest public opinion which was going against him, by shewing that his question was a proper question; but he might do so by proving at once how tender was his own heart.

"It is a pain and grief to me," said he, "to bring sorrow upon any one. But look at those prisoners at the bar, whose lives are committed to my charge, and know that I, as their advocate, love them while they are my clients as well as any father can love his child. I will spend myself for them, even though it may be at the risk of the harsh judgment of those around me. It is my duty to prove to the jury on their behalf that the life of this young woman has been such as to invalidate her testimony against them;—and that duty I shall do, fearless of the remarks of any one. Now I ask you again, Caroline Brattle, whether you are not one of the unfortunates?"

This attempt of the burly barrister was to a certain extent successful. The juryman who had daughters of his own had been put down, and the barrister had given, at any rate, an answer to the attack that had been silently made on him by the feeling of the court. Let a man be ready with a reply, be it ever so bad a reply, and any attack is parried. But Carry had given no answer to the question, and those who looked at her thought it very improbable that she would be able to do so. She had clutched the arm of the man who stood by her, and in the midst of her sobs was looking round with snatched, quick, half-completed glances for protection to the spot on which her father and brother were standing. The old man had moaned once; but after that he uttered no sound. He stood leaning on his stick with his eyes fixed upon the ground, quite motionless. Sam was standing with his hands grasping the woodwork before him and his bold gaze fastened on the barrister's face, as though he were about to fly at him. The burly barrister saw it all and perceived that more was to be gained by sparing than by persecuting his witness, and resolved to let her go.

"I believe that will do," he said. "Your silence tells all that I wish the jury to know. You may go down." Then the man who had acted as mouthpiece led Carry away, delivered her up to her father, and guided them both out of court.

They went back to the room in which they had before been seated, and there they waited for Sam, who was called into the witness-box as they left the court.

"Oh, father," said Carry, as soon as the old man was again placed upon the bench. And she stood over him, and put her hand upon his neck.

"We've won through it, girl, and let that be enough," said the miller. Then she sat down close by his side, and not another word was spoken by them till Sam returned.

Sam's evidence was, in fact, but of little use. He had had dealings with Acorn, who had introduced him to Burrows, and had known the two men at the old woman's cottage on the Common. When he was asked, what these dealings had been, he said they were honest dealings.

"About your sister's marriage?" suggested the crown lawyer.

"Well,—yes," said Sam. And then he stated that the men had come over to Bullhampton and that he had accompanied them as they walked round Farmer Trumbull's house. He had taken them into the Vicar's garden; and then he gave an account of the meeting there with Mr. Fenwick. After that he had known and seen nothing of the men. When he testified so far he was handed over to the burly barrister.

The burly barrister tried all he knew, but he could make nothing of this witness. A question was asked him, the true answer to which would have implied that his sister's life had been disreputable. When this was asked Sam declared that he would not say a word about his sister one way or the other. His sister had told them all she knew about the murder, and now he had told them all he knew. He protested that he was willing to answer any questions they might ask him about himself; but about his sister he would answer none. When told that the information desired might be got in a more injurious way from other sources, he became rather impudent.

"Then you may go to—other sources," he said.

He was threatened with all manner of pains and penalties; but he made nothing of these threats, and was at last allowed to leave the box. When his evidence was completed the trial was adjourned for another day.

Though it was then late in the afternoon the three Brattles returned home that night. There was a train which took them to the Bullhampton Road station, and from thence they walked to the mill. It was a weary journey both for the poor girl and for the old man; but anything was better than delay for another night in Trotter's Buildings. And then the miller was unwilling to be absent from his mill one hour longer than was necessary. When there came to be a question whether he could walk, he laughed the difficulty to scorn in his quiet way. "Why shouldn't I walk it? Ain't I got to 'arn my bread every day?"

It was ten o'clock when they reached the mill, and Mrs. Brattle, not expecting them at that hour, was in bed. But Fanny was up, and did what she could to comfort them. But no one could ever comfort old Brattle. He was not susceptible to soft influences. It may almost be said that he condemned himself because he gave way to the daily luxury of a pipe. He believed in plenty of food, because food for the workman is as coals to the steam-engine, as oats to the horse,—the raw material out of which the motive power of labour must be made. Beyond eating and working a man had little to do, but just to wait till he died. That was his theory of life in these his latter days; and yet he was a man with keen feelings and a loving heart.

But Carry was comforted when her sister's arms were around her. "They asked me if I was bad," she said, "and I thought I should a' died, and I never answered them a word,—and at last they let me go." When Fanny inquired whether their father had been kind to her, she declared that he had been "main kind." "But, oh, Fanny! if he'd only say a word, it would warm one's heart; wouldn't it?"

On the following evening news reached Bullhampton that the Grinder had been convicted and sentenced to death, but that Lawrence Acorn had been acquitted. The judge, in his summing up, had shown that certain evidence which applied to the Grinder had not applied to his comrade in the dock, and the jury had been willing to take any excuse for saving one man from the halter.

CHAPTER LXX.

THE FATE OF THE PUDDLEHAMITES.

Fenwick and Gilmore breakfasted together on the morning that the former left London for Bullhampton; and by that time the Vicar had assured himself that it would be quite impossible to induce his friend to go back to his home. "I shall turn up after some years if I live," said the Squire; "and I suppose I shan't think so much about it then; but for the present I will not go to the place."

He authorised Fenwick to do what he pleased about the house and the gardens, and promised to give instructions as to the sale of his horses. If the whole place were not let, the bailiff might, he suggested, carry on the farm himself. When he was urged as to his duty, he again answered by his illustration of the man without a leg. "It may be all very true," he said, "that a man ought to walk, but if you cut off his leg he can't walk." Fenwick at last found that there was nothing more to be said, and he was constrained to take his leave.

"May I tell her that you forgive her?" the Vicar asked, as they were walking together up and down the station in the Waterloo Road.

"She will not care a brass farthing for my forgiveness," said Gilmore.

"You wrong her there. I am sure that nothing would give her so much comfort as such a message."

Gilmore walked half the length of the platform before he replied. "What is the good of telling a lie about it?"—he said, at last.

"I certainly would not tell a lie."

"Then I can't say that I forgive her. How is a man to forgive such treatment? If I said that I did, you wouldn't believe me. I will keep out of her way, and that will be better for her than forgiving her."

"Some of your wrath, I fear, falls to my lot?" said the Vicar.

"No, Frank. You and your wife have done the best for me all through,—as far as you thought was best."

"We have meant to do so."

"And if she has been false to me as no woman was ever false before, that is not your fault. As for the jewels, tell your wife to lock them up,—or to throw them away if she likes that better. My brother's wife will have them some day, I suppose." Now his brother was in India, and his brother's wife he had never seen. Then there was a pledge given that Gilmore would inform his friend by letter of his future destination, and so they parted.

This was on the Tuesday, and Fenwick had desired that his gig might meet him at the Bullhampton Road station. He had learned by this time of the condemnation of one man for the murder, and the acquittal of the other, and was full of the subject when his groom was seated beside him. Had the Brattles come back to the mill? And what of Sam? And what did the people say about Acorn's escape? These, and many other questions he asked, but he found that his servant was so burdened with a matter of separate and of infinitely greater interest, that he could not be got to give his mind to the late trial. He believed the Brattles were back; he had seen nothing of Sam; he didn't know anything about Acorn; but the new chapel was going to be pulled down.

"What!" exclaimed the Vicar;—"not at once?"

"So they was saying, sir, when I come away. And the men was at it,—that is, standing all about. And there is to be no more preaching, sir. And missus was out in the front looking at 'em as I drove out of the yard."

Fenwick asked twenty questions, but could obtain no other information than was given in the first announcement of these astounding news. And as he entered the vicarage he was still asking questions, and the man was still endeavouring to express his own conviction that that horrible, damnable, and most heart-breaking red brick building would be demolished, and carted clean away before the end of the week. For the servants and dependents of the vicarage were staunch to the interests of the church establishment, with a degree of fervour of which the Vicar himself knew nothing. They hated Puddleham and dissent. This groom would have liked nothing better than a commission to punch the head of Mr. Puddleham's eldest son, a young man who had been employed in a banker's office at Warminster, but had lately come home because he had been found to have a taste for late hours and public-house parlours; and had made himself busy on the question of the chapel. The maid servants at the vicarage looked down as from a mighty great height on the young women of Bullhampton who attended the chapel, and the vicarage gardener, since he had found out that the chapel stood on glebe land, and ought therefore, to be placed under his hands, had hardly been able to keep himself off the ground. His proposed cure for the evil that had been done,—as an immediate remedy before erection and demolition could be carried out, was to form the vicarage manure pit close against the chapel door,—"and then let anybody touch our property who dares!" He had, however, been too cautious to carry out any such strategy as this, without direct authority from the Commander-in-Chief. "Master thinks a deal too much on 'em," he had said to the groom, almost in disgust at the Vicar's pusillanimity.

When Fenwick reached his own gate there was a crowd of men loitering around the chapel, and he got out from his gig and joined them. His eye first fell upon Mr. Puddleham, who was standing directly in front of the door, with his back to the building, wearing on his face an expression of infinite displeasure. The Vicar was desirous of assuring the minister that no steps need be taken, at any rate, for the present, towards removing the chapel from its present situation. But before he could speak to Mr. Puddleham he perceived the builder from Salisbury, who appeared to be very busy,—Grimes, the Bullhampton tradesman, so lately discomfited, but now triumphant,—Bolt, the elder, close at Mr. Puddleham's elbow,—his own churchwarden, with one or two other farmers,—and lastly, Lord St. George himself, walking in company with Mr. Packer, the agent. Many others from the village were there, so that there was quite a public meeting on the bit of ground which had been appropriated to Mr. Puddleham's preachings. Fenwick, as soon as he saw Lord St. George, accosted him before he spoke to the others.

"My friend Mr. Puddleham," said he, "seems to have the benefit of a distinguished congregation this morning."

"The last, I fear, he will ever have on this spot," said the lord, as he shook hands with the Vicar.

"I am very sorry to hear you say so, my lord. Of course, I don't know what you are doing, and I can't make Mr. Puddleham preach here, if he be not willing."

Mr. Puddleham had now joined them. "I am ready and willing," said he, "to do my duty in that sphere of life to which it has pleased God to call me." And it was evident that he thought that the sphere to which he had been called was that special chapel opposite to the vicarage entrance.

"As I was saying," continued the Vicar, "I have neither the wish nor the power to control my neighbour; but, as far as I am concerned, no step need be taken to displace him. I did not like this site for the chapel at first; but I have got quit of all that feeling, and Mr. Puddleham may preach to his heart's content,—as he will, no doubt, to his hearers' welfare, and will not annoy me in the least." On hearing this, Mr. Puddleham pushed his hat off his forehead and looked up and frowned, as though the levity of expression in which his rival indulged, was altogether unbecoming the solemnity of the occasion.

"Mr. Fenwick," said the lord, "we have taken advice, and we find the thing ought to be done,—and to be done instantly. The leading men of the congregation are quite of that view."

"They are of course unwilling to oppose your noble father, my lord," said the minister.

"And to tell you the truth, Mr. Fenwick," continued Lord St. George, "you might be put, most unjustly, into a peck of troubles if we did not do this. You have no right to let the glebe on a building lease, even if you were willing, and high ecclesiastical authority would call upon you at once to have the nuisance removed."

"Nuisance, my lord!" said Mr. Puddleham, who had seen with half an eye that the son was by no means worthy of the father.

"Well, yes,—placed in the middle of the Vicar's ground! What would you say if Mr. Fenwick demanded leave to use your parlour for his vestry room, and to lock up his surplice in your cupboard?"

"I'm sure he'd try it on before he'd had it a day," said the Vicar, "and very well he'd look in it," whereupon the minister again raised his hat, and again frowned.

"The long and the short of it is," continued the lord, "that we've, among us, made a most absurd mistake, and the sooner we put it right the better. My father, feeling that our mistake has led to all the others, and that we have caused all this confusion, thinks it to be his duty to pull the chapel down and build it up on the site before proposed near the cross roads. We'll begin at once, and hope to get it done by Christmas. In the mean time, Mr. Puddleham has consented to go back to the old chapel."

"Why not let him stay here till the other is finished?" asked the Vicar.

"My dear sir," replied the lord, "we are going to transfer the chapel body and bones. If we were Yankees we should know how to do it without pulling it in pieces. As it is, we've got to do it piecemeal. So now, Mr. Hickbody," he continued, turning round to the builder from Salisbury, "you may go to work at once. The Marquis will be much obliged to you if you will press it on."

"Certainly, my lord," said Mr. Hickbody, taking off his hat. "We'll put on quite a body of men, my lord, and his lordship's commands shall be obeyed."

After which Lord St. George and Mr. Fenwick withdrew together from the chapel and walked into the vicarage.

"If all that be absolutely necessary—" began the Vicar.

"It is, Mr. Fenwick; we've made a mistake." Lord St. George always spoke of his father as "we," when there came upon him the necessity of retrieving his father's errors. "And our only way out of it is to take the bull by the horns at once and put the thing right. It will cost us about £700, and then there is the bore of having to own ourselves to be wrong. But that is much better than a fight."

"I should not have fought."

"You would have been driven to fight. And then there is the one absolute fact;—the chapel ought not to be there. And now I've one other word to say. Don't you think this quarrelling between clergyman and landlord is bad for the parish?"

"Very bad indeed, Lord St. George."

"Now I'm not going to measure out censure, or to say that we have been wrong, or that you have been wrong."

"If you do I shall defend myself," said the Vicar.

"Exactly so. But if bygones can be bygones there need be neither offence nor defence."

"What can a clergyman think, Lord St. George, when the landlord of his parish writes letters against him to his bishop, maligning his private character, and spreading reports for which there is not the slightest foundation?"

"Mr. Fenwick, is that the way in which you let bygones be bygones?"

"It is very hard to say that I can forget such an injury."

"My father, at any rate, is willing to forget,—and, as he hopes, to forgive. In all disputes each party of course thinks that he has been right. If you, for the sake of the parish, and for the sake of Christian charity and goodwill, are ready to meet him half way, all this ill-will may be buried in the ground."

What could the Vicar do? He felt that he was being cunningly cheated out of his grievance. He would have had not a minute's hesitation as to forgiving the Marquis, had the Marquis owned himself to be wrong. But he was now invited to bury the hatchet on even terms, and he knew that the terms should not be even. And he resented all this the more in his heart because he understood very well how clever and cunning was the son of his enemy. He did not like to be cheated out of his forgiveness. But after all, what did it matter? Would it not be enough for him to know, himself, that he had been right? Was it not much to feel himself free from all pricks of conscience in the matter?

"If Lord Trowbridge is willing to let it all pass," said he, "so am I."

"I am delighted," said Lord St. George, with spirit; "I will not come in now, because I have already overstayed my time, but I hope you may hear from my father before long in a spirit of kindness."

CHAPTER LXXI.

THE END OF MARY LOWTHER'S STORY.

Sir Gregory Marrable's headache was not of long duration. Allusion is here made to that especial headache under the acute effects of which he had taken so very unpromising a farewell of his nephew and heir. It lasted, however, for two or three days, during which he had frequent consultations with Mrs. Brownlow, and had one conversation with Edith. He was disappointed, sorry, and sore at heart because the desire on which he had set his mind could not be fulfilled; but he was too weak to cling either to his hope or to his anger. His own son had gone from him, and this young man must be his heir and the owner of Dunripple. No doubt he might punish the young man by excluding him from any share of ownership for the present; but there would be neither comfort nor advantage in that. It is true that he might save any money that Walter would cost him, and give it to Edith,—but such a scheme of saving for such a purpose was contrary to the old man's nature. He wanted to have his heir near him at Dunripple. He hated the feeling of desolation which was presented to him by the idea of Dunripple without some young male Marrable at hand to help him. He desired, unconsciously, to fill up the void made by the death of his son with as little trouble as might be. And therefore he consulted Mrs. Brownlow.

Mrs. Brownlow was clearly of opinion that he had better take his nephew, with the encumbrance of Mary Lowther, and make them both welcome to the house. "We have all heard so much good of Miss Lowther, you know," said Mrs. Brownlow, "and she is not at all the same as a stranger."

"That is true," said Sir Gregory, willing to be talked over.

"And then, you know, who can say whether Edith would ever have liked him or not. You never can tell what way a young woman's feelings will go."

On hearing this Sir Gregory uttered some sound intended to express mildly a divergence of opinion. He did not doubt but what Edith would have been quite willing to fall in love with Walter, had all things been conformable to her doing so. Mrs. Brownlow did not notice this as she continued,—"At any rate the poor girl would suffer dreadfully now if she were allowed to think that you should be divided from your nephew by your regard for her. Indeed, she could hardly stay at Dunripple if that were so."

Mrs. Brownlow in a mild way suggested that nothing should be said to Edith, and Sir Gregory gave half a promise that he would be silent. But it was against his nature not to speak. When the moment came the temptation to say something that could be easily said, and which would produce some mild excitement, was always too strong for him. "My dear," he said, one evening, when Edith was hovering round his chair, "you remember what I once said to you about your cousin Walter?"

"About Captain Marrable, uncle?"

"Well,—he is just the same as a cousin;—it turns out that he is engaged to marry another cousin,—Mary Lowther."

"She is his real cousin, Uncle Gregory."

"I never saw the young lady,—that I know of."

"Nor have I,—but I've heard so much about her! And everybody says she is nice. I hope they'll come and live here."

"I don't know yet, my dear."

"He told me all about it when he was here."

"Told you he was going to be married?"

"No, uncle, he did not tell me that exactly;—but he said that—that—. He told me how much he loved Mary Lowther, and a great deal about her, and I felt sure it would come so."

"Then you are aware that what I had hinted about you and Walter—"

"Don't talk about that, Uncle Gregory. I knew that it was ever so unlikely, and I didn't think about it. You are so good to me that of course I couldn't say anything. But you may be sure he is ever so much in love with Miss Lowther; and I do hope we shall be so fond of her!"

Sir Gregory was pacified and his headache for the time was cured. He had had his little scheme, and it had failed. Edith was very good, and she should still be his pet and his favourite,—but Walter Marrable should be told that he might marry and bring his bride to Dunripple, and that if he would sell out of his regiment, the family lawyer should be instructed to make such arrangements for him as would have been made had he actually been a son. There would be some little difficulty about the colonel's rights; but the colonel had already seized upon so much that it could not but be easy to deal with him. On the next morning the letter was written to Walter by Mrs. Brownlow herself.

About a week after this Mary Lowther, who was waiting at Loring with an outward show of patience, but with much inward anxiety for further tidings from her lover, received two letters, one from Walter, and the other from her friend, Janet Fenwick. The reader shall see those, and the replies which Mary made to them, and then our whole story will have been told as far as the loves, and hopes, and cares, and troubles of Mary Lowther are concerned.

Bullhampton, 1st September.

DEAREST MARY,

I write a line just because I said I would. Frank went up to London last week and was away one Sunday. He found his poor friend in town and was with him for two or three days. He has made up his mind to let the Privets, and go abroad, and nothing that Frank could say would move him. I do not know whether it may not be for the best. We shall lose such a neighbour as we never shall have again. He was the same as a brother to both of us; and I can only say, that loving him like a brother, I endeavoured to do the best for him that I could. This I do know;—that nothing on earth shall ever tempt me to set my hand at match-making again. But it was alluring,—the idea of bringing my two dearest friends near me together.

If you have anything to tell me of your happiness, I shall be delighted to hear it; I will not set my heart against this other man;—but you can hardly expect me to say that he will be as much to me as might have been that other. God bless you,

Your most affectionate friend,

JANET FENWICK.

I must tell you the fate of the chapel. They are already pulling it down, and carting away the things to the other place. They are doing it so quick, that it will all be gone before we know where we are. I own I am glad. As for Frank, I really believe he'd rather let it remain. But this is not all. The Marquis has promised that we shall hear from him "in a spirit of kindness." I wonder what this will come to? It certainly was not a spirit of kindness that made him write to the bishop and call Frank an infidel.

And this was the other letter.

Barracks, 1st September, 186—.

DEAREST LOVE,

I hope this will be one of the last letters I shall write from this abominable place, for I am going to sell out at once. It is all settled, and I'm to be a sort of deputy Squire at Dunripple, under my uncle. As that is to be my fate in life, I may as well begin it at once. But that's not the whole of my fate, nor the best of it. You are to be admitted as deputy Squiress,—or rather as Squiress in chief, seeing that you will be mistress of the house. Dearest Mary, may I hope that you won't object to the promotion?

I have had a long letter from Mrs. Brownlow; and I ran over yesterday and saw my uncle. I was so hurried that I could not write from Dunripple. I would send you Mrs. Brownlow's letter, only perhaps it would not be quite fair. I dare say you will see it some day. She says ever so much about you, and as complimentary as possible. And then she declares her purpose to resign all rights, honours, pains, privileges, and duties of mistress of Dunripple into your hands as soon as you are Mrs. Marrable. And this she repeated yesterday with some stateliness, and a great deal of high-minded resignation. But I don't mean to laugh at her, because I know she means to do what is right.

My own, own, Mary, write me a line instantly to say that it is right,—and to say also that you agree with me that as it is to be done, 'twere well it were done quickly.

Yours always, with all my heart,

W. M.

It was of course necessary that Mary should consult with her aunt before she answered the second letter. Of that which she received from Mrs. Fenwick she determined to say nothing. Why should she ever mention to her aunt again a name so painful to her as that of Mr. Gilmore? The thinking of him could not be avoided. In this, the great struggle of her life, she had endeavoured to do right, and yet she could not acquit herself of evil. But the pain, though it existed, might at least be kept out of sight.

"And so you are to go and live at Dunripple at once," said Miss Marrable.

"I suppose we shall."

"Ah, well! It's all right, I'm sure. Of course there is not a word to be said against it. I hope Sir Gregory won't die before the Colonel. That's all."

"The Colonel is his father, you know."

"I hope there may not come to be trouble about it, that's all. I shall be very lonely, but of course I had to expect that."

"You'll come to us, Aunt Sarah? You'll be as much there as here."

"Thank you, dear. I don't quite know about that. Sir Gregory is all very well; but one does like one's own house."

From all which Mary understood that her dear aunt still wished that she might have had her own way in disposing of her niece's hand,—as her dear friends at Bullhampton had wished to have theirs.

The following were the answers from Mary to the two letters given above;—

Loring, 3rd September, 186—.

DEAR JANET,

I am very, very, very sorry. I do not know what more I can say. I meant to do well all through. When I first told Mr. Gilmore that it could not be as he wished it, I was right. When I made up my mind that it must be so at last, I was right also. I fear I cannot say so much of myself as to that middle step which I took, thinking it was best to do as I was bidden. I meant to be right, but of course I was wrong, and I am very, very sorry. Nevertheless, I am much obliged to you for writing to me. Of course I cannot but desire to know what he does. If he writes and seems to be happy on his travels, pray tell me.

I have much to tell you of my own happiness,—though, in truth, I feel a remorse at being happy when I have caused so much unhappiness. Walter is to sell out and to live at Dunripple, and I also am to live there when we are married. I suppose it will not be long now. I am writing to him to-day, though I do not yet know what I shall say to him. Sir Gregory has assented, and arrangements are to be made, and lawyers are to be consulted, and we are to be what Walter calls deputy Squire and Squiress at Dunripple. Mrs. Brownlow and Edith Brownlow are still to live there, but I am to have the honour of ordering the dinner, and looking wise at the housekeeper. Of course I shall feel very strange at going into such a house. To you I may say how much nicer it would be to go to some place that Walter and I could have to ourselves,—as you did when you married. But I am not such a simpleton as to repine at that. So much has gone as I would have it that I only feel myself to be happier than I deserve. What I shall chiefly look forward to will be your first visit to Dunripple.

Your most affectionate friend,

MARY LOWTHER.

The other letter, as to which Mary had declared that she had not as yet made up her own mind when she wrote to Mrs. Fenwick, was more difficult in composition.

Loring, 2nd September, 186—.

DEAREST WALTER,

So it is all settled, and I am to be a deputy Squiress! I have no objection to urge. As long as you are the deputy Squire, I will be the deputy Squiress. For your sake, my dearest, I do most heartily rejoice that the affair is settled. I think you will be happier as a county gentleman than you would have been in the army; and as Dunripple must ultimately be your home,—I will say our home,—perhaps it is as well that you, and I also, should know it as soon as possible. Of course I am very nervous about Mrs. Brownlow and her daughter; but though nervous I am not fearful; and I shall prepare myself to like them.

As to that other matter, I hardly know what answer to make on so very quick a questioning. It was only the other day that it was decided that it was to be;—and there ought to be breathing time before one also decides when. But, dear Walter, I will do nothing to interfere with your prospects. Let me know what you think yourself; but remember, in thinking, that a little interval for purposes of sentiment and of stitching is always desired by the weaker vessel on such an occasion.

God bless you, my own one,

Yours always and always, M. L.

In real truth, I will do whatever you bid me.

Of course, after that, the marriage was not very long postponed. Walter Marrable allowed that some grace should be given for sentiment, and some also for stitching, but as to neither did he feel that any long delay was needed. A week for sentiment, and two more for the preparation of bridal adornments, he thought would be sufficient. There was a compromise at last, as is usual in such cases, and the marriage took place about the middle of October. No doubt, at that time of year they went to Italy,—but of that the present narrator is not able to speak with any certainty. This, however, is certain,—that if they did travel abroad, Mary Marrable travelled in daily fear lest her unlucky fate should bring her face to face with Mr. Gilmore. Wherever they went, their tour, in accordance with a contract made by the baronet, was terminated within two months. For on Christmas Day Mrs. Walter Marrable was to take her place as mistress of the house at the dinner table.

The reader may, perhaps, desire to know whether things were made altogether smooth with the Colonel. On this matter Messrs. Block and Curling, the family lawyers, encountered very much trouble indeed. The Colonel, when application was made to him, was as sweet as honey. He would do anything for the interests of his dearest son. There did not breathe a father on earth who cared less for himself or his own position. But still he must live. He submitted to Messrs. Block and Curling whether it was not necessary that he should live. Messrs. Block and Curling explained to him very clearly that his brother, the baronet, had nothing to do with his living or dying,—and that towards his living he had already robbed his son of a large property. At last, however, he would not make over his life interest in the property, as it would come to him in the event of his brother dying before him, except on payment of an annuity on and from that date of £200 a year. He began by asking £500, and was then told that the Captain would run the chance and would sue his father for the £20,000 in the event of Sir Gregory dying before the Colonel.

Now the narrator will bid adieu to Mary Lowther, to Loring, and to Dunripple. The conduct of his heroine, as depicted in these pages, will, he fears, meet with the disapprobation of many close and good judges of female character. He has endeavoured to describe a young woman, prompted in all her doings by a conscience wide awake, guided by principle, willing, if need be, to sacrifice herself, struggling always to keep herself from doing wrong, but yet causing infinite grief to others, and nearly bringing herself to utter shipwreck, because, for a while, she allowed herself to believe that it would be right for her to marry a man whom she did not love.

CHAPTER LXXII.

AT TURNOVER CASTLE.

Mrs. Fenwick had many quips and quirks with her husband as to those tidings to be made in a pleasant spirit which were expected from Turnover Castle. From the very moment that Lord St. George had given the order,—upon the authority chiefly of the unfortunate Mr. Bolt, who on this occasion found it to be impossible to refuse to give an authority which a lord demanded from him,—the demolition of the building had been commenced. Before the first Sunday came any use of the new chapel for divine service was already impossible. On that day Mr. Puddleham preached a stirring sermon about tabernacles in general. "It did not matter where the people of the Lord met," he said, "so long as they did meet to worship the Lord in a proper spirit of independent resistance to any authority that had not come to them from revelation. Any hedge-side was a sufficient tabernacle for a devout Christian. But—," and then, without naming any name, he described the Church of England as a Upas tree which, by its poison, destroyed those beautiful flowers which strove to spring up amidst the rank grass beneath it and to make the air sweet within its neighbourhood. Something he said, too, of a weak sister tottering to its base, only to be followed in its ruin by the speedy prostration of its elder brother. All this was of course told in detail to the Vicar; but the Vicar refused even to be interested by it. "Of course he did," said the Vicar. "If a man is to preach, what can he preach but his own views?"

The tidings to be made in a pleasant spirit were not long waited for,—or, at any rate, the first instalment of them. On the 2nd of September there arrived a large hamper full of partridges, addressed to Mrs. Fenwick in the Earl's own handwriting. "The very first fruits," said the Vicar, as he went down to inspect the plentiful provision thus made for the vicarage larder. Well;—it was certainly better to have partridges from Turnover than accusations of immorality and infidelity. The Vicar so declared at once, but his wife would not at first agree with him. "I really should have such pleasure in packing them up and sending them back," said she.

"Indeed, you shall do nothing of the kind."

"The idea of a basket of birds to atone for such insults and calumny as that man has heaped on you!"

"The birds will be only a first instalment," said the Vicar,—and then there were more quips and quirks about that. It was presumed by Mr. Fenwick that the second instalment would be the first pheasants shot in October.

But the second instalment came before September was over in the shape of the following note:—

> Turnover Park, 20th September, 186—.
>
> The Marquis of Trowbridge and the Ladies Sophie and Carolina Stowte request that Mr. and Mrs. Fenwick will do them the honour of coming to Turnover Park on Monday the 6th October, and staying till Saturday the 11th.

"That's an instalment indeed," said Mrs. Fenwick. "And now what on earth are we to do?" The Vicar admitted that it had become very serious. "We must either go, and endure a terrible time of it," continued Mrs. Fenwick, "or we must show him very plainly that we will have nothing more to do with him. I don't see why we are to be annoyed, merely because he is a Marquis."

"It won't be because he is a Marquis."

"Why then? You can't say that you love the old man, or that the Ladies Sophie and Carolina Stowte are the women you'd have me choose for companions, or that that soapy, silky, humbugging Lord St. George is to your taste."

"I am not sure about St. George. He can be everything to everybody, and would make an excellent bishop."

"You know you don't like him, and you know also that you will have a very bad time of it at Turnover."

"I could shoot pheasants all the week."

"Yes,—with a conviction at the time that the Ladies Sophie and Carolina were calling you an infidel behind your back for doing so. As for myself I feel perfectly certain that I should spar with them."

"It isn't because he's a Marquis," said the Vicar, carrying on his argument after a long pause. "If I know myself, I think I may say that that has no allurement for me. And, to tell the truth, had he been simply a Marquis, and had I been at liberty to indulge my own wishes, I would never have allowed myself to be talked out of my righteous anger by that soft-tongued son of his. But to us he is a man of the very greatest importance, because he owns the land on which the people live with whom we are concerned. It is for their welfare that he and I should be on good terms together; and therefore if you don't mind the sacrifice, I think we'll go."

"What;—for the whole week, Frank?"

The Vicar was of opinion that the week might be judiciously curtailed by two days; and, consequently, Mrs. Fenwick presented her compliments to the Ladies Sophie and Carolina Stowte, and expressed the great pleasure which she and Mr. Fenwick would have in going to Turnover Park on the Tuesday, and staying till the Friday.

"So that I shall only be shooting two days," said the Vicar, "which will modify the aspect of my infidelity considerably."

They went to Turnover Castle. The poor old Marquis had rather a bad time of it for the hour or two previous to their arrival. It had become an acknowledged fact now in the county that Sam Brattle had had nothing to do with the murder of Farmer Trumbull, and that his acquaintance with the murderers had sprung from his desire to see his unfortunate sister settled in marriage with a man whom he at the time did not know to be disreputable. There had therefore been a reaction in favour of Sam Brattle, whom the county now began to regard as something of a hero. The Marquis, understanding all that, had come to be aware that he had wronged the Vicar in that matter of the murder. And then, though he had been told upon very good authority,—no less than that of his daughters, who had been so informed by the sisters of a most exemplary neighbouring curate,—that Mr. Fenwick was a man who believed "just next to nothing," and would just as soon associate with a downright Pagan like old Brattle, as with any professing Christian,—still there was the fact of the Bishop's good opinion; and, though the Marquis was a self-willed man, to him a bishop was always a bishop. It was also clear to him that he had been misled in those charges which he had made against the Vicar in that matter of poor Carry Brattle's residence at Salisbury. Something of the truth of the girl's history had come to the ears of the Marquis, and he had been made to believe that he had been wrong. Then there was the affair of the chapel, in which, under his son's advice, he was at this moment expending £700 in rectifying the mistake which he had made. In giving the Marquis his due we must acknowledge that he cared but little about the money. Marquises, though they may have large properties, are not always in possession of any number of loose hundreds which they can throw away without feeling the loss. Nor was the Marquis of Trowbridge so circumstanced now. But that trouble did not gall him nearly so severely as the necessity which was on him to rectify an error made by himself. He had done a foolish thing. Under no circumstances should the chapel have been built on that spot. He knew it now, and he knew that he must apologise. Noblesse oblige. The old lord was very stupid, very wrong-headed, and sometimes very arrogant; but he would not do a wrong if he knew it, and nothing on earth would make him tell a wilful lie. The epithet indeed might have been omitted; for a lie is not a lie unless it be wilful.

Lord Trowbridge passed the hours of this Tuesday morning under the frightful sense of the necessity for apologising;—and yet he remembered well the impudence of the man, how he had ventured to allude to the Ladies Stowte, likening them to—to—to—! It was terrible to be thought of. And his lordship remembered, too, how this man had written about the principal entrance to his own mansion as though it had been no more than the entrance to any other man's house! Though the thorns still rankled in his own flesh, he had to own that he himself had been wrong.

And he did it,—with an honesty that was beyond the reach of his much more clever son. When the Fenwicks arrived, they were taken into the drawing-room, in which were sitting the Ladies Sophie and Carolina with various guests already assembled at the Castle. In a minute or two the Marquis shuffled in and shook hands with the two new comers. Then he shuffled about the room for another minute or two, and at last got his arm through that of the Vicar, and led him away into his own sanctum. "Mr. Fenwick," he said, "I think it best to express my regret at once for two things that have occurred."

The drawing-room at Turnover Castle.

"It does not signify, my lord."

"But it does signify to me, and if you will listen to me for a moment I shall take your doing so as a favour added to that which you have conferred upon me in coming here." The Vicar could only bow and listen. "I am sorry, Mr.

Fenwick, that I should have written to the bishop of this diocese in reference to your conduct." Fenwick found it very difficult to hold his tongue when this was said. He imagined that the Marquis was going to excuse himself about the chapel,—and about the chapel he cared nothing at all. But as to that letter to the bishop, he did feel that the less said about it the better. He restrained himself, however, and the Marquis went on. "Things had been told me, Mr. Fenwick;—and I thought that I was doing my duty."

"It did me no harm, my lord."

"I believe not. I had been misinformed,—and I apologise." The Marquis paused, and the Vicar bowed. It is probable that the Vicar did not at all know how deep at that moment were the sufferings of the Marquis. "And now as to the chapel," continued the Marquis.

"My lord, that is such a trifle that you must let me say that it is not and has not been of the slightest consequence."

"I was misled as to that bit of ground."

"I only wish, my lord, that the chapel could stand there."

"That is impossible. The land has been appropriated to other purposes, and though we have all been a little in the dark about our own rights, right must be done. I will only add that I have the greatest satisfaction in seeing you and Mrs. Fenwick at Turnover, and that I hope the satisfaction may often be repeated." Then he led the way back into the drawing-room, and the evil hour had passed over his head.

Upon the whole, things went very well with both the Vicar and his wife during their visit. He did go out shooting one day, and was treated very civilly by the Turnover gamekeeper, though he was prepared with no five-pound note at the end of his day's amusement. When he returned to the house, his host congratulated him on his performance just as cordially as though he had been one of the laity. On the next day he rode over with Lord St. George to see the County Hunt kennels, which were then at Charleycoats, and nobody seemed to think him very wicked because he ventured to have an opinion about hounds. Mrs. Fenwick's amusements were, perhaps, less exciting, but she went through them with equanimity. She was taken to see the parish schools, and was walked into the parish church,—in which the Stowte family were possessed of an enormous recess called a pew, but which was in truth a room, with a fireplace in it. Mrs. Fenwick thought it did not look very much like a church; but as the Ladies Stowte were clearly very proud of it she held her peace as to that idea. And so the visit to Turnover Park was made, and the Fenwicks were driven home.

"After all, there's nothing like burying the hatchet," said he.

"But who sharpened the hatchet?" asked Mrs. Fenwick.

"Never mind who sharpened it. We've buried it."

CHAPTER LXXIII.

CONCLUSION.

There is nothing further left to be told of this story of the village of Bullhampton and its Vicar beyond what may be necessary to satisfy the reader as to the condition and future prospects of the Brattle family. The writer of these pages ventures to hope that whatever may have been the fate in the readers' mind of that couple which are about to settle themselves peaceably at Dunripple, and to wait there in comfort till their own time for reigning shall have come, some sympathy may have been felt with those humbler personages who have lived with orderly industry at the mill,—as, also, with those who, led away by disorderly passions, have strayed away from it, and have come back again to the old home.

For a couple of days after the return of the miller with his daughter and son, very little was said about the past;—very little, at least, in which either the father or Sam took any part. Between the two sisters there were no doubt questions and answers by the hour together as to every smallest detail of the occurrences at Salisbury. And the mother almost sang hymns of joy over her child, in that the hour which she had so much dreaded had passed by. But the miller said not a word;—and Sam was almost equally silent. "But it be all over, Sam?" asked his mother, anxiously one day. "For certain sure it be all over now?"

"There's one, mother, for whom it ain't all over yet;—poor devil."

"But he was the—murderer, Sam."

"So was t'other fellow. There weren't no difference. If one was more spry to kill t'old chap than t'other, Acorn was the spryest. That's what I think. But it's done now, and there ain't been much justice in it. As far as I sees, there never ain't much justice. They was nigh a-hanging o' me; and if those chaps had thought o' bringing t'old man's box nigh the mill, instead of over by t'old woman's cottage, they would a hung me;—outright. And then they was twelve months about it! I don't think much on 'em." When his mother tried to continue the conversation,—which she would have loved to do with that morbid interest which we always take in a matter which has been nearly fatal to us, but from which we have escaped,—Sam turned into the mill, saying that he had had enough of it, and wouldn't have any more.

Then, on the third day, a report of the trial in a county newspaper reached them. This the miller read all through, painfully, from the beginning to the end, omitting no detail of the official occurrences. At last, when he came to the account of Sam's evidence, he got up from the chair on which he was sitting close to the window, and striking his fist upon the table, made his first and last comment upon the trial. "It was well said, Sam. Yes; though thou be'est my own, it was well said." Then he put the paper down and walked out of doors, and they could see that his eyes were full of tears.

But from that time forth there came a great change in his manner to his youngest daughter. "Well, Carry," he would say to her in the morning, with as much outward sign of affection as he ever showed to any one; and at night, when she came and stood over him before he lifted his weary limbs out of his chair to take himself away to his bed, he turned his forehead to her to be kissed, as he did to that better daughter who had needed no forgiveness from him. Nevertheless, they who knew him,—and there were none who knew him better than Fanny did,—were aware that he never for a moment forgot the disgrace which had fallen upon his household. He had forgiven the sinner, but the shame of the sin was always on him; and he carried himself as a man who was bound to hide himself from the eyes of his neighbours because there had come upon him a misfortune which made it fit that he should live in retirement.

Sam took up his abode in the house, and worked daily in the mill, and for weeks nothing was said either of his going away or of his return. He would talk to his sisters of the manner in which he had worked among the machinery of the Durham mine at which he had found employment; but he said nothing for awhile of the cause which had taken him north, or of his purpose of remaining where he was. He ate and drank in the house, and from time to time his father paid him small sums as wages. At last, sitting one evening after the work of the day was done, he spoke out his mind. "Father," said he, "I'm about minded to get me a wife." His mother and sisters were all there and heard the proposition made.

"And who is the girl as is to have thee, Sam?" asked his mother.

As Sam did not answer at once, Carry replied for him. "Who should it be, mother;—but only Agnes Pope?"

"It ain't that 'un?" said the miller, surlily.

"And why shouldn't it be that 'un, father? It is that 'un, and no other. If she be not liked here, why, we'll just go further, and perhaps not fare worse."

There was nothing to be said against poor Agnes Pope,—only this, that she had been in Trumbull's house on the night of the murder, and had for awhile been suspected by the police of having communicated to her lover the tidings of the farmer's box of money. Evil things had of course been said of her then, but the words spoken of her had been proved to be untrue. She had been taken from the farmer's house into that of the Vicar,—who had, indeed, been somewhat abused by the Puddlehamites for harbouring her; but as the belief in Sam's guilt had gradually been abandoned, so, of course, had the ground disappeared for supposing that poor Agnes had had ought to do in bringing about the murder of her late master. For two days the miller was very gloomy, and made no reply when Sam declared his purpose of leaving the mill before Christmas unless Agnes should be received there as his wife;—but at last he gave way. "As the old 'uns go into their graves," he said, "it's no more than nature that the young 'uns should become masters." And so Sam was married, and was taken, with his wife, to live with the other Brattles at the mill. It was well for the miller that it should be so, for Sam was a man who would surely earn money when he put his shoulder in earnest to the wheel.

As for Carry, she lived still with them, doomed by her beauty, as was her elder sister by the want of it, to expect that no lover should come and ask her to establish with him a homestead of their own.

Our friend the Vicar married Sam and his sweetheart, and is still often at the mill. From time to time he has made efforts to convert the unbelieving old man whose grave is now so near to his feet; but he has never prevailed to make the miller own even the need of any change. "I've struv' to be honest," he said, when last he was thus attacked, "and I've wrought for my wife and bairns. I ain't been a drunkard, nor yet, as I knows on, neither a tale-bearer, nor yet a liar. I've been harsh-tempered and dour enough I know, and maybe it's fitting as they shall be hard and dour to me where I'm going. I don't say again it, Muster Fenwick;—but nothing as I can do now 'll change it." This, at any rate, was clear to the Vicar,—that Death, when it came, would come without making the old man tremble.

Mr. Gilmore has been some years away from Bullhampton; but when I last heard from my friends in that village I was told that at last he was expected home.

Milton Keynes UK
Ingram Content Group UK Ltd.
UKHW031955281024
450365UK00009B/526